Human Bondage and Abolition

Slavery's expansion across the globe often escapes notice because it operates as an underground criminal enterprise, rather than as a legal institution. In this volume, Elizabeth Swanson and James Brewer Stewart bring together scholars from across disciplines to address and expose the roots of modern-day slavery from a historical perspective as a means of supporting activist efforts to fight it in the present. They trace modern slavery to its many sources, examining how it is sustained and how today's abolitionists might benefit by understanding their predecessors' successes and failures. Using scholarship also intended as activism, the volume's authors analyze how the history of African American enslavement might illuminate or obscure the understanding of slavery today and show how the legacies of earlier forms of slavery have shaped human bondage and social relations in the twenty-first century.

ELIZABETH SWANSON is Professor of English at Babson College. She has published extensively in the areas of slavery, human rights, and literature, and has worked to help rebuild the lives of survivors of brothel slavery in India, Nepal, and the US.

JAMES BREWER STEWART is the James Wallace Professor of History Emeritus at Macalester College. He is the founder and director emeritus of Historians Against Slavery, an international network that advocates for contemporary antislavery and antiracism (historiansagainstslavery. org). He co-edits Louisiana State University's book series *Abolition, Antislavery and the Atlantic World*, and is the author or editor of thirteen scholarly books bearing on the historical problem of slavery.

Slaveries since Emancipation

General Editors
Randall Miller, *St. Joseph's University*
Zoe Trodd, *University of Nottingham*

Slaveries since Emancipation publishes scholarship that links slavery's past to its present, consciously scanning history for lessons of relevance to contemporary abolitionism, and that directly engages current issues of interest to activists by contextualizing them historically.

Also in this series:

Human Bondage and Abolition

New Histories of Past and Present Slaveries

Edited by

ELIZABETH SWANSON

Babson College

JAMES BREWER STEWART

Macalester College

POR Luis —
Con Muchissimo
Apreciación & en
gratitud Por
Tu Amistad —

Jim

CAMBRIDGE
UNIVERSITY PRESS

CAMBRIDGE
UNIVERSITY PRESS

University Printing House, Cambridge CB2 8BS, United Kingdom

One Liberty Plaza, 20th Floor, New York, NY 10006, USA

477 Williamstown Road, Port Melbourne, VIC 3207, Australia

314–321, 3rd Floor, Plot 3, Splendor Forum, Jasola District Centre,
New Delhi – 110025, India

79 Anson Road, #06-04/06, Singapore 079906

Cambridge University Press is part of the University of Cambridge.

It furthers the University's mission by disseminating knowledge in the pursuit of
education, learning, and research at the highest international levels of excellence.

www.cambridge.org
Information on this title: www.cambridge.org/9781107186620
DOI: 10.1017/9781316890790

© Cambridge University Press 2018

First published 2018

Printed in the United States of America by Sheridan Books, Inc.

A catalogue record for this publication is available from the British Library.

Library of Congress Cataloging-in-Publication Data
Names: Goldberg, Elizabeth Swanson, 1966– editor. | Stewart, James Brewer, editor.
Title: Human bondage and abolition : new histories of past and present slaveries /
edited by Elizabeth Swanson, Babson College,
James Brewer Stewart, Macalester College.
Description: Cambridge, United Kingdom; New York, NY:
Cambridge University Press, 2018. | Series: Slaveries since emancipation |
Includes bibliographical references and index.
Identifiers: LCCN 2018013743 | ISBN 9781107186620 (hardback)
Subjects: LCSH: Slavery – History. | Slavery – History – 21st century.
Classification: LCC HT867.H86 2018 | DDC 306.3/6209–dc23
LC record available at https://lccn.loc.gov/2018013743

ISBN 978-1-107-18662-0 Hardback
ISBN 978-1-316-63736-4 Paperback

Contents

Figures

Contributors

Dave Blair holds a PhD in International Relations from Georgetown University, and a Masters in Public Policy from the Harvard Kennedy School. He is a graduate of the United States Air Force Academy, a veteran of Air Force Special Operations Command, and a combat pilot with experience in several conflicts. He has published on network theory, historical and contemporary unconventional conflict, strategy, and technology. His research interests include datacentric approaches to defeating modern slavery.

David Blight is Class of 1954 Professor of American History at Yale University and Director of the Gilder Lehrman Center for the Study of Slavery, Resistance, and Abolition at Yale. He is the author of *Race and Reunion: The Civil War in American Memory* (2001), which received eight book awards from prominent learned societies. Among his many other publications are *Beyond the Battlefield: Race, Memory, and the American Civil War* (2002) and *Frederick Douglass's Civil War: Keeping Faith in Jubilee* (1989).

Monti Narayan Datta is Associate Professor of Political Science at the University of Richmond, where he teaches classes on international relations, research methods, human rights, and modern slavery. He is the author of several articles on modern slavery, published in *Human Rights Quarterly*, *The Brown Journal of International Affairs*, *The SAIS Review of International Affairs*, and *Significance*. His current work examines the extent to which antislavery NGOs in Southeast Asia are successfully helping survivors of modern slavery reintegrate into society. He is also the author of *Anti-Americanism: The Rise of World Opinion* (Cambridge University Press, 2014).

John Donoghue is Associate Professor of History at Loyola University Chicago. He is the author of *Fire under the Ashes: An Atlantic History of the English Revolution* (Chicago: University of Chicago Press, 2013) and co-editor, with Evelyn Jennings, of *Building the Atlantic Empires: Unfree Labor and Imperial States in the Political Economy of Capitalism, ca. 1500–1914* (Leiden: Brill, 2015).

Anna Mae Duane is Associate Professor of English at the University of Connecticut. She is the author, editor, or co-editor of four books focusing on childhood in early American literature and culture. She is the co-editor of *Common-place*, the journal of early American life.

Allison Mileo Gorsuch received her PhD in History from Yale University in 2013 and her J.D. from Yale Law School in 2015. She is also the author of "To Indent Oneself: Ownership, Contracts, and Consent in Antebellum Illinois," in *The Legal Understanding of Slavery: From the Historical to the Contemporary*, ed. Jean Allain (Oxford University Press, 2012) and "Legacies of Empire: Race and Labor Contracts in the Upper Mississippi River Valley," in *The Legal Histories of the British Empire*, eds. Shaunnagh Dorsett and John McLaren (London: Routledge, 2014).

Jessica R. Pliley is an Associate Professor of Women's, Gender and Sexuality History at Texas State University. She is the author of *Policing Sexuality: The Mann Act and the Making of the FBI* (Harvard University Press, 2014) and co-editor of *Global Anti-Vice Activism, 1890–1950: Fighting Drink, Drugs, and 'Immorality'* (Cambridge University Press, 2016). Her articles have appeared in the *Journal of Women's History*, the *Journal of the Gilded Age and Progressive Era*, and the *Journal of the History of Sexuality*.

David Richardson is Professor of Economic History at the University of Hull (UK) and founder and former Director of the University's Wilberforce Institute for the Study of Slavery and Emancipation. Among his many publications is the multiple award-winning *Atlas of the Transatlantic Slave Trade* (Yale University Press, 2010), which he co-authored with David Eltis. He is co-editor of the final two volumes of the four-volume *Cambridge World History of Slavery*, scheduled to appear in 2017 and 2018.

James Sidbury is the Andrew W. Mellon Distinguished Professor of the Humanities in the Department of History at Rice University. He is the author of *Ploughshares into Swords: Race, Rebellion and Identity in Gabriel's Virginia, 1730–1810* (Cambridge University Press, 2008) and *Becoming African in America: Race and Nation in the Early Black Atlantic* (Oxford University Press, 2009), and the co-editor of *The Black Urban Atlantic in the Age of the Slave Trade* (University of Pennsylvania Press, 2016). He has also published a number of essays on race and slavery in the eighteenth-century Atlantic world.

James Brewer Stewart is James Wallace Professor of History Emeritus, Macalester College. He has written or edited thirteen books addressing the problem of slavery's abolition, is co-editor of Louisiana State University's book series *Antislavery and Abolition in the Atlantic World*, has worked as a consultant for several museums and public history sites, and is the founder of Historians Against Slavery, an international network of scholars and activists that brings historical knowledge to bear on the problem of contemporary slavery.

Elizabeth Swanson is Professor of English at Babson College. Author of *Beyond Terror: Gender, Narrative, Human Rights* (Rutgers University Press, 2007), she is co-editor of several edited collections on literature and human rights and the author of many articles on human rights, gender studies, and literature. Elizabeth has worked directly with survivors of brothel slavery in India and Nepal, partnering to rebuild lives with dignified, creative, high-wage livelihood solutions in her capacity as Board Chair for the international NGO Her Future Coalition from 2008 to 2016.

Kerry Ward is Associate Professor of World History at Rice University and an Editor of the *Journal of World History*. She is the author of *Networks of Empire: Forced Migration in the Dutch East India Company* (Cambridge University Press, 2009) and co-author with Ross Dunn and Laura Mitchell of *The New World History: A Field Guide for Teachers and Researchers* (University of California Press, 2016). She co-directed the 2012–2013 Rice Seminar on "Human Trafficking Past and Present: Crossing Borders, Crossing Disciplines" with Jim Sidbury. She was the Modern Slavery and Human Trafficking Fellow at the Gilder Lehrman Center for the Study of Slavery, Resistance, and Abolition at Yale University in 2013–2014.

Preface: Solidarity of the Ages

David Blight

Contrary to popular belief, the past was not more eventful than the present. If it seems so it is because when you look backward things that happened years apart are telescoped together, and because very few of your memories come to you genuinely virgin.

George Orwell, *"My Country, Right or Left,"* 1940

To find, to know, to narrate, and to explain the past is an ever-daunting task. In sheer metaphysical terms, it may even be impossible. But we historians, and our readers, love this task; we believe in it, cannot resist its charms, insist on climbing its unreachable peaks, descend into its darkest valleys, hack our way through its jungles, and, every once in a while, a few of us find one of its shining lost cities. We do so for countless reasons, not least of which we hope are our insatiable curiosity and need for human stories, as well as our quest to comprehend the depths of human nature. As Herodotus seemed to know in the opening sentence of his *Histories*, some at least in our unique species are driven to tell a tale and interpret it. Like Herodotus, we are compelled to research and write the past perhaps above all because we live in a sovereign present, our own time which ever shapes us as it demands our understanding.[1]

This remarkable book of essays, taking a place like no other work of its kind in this new field of modern slavery studies, calls us to, in the

---

[1] Herodotus, *The History*, trans. David Grene (Chicago, IL: University of Chicago Press, 1987), 33. Those opening lines are "I, Herodotus of Halicarnassus, am here setting forth my history, that time may not draw the color from what man has brought into being, nor those great and wonderful deeds, manifested by both Greeks and Barbarians, fail of their report, and, together with all this, the reason why they fought one another."

editors' apt phrase, an "ethical empathy ... then and now." With clear-eyed openness and the courage for debate about a "chameleon-like" phenomenon, as one author nicely puts it, this collection demands that we use and know the history of forms of enslavement since the great national and imperial emancipations of the nineteenth century in order to develop research agendas and write the history of slavery and human trafficking in our own time. Past and present meet here in these pieces, some based in deep research and others offered as challenging argument essays, with intensity, explicitness, and comparative fervor. History can and must be *used* to inform the present; the public and its political leaders do it every day. Historians should offer them a lead, as a "lantern," wrote the historian Allan Nevins idealistically in 1938, "carried by the side of man moving forward with every step taken."[2] How desperately the world needed such lanterns in the late 1930s; and how desperately we need them now!

Historians can seem preachy when we caution, or sometimes demand, that contemporary debates take time out to learn a little history first. We burn with indignation when we see blatant historical ignorance prevail in a presidential news conference or a tweet, in a pundits' discussion, or in the public square. Historians sometimes desperately feel the need, within our limited domains, to put our hands on the scale and tip it toward knowledge, thoughtfulness about cause and consequence, and, dare we admit it, truth. The works in this book do not claim high-minded or irreversible truths, but they do offer bracing, informed perspectives on how and why exploitive forms of labor grew in the late nineteenth century in illegal environments, and why sex trafficking and abolition movements against it emerged out of "moral panics" in the early twentieth century. Current, "new abolitionists" ought not be left alone in their conflicted worlds of moral outrage, NGO fund-raising, and strategic free-for-alls. They have an abundance of empathy and commitment, but they need a historically informed empathy, and a clear-headed commitment that stops to grasp, as the authors demonstrate here, that forms of slavery since ancient times have always grown out of "greed, autocracy, tyranny, war, disruption, and disaster."[3] There is nothing new under the sun, even as the details always change. 9/11 was not new; it happened in the Trojan War. The slaughter and displacement in Syria today is not new; it happened

---

[2] Allan Nevins, "A Proud Word for History," 1938, reprinted in Stephen Vaughn, ed., *The Vital Past: Writings on the Uses of History* (Athens, GA: University of Georgia Press, 1985), 237.

[3] See Introduction by Stewart and Swanson, and Chapter 1 by David Richardson.

in the Hundred Years War. Massive supply chains exploiting forced labor are not new; only the commodities and the scale may be mostly new.

Historians, it turns out, do need to preach once in a while. We simply need to have our theology down solid – meaning our facts rooted in research – and then we can, carefully, be that lantern of intellectual and ethical guidance. We might even prod the unknowing to action. As the great social scientist James Scott writes in his latest work, "History at its best, in my view, is the most subversive discipline inasmuch as it can tell us how things that we are likely to take for granted came to be."[4] Scott's is a gentle but powerful call for useful histories that push us into our present, like it or not, armed with data, and maybe even a little wisdom.

Although so much of the best research about modern slavery – both about the supply chains in forced labor regimes that have ensnarled millions on all continents, or in the bewildering, gruesome, and seemingly countless precincts of sex trafficking (or "work") around the world – is stunning in its capacity to build awareness, most people prefer to ignore these realities. The "indifference," shown in some of these essays, that formed so much of the environment in which new forms of enslavement thrived in the late nineteenth and early twentieth centuries prevails today as well. In a world of terror, mass murder, refugee displacement, and war on civilians, one can only look at so much pain. In the educated classes we often prefer irony as the antidote for our awkward comfort, not horror. We perhaps prefer subjects to which we can apply satire, rather than revelation. The sheer cunning of evil can overwhelm our empathic and strategic imaginations.

If the present may terrify people, they simply may never seek to know the history of how they got here. But we have to find ways to light the lanterns and keep them marching. Few ever wrote about the connections of past and present with quite the insight and poignancy of Marc Bloch. One of the best, and certainly most heroic, books ever produced on the nature of historians' work is *The Historian's Craft*, written in great part while surviving and fighting in the French resistance in the Second World War. The great French historian of feudalism and other broad subjects, Bloch, a veteran of the First World War, fled from his professorship at the Sorbonne into hiding in Strasbourg after the fall of France to the Nazis in 1940. He began writing his masterful meditation on the historian's art in 1941. Chased further into hiding, he finished perhaps only about

---

[4] Lecture by James Scott, April 13, 2017, sponsored by Gilder Lehrman Center for the Study of Slavery and Abolition, Yale University.

two-thirds of the book he had planned, until the Nazis captured, imprisoned, and tortured him, and finally shot him in an open field with twenty-six other French patriots in June, 1944. But in that text he left, Bloch could write under unbearable circumstances with such a sense of humor. "A good cataclysm," he said, "suits our business."[5]

Block found the poise to write about how history intrudes, indeed roars, into the present. The writing and imagination of history cannot be spared "present controversy," Bloch wrote. "Once an emotional chord has been struck, the line between present and past is no longer strictly regulated by a mathematically measureable chronology." Bloch deeply understood the pain and pleasure of knowing and doing history, as well as the marvelous joy of transforming research into writing. And he certainly grasped how the past is so often that thing we cannot live without, but also sometimes we cannot live with as well. Its double-edged cuts may leave us wounded and stranded. "The solidarity of the ages," declared Bloch, "is so effective that lines of connection work both ways. Misunderstanding of the present is the inevitable consequence of ignorance of the past. But a man may wear himself out just as fruitlessly in seeking to understand the past, if he is totally ignorant of the present."[6] We are bound by our craft and our humanity to engage both past and present, whatever the pain or pleasure. Historians are often reticent in linking then and now, shy of instrumental parallels and analogies that often do not work. But we have no choice; the path to understanding goes through shaky parallels and dimly lit analogies. This book provides a great deal of illumination of these pathways.

The essays in this volume have much to suggest about how to think in time about analogies. Debt peonage in the late nineteenth century is today's forced labor systems in everything from tea to cocoa production; the convict lease system of a century ago is today's "guest workers" shipped from South Asia to Qatar and a dozen other less visible places; and the moral panic over "white slavery" in the 1920s is something akin to today's moral absolutism over prostitution and sex work. We have to think in these terms even when we find difference colliding with similarity.

Sometimes we need the assistance of art to help us particularize and grasp the cunning of evil and how to think about the past. A case in point is the novel by Nigerian-born writer Chimamanda Ngozi Adichie, *Half*

---

[5] Marc Bloch, *The Historian's Craft*, intro. Joseph R. Strayer, trans. Peter Putnam (New York: Vintage, 1953), 75.

[6] Ibid., 37, 43.

of a Yellow Sun. Adichie's book is not explicitly written to engage the current dilemmas of modern forms of slavery, but it is richly historical, resonant of our recurring present in countless ways, and genuinely tragic as it instructs with resolutions through blood and loss. *Half a Yellow Sun* is a harrowing tale of the Biafran Civil War in the 1960s. All the brutalities and devastation, much of it invisible to or suppressed in modern historical memory now, are on display in this book. A teenager, Ugwu, comes of age as the civil war breaks out and takes over the land. He is torn from his family and conscripted into the army to fight for Igbo independence in the three-year bloodbath. Ugwu undergoes great suffering, wounds, despair, and both witnesses and participates in the rape of a young woman among his fellow soldiers. The look in her eyes haunts his boyish conscience and nightmares. Under gunpoint, Ugwu is kidnapped, taken to a former primary school turned into a training camp. His hair is shaved with a piece of broken glass, leaving his "scalp tender, littered with nicks." The terrified youth is punished by the "skinny soldiers – with no boots, no uniforms, no half a yellow sun on their sleeves" [symbol of the rebels] who – "kicked and slapped and mocked Ugwu during physical training." Ugwu nearly succumbed to this brutalization. "The obstacle training left his calves throbbing. The rope-climbing left his palms bleeding. The wraps of *garri* he stood in line to receive, the thin soup scraped from a metal basin once a day, left him hungry. And the casual cruelty of this new world in which he had no say grew a hard clot of fear inside of him."[7] A world in which he *had no say*. Such a circumstance, as Adichie portrays it, fits firmly into both the 1956 United Nations Supplementary Convention on the Abolition of Slavery, as well as even more so into the 2016 Bellagio working group's updated definition. Ugwu was enslaved by war, an automatic machine gun-toting child soldier.

War itself becomes a monstrous character in Adichie's nimble writing, even as she humanizes other people in her story. War corrupts or ravages all good will in its path, it seems, and especially in this case the meaning of books, learning, and education. At least almost all. Ugwu, who has been educated and loves to read, searches for scraps of paper on which to write down his thoughts, in part as a means of sustaining his sanity, of keeping his mind alive whatever happens to his body. One day in the abandoned schoolhouse, Ugwu finds wedged behind a blackboard a copy of *Narrative of the Life of Frederick Douglass, an American Slave*.

[7] Chimamanda Ngozi Adichie, *Half of a Yellow Sun* (New York: Random House, 2006), 449–50.

The boy sits on the floor and reads the book for two days; he then continues reading it over and over as his unit moves to other locations. *The Narrative* becomes Ugwu's sacred possession and psychological sustenance. He declares himself "so sad and angry for the writer," whose experiences in slavery become a metaphor for his existence in the enslavement of soldiering. He discovers that he and Douglass wrote for many of the same reasons. One day Ugwu explodes in rage as he sees a fellow soldier rolling a cigarette in torn out pages of the *Narrative*. Ugwu's despair becomes almost unbearable after watching and then joining in during the rape of a barmaid. He witnesses people whipped brutally, feels the inner weakness of hopelessness. He manages to carry on by continuing to collect scraps of paper on which he writes of his own experiences with Douglass's classic slave narrative as his model.[8] Adichie demonstrates in wonderful imagery the now universal reach and appeal of Douglass's powerful tale of survival and reinvention through literacy. It is a great distance and no distance at all between these pasts and presents, between Frederick Bailey's "dark night of slavery" on Maryland's eastern shore and a Nigerian teenager's ravaged spirit in the Biafran War of the 1960s. Douglass still speaks across all time and all borders.

Ugwu memorized some sentences in Douglass's *Narrative*. As he tried to attack the soldier rolling a cigarette in a page of the book, others grabbed him, and "dragged him away, said it was just a book after all, told him to drink some more gin." When combat operations "overwhelmed him, froze him," he would return to his copy of Douglass and read "pages of his book over and over." Wounded and convalescing, sitting under a flame tree, a journalist named Richard keeps trying to interview Ugwu about his experiences, wondering about the boy's visible efforts to write and hide his manuscript, such as it is, scribbled on old newspapers and anything resembling paper. Richard finds the discovery of the Douglass *Narrative* a very useful "anecdote." Ugwu cannot sleep because of his wounds and because of the "dead hate in the eyes of that girl" that awakens him. Ugwu survives and returns home at the end of the war to his destroyed town. He seems to have lost most of his health and his precious copy of the American slave narrative. He sees a huge pile of blackened books that have been burned. Ugwu laments: "I wish I had that Frederick Douglass book." After the interviewer sees and reads

---

[8] Ibid., 451–2. There are many editions of Douglass. See *Narrative of the Life of Frederick Douglass, an American Slave, Written by Himself*, 3rd ed., ed. David W. Blight (Boston, MA: Bedford Books, 2017).

some of the "sheets of paper" Ugwu has been writing on, left on a table, he remarks that they are "fantastic." "Yes sah," replies the young writer, "I will call it 'Narrative of the Life of a Country.'"[9]

In today's brooding world of multiple forms of contemporary enslavement and exploitation, which end in no exits for so many victims, survivors have nevertheless found ways to tell their stories. In all this loss there are renewals. In all the endings there are beginnings; survivals, if never utopias. It has ever been thus despite all the darkness of human conduct. We have to keep solidarity with the ages. There are pasts that will help us prepare if not prescribe for the present. There is a book behind that abandoned blackboard.

[9] Adichie, *Half of a Yellow Sun*, 456–8, 495–6, 530.

Acknowledgments

This volume is dedicated to

all those lost to slavery and slaving, then and now;
all those who have survived slavery, past and present; and
all those who have dedicated their lives to ending slave systems
wherever they manifest.

For Dottie and for Mike and Marcelle.

We gratefully acknowledge the team at Cambridge University Press, especially Deborah Gershenowitz, who has so assiduously shepherded this volume from idea to fruition. We are also deeply indebted to Series Editors Randall Miller and Zoe Trodd, whose careful and thoughtful readings have done much to strengthen our work. Additionally, the community of scholars comprising the international NGO Historians Against Slavery, whose work on slavery and abolition straddles past and present, has provided foundation and support for this volume, and more significantly, to the endeavor to mine usable pasts for academic and activist purposes in the present. We thank especially HASers Jason Allen, Michael Todd Landis, Talitha LeFlouria, Matthew Mason, Stacey Robertson, Stephen Rozman, and Robert Wright. Finally, we offer our sincere gratitude to the many individuals whose ideas, critical readings, and activism have invigorated this work, especially Kevin Bales, Nikki Berg Burgin, Douglas Blackmon, Shakti Jaisingh, Siddarth Kara, Greg Mullins, Laura Murphy, Alexandra Schultheis Moore, John Pepper, Louise Shelley, and Zoe Trodd.

Introduction

Getting beyond Chattel Slavery

James Brewer Stewart and Elizabeth Swanson

OLD AND NEW ABOLITIONISTS: SYMMETRIES OF
PAST WITH PRESENT

The 2016 Global Slavery Index's annual *Report* declared that close to 46 million people the world over had been forced into human bondage, a disputed but nevertheless deeply dismaying figure. Of course, it is notoriously difficult to ascertain and process definitive data regarding a trade that is wholly illegal and underground; however, whatever the exact numbers may be, it is clear that as we advance further into the twenty-first century, an ever increasingly large host of oppressors continues exploiting an ever larger number of their fellow humans by reducing them to slavery. How can we obliterate these morally repugnant and socially debilitating practices, or at least limit their spread? This question, as obvious as it is urgent, continues to be pressed by governments, activists, business, labor, and religious leaders, academics, and concerned citizens all over the globe.[1]

The same question should rightly preoccupy the readers addressed by this volume, particularly scholars, teachers, students, and activists interested in the histories of Great Britain and the United States, two nations with histories deeply tainted by centuries of enslavement, ennobled by the Western world's most powerful abolitionist movements, and noteworthy for their dramatic acts of mass emancipation. Great

---

[1] Please see www.globalslaveryindex.org/findings/ for more about the 46 million figure. A critique of this claim can be found in www.theguardian.com/global-development/poverty-matters/2014/nov/28/global-slavery-index-walk-free-human-trafficking-anne-gallagher.

Britain's "emancipation" came to pass in 1833 when compensated emancipation approved by Parliament liberated over 800,000 people. In the United States, the moment arrived in 1865 when freedom for roughly 4 million enslaved people was ratified by the Constitution's 13th Amendment. Thus it was that long ago, slavery embedded itself deeply within both nations' histories – and so did slavery's abolition. It is therefore not surprising that Anglo-American antislavery activists today equate the slaveries they seek to destroy with the kind of slavery that their forebears abolished; take inspiration from epochal figures such as Harriet Tubman, Frederick Douglass, Harriet Beecher Stowe, Olaudah Equiano, and William Wilberforce; and refer to themselves collectively as the "the new abolitionist movement."[2]

Such close identification with this deeply inspirational antislavery past goes far to explain the modern-day, or "new" abolitionists' accomplishments and why they are closely emulating the work of their ancestors. Today their non-governmental organizations (NGOs) number in the hundreds and continue proliferating; many are deservedly praised for their sophisticated approaches and impressive results. Over a century and a half ago, their forebears likewise created networks of antislavery societies that linked them closely together even as they crisscrossed the Atlantic. Today, in libraries all over the country, one encounters in increasing numbers the new abolitionists' gripping exposés of enslavement, along with analytical studies by serious academicians and governmental reports of all sorts. The original abolitionists likewise published innumerable rhetorical tracts and substantial volumes with damning testimony from escapees from slavery. Today, documentary films of widely varying quality for which new abolitionists are responsible continue multiplying, some narrated by high-profile media personalities and almost all having some testimony from a survivor of modern-day bondage. Before the Civil War, the original abolitionists turned themselves into speechmaking celebrities, performed popular antislavery

---

[2] For typical examples of this attribution that can be multiplied many times over, see https://thesocietypages.org/sexuality/2009/10/21/the-new-abolitionists-and-their-critics-second-in-a-series-on-anti-trafficking-efforts/; www.facebook.com/nynewabolitionists/; Joy James, ed., *The New Abolitionists: (Neo) Slave Narratives and Contemporary Prison Writings* (Albany, NY: State University of New York Press, 2005); www.christianpost .com/news/in-the-new-abolitionist-movement-to-stop-sex-trafficking-christians-are-still-key-players-97004/; www.vsconfronts.org/blog/we-are-the-new-abolitionists-an-education-and-action-event-to-end-human-trafficking-in-new-york-city/; www.antislavery .org/english/what_you_can_do/set_up_or_join_an_antislavery_group/join_an_existing_antislavery_group.aspx.

music, and developed eye-catching antislavery art work and ear-catching poetry. Responding (at least in part) to today's abolitionists' demands, our politicians design and our governments enact stringent laws against slavery and human trafficking. More than a century and a half ago, their predecessors flooded the halls of Congress and Parliament with antislavery petitions signed by tens of thousands of ordinary people.[3]

Propelling all this activism is the grass roots energy of everyday citizens, who behave in very similar ways as did their abolitionist predecessors when learning and teaching others about slavery, pressuring local officials, demanding action from their churches, synagogues, and mosques, monitoring their neighborhoods for evidence of enslavement, and taking care to consume as few goods produced by enslaved people as possible. It feels almost as if the new abolitionist movement has us living our antislavery history all over again. In a burst of zeal (never mind the daunting statistics), one particularly over-promising NGO, Not for Sale, goes as far as to exhort the new abolitionists that "Together we can end slavery in our lifetimes!"[4] Over 150 years ago, William Lloyd Garrison and Joseph Clarkson were given to making similar pronouncements.

The response of any serious historian to such over-the-top predictions is "simply impossible" – for this very good reason. As David Richardson makes clear in his contribution to this volume, "Contemporary Slavery in Historical Perspective," and as will be discussed more extensively later on, from at least biblical times, if not before, the heavy influences of slavery are documented throughout recorded history, leaving no assurance that it will ever be "ended," let alone "in our lifetimes." Richardson's essay also offers thoughtful assessments for modern abolitionists of how to respond constructively to slavery's persistence.

At the same time, the value of such embellishment is hard to deny. Not so long ago, in defiance of massive white hostility, it directly inspired the epochal Civil Rights struggles of the 1950s and 1960s in the United States,[5] much as it fires the imaginations and undergirds the endurance of

---

[3] James Brewer Stewart, *Holy Warriors: The Abolitionists and American Slavery* (New York: Hill and Wang, 1996), 51–125.

[4] Michelle Garza, "Not for Sale: End Human Trafficking and Slavery," Texas A&M Corpus Christi Wiki, www.tamucc.edu/wiki/MichelleGarza/NotForSaleEndHumanTrafficking AndSlavery.

[5] The classic formulation of these historical connections is Howard Zinn, *SNCC: The New Abolitionists: Racism and Civil Rights* (Chicago, IL: Haymarket Press, 1964; reprinted 2013). That racists have just as easily elided a vision of the antebellum Southern past with their sense of the present by turning themselves into "Neo-Confederates" when opposing

abolitionists today in the face of truly dismaying material circumstances. When specifying these dismaying circumstances, historical analogies continue to ring true.

Much as was the case during the nineteenth century, powerful social and economic forces are combining today to drive a staggering number of people into circumstances that make them highly vulnerable to enslavement, far more in raw numbers than at any previous time in history. Back in Frederick Douglass's day, the drivers of enslavement were basic commodities: cotton, rice, sugar, and tobacco traded in huge volumes across the greater Atlantic basin. The population vulnerable to enslavement was a seemingly limitless supply of West Africans, mostly from present day Congo, Mali, Côte d'Ivoire, Nigeria, Ghana, and Angola.[6] In our day, the drivers are goods and services of every kind imaginable and seemingly from everywhere (reflect on any Walmart store's inventory).[7] The vulnerable population is now spread across the globe and almost too enormous to calculate. The United Nations, for example, reported in 2016 that among the world's population are over 63 million refugees, more than were displaced by the Second World War, and that around 795 million people in the world do not have enough food to lead a healthy life. The continuing degradation of the natural environment caused by hyper-development all over the globe has been closely linked to spreading patterns of enslavement.[8] During the eighteenth and nineteenth centuries, slavery's environmental scourge was severe deforestation and all but unrelenting soil exhaustion. Just as was true then, the plain fact today is that the new abolitionist movement is exactly the

black civil rights is amply demonstrated in David Blight, *Race and Reunion: The Civil War in American Memory* (Cambridge, MA: Harvard University Press, 2002).

[6] The essential source for all aspects of the African slave trade is David Eltis and David Richardson, *The Atlas of the Transatlantic Slave Trade* (New Haven, CT: Yale University Press, 2009).

[7] For a highly useful study that examines modern slavery in depth and transnationally, see Louise Shelley, *Human Trafficking: A Global Perspective* (Cambridge and New York: Cambridge University Press, 2013). Limitations of space do not allow descriptions of the many goods and services that are most commonly associated with enslavement or detailed information on demographics, profitability, and so forth. Such limitations also make it impossible to offer detailed descriptions of specific new abolitionists' programs and initiatives. Three websites are particularly useful sources of such information: www.endslaverynow.org/, www.walkfree.org/, and https://polarisproject.org/.

[8] Kevin Bales, *Blood and Earth: Slavery, Econocide and the Secret to Saving the World* (New York: Spiegel & Grau, 2016).

proper response to one of our time's most agonizing and multifaceted moral and ethical challenges.

Thus far, the parallels between past and present seem straightforward, and so does the inspiration they offer today's abolitionists. As we continue to explore them, however, they mutate into conundrums that challenge the new abolitionists. As is usually the case, history, when deeply studied, complicates and (one hopes) deepens our understanding of our current circumstances. The goal of our volume is precisely this.

OLD AND NEW SLAVERY: COLLISIONS OF PAST WITH PRESENT

History's complications for today's abolitionists originate in this one deeply disruptive fact: the forms of enslavement found across the world today have almost nothing in common with nineteenth-century plantation slavery. Apart from their inherent brutality and enrichment for enslavers, plantation slavery "then" and slavery "now" reside in seemingly alternate universes. The antislavery work accomplished by Frederick Douglass and William Wilberforce went forward under circumstances almost wholly at odds with those facing today's abolitionists.[9]

Unimpeachable legal codes, massive capital investments, and unswerving state power undergirded all aspects of nineteenth-century plantation slavery. Overturning it required abolitionists to demand an entire body of existing law be overthrown and a staggering amount of private (human) property be alienated from its owners. When they demanded precisely this, they provoked explosive controversy, disrupting politics and religious denominations and vastly multiplying their influence on public opinion.[10]

Today's abolitionists enjoy none of these advantages because modern slavery enjoys no legal protections. Instead, it is criminal enterprise, outlawed (in theory) all across the globe. Suppressing it requires abolitionists to demand the stringent application of existing laws, the enactment of more effective laws and the cooperation of multinational

---

[9] Important examinations of the history of abolitionist movements and their evolution are Seymour Drescher, *Abolition: A History of Slavery and Antislavery* (Cambridge and New York: Cambridge University Press, 2009) and Joel Quirk, *The Antislavery Project: From the Slave Trade to Human Trafficking* (Philadelphia, PA: University of Pennsylvania Press, 2011).

[10] Stewart, *Holy Warriors*, 51–96. Manisha Sinha, *The Slave's Cause: A History of Abolition* (New Haven, CT: Yale University Press, 2016).

agencies and businesses of all sorts. In perhaps the most revealing contrast to the situations of their controversial forebears, abolitionists today find that most everyone already gives lip service to such laws and that businesses sensitive about their public images do the same as well.[11] In brief, they lack powerful proslavery opponents who would fan the flames of controversy and help them to generate headlines. Who is today's John C. Calhoun? Who, today, openly defends slavery, as did Calhoun in his infamous 1837 speech before the US Senate entitled "The Positive Good of Slavery"?[12] This question raises one of modern abolitionism's most daunting problems: the fact that modern slavery remains difficult for the vast majority of scholars to define exactly, and for abolitionists' fellow citizens to respond to with empathy and a sense of urgency.

Deeply aware of this problem, modern abolitionists often lament that most of their country people truly believe that slavery ended forever in 1833 or 1865, strongly denying its ongoing existence in a variety of forms into the present time. Highly promoted films such as *Amazing Grace* (2007) and *Lincoln* (2012) simply ratify the deeply embedded historical memories which maintain that Great Britain and the United States triumphed in glorious moral wars that swept the scourge forever from the face of the Earth.[13] And why should not ordinary citizens believe exactly this? For Great Britain and the United States, as historians have told them time out of mind and quite correctly, emancipation marked truly epochal moments not only for those liberated (a combined total of 4,800,000) and for their former slaveholders, but also for practically everyone alive at the time. The costs included a catastrophic 750,000 Civil War casualties for the United States and an expenditure of as much as a jaw-dropping 2 billion, 180 million inflation-adjusted pounds for the British.[14] As the powerful myths and memories generated by such watershed events

---

[11] A useful introduction to this problem and efforts to address it is found in www.cips.org/Documents/About%20CIPS/Ethics/CIPS_ModernSlavery_Broch_WEB.pdf.

[12] J. C. Calhoun, "Speech on the Reception of Abolition Petitions, Delivered in the Senate, February 6th, 1837," in R. Cralle, ed., *Speeches of John C. Calhoun, Delivered in the House of Representatives and in the Senate of the United States* (New York: D. Appleton, 1853), 625–33. Retrieved from www.stolaf.edu/people/fitz/COURSES/calhoun.html.

[13] For illuminating analyses of the Civil War in American historical memory, consult Blight, *Race and Reunion*, and Gaines M. Foster, *Ghosts of the Confederacy: Defeat, the Lost Cause and the Emergence of the New South* (Oxford and New York: Oxford University Press, 1988).

[14] See www.in2013dollars.com/1833-GBP-in-2016?amount=20000000 for calculations approximating those above based on 20 million 1833 pounds adjusted to 2016 rates.

reverberate into our time, is it a surprise that many find it hard to believe that slavery persists?

In the United States, for example, mention of slavery today leads Americans to fasten instinctively on Abraham Lincoln, Robert E. Lee, Frederick Douglass, or Jefferson Davis; some may extend their thinking to include Martin Luther King, Jr. and Malcolm X, or the 1964 Civil Rights Act; and even the presidency of Barack Obama. Little wonder, then, that people enslaved in so many differing circumstances remain all but unrecognizable to most Americans and so challenging for scholars to generalize about: manacled woodcutters in Manaos, Brazil; children peering through barbwire fences on West African cacao plantations; multiple generations of Indian families held in debt bondage; Pakistani children chained to carpet looms; profoundly traumatized child soldiers in the Democratic Republic of Congo; enslaved vegetable pickers in the Florida "panhandle"; kidnapped South Asian men and boys enslaved on Thai fishing boats; and prostituted people of every age, gender, and sexual orientation put up for sale in Bangkok, Minneapolis, and London. Indeed, these staccato descriptions illustrate perfectly why modern slavery defies easy generalization and straightforward definitions.

Powerful as it is, historical memory is but one of several factors that explain why mobilization of antislavery knowledge and opinion is so much more difficult now than it was in the nineteenth century, and also why slavery today is so much more challenging to describe.[15] To explain: back in the nineteenth century plantation slaves were reflexively lumped together by a racist white society into a single "black race." Exposed to outside observation, the lives and work of those enslaved were regionally centered over several generations. They resided in familiar places. They were openly bought and sold. They sustained their own communities, built their own cultural defenses, engaged in

---

[15] Exceptions to these generalizations about modern slavery's invisibility are long-sanctioned slavery systems such as those found in Mauritania, India, Pakistan, and other locales where tradition has sustained the practice with very little change, deeply rooting it across generations. For different reasons, exceptions also include locations where sexually enslaved individuals are put on public display for commercial purposes. Although these forms of enslavement are easily visible, for most citizens of Great Britain and the United States the lived experiences of those enslaved remain worlds away. As emigration from slavery-ridden regions to Great Britain and the United States continues, however, it is likely that these "worlds away" will begin to converge. For descriptions of these locales and explanation of their forms of enslavement see Kevin Bales, *Disposable People: The New Slavery and the Global Economy* (Berkeley, CA: University of California Press, 1999).

day-to-day resistance, organized collective rebellion, and liberated themselves and one another. In short, they lived in plain sight, made endless trouble, created headlines, and brought still more attention to their abolitionist allies. Today's enslaved and their exploiters, by contrast, are all but invisible to anyone other than themselves and the activists working directly with them.[16] Because they represent every imaginable race and nationality, and are geographically dispersed and highly mobile, the enslaved cannot be lumped into a single racial stereotype. Since slavery is everywhere illegal, they are bought and sold in secret and forced to live "under the radar," where it is next to impossible to sustain multigenerational communities that support individual and collective solidarity and resistance, let alone mass rebellion. By the same token, many of today's enslavers live as marginalized outlaws. Back then, they sat in Parliament or resided in the White House.

With today's slavery virtually outlawed and operating only in the form of criminal conspiracies, anything goes. In absolute contrast to the old plantation complex, slavery today involves no fixed rules, no shared understandings of limits, no guiding precepts or precedents, no long-term planning and no accountability. It's all up for grabs. Many decades of improvisation and untrammeled entrepreneurship under widely varying conditions have caused modern slavery to mutate into multiple forms of exploitation as distinct from one another as they are from the nineteenth-century plantation complex. Attorneys, activists, scholars, and public policy experts often disagree over legal definitions of slavery today and, as a result, an opaque legal and cultural curtain shields the realities of modern slavery from the lived experiences of most white people in America, as well as from straightforward legal codification.[17]

Back in John C. Calhoun's day, everyone knew slavery when they saw it; abolitionists also knew how to litigate over it, which was frequently. Whatever one's ethical views of the institution, it was easy to define its standing in law and its substance in social reality. Today, all these certainties have vanished, as has the myth that emancipation in 1865 meant the end of slave systems in the United States. In considering modern slavery, then, scholars must attend both to its perpetuation as a global system *and* to its transformations in the United States into reconstruction-era

---

[16] Kevin Bales, *Ending Slavery: How We Free Today's Slaves* (Berkeley and Los Angeles: University of California Press, 2007), 51–2.

[17] For an incisive analysis and critique of current definitions of slavery, see Julia O'Connell Davidson, *The Margins of Freedom: Modern Slavery* (New York: Palgrave MacMillan, 2015), 28–55.

debt bondage and convict leasing; Jim Crow segregation and racial terror backed by lynching; and mass incarceration, the prison-industrial complex, the school-to-prison pipeline, and racialized policing.[18] Clearly, then, a description of modern slavery that is easily grasped by average citizens and firmly fixed for legal experts and makers of public policy can seem as difficult to pin down as trying to capture a blob of mercury with a teaspoon as it darts across a highly polished dinner table.

CATCHING MERCURY: RULES AND REGULATIONS

A wise historian might suggest that cornering this blob of mercury requires holding simultaneously to two quite contradictory approaches to slavery in the British and American past, observing what each reveals about modern slavery. The first contends that looking deeply into nineteenth-century Anglo-American slavery and weighing it against slavery today yields a wealth of understanding. The second holds precisely the opposite, insisting that focus on the plantation complex seriously hinders coming to grips with slavery in its current forms; hence, we should banish it from our attempts to mobilize historical knowledge in service of ending current oppressions.[19] Which approach succeeds more fully in removing the legal and cultural veil? Happily, both have great value. For all their differences, both render today's forms of slavery highly visible and far more open to critical analysis and generalization. And both are guided by the axiom emphasized thus far – that the old plantation slavery and modern human bondage have little in common beyond cruelty and exploitation. Whether weighing comparative profitability, methods of enslavement and slave trading, the biological and

---

[18] To trace the transformation of plantation slavery in the US into disparate forms of oppression, brutality, and exploitation over time see Michelle Alexander, *The New Jim Crow: Mass Incarceration in the Age of Colorblindness* (New York: The New Press, 2010); Douglas A. Blackmon, *Slavery by Another Name: The Re-Enslavement of Black Americans from the Civil War to World War II* (New York: Doubleday, 2008); Dennis Childs, *Slaves of the State: Black Incarceration from the Chain Gang to the Penitentiary* (Minneapolis, MN: University of Minnesota Press, 2015); Talitha LeFlouria, *Chained in Silence: Black Women and Convict Labor in the New South* (Chapel Hill, NC: University of North Carolina Press, 2015).

[19] Bales develops these contrasts in *Disposable People*, 7–11, and in Kevin Bales, Zoe Trodd, and Alex Kent Williamson, *Modern Slavery: The Secret World of 27 Million People* (New York: Oneworld Press, 2009), 27–34. Joseph C. Miller, *The Problem of Slavery as History: A Global Approach* (New Haven, CT: Yale University Press, 2009), 1–35, elucidates these contrasts with great clarity – and then recommends banishment of the descriptor "slavery" for reasons discussed in the following pages.

social reproduction of the enslaved, or slavery's ideological justifications, in this respect, contrast overwhelms commonality and, for this reason, there is much to learn from it. Precisely because the contrasts between "now" and "then" are so undeniable, they help to render modern slavery starkly visible, shredding the curtain that camouflages modern slavery and obliterating the tidy narrative of progress from slavery to freedom. Thus, the importance of fixing on the plantation complex in order, by contrast, to describe modern slavery is essential.

Just as important – perhaps more so – comparing and contrasting nineteenth-century race-based plantation slavery and slavery as practiced today directly addresses one of the modern abolitionist movement's most consequential failures. Its problem, bluntly, is that while contemporary abolitionists constantly mine nineteenth-century abolitionism for symbols that legitimize their cause, they seem unable to recognize that the history of African enslavement and liberation is powerfully implicated in their mission. Close inspection of high-profile websites reveals no leading African American intellectuals or activists among their spokespeople, and they demonstrate no observable interest in attracting African American supporters. The slavery that fires their opposition leads them to no substantial engagement with the slavery so central to African American history. The problem, then, is not academic; instead, it involves the new abolitionists' racial astigmatism, and, crucially, the obligation of historians is to offer remedies. At the same time, it is also about the integrity of this volume. Having promised to take its readers "beyond chattel slavery," our book will do so only by grappling with the African American past and its pertinence for the problem of slavery today, at least in terms of British and American interest and involvement. As with any such massive historical wound, getting "beyond chattel slavery" first requires dealing directly with it.[20]

CATCHING MERCURY: A THOUGHT EXPERIMENT

The following thought experiment addresses this welter of problems, illustrates the value of our two antithetical approaches to modern slavery, and simplifies the task of introducing our volume's essays.

---

[20] The problem of racial blindness within "new abolitionism" is detailed at length in James Brewer Stewart, "'Using History to Make Slavery History': The African American Past and the Challenge of Contemporary Slavery," *Social Inclusion* 3, no. 1 (2015), 125–35. www.cogitatiopress.com/ojs/index.php/socialinclusion/article/download/.../pdf_21.

Imagine yourself giving a talk entitled "Challenges of the New Global Slavery" before the US Congressional Black Caucus. Some audience members are renowned civil rights veterans, and many trace their genealogies to enslaved ancestors. All know their American history. They are powerfully placed to advance the agendas of modern abolitionism. But if you fail to connect the "new" slavery with the "old," your listeners will likely believe that you understand the history of enslavement that they consider central to their lives as fundamentally disconnected from the "global" slavery you are about to describe. They might further suspect, as a result of your elision of these connections, that you harbor certain racial and historical insensitivities. Fortunately, your best strategy for success is also the central theme of this essay, which is to show that modern forms of enslavement are vastly different from British West Indian or United States plantation slavery. At the same time, you are also about to demonstrate how the African American past powerfully illuminates slavery in the present, and vice versa, as well as the value of our two opposing approaches. With that settled, we move on, then, to the lecture.

Once you have elucidated our now familiar contrasts (our first approach) and have shredded modern slavery's veil of invisibility, you turn next to demonstrating how to dismember the popular belief that dramatic mass emancipations like the one that accompanied the US Civil War permanently ended slavery. You accomplish this by banishing the antebellum US South from your thoughts and dwelling instead on the re-enslavement of those recently emancipated in the post-Civil War era. The fact you stress above all others is that human bondage in the United States survived the 13th Amendment in various forms and continued well into our own day. With this segue, the old plantation complex as a benchmark for assaying modern slavery becomes irrelevant, because you have shown that its full abolition was nothing more than a myth designed to obscure the truth of its persistence into the present. Now the enslavement of African Americans you are detailing looks much like the fraternal twin of some of the most widespread forms of slavery today – not to mention mirroring the problem of their invisibility, and the denial of many that they in fact exist. The second approach – comparison instead of contrast – rightly takes front and center. Contrasts vanish. Symmetries dominate.

Your audience knows well the history of post-emancipation re-enslavement, or "slavery by another name," as it is often described. Some of their forebears were ensnared in it; it is exhaustively documented; and it is often seen as foreshadowing the devastating US "prison industrial complex," which not coincidentally continues to be a site of profit from the unpaid or extremely poorly paid labor of prisoners, the vast majority of whom (despite representing only 13 percent of the US population) are African American. It took the form of debt peonage and the exploitation of fraudulently convicted and imprisoned black citizens. These practices also ensnared a much smaller number of vulnerable whites. Although it was outlawed by the United States Constitution, debt peonage and convict labor exploited tens of thousands and remained entrenched until the end of the Second World War.[21]

The key descriptor here, you stress to your audience, is *outlawed*, which signals strongly that the African American experience with postwar re-enslavement and the ways in which enslavement is being practiced today have a surprising amount in common, at least in terms of their standing under the law. This point is critical. Both are transacted outside the law and too often treated by governments with a wink and a nod. Enslavers see those they cast into bondage as cheap, malleable, short-term, or, worse, short-lived workers, not as valuable (human) property to be retained as it reproduces over generations. Improvisation drives slaveholders' behavior in both instances. Tradition and fixed rules no longer prevail. If transported back to a time between the 1880s and the end of the Second World War, many of today's enslavers would instantly recognize exactly what their white Southern counterparts were up to – and would likely eagerly join in.

From the moment of emancipation, former American slaveholders did everything they could think of to force their former "property" back into servitude. First, they attempted to enforce so called "Black Codes" that punished African Americans for often trumped up charges of debt, vagrancy, petty larceny, and even "lurking" by returning them to the plantations they had recently left, manacled and chained. After federal intervention suppressed such practices, former slaveholders and other entrepreneurs turned to re-enslaving African American "debtors," whom they saddled with impossible sums with rapidly compounding interest for "services rendered." This practice of debt peonage is of course precisely what enslavers the world over use to extort labor from vulnerable people today. Using fraudulent pretenses, today's slaveholders keep their

---

[21] Excellent studies of post-Civil War re-enslavement include Pete Daniels, *In the Shadow of Slavery: Peonage in the New South, 1901–1969* (Champaign-Urbana, IL: University of Illinois Press, 1960); Blackmon, *Slavery by Another Name*; David Oshinski, *Worse than Slavery: Parchman Farm and the Ordeal of Jim Crow* (New York: Free Press, 1977); and Leflouria, *Chained in Silence*.

indebted victims close at hand, or move them across national borders for enslavement by others for sexual exploitation and for brutalizing labor on farms, in factories, and in private residences.

A second method of Southern re-enslavement, the convict lease system, also replicates itself today wherever unscrupulous governments and private recruiters enslave "guest workers" after luring them with promises of employment. It is no accident that Louisiana's maximum security prison, Angola (the name is telling, recalling the country of origin of many of the enslaved persons who labored there in the antebellum period; the prison is also known as "the Alcatraz of the South"), is situated on what was once an enormous cotton plantation.[22] There and throughout the South, enslavement meant labor in chain gangs or within the prisons themselves. Today, what awaits those convicted of any number of crimes is exploitation in public works projects, agribusiness operations, retail manufacturing, and other industries.[23]

These stark similarities between slavery in the past and slavery today prompt a member of your audience to inquire how and why re-enslavement developed in the post-emancipation South? In reply, you quote the deeply thoughtful American abolitionist Wendell Phillips, who offered this blunt warning in response to the ratification of the 13th Amendment: "We have abolished the slave. The master remains." What so concerned Phillips, you explain, is what economists have termed "labor substitution"; that is, in this context, the sharp economic imperative felt by the growers of major commodities such as sugar, cotton, rice, and tobacco to find new sources of exploitable labor as rapidly as possible to replace their former slaves. For the great planters in the American South, the answer, along with sharecropping, was re-enslavement. For commodity growers in Central American nations, the British Caribbean Islands, and the Philippines, each a major exporter of "enslaveable" people today, the initial answer was the substitution of Asian and Amerindian "contract laborers." In Haiti, "slavery by almost the same name" was the eventual

---

[22] "History of Angola," Angola Museum: Louisiana State Penitentiary Museum Foundation, www.angolamuseum.org/history/history/.

[23] The most profoundly unconscionable varieties of imprisonment as slavery take us to Nazi Germany, North Korea, the Soviet gulags, Boko Haram, and the Islamic State, systems so barbaric that it is impossible to consider them in the analysis developed here. For more on prison labor, see Earl Smith and Angela J. Hattery, "Incarceration: A Tool for Racial Segregation and Labor Exploitation," *Race, Gender, and Class* 15, no. 1–2 (2008), 79–97; Jaron Browne, "Rooted in Slavery: Prison Labor Exploitation," *Race, Poverty & the Environment* 14, no. 1 (Spring 2008), 42–4; Childs, *Slaves of the State*.

answer.[24] In China and India, deeply rooted traditions, not labor substitution, explain why debt peonage today enslaves millions, some of whom flee only to be re-enslaved elsewhere. But labor substitution as a springboard to enslavement is hardly a closed chapter within the United States. In Florida, for instance, fruit and vegetable growers who exploit undocumented Central American workers have made that area infamous as (quoting the Justice Department) "ground zero for slavery." All over the country, foreign workers are brought in under the H1 and H2A (non-agricultural workers) and H2B (agricultural workers) visa system, programs which have been identified with exploitative and "slave-like" practices by a range of NGOs and investigative journalists.[25] In such instances, the "slavery by another name" endured by African Americans casts a harsh but helpful illumination on various forms of enslavement today. This point of comparison overcomes modern slavery's current invisibility, puts African American history front and center for today's abolitionists, and powerfully reinforces black Americans' demands for racial justice in what Amiri Baraka (Leroy Jones) refers to as the "changing same" of racism as it manifests in our current historical moment.[26]

Presentation before the Congressional Black Caucus concluded, members of your distinguished audience express appreciation for your clarity when demonstrating how the African American experience of post-Civil War re-enslavement illuminates the circumstances of the enslaved today, how precisely the reverse is also true, and why it is that the echoes of post-plantation slavery reverberate so powerfully into our time. Your hope is that they move next to consulting about new legislation to combat the legacies of slavery from the past and the challenges of slavery today.

---

[24] Excellent discussions of labor substitution include Eric Foner, *Nothing but Freedom: Emancipation and its Legacies* (Baton Rouge, LA: State University of Louisiana Press, 1987) and Suzanne Miers, *Slavery in the 20th Century: The Evolution of a Global Problem* (New York: Rowman Altimira, 2003).

[25] See the Southern Poverty Law Center report "Close to Slavery: Guestworker Programs in the United States" (February 13, 2013), www.splcenter.org/20130218/close-slavery-guestworker-programs-united-states; Polaris Project, "Labor Trafficking in the US: A Closer Look at Temporary Work Visas," n.d., https://polarisproject.org/sites/default/files/Temp%20Visa_v5%20(1).pdf; Jessica Garrison et al., "The New American Slavery: Invited to the US, Workers Find a Nightmare," *Buzzfeed* (July 24, 2015), www.buzzfeed.com/jessicagarrison/the-new-american-slavery-invited-to-the-us-foreign-workers-f?utm_term=.avLWvbqYE#.pmKPLoJ1N.

[26] Amiri Baraka (LeRoi Jones), "The Changing Same: R&B and the New Black Music," in William H. Harris, ed., *The LeRoi Jones/Amiri Baraka Reader* (New York: Thunder's Mouth Press, 1960), 186–209.

CONTEMPORARY SLAVERY: A CONTESTABLE CONCEPT

Having established the value of understanding post-emancipation re-enslavement and labor substitution in order to remove modern slavery's curtain of invisibility, what else might historical approaches contribute to the work of modern abolitionism? One quite pressing issue involves responding as historians to a string of urgent questions that open modern abolitionism to stringent criticism. To explain:

Skeptics want to know what, exactly, distinguishes slavery from other profound forms of deprivation, suffering, and gross exploitation. What bright line, if any, should morally responsible people draw between the enslaved and those who, though technically "free," remain no less profoundly oppressed? If that line cannot be confidently established, how can it be claimed that the world today contains 46 million enslaved, or any other number, for that matter? These questions yield no easy answers because, as we know, today's slavery can defy generalization by displaying so many variations while operating so far under the radar. Then there is the complication of what the term "slavery" has come to represent in today's public discourse, where it is highly politicized and endlessly invoked to decry all manner of social practices which have nothing in common with actual human bondage. Louis Farrakhan, leader of the Nation of Islam, demonstrates this problem perfectly when making the following assertion: NBA superstar LeBron James (2016 salary, including promotional fees, $90,365,000) is, according to Farrakhan's rhetoric "nothing but a modern day slave – owned by the white man – in a system designed to chew him up and spit him out."[27] To apply Farrakhan's rhetoric much more mundanely, why are we incessantly cautioned that smart phones, play stations, controlled substances, pornography, Netflix binges, destructive relationships, and even shopping all possess the power to "enslave" us? Such assertions drain "slavery" of its ethical and emotional resonance and analytical meaning. The curtain of invisibility shrouding the practice in its current forms grows all the more weighty.

To be sure, linking one's righteous cause to accusations of enslavement has, from at least the seventeenth century, empowered epochal struggles for social justice such as feminism ("the slavery of sex"), labor organizing ("wage slavery"), and revolutions against political oppression (the

---

[27] "NBA is Modern-Day Slavery: They Buy Us, They Trap Us," TMZ Sports (February 22, 2016), www.tmz.com/2016/02/22/louis-farrakhan-nba-is-modern-day-slavery-they-buy-us-trap-us/.

"slavery" of kings, autocrats, and dictators). Across the millennia, fervent Christians have embraced the transformative promise of personal liberation from enslavement to sin, and such linkages continue to be articulated today. Cut close to the bone, however, and the problems associated with invoking slavery to highlight oppression can be as deeply troubling as they are illuminating.

Consider these questions: What, if anything, distinguishes what abolitionists call "slavery" from conditions facing technically "free" people who endure lifetimes that are every bit as full of grinding poverty, harsh manual labor, sub-subsistence wages, and profound abuse from employers? Could it be that by concentrating entirely on what they perceive to be enslavement, abolitionists are ignoring or even enabling other equally heinous assaults against human dignity? Could it be that there are enslaved people today who actually live better than others who are free? And if so, should not humanitarians champion such unfortunates over the more protected of the enslaved? Are there people who have voluntarily chosen to become sex workers whose employment abolitionists jeopardize when campaigning to eliminate prostitution? Could it be that self-interested governments are conflating "slavery" with "human trafficking" in order to enflame nativists and bigots to demand the sealing of national borders against the "threats" of refugees and asylum seekers? Might, then, today's abolitionist movement be used as a pawn by governments bent on exclusion and internal repression? These are urgent questions, too often avoided by too many of today's abolitionist activists, which was often true for yesteryear's abolitionists as well.[28]

To explain: once compensated emancipation had been achieved in 1833, British abolitionists wrestled with just these conundrums as they embarked on their new mission of eradicating slavery all over the globe, a quest that continued well into the twentieth century. When picking their next targets, they fixed on forms of enslavement that resembled the once-legal plantation system they had so recently vanquished. Slavery that differed markedly by relying on custom, not legal codes, failed to attract their opposition. They likewise failed to grasp the significance of labor substitution, even as new, illegal forms of enslavement replaced legalized systems being overturned.[29] Some critics condemned these abolitionists

[28] These questions are most incisively developed in O'Connell, *The Margins of Freedom*, 28–80.

[29] These critiques of British abolitionism are extensively discussed in Quirk, *The Antislavery Project*, 56–125.

as pawns of imperialist governments because of their intrusions into the affairs of other nations and cultures. Others asserted that the supposedly enslaved were actually working of their own free wills and that abolitionists were actually stimulating mass unemployment. Drastically exploited British industrial workers, many of them children, condemned the abolitionists as hypocrites for maintaining that their poverty was not slavery because they were legally "free." "Slaves without masters" was an abolitionist oxymoron; selective perceptions of suffering and exploitation were no less widespread back then than they seem to skeptics today.[30]

Julia O'Connell Davidson's powerfully argued *The Margins of Freedom: Modern Slavery* sets forth these critiques and challenges today's abolitionists to overcome them. How? By combating state efforts to pervert antislavery ideology to justify closing borders against refugees and to foster racial bigotry and nativism. By resisting paternalism and racial blindness in their own antislavery appeals. By insisting that "if poverty is not [technically] slavery," it nevertheless propels slavery's terrifying expansion. By objecting vociferously when the sufferings of those nominally free are as horrific as those enslaved. In other words, in order to succeed with integrity, abolitionists must embrace an expansive mandate, not a strictly legalistic one.[31]

MARKING SLAVERY'S BLURRY BOUNDARIES

Still, even under the conditions of such a mandate, we remain troubled by that vexing question: where do we draw the elusive line between slavery and freedom? For at least the past half century, the task of defining slavery has puzzled policy makers and activists, spurred political discord, and generated academic contestation. At first, the history of determining slavery's status in international law was straightforward. In 1926, the League of Nations Slavery Convention ratified precisely the same definition that the old abolitionists had always embraced. Slavery

---

[30] For an extended treatment of nineteenth-century distinctions between poverty and enslavement see Jonathan Glickstein, "Poverty Is Not Slavery: The Abolitionists and the Competitive Labor Market," in Michael Fellman and Lewis Perry, eds., *Antislavery Reconsidered: New Essays on the Abolitionists* (Baton Rouge, LA: Louisiana State University Press, 1979), 195–218.

[31] We urge readers to consider carefully the fine critical analysis of the contested concept of slavery throughout Davidson's *The Margins of Freedom*. Limitations of space permit neither as full a consideration of this problem as her work addresses it, nor as it – and her work – deserve.

meant chattel slavery, legalized slavery, and nothing else. Wherever one found slavery anywhere in the world, positive law supported it, just as it had in Frederick Douglass's day. An enslaved person, according to the Convention, was someone over whom "any or all the powers attaching to the rights of ownership are exercised."[32] The Convention gave no overt recognition to "slavery by another name" and after the passage of thirty years it became all too obvious that this restrictive definition needed significant expansion.[33]

In 1956, the United Nation's Supplementary Convention on the Abolition of Slavery acted accordingly by concluding quite rightly that today's slavery takes a variety of forms and rests far more often on custom, entrepreneurship, and criminal conspiracies than on codified law and property relations. It then went on to define slavery to include debt bondage, serfdom, forced marriages, coerced prostitution, and the exploitation for any purpose of a child less than eighteen years of age. Paradoxically, this more realistic definition of slavery is also highly susceptible to being flouted, misinterpreted, and politicized. By 2016, practically every nation had signed up to this document, but some who have pledged to suppress slavery also connive to sponsor it. (The 1957 Convention has no enforcement mechanisms.) Further complications arise when politicians and popular media incorrectly conflate slavery with human trafficking, and when activists insist that colonialism, incest, the incarceration of children, organ harvesting, and other evils quite distinct from modern slavery, are, nevertheless, modern slavery. Little wonder that confusion surrounds the question of what modern slavery is and is not.[34]

How might historical approaches bring clarity? The widely cited historian Orlando Patterson took an important step when arguing that the irreducible commonality shared by all enslaved, past and present, is the condition of "social death," defined as a parasitic "relation of domination, approaching the limits of total power." To be socially dead is

---

[32] *Convention to Suppress the Slave Trade and Slavery*, Geneva, September 25, 1926, *United Nations Treaty Series*, vol. 212, no. 2861, p. 17. Available at https://treaties.un.org/pages/ViewDetails.aspx?src=TREATY&mtdsg_no=XVIII-2&chapter=18&clang=_en.

[33] For a full account of these developments, see Jean Allain and Kevin Bales, "Slavery and Its Definitions," *Global Dialogue* 14, no. 2 (Summer/Autumn 2012), Queen's University Belfast Law Research Paper No. 12-06.

[34] Human trafficking and slavery are constantly being described as identical problems, which they are not. Trafficking refers only to the illegal movement of people such as refugees from the Middle East being trafficked across the Mediterranean to Italy. Such persons are not enslaved, but the fact of their being trafficked surely makes them vulnerable to enslavement, which is what often happens when they arrive at their destinations.

to be stripped of all autonomy, support from kin, honor, and claims of humanity. According to Patterson, enslaved people are transformed into physical representations of their masters and exercise no independent power. Patterson's critics regard his generalizations as far too restrictive, noting correctly that very large numbers of the enslaved today remain connected to family; for example, those millions held in debt bondage. Family ties, moreover, often remain crucial for both slaveholders and the enslaved. The former threaten and abuse them in order to force obedience and garner profit. The latter protect them, sometimes fiercely, to the point of open resistance.[35]

Whatever one's view of slavery as social death, attempts to develop a comprehensive definition of modern slavery remained academic exercises until 2012, when a veritable squadron of distinguished historians and world-renowned activists gathered in Italy at Lake Como's Bellagio Conference Center and took on the task of establishing a legally binding description suitable for prosecuting today's "real world" enslavers. With this goal in mind they reinterpreted for twenty-first-century purposes the 1926 League of Nations Slavery Convention's original definition of slavery's essence as "the status or condition of a person over which any or all of the powers attached to the right of ownership are exercised." Back in 1926, as we have seen, the authors of this rubric intended to describe only forms of legalized chattel slavery reminiscent of the old Western Hemisphere's plantation model. Viewing this description from twenty-first-century vantage points, however, the historically minded Bellagio working group concluded that the phrase "rights of ownership" had a deeper implicit meaning that applied directly to enslavement in our time. To be enslaved in every variety of human bondage meant much more than being defined by a legally binding bill of sale. It also involved being under constant surveillance, having your family threatened and held hostage, having your children exploited, suffering sexual abuse, and surviving brutal corporeal abuse and semi-starvation as forms of punishment. The working group consolidated this litany of exploitation into a single generalization that defines, in their view, the essence of enslavement. A key paragraph in the working group's report, the *Bellagio-Harvard Guidelines on the Legal Parameters of Slavery*, defines slavery as follows:

... control over a person in such a way as to significantly deprive that person of his or her personal liberty, with the intent of exploitation through the use,

---

[35] Orlando Patterson, *Slavery and Social Death: A Comparative Study* (Cambridge, MA: Harvard University Press, 1982).

management, transfer or disposal of that person. Usually this exercise will be supported by and obtained through means such as violent force, deception or coercion.[36]

In short, these historians transformed the 1926 rubric into a prosecutorial weapon against "under the radar" slave dealers the world over by applying the first of our two approaches; that is, by investigating through both comparison and contrast how plantation slavery illuminates slavery as practiced today. David Richardson's capacious essay in this volume, "Contemporary Slavery in Historical Perspective," confirms precisely this formulation. It demonstrates the applicability of the working group's definition as he describes, compares, contrasts, and differentiates among varieties of enslavement from classical times onward, including in the Middle East, East Africa, India, the far East, and South Asia, as well as throughout the plantation systems of the Western Hemisphere. Richardson's essay demonstrates the enormous value for academicians and activists alike of "thinking big" about slavery's history and its implications.

But for all the technical value of the Bellagio working group's definition, it does not succeed in raising slavery's curtain of invisibility in some dramatic way for the larger political culture. James Sidbury corrects this deficiency by employing biography to argue convincingly that the condition of "civil death" should replace Patterson's "social death" as the universal descriptor of enslavement. His contribution to this volume, "Slavery and Civic Death: Making Sense of Modern Slavery in Historical Context," holds that the enslaved are invariably cut off from any appeal for justice to or even recognition from state authority. For enslaved people, there can be no appeal for redress of grievances, no legitimate access to the public sphere. The practices enforcing "civic death," as Sidbury defines it, are also part and parcel of the working group's definition of slavery.

Sidbury anchors the concept of "civic death" in historical analysis and employs it when bringing to life the quests for self-liberation of a dozen truly remarkable survivors of contemporary slavery from all over the globe. These forays into biography add flesh-and-blood urgency to the working group's legal reasoning, much as Frederick Douglass's *Narrative* infused urgency into the original abolitionists' appeals. The example has great value for abolitionists today in raising the veil that obscures

---

[36] The *Bellagio-Harvard Guidelines* are found on www.law.qub.ac.uk/schools/SchoolofLaw/FileStore/Filetoupload,651854,en.pdf.

contemporary slavery, which was precisely the intent of the National Underground Freedom Center when it collaborated with the US State Department in producing *Journey to Freedom*, a moving documentary featuring this same exceptional group of escapees from slavery.[37]

Another contributor to our volume, Allison Mileo Gorsuch, an attorney and a historian, has publicly endorsed the working group's description of slavery. Her essay, "From Statute to Amendment and Back Again: The Evolution of American Slavery and Anti-Slavery Law," demonstrates the value of the Bellagio description for developing a clear historical understanding of how antislavery jurisprudence and legislation in the United States has addressed the problem of "slavery by another name." Well into the twentieth century, some judicial findings held to a restricted understanding of the old chattel slavery, using physical coercion and formal ownership as the criteria for defining human bondage. Increasingly, however, judges and legislators found in the 13th Amendment ample precedent for moving against sexual enslavement, debt bondage, profoundly coerced labor, and the illegal trafficking of enslaved persons across national boundaries. This trend was well established even before the passage of the Trafficking Victims Protection Act in 2000, federal legislation that anticipated the conclusions of the working group that the "old" slavery and the "new" have many oppressive features in common that go far beyond bills of sale and tools of violence, including psychological manipulation, geographic isolation, threats to family, harsh surveillance, physical and sexual abuse, and the confiscation of documents proving citizenship. The working group's findings, according to Gorsuch, now provide guiding principles through which antislavery legislation is adjudicated and enforced. How effective those laws are and how rigorous that enforcement is depends entirely on the new abolitionists' degree of success in provoking public opinion to demand change and accountability, and in understanding and using the law, as did abolitionists to sometimes good effect in the eighteenth and nineteenth centuries.

---

37 *Journey to Freedom*, Dir. Justin Dillon (2012), http://freedomcenter.org/enablingfreedom/journeytofreedom. A rich compilation of survivor narratives is Laura Murphy's *Survivors of Slavery: Modern-Day Slave Narratives* (New York: Columbia University Press, 2014); her Introduction presents a lucid examination of the characteristics of modern slavery and of the echoes of the antebellum slave narrative in today's narratives of enslavement. Also see Kevin Bales and Zoe Trodd, *To Plead Our Own Cause: Personal Stories by Today's Slaves* (New York: Columbia University Press, 2008); and Bales, Trodd, and Williamson, *Modern Slavery*.

SLAVING, NOT SLAVERY: GERUNDS, NOT NOUNS

So have the working group's conclusions settled the question of slavery's definition to historians' satisfaction? Not according to the eminent African historian Joseph C. Miller, whose brilliantly argued monograph *The Problem of Slavery as History: A Global Approach* (2009) should be of great interest to twenty-first-century abolitionists. Miller insists that to better understand how slavery actually worked, still works, and should be worked against today, historians must abandon the noun "slavery" and all attempts to describe slavery as an "institution." These, Miller argues, are static characterizations that convey none of slavery's dynamism, durability, variability, and evolution across the centuries. Historians have habitually constructed abstract "models" of nineteenth-century plantation slavery, he contends, which they then apply ahistorically when attempting to understand slavery in all its bewildering variety, wherever it might be found. To solve this problem, Miller advocates our second approach, which is that in order to grasp modern slavery, we must jettison all thoughts of the plantation complex. To this injunction, Miller adds the jolting recommendation that we also scrap the term "slavery" altogether. Instead, Miller recommends employing the gerund "slaving," which forces us to recognize that human bondage is above all an ongoing historical process carried forward dynamically by highly active agents – in his terminology, "slavers" – in response to ever-changing circumstances over the centuries.[38] Miller's analysis invites criticism.[39] Nevertheless, his explanation of what slaving constitutes, who slavers were, and what has motivated them over the millennia holds great import for anyone seeking to grapple with slavery today. "The definable and distinguishing position of slavers is their marginality," Miller explains. "It is a very precise situation in terms of historical contexts that both motivated and enabled slavers to enslave." Moving from the margins to positions of power meant acquiring people, growing rich from their labor, deriving status and patronage from their dependency, and using all this to secure positions of otherwise unattainable authority and economic power. Slaving, Miller insists, has served as a time-honored

---

[38] Miller, *The Problem of Slavery as History*, 68–72.

[39] It can be argued that plantation slavery did organize itself into highly articulated systems because they were so heavily supported by the state and the workings of global capitalism. Certainly the original abolitionists saw their task as the destruction of oppressive systems, not the suppressing of individual slavers.

way for ambitious outsiders to secure wealth, deference, and honor. "Strategic slaving" is Miller's term of choice.

Although Miller's name appears nowhere in their citations, three essays in this volume validate his recommendations. Each closely examines the evolution of a specialized form of slaving (as Miller would have it) from its historical beginnings into the present; specifically, the enslaving of children, the seizing of men and boys for enslavement in the seaborne fishing industry, and the capturing of vulnerable people who are trafficked into bondage across international borders. Each essay closely tracks what Miller would term strategic enslavement, and each links it in illuminating ways to events taking place today. What explains the presence of the uncited Miller in these essays? Simply the fact that thoughtful scholars, working independently, can easily hit upon similar strategies when pursuing a shared historical interest, in this instance approaching the problem of enslavement as a dynamic process, not as an institution.

A clear exemplar of this procedure is historian John Donoghue, whose chapter in this volume offers powerful substantiation of Miller's conclusions. His "Kidnappers and Subcontractors: Historical Perspectives on Human Trafficking" demonstrates that the "indentured servants" upon whom the British relied in the late seventeenth and early eighteenth centuries to build their colonial empire were provided by ruthless slavers whose work is most faithfully captured by employing gerunds. They spent their time practicing strategic slaving, combing the streets and waterfronts of England's cities, capturing vulnerable adults and children and selling them off for shipment overseas. Whether misleading the desperate and gullible with false promises or physically overpowering them, slavers flouted laws that Parliament failed to enforce even in the face of widespread protests. Donoghue correctly draws sharp distinctions between British citizens held captive for specific terms of enslavement, on the one hand, and the enslaved from Africa, whose perpetual bondage passed on to their descendants, on the other. He also demonstrates how vital the enslavement of Englanders by their fellow citizens was to the concurrent development of the African slave trade. Here again, as Miller contends, shifting patterns of enslaving quite different populations interacted and evolved to create a colonial empire heavily dependent on multiple forms of profoundly coerced labor. And, as per Miller, such strategic slaving continues to this day, as Donoghue confirms when comparing forced indentured servitude in the British Empire to the exploitation of coerced South Asian laborers supplied by American corporations to wealthy Middle Eastern countries in the twenty-first century. Since the

Government of Qatar is not inclined to move against exploiters within their borders, it seems logical for abolitionists to demand the prosecutors of their American suppliers, most notably KBR, Inc. (formerly Kellogg Brown & Root), a spin-off of the Halliburton Corporation.[40]

The value of approaching slavery dynamically is also confirmed in Anna Mae Duane's essay, "'All Boys are Bound to Someone': Reimagining Freedom in the History of Child Slavery," but for quite different reasons. These have everything to do with how to plot that ethically troublesome line between slavery and freedom. First, Duane reminds readers that slavery – both "then" and "now" – usually involves a disproportionately large number of children. Next, she examines slaveholders' (slavers') self-exculpating claims of benevolence toward their "childlike" slaves and the all but universally accepted cultural assumption that the family constitutes a haven that protects children from marketplace exploitation and sexual degradation. Victims who have been stripped of such protection include enslaved children harvesting cacao and coffee beans, mining precious metals, laboring for agribusiness, working in brick yards, carrying automatic weapons as child soldiers, and being raped by sexual predators and "customers." For many modern abolitionists, as for their nineteenth-century predecessors, this form of predation against the most "innocent" is what it is all about, retrieving the victimized, particularly children, and restoring them by bringing them "home." While Duane is emphatic that the suffering of enslaved children is truly horrific and screams for intervention, she also invites us to expand our attention to include children who are nominally free as well as those in bondage. There are millions of children whose equally grievous suffering

---

[40] Donoghue attends to this and similar cases in his essay; see p. 000. KBR was sued under the US Trafficking Victims' Protection Reauthorization Act (TVPRA) and the Alien Tort statute in the case *Ramchandra Adhikari, et al., Plaintiffs, v. Daoud & Partners, et al., Defendants* for its role in the deaths of eleven Nepali workers in Iraq, although after multiple appeals, relief was not granted – largely for issues of jurisdiction. For more information on this case and on accusations against KBR and other US corporations for trafficking, see *Ramchandra Adhikari, et al., Plaintiffs, v. Daoud & Partners, et al., Defendants*, United States District Court, S.D. Texas, Houston Division, signed March 24, 2015, www.leagle.com/decision/infdco20150327a50; "KBR Lawsuit in Iraq (re Human Trafficking)," Business and Human Rights Resource Center, n.d., https://business-humanrights.org/en/kbr-lawsuit-re-human-trafficking-in-iraq; Sarah Stillman, "The Invisible Army," *The New Yorker* (June 6, 2011), www.newyorker.com/magazine/2011/06/06/the-invisible-army; ACLU and Allard K. Lowenstein International Human Rights Clinic, Yale University, "Victims of Complacency: The Ongoing Trafficking and Abuse of Third Country Nationals by US Government Contractors" (June 2012), www.aclu.org/report/victims-complacency-ongoing-trafficking-and-abuse-third-country-nationals-us-government.

is overlooked by an abolitionist movement transfixed by the distinction between bondage and liberation and by sentimental notions of enslaved childhood: nominally free children who are sexually exploited within their own families, worked to exhaustion as factory laborers and field hands, caught up in terrorism, fleeing famine and warfare (note all the gerunds). In the face of these heartbreaking realities, Duane inquires, how can today's abolitionists ethically privilege only the suffering of the enslaved child? Would it not be morally preferable, she asks, to attack slavery by questioning the claim that presumably "autonomous" adults have the absolute right to rule over "dependent" children? She endows these questions with flesh-and-blood urgency that raises the curtain of slavery's invisibility when evoking the childhood memories of Frederick Douglass and his contemporary Haitian counterpart, Jean Cadet, both antislavery heroes who, upon achieving manhood, cast off the debilities of childhood and achieved self-liberation.

One can well imagine an appreciative Joseph Miller reading with satisfaction Kerry Ward's examination of seaborne enslavement, "Maritime Bondage: Comparing Past and Present." Strategic enslavers and their captive resistors behave much as Miller described as they take center stage in this explanation of how and why maritime slavery has changed so little over the centuries, and also why it continues expanding in our time. Since the oceans are an enormous common space, open to all and challenging to regulate, they have always given enslavers expanded freedom to innovate and unusual opportunities for their enslaved to free themselves. Ward anchors her historical examination with the seaborne escape narrative of Frederick Douglass, bringing the drama into the present with the self-liberation of his twenty-first-century Cambodian fisherman counterpart, Vannack Anan Prum. Their stories bracket over two centuries of strategic slaving that transferred its focus from capturing Africans during the transatlantic slave trade, to the "shanghaiing" of vulnerable people from many regions in the early and mid twentieth century, and finally to exploiting captive laborers on fishing ships all over the globe. As shipping technology shifted from sail to steam power, strategy-minded slavers adapted time-honored methods of kidnapping to new theaters of operation across the Great Lakes region of Central Africa, throughout the east, and finally wherever small-scale commercial fishing boats operate today. Meantime, antislavery measures undertaken by lawmakers, labor unions, international agencies, and multinational treaties have done little to impede the spread of slaving into the seafood industry. The lesson for abolitionists to draw from this narrative is the magnified importance of boycotting offending distributors and pushing major corporations to insure uncorrupted supply chains.

THE SLAVERY OF SEX

Inquire of your activist acquaintances whether or not sex work, prostitution, or commercial sexual exploitation (these terms are very much up for debate among different communities of activists) is, in fact, slavery ... then ... run for cover. No other question so fiercely sets today's abolitionists against their severest critics than this one: where to draw this particular line between freedom and bondage? Back in Wendell Phillips's day, such debates were unthinkable. The Victorian moral codes of his time decreed that prostitutes were tragically "fallen" women, a moral category which, unsurprisingly, often intersected the designations of "lesser" races and ethnicities as professed by the racialized science of the day. The "ruin" of such women, according to the reigning ideology, was rooted in their own moral frailty – revealed by their presence in gin mills, opium dens, and gambling halls – as well as in malignant male motives. Prostitution led to personal degradation, but generally not to enslavement. The sexual abuses that planters inflicted on their bondspeople were, however, an entirely different matter for abolitionists of the time. On Southern plantations, sexual exploitation and slavery were synonyms. That abolitionists came to this conclusion is certainly no surprise. Nevertheless, a review of how they built their case does much to clarify today's controversies over whether or not prostitution does in fact constitute slavery (or slaving, as per Miller).[41]

For abolitionists, the mixed-race children so commonly found on large plantations proved beyond question that sexual exploitation constituted the irreducible essence of what made human bondage such a blasphemous sin. The unassailable fact of forced miscegenation established a sturdy platform for constructing an expansive indictment of the planter class that featured in no-holds-barred reportage laced with detailed descriptions of extreme violence. This sweeping bill of particulars came complete with

[41] Highly lucid analyses of abolitionists' beliefs regarding sexual exploitation and the South can be found in Ronald Walters, *The Antislavery Appeal: Abolition after 1831* (New York: W.W. Norton, 1978); Walters, "The Erotic South: Civilization and Sexuality in American Abolitionism," *American Quarterly* (May 1973), 177–201; a more comprehensive treatment of this theme in relation to other Northern responses to slavery is Saidiya V. Hartman, *Scenes of Subjection: Terror, Slavery and Self-Making in Nineteenth Century America* (New York: Oxford University Press, 1997).

visual images of slaveholders wielding lethally flaying lashes, wrenching babies from enslaved mothers while forcing them onto the auction block, loosing hunting dogs on desperate fugitives, searing the flesh of enslaved persons with red hot branding irons, and raping terrorized black women.[42] Since abolitionists scrupulously documented these atrocities, historians today find little reason to doubt them. Historians do, however, divide sharply over the abolitionists' deeper motivations for developing such harrowing – and eroticized – descriptions of the suffering of enslaved people.

These disagreements, important in their own right, carry added significance because they help to explain the conflict between twenty-first-century abolitionists and their critics over whether prostitution constitutes slavery. They also speak to one of the most challenging questions historians can ask: what prompts us to transcend our emotional distance from others who suffer grievously, even though they are often quite unlike us and often far beyond our direct fields of vision? Or, to put the matter much more pointedly, what compelled privileged white abolitionists suddenly to portray the suffering of enslaved African Americans in such viscerally tortured terms? Put this way, the question reveals itself to be fundamentally about the nature of empathy: what is it, how is it activated, and with what effects?

One explanation, to summarize ruthlessly, is that empathy arises from economics. This is the conclusion of Thomas Haskell, who posits

[42] While women and girls were far and away the primary victims of sexual violence under the plantation system of slavery in the Americas, men and boys were also vulnerable to sexual exploitation in various forms, many less overt than the rape of women by slaveholders. One primary text that recounts the story of sexualized violence against a male slave (Luke) by his slaveholder is Chapter XL, "The Fugitive Slave Law," in Harriet Jacobs, *Incidents in the Life of a Slave Girl* (New York: Dover Publications, 2012). For a brilliant analysis of the multiple spectacles of eroticized pain, as well as performances of "pleasure," demanded of enslaved persons by slaveholders, see Hartman, *Scenes of Subjection*; see also Christina Sharpe's incisive critique of the intertwining of violence and subjectivity within the institution of slavery in *Monstrous Intimacies: Making Post-Slavery Subjects* (Durham, NH: Duke University Press, 2010). Significantly, both Hartman and Sharpe link the systemic and sadistic violence of slavery to the making of subjects and subjectivity – of enslaved persons and slavers alike. Both show how violence not coded as explicitly sexual (especially floggings) were in fact deeply sexualized and infused with the power relations that also characterize rape. And both show how quotidian practices of slaving and slaveholding – such as the forced nudity of the auction block, the touching that accompanied the act of inspecting an enslaved person for purchase, or the common practice of forcing enslaved persons to sleep near the bedside of the slaveholder – also constituted forms of eroticized violence, if less explicitly than overt sexual violence.

that humanitarian sensibilities arose in the late seventeenth century and spread in tandem with the network of contractual obligations that was part and parcel of British capitalism's rapid expansion across the globe.[43] As ever larger populations became entangled with one another's conduct and decision-making over ever greater distances, so did intensifying impulses to monitor and judge the moral conduct of those who were otherwise remote strangers. The point for our purposes is that by this estimate (and contrary to what abolitionists had always believed about themselves) empathy had little to do with conscious moral choice and basic human rights, and everything to do with responding to impersonal market forces and the social labyrinths in which they are enmeshed.[44]

Next we turn to social psychology and to Karen Halttunen's conclusion that, rather than expressing a substantial concern for the rights of others, or the straightforward responsibility to represent the suffering of such "others" when they cannot speak for themselves, what empathy actually communicates is the "pornography of pain." Halttunen argues that empathy emerged in the eighteenth century thanks to a rising revulsion toward physical pain (particularly as expressed in the act of torture, a practice which was also under strong protest at this time) mixed with a prurient attraction to it that reflected the rise of bourgeois values of civility, gentility, and respectability in Great Britain, France, and the United States. In her account, the abolitionists' chronicles of abuse registered their voyeuristic desires and those of their wider audiences to participate at one remove in the titillating agony of the enslaved. According to Halttunen, "the pornography of pain" in which the abolitionists trafficked was in no way an aberration, but rather, in her words, "an integral aspect of humanitarian sensibility" (304). To follow Halttunen's argument, the abolitionists' searing critiques were less about identifying with the enslaved and more about serving their own, if unconscious, desire for the very same spectacles of pain that Saidiya V. Hartman describes in *Scenes of Subjection*.[45]

---

[43] Historian Lynn Hunt adds dimension to this claim by tracing how such humanitarian sensibilities arose in tandem with and were helpfully disseminated by the rise of the novel form, which permitted readers, who were largely of the upper classes, an opportunity to identify with protagonists from the working or "poor" classes. See Lynn Hunt, *Inventing Human Rights: A History* (New York: W.W. Norton & Co., 2007).

[44] Thomas Haskell, "Capitalism and the Origins of Humanitarian Sensibility, Part I," *American Historical Review* 90, no. 2 (April 1995), 339–61; "Part II," 90, no. 2 (April 1995), 547–66.

[45] Karen Halttunen, "Humanitarianism and the Pornography of Pain in Anglo-American Culture," *American Historical Review* 110, no. 2 (April 1995), 303–34. See n. 42 for

We arrive finally at the scholarship of Elizabeth Clark, who takes the position that the abolitionists' motives are best understood much as they, themselves, understood them. When portraying slavery in all its gruesome dimensions, they were, according to Clark, describing what they knew they could prove was transpiring on the ground all over the plantation South. The title of Theodore Dwight Weld's justly famous, scrupulously documented compendium of planter class atrocities (published by the American Anti-Slavery Society in 1839 and based exclusively on Southern newspaper sources), *American Slavery as it Is: The Testimony of a Thousand Witnesses*, captures Clark's argument that abolitionists' reports were well grounded in evidence.[46] Equally persuasive documentation, Clark observes, was found in the grim realities reported by candid African American autobiographers such as Solomon Northup, Frederick Douglass, William and Ellen Craft, Harriet Jacobs, and so many others. According to Clark, it was neither prurient voyeurism nor globalizing capitalist expansion and its accompanying exportation of pious moralities that generated abolitionist empathy; rather, the forces of theology, religious imagination, pious church-centered sociability, and rapidly expanding networks of literacy and communication during the 1820s and 1830s engendered such sentiment and concern for others. Emerging from such incubators of human concern, the abolitionists turned themselves into powerful and authentic advocates for basic human rights and individual liberties.[47]

How do these academic disagreements pertain to today's debates about prostitution and enslavement? For some answers, look to the late nineteenth and early twentieth centuries, consider Halttunen's concept of "the pornography of pain" alongside Haskell's emphasis on capitalism and colonialism, and then review Jessica Pliley's essay, "From White Slavery to Anti-Prostitution, the Long View: Law, Policy, and Sex Trafficking," in this volume. Such a reading reveals the dark undersides of empathy, and also does much to explain why certain activists today deny the connection between prostitution and enslavement; disparage

explication of the role of eroticized violence in US slave systems and its influence upon the subjectivities of people living within them.

[46] Theodore D. Weld, *Slavery as It Is: Testimony of a Thousand Witnesses*, in Documenting the American South, University of North Carolina Digitization Project (2000), http://docsouth.unc.edu/neh/weld/weld.html.

[47] Elizabeth B. Clark, "'The Sacred Rights of the Weak': Pain, Sympathy and the Culture of Individual Rights in Antebellum America," *The Journal of American History* 82, no. 2 (September 1995), 463–93.

contemporary anti-trafficking campaigns as extensions of earlier, moralizing purity crusades, or as expressions of an exploitative, sentimentalized, self-serving "rescue" industry that infantilizes and coerces the objects of its efforts; and most significantly, campaign for the legalization (or decriminalization) of sex work.

During the late nineteenth and early twentieth centuries, as Pliley explains, large slices of public opinion – first in England, next in the United States, and finally in many Western Hemisphere and European nations – became convinced that the scourge of white slavery was victimizing untold numbers of vulnerable women. Moral empathy dictated not only the rescue of these victims of enslavement, but also the suppression of prostitution itself through stringent antislavery legislation and its enforcement. The lurid pictures these "new abolitionists" painted of what befell prostituted women echoed the indictments made by their abolitionist predecessors. But at the same time their antislavery arguments denigrated women for exhibiting what they construed as numerous "weaknesses"; broadcast white racism through their descriptor of choice ("white" slavery); castigated immigrants and ethnic minorities as sources of corruption; and denied basic human rights when legislating ethnocentric state surveillance and immigration policies. In this instance, "empathy" for the "plight" of "prostituted women" constituted "moral panic" (scare quotes indicating the contested nature of each of those terms) and an upwelling of anxiety over the perpetrators of sex trafficking, who were, not surprisingly, mostly immigrants and ethnic minorities – precisely the arguments made by many critics of the anti-trafficking movement today.

Pliley closes her essay with the crucial point that the legacies of this history extend directly into the present day, which helps to explain why anti-sex trafficking policies of governments all over the globe prioritize state security over human rights by emphasizing border control over prevention, suppressing and expelling refugees, and criminalizing those caught up in human trafficking. Little wonder, given these outcomes, that those who insist that sex work is not enslavement and who demand the decriminalization of prostitution ground their arguments in examples drawn from the inglorious history of white slavery.

The problem, however, is that many prostituted women and children today most certainly do labor under conditions that fit the Bellagio definition of enslavement, although this certainly does not accurately describe the conditions of all work in the commercial sex industry.[48] Many sex

---

[48] Conditions for some people working in the commercial sex industry have shifted with the

workers enter the trade as adults and without coercion, driven by economic expediency or desire. For them, it's much more about money, autonomy, and even service than about exploitation or criminal enslaving. But at the same time, complications multiply. Some who make this choice subsequently find themselves being bought, sold, and coerced by pimps who claim first to love them, then to own them. Others make a putatively free will choice to trust the promises of labor recruiters who then seize their documentation, hold them hostage, and force them into prostitution. And finally, there is the fact that most of the young people found in the sex trade come from families shattered by poverty, substance abuse, racism, sexual abuse, incarcerated parents, and dysfunctional social welfare programs.[49] Sustained efforts to reduce these drivers of sexual exploitation are much more effective than reactive responses driven by empathizing moral panic.

Freely granting all these complications and exceptions, the plain fact remains that much sex work does come down to enslavement. Were that original abolitionist mentioned earlier, Theodore Dwight Weld, whisked forward into our time, he could easily write a globally based sequel to his precisely documented *Slavery as It Is: The Testimony of a Thousand Witnesses*. All the necessary evidence is readily available. He would turn to a profusion of personal testimonies that match the veracity of what Frederick Douglass made plain in his 1845 *Narrative*. He would also discover twenty-first-century equivalents of his old abolitionist colleagues who trekked south and reported on slavery first hand, and who assisted those in bondage to make their escapes and restore their lives. Those

move of the trade from the street to online, where most transactions are now conducted. Sociologist Elizabeth Bernstein correlates the shift of commercial sex from street to internet with other socio-economic trends, including the rise of the post-industrial service and technology industries and the deconstruction of traditional marriage and family ties, arguing that the trend toward transactional socio-sexual relations extends far beyond the world of commercial sex into quotidian life in the "developed" world. See Elizabeth Bernstein, *Temporarily Yours: Intimacy, Authenticity, and the Commerce of Sex* (Chicago, IL: University of Chicago Press, 2007).

49 A multi-city study from the Field Center for Children's Policy, Practice, & Research at the University of Pennsylvania has found in interviews with homeless youth exploited in the commercial sex trade (either through trafficking or through engagement in "survival sex") that fully 95 percent reported experiencing child abuse or neglect, and 63 percent had at some point been involved in the child welfare system. Debra Schilling Wolfe, "95% of Homeless Youth Who Experienced Sex Trafficking Say They Were Maltreated as Children," *Chronicle of Social Change* (September 14, 2017), https://chronicleofsocialchange.org/research-news/majority-of-homeless-youth-who-experienced-sex-trafficking-say-they-were-maltreated-as-children.

equivalents to Theodore Weld are the new abolitionists who work against sexual enslavement and exploitation in well-established NGOs, legal services, and law enforcement agencies.[50] In addition to quoting scripture, Weld's abolitionist comrades built their antislavery arguments by immersing themselves in constitutional law, property law, tort law, international law, state-level jurisprudence, and criminal procedure. Their successors today marshal precisely the same sources, including, for some of them, the same scriptural injunctions.

By now the larger generalization should be clear. What historian Elizabeth Clark concludes as regards the motives of the original abolitionists applies with equal force to these contemporary anti-sex trafficking activists. In both instances, the ideal personal commitment results from empathy tempered by critical attention to the dangers of moral panic and marketplace considerations, both. Such commitments constitute an ethically informed response to well-documented enslavement. Today, as in the past, those so motivated often become perceptive social critics and advocates of human rights. Continuity between past and present is unmistakable.

The question now becomes what leads those demanding the decriminalization of prostitution to express such disinterest in the suffering of the sexually enslaved? How does one explain empathy's opposite? The essay by Elizabeth Swanson and James Brewer Stewart, "Defending Slavery,

---

[50] It is well beyond the scope of this essay to parse the missions and visions of the various organizations and NGOs fighting sex trafficking in order to discern their susceptibility to such "moral panic"; the motivations for their work; the extent to which such work is informed by religious principles, etc.; however, the larger point that we insist upon is that the "anti-sex trafficking movement" is not a monolith, and neither are the people working within it. Criticism of efforts to prevent and address sex trafficking and commercial sexual exploitation often paints all participants with the same unnuanced brush: as right-wing, evangelical, anti-sex, moralizing purists who seek to control the movement of women and migrants; who participate in negatively racialized power dynamics; who raise funds for specious purposes; and who cynically construct "innocent victims" as the only legitimate recipients of their largesse. On the other hand, those who oppose the commercial sex trade and conflate all sex work with trafficking contribute to the same problem, by refusing to acknowledge the existence of people who enter the commercial sex trade for a range of reasons, including serving the needs of some whose desires fall outside the mainstream hetero- (or even homo-) normative culture. Simply put, such generalizations on either "side" cannot capture the breadth of motives, politics, and commitments at play in the struggle against exploitation. Such generalizations can be traced to the culture wars around pornography in the 1980s and sex work/commercial sexual exploitation in the 1990s, and they continue to be a distraction from the work of preventing and addressing exploiting and slaving in the real, nuanced, and infinitely varied circumstances under which it occurs.

Denying Slavery: Rhetorical Strategies of the Contemporary Sex Worker Rights Movement in Historical Context," addresses this question through a comparative examination of antebellum planters' defenses of African American bondage and arguments advanced by advocates of legalized sex work in the current moment. To be clear, this essay suggests not even a whisper of an inference that advocates of legalizing sex work implicate themselves in actual slaveholding. Instead, the essay's simple premise is that some vocal sex worker rights advocates today share one important characteristic with some antebellum planters. Both advance their most compelling interests with emphatic claims to their legality: slaveholders to protect the legality of human bondage, critics of new abolitionists to secure the legality (or more precisely, the decriminalization) of all sex work.[51] The ends sought are wildly different. The method employed, however, bears important similarities; inherent in their arguments is a consistent dismissal of the documented suffering of those enslaved and exploited.

Three quite distinct tactics serve this purpose, the first of which is to expose the opponent's evidence as fraudulently manufactured. The second involves characterizing the opponent's case as a distraction from a truly serious injustice that must be attended to instead. The third contends that the persons who suffer are better off under the present circumstances than would they be subject to the controlling impulses of the anti-trafficking movement. These three arguments, Swanson and Stewart contend, are premised on indifference to the verifiable suffering of those enslaved. In this respect, the case for decriminalizing sex work, Swanson and Stewart suggest, unintentionally reprises the proslavery argument of the antebellum era. Learning from the past in an effort to solve this problem, they conclude, requires redefining sex work, enslaved/exploited or not, as a profoundly important human rights issue with breadth to include all those impacted by it, not a narrowly argued legal or rhetorical dispute with clear "sides."

SOLUTIONS

Many historians flinch when asked to apply their knowledge directly to contemporary social problems – but not three contributors to this

---

[51] Decriminalization generally means the removal of any laws rendering prostitution a criminal offense, whereas legalization removes criminal penalties for the act but also could involve government regulation and control of prostitution as an industry.

volume. Two have written essays that detail what abolitionists today can learn from the success of the British government in bringing an end to the Atlantic slave trade and to slavery in its West Indian colonies. A third teams up with a political scientist to present a micro-study of how a city's historical roots in antebellum slavery can be made to mobilize its citizens against racial oppression and enslavement today. After presenting summaries of these essays, this introduction closes with a review of suggested solutions to the problems of slavery and exploitation currently under development by activists and by civil authorities.

For suggested solutions drawn from the past, we turn again to David Richardson's essay in this volume, "Modern Slavery in Historical Perspective," this time because it reminds us of just how enormous the problem of slavery has been, and because it outlines the equally enormous undertaking required to suppress it today. The essay tracks slavery's history all over the globe in a manner of which Joseph Miller would surely approve, particularly since it richly documents the "chameleon-like nature" of human bondage as it developed over time. It thrives today as it always has, Richardson reminds us, on greed, autocracy, tyranny, war, disruption, and disaster, adapting to changing circumstances and slipping past stratagems to suppress it. What is required, Richardson asks, to get the better of this shape-shifter? His recommendations, addressed to nation states, go as follows. Start with record-setting government financing and work to rid your own nation of slavery. Next, add ceaselessly aggressive global diplomacy, multinational alliance-building, and the deployment of a very powerful military. Undergird it all with a militant public opinion that embraces abolition as its nation's glorious destiny. What is being described is a recipe for twenty-first-century antislavery that was first put into practice by Great Britain during the nineteenth century when it sought to peacefully end West Indian slavery and devoted nearly a century to destroying the Atlantic slave trade. Although we are no longer challenged, as the British were, by systems of plantation slavery that can be uprooted in one fell swoop, it is nevertheless an approach with pertinence for our time – all the more so because rarely are these kinds of interventions explored in contemporary antislavery circles, perhaps because of a realpolitik in the current moment that renders such government intervention nearly unthinkable. Richardson sets in bold relief the enormous commitment required of national governments that claim today to pursue antislavery policies, challenging them to indeed follow through on their responsibilities.

David Blair, one imagines, surely agrees to this proposition, since his contribution to this volume, "All the Ships that Never Sailed: Lessons for the Modern Antislavery Movement from the British Naval Campaigns against the Atlantic Slave Trade," directly addresses the question of what today's abolitionists can learn from Great Britain's antislavery past. Expert in the field of security studies and a specialist in counterterrorism research, Blair presents a truly original explanation of why Great Britain's campaign against the African slave trade was ultimately successful, drawing from that historical example strategic axioms for attacking slavery today. As it turns out, moreover, Blair's approach resonates again with Joseph Miller's, since it portrays abolition as an evolving process, not as a unitary project, a decades long exercise in *antislaving*, not antislavery.

Much as does contributor Kerry Ward, Blair understands the ocean as a vast commons. He also notes basic qualities that make it similar to the internet; that is, it is open to be freely used by one and all. During the transatlantic slave trade, seafaring slavers exploited the oceans to transport captive Africans, and today, their technologically adept counterparts do likewise by setting up websites and communicating over smart phones. For this reason, Blair contends, the evolving strategies and tactics deployed by the British Navy forced slavers into what is best characterized as a chess-like game governed by ever-changing rules in which antislaving slowly gained the upper hand. Might not a similar chess game be devised to combat the online components of human trafficking now?

To explain how this idea is grounded in history, Blair aggregates information from the Atlantic Slave Trade Data Base and numerous other sources to develop a fine-grained analysis of how this strategic struggle evolved over the decades as the British adjusted their tactics and forced slavers into increasingly untenable positions. What, Blair asks, would be required by national governments and international agencies in order to adapt this highly coordinated British example to slaving today? His answers are surely worth serious evaluation.

Unlike the large-scale solutions put forward by Richardson and Blair, Monti Narayan Datta and James Brewer Stewart think smaller in their essay, "The Power of the Past in the Present: The Capitol of the Confederacy as an Antislavery City." But thinking small allows them to offer a gloss on that imaginary lecture presented to the Congressional Black Caucus and reprised so many pages earlier in this Introduction. One might recall that this hypothetical exercise engaged these influential politicians with the proposition that to be successful (and to be rid of racist warrants), today's antislavery activism in the United States must be rooted in the history of plantation slavery and its consequences. To that end, Datta and Stewart's essay fixes on the city of Richmond, Virginia, which was once the capital of the slaveholders' Confederacy during the Civil War.

Beset with a full array of urban problems, today's Richmond is also the scene of bitter contestation between virulent white supremacists and fully engaged African American activists over the meaning of gargantuan statues of slaveholding Confederate "heroes" (Robert E. Lee, Jefferson Davis, and "Stonewall" Jackson) that dominate its public space. At the same time, Richmond is also a major hub for transporting women who have been coerced into the sex trade to destinations all over the Southern United States. Richmond, in short, is equally afflicted by the oppressive legacies of the old plantation slavery and the equally intolerable consequences of the new.

Datta and Stewart's essay proposes linked solutions to both sets of problems, after first bringing to the fore as an antidote to the city's racist atmosphere the remarkable history of its African American citizens from slaving times onward. The motive for so doing is academic – but also much more than that. It is a history meant to be owned and enriched by Richmond's citizens as they continue a concerted grass roots initiative already under way. Their goal is the establishment of a memorial park in memory of the approximately 300,000 enslaved people who, between the years 1830 and 1865, were forcibly marched from Richmond into the deep South and resold. Written in consultation with antiracist activists, Richmond's African American past is presented in this essay with a view to supporting the memorial park by making it accessible through popular media – theater, music, poetry, MP3 videos, logos, Facebook blogs, and so forth. The memorial park itself is designed as a site for racial reconciliation and reparation, and the essay's specific policy recommendations are tailored to support these objectives – key among them the goal of forging alliances between African American activists and the city's new abolitionists. As has been heavily emphasized early in this introduction, to get "beyond chattel slavery" first requires Americans to face up to it and push back against its destructive legacies.

This volume is a first attempt at supporting teachers, students, scholars, activists, and citizens in doing just that. Our goal has been to show how both similarities and divergences between contemporary slavery/abolition and past slaving/antislaving are instructive in the fight against slavery today. We have sought to identify two urgent pathways for antislavery activism today: first, recognition of and struggle against the transmogrification of American plantation slavery systems into new forms of brutality and impression such as mass incarceration, the school-to-prison pipeline, and the overarching "vulnerability to premature death" endured by African American citizens; and second, recognition of and struggle against systems of global slavery that take multiple forms and are all but invisible within the legal proscription against slavery. The essays in this volume suggest a wealth of future research agendas for those motivated to engage with "antislavery's usable past," exploring synergies and divergences between past and present usages of law, economics, and rhetorical appeals to end slavery. They notice and build upon connections between problems of environmental degradation and slavery, population and the biological and social reproduction of the enslaved, and slavery's ideological justifications, and most especially, they emphasize the role of vulnerability and precarity in the problem of slaving over time and space. It is our intention that this volume not only provide new knowledge, but also, and equally significant, new methods to mobilize in the ongoing struggle against the enslavement and exploitation of humans, anywhere it is found.

PART I

UNDERSTANDING AND DEFINING SLAVERY, THEN AND NOW

Contemporary Slavery in Historical Perspective

David Richardson*

> There is not much point in recalling all this ancient history ... So let us
> leave ancient history out of it, and come to the present.
>
> *Herodotus*

DEFINING SLAVERY OVER THE CENTURIES

Slavery, coerced labor, and dependency are as old as human history,
although their scale and relative importance across time and place have
varied considerably. Since 1800, however, chattel slavery and what the
United Nations Supplementary Convention on the Abolition of Slavery
of 1956 called "Institutions and Practices Similar to Slavery" have been
outlawed across the world.[1] The 1956 convention was supplementary to
the 1926 League of Nations one, which first legally defined slavery.[2] Yet
today an estimated 46 million people globally are thought to live under
slave-like or forced labor conditions. The number of children in child
labor, condemned under the 1930 Forced Labor Convention, runs even

* I thank Gary Craig, Judith Spicksley, and James Stewart for commenting on earlier drafts
  of this essay. The usual disclaimer applies. An earlier version was delivered as the annual
  Alderman Sydney Smith lecture at the Wilberforce Institute for the Study of Slavery and
  Emancipation, University of Hull, in October 2016.

[1] *Supplementary Convention on the Abolition of Slavery, the Slave Trade, and Institutions
and Practices Similar to Slavery*, Geneva, September 7, 1956, *United Nations Treaty
Series* vol. 226, no. 3822, p. 3. Available from https://treaties.un.org/Pages/ViewDetailsIII
.aspx?src=IND&mtdsg_no=XVIII-4&chapter=18&Temp=mtdsg3&clang=_en.

[2] *Convention to Suppress the Slave Trade and Slavery*, Geneva, September 25, 1926, *United
Nations Treaty Series* vol. 212, no. 2861, p. 17. Available at https://treaties.un.org/Pages/
ViewDetails.aspx?src=TREATY&mtdsg_no=XVIII-2&chapter=18&clang=_en.

higher. Even in an emancipatory age, therefore, slavery, however defined, remains a robust institution. Global population growth and other changes over the last two centuries mean that its incidence today is low within recorded human history, but it is still endemic and entrenched in some societies, and only absent, if at all, from a small minority. Reflecting the greed that typically encourages attempts to circumvent laws banning specific behaviors, the human trafficking that helps sustain contemporary slavery is among the principal forms of internationally organized crime, matched only by drug trafficking and illegal arms sales in scale and significance. Human trafficking, like its drug and arms counterparts, poses a fundamental challenge to efforts to promote equity, human rights, and social justice across the world.

As a contribution toward understanding the difficulties in confronting that challenge, I shall adopt a "businesslike" approach to an issue of 'spiritual" (or moral) accountancy, placing the incidence of contemporary slavery in historical perspective.[3] Unlike Herodotus in the epigraph to this essay, I embrace rather than "leave ancient history out of it," seeking to highlight processes that made and continue to make people vulnerable to enslavement. I explore, too, historical challenges to slavery from abolitionist movements that culminated in the global outlawing of slavery and similar practices. Among the lessons of historical abolitionism is the need, in the face of slavery's variable character in different localities and settings, to mobilize the collective will of people around defined, coherent programs of intervention. History reminds us, too, how inertia and even resistance to externally imposed human rights agendas can inhibit the pursuit of such programs. Accordingly, successful outcomes for modern-day antislavery movements, like their predecessors, are necessarily intertwined with larger sociopolitical forces of change.

A historically based comparative review of slavery requires consistency of definition over time. Throughout recorded history, the legal understanding of slavery, an extreme form of forced labor, has typically been defined in terms of property, or the exclusive ownership of one person by another. Aristotle argued that "anyone who by his nature is not his own man, but another's, is by his nature a slave; anybody who, being a man, is an article of property is another's man."[4] Slaves as property found sanction too in the Bible, where in Exodus 20:20–1 it is stated that a master could escape punishment for killing his slave, "for he is his

---

[3] Cf. James Joyce, *Dubliners* (1914; London: Penguin Books, 2000), 174.
[4] Aristotle, *Politics*, ed. R. F. Stalley (Oxford: Oxford University Press, 1995), 14.

property." It was the Romans, however, who provided the clearest and most consistent property-based rational for slavery. According to British legal expert Antony Honoré, Roman jurists assumed all people were naturally born free and that Roman law favored freedom. But, he argues, ownership of people was clearly recognized in Roman law as part of "general political practice" and, as such, came to be embodied in the Justinian code.[5] That, Honoré suggests, was the foundation for subsequent thinking in Europe about the legal status of slavery, although he also suggests that the Justinian code's recognition of slavery as contrary to nature ultimately may have "paved the way ... for the movement to outlaw the slave trade and, ultimately, slavery itself."[6] Be that as it may, slavery's identification with property rights in people transcended the emergence of antislavery movements from the 1780s. In 1833, Britain compensated slave owners in the British Empire for liberating their chattels. In 1926, the League of Nations defined slavery as "the status or condition of a person over whom any or all of the powers attaching to the right of ownership are exercised." That definition subsequently underpinned the protocols of other international bodies against slavery and similar practices.

Nevertheless, the rise of antislavery ultimately determined a reversal of the general practice of ownership that Honoré saw as legitimizing slavery from ancient Rome onwards. Despite its outlawing globally, however, slavery persists. That persistence has encouraged rethinking of the meaning of slavery past and present, prompting suggestions that "modern slavery" extends beyond people as property, now universally outlawed, and instead involves "one person possessing or controlling another person in such as a way as to significantly deprive that person of their individual liberty, with the intention of exploiting that person through their use, management, profit, transfer, or disposal."[7] The rethinking also prompted the *Bellagio-Harvard Guidelines on the Legal Parameters of Slavery*, which seek to reconcile contemporary slavery-like practices with existing international law, notably the 1926 League of Nations Slavery Convention. The Guidelines offer a working definition of slavery that, as one of their leading architects, Jean Allain, notes,

---

[5] Antony Honoré, "The Nature of Slavery," in Jean Allain, ed., *The Legal Understanding of Slavery: From the Historical to the Contemporary* (Oxford: Oxford University Press, 2012), 9–16.

[6] Ibid., 12.

[7] Global Slavery Index 2014; Kevin Bales, "Slavery in its Contemporary Manifestations," in Jean Allain, ed., *Legal Understanding*, 282–3.

"marries the property paradigm, which is at the heart of the legal definition, with the essence of the lived experience of contemporary slavery."[8]
The concept of "lived experience" provides a means to relate slavery
past and present, and also suggests an approach consistent with Joseph
Miller's plea to historicize *slaving* (or "the human meanings that have
motivated people's actions") and to "add the political and intellectual
contexts of slaving to the primarily economic analyses that have otherwise tended to prevail."[9]

My approach here naturally draws on sociologically based interpretations of slavery, most commonly identified with Orlando Patterson and
Kevin Bales.[10] Highlighting the diversity of enslaved persons' experiences,
past and present, Patterson and Bales recognize the power of some, even
without legal sanction, to control or take possession of the lives of others
through untrammeled violence and the dehumanization or social marginalization of their victims. Although technically not the property of
others, the victims of such controlling relationships are nevertheless *de
facto* slaves, being subject to "any or all of the powers attaching to the
right of ownership."

Intended to illuminate contemporary slavery, this reformulation of
slavery's meaning, with its emphasis on control and on the experiences
of enslaved persons – or their shared "common essence"[11] – is equally
relevant to historical slavery, a point underlined by Patterson's sweeping
analysis.[12] It is consistent too with some more recent and regionally
specific assessments of historic slavery, including Richard Easton's analysis of South Asia. Easton notes the variety of indigenous terms used
to describe people considered enslaved in this context. He sees them as
"uprooted outsiders, impoverished insiders – or the descendants of both –
serving persons or institutions on which they are wholly dependent."[13]
Moreover, although degrees of dependency existed between "masters"

---

[8] Jean Allain, "Introduction," in Allain, ed., *Legal Understanding*, p. 5.
[9] Joseph C. Miller, *The Problem of Slavery as History: A Global Approach* (New Haven,
CT: Yale University Press, 2012), 3–4.
[10] Orlando Patterson, *Slavery and Social Death: A Comparative Study* (Cambridge,
MA: Harvard University Press, 1982); Kevin Bales, *Disposable People: New Slavery in
the Global Economy* (Berkeley, CA: University of California Press, 2000).
[11] Michael Frayn, *Headlong* (London: Faber, 1999), 24.
[12] Patterson, *Slavery and Social Death*.
[13] Richard M. Easton, "Introduction," in Indrani Chatterjee and Richard M. Easton,
eds., *Slavery and South Asian History* (Bloomington, IN: Indiana University Press,
2006), 2.

and "slaves," Easton believes those in bondage to be almost invariably "more dependent on the will and the power of someone else than were non-slaves."[14] The relative importance of distinctions between outsiders and insiders to slavery's persistence today in some parts of the world is an issue I explore later. Here, suffice to observe that Easton's use of *dependency* to define South Asian historic slavery echoes notions of control that inform Allain's definition of contemporary slavery. The *Bellagio-Harvard Guidelines* therefore offer a foundation upon which to study contemporary slavery in long-term historical perspective. They enable us better to understand the commonalities of contemporary and historic slavery while helping to expose constraints on the global community's ability finally to eradicate the former. In short, they allow us to put "pressing contemporary issues into historical perspective."[15]

DESCRIBING MODERN SLAVERY HISTORICALLY

The International Labour Organization (ILO) and the Global Slavery Index (GSI) provide the two most comprehensive surveys of the scale and nature of modern-day slavery and the factors that shape them. Their latest assessments appeared in 2012 and 2016, respectively.[16] The ILO survey concerns forced labor, defined as "all work or service which is extracted from any person under the menace of any penalty and for which the said person has not offered himself voluntarily." The definition encompasses "the full realm of forced labor and human trafficking for labor and sexual exploitation, or what some call 'modern-day slavery.'" The ILO estimates that 20.9 million people experienced forced labor in 2012, a rise of 8.6 million from its previous assessment in 2005. This outcome, it claims, reflects improvements in data collection and analysis, as opposed to increases in such labor in 2005–12.

Alternatively, the GSI 2016 estimates that there are 45.8 million people globally in "modern-day slavery." That figure is 16 million higher than it projected in 2013 and 10 million higher than in 2014. Embracing

---

[14] Ibid., 3.

[15] Benjamin N. Lawrance and Richard L. Roberts, "Contextualizing Trafficking in Women and Children in Africa," in Benjamin Lawrance and Richard L. Roberts, eds., *Trafficking in Slavery's Wake: Law and the Experience of Women and Children in Africa* (Athens, OH: Ohio University Press, 2012), 17–18; Louise Shelley, *Human Trafficking: A Global Perspective* (Cambridge and New York: Cambridge University Press, 2010).

[16] See International Labor Organization, *Global Estimate of Forced Labor*, June 1, 2012; Walk Free Foundation, Globalslaveryindex.org, 2016.

people living in conditions of forced labor, debt bondage, forced or servile marriage, and commercial sexual exploitation, all GSI estimates lie well outside the standard error of 1.4 million of ILO's median "conservative estimate" of 2012. Their rising total in 2013–16 is, again, said to reflect improved data and estimation procedures. Both ILO and GSI estimates, however, underscore the difficulties of measuring what is internationally a very shadowy (if only because totally illicit) business.[17] On the most readily available estimates, nonetheless, 20–46 million people worldwide may be living in conditions of modern-day slavery.

Although estimates of such slavery are more than exercises in turning sunbeams into cucumbers, they have been criticized on methodological and policy-making grounds. GSI has attracted particularly heavy criticism. Some see its value as more "political and organisational" than "analytical." Its methods are said to involve reducing "different forms of complex and case-specific phenomena into more easily comparable and accessible numerical values and statistical tables," which are then considered "facts." Others see the GSI as harnessing the "power of statistics and numbers in order to create an illusion of concreteness that masks the slipperiness of what we are counting and how."[18] Historians of slavery recognize the force of such arguments, the need to treat measurements of slavery's scale and distribution cautiously, and the importance of treating them as orders of magnitude, not precise numbers. Even so, acknowledging that overall calculations of those in slavery may be subject to wide variances, the temporal and geographical patterns underlying those calculations may shift rather less. This is true of historic slavery and appears to be the case

---

[17] A partnership between the ILO and Walk Free, the organization that produces the Global Slavery Index, was announced in March 2017, with the goal of pooling resources and methodologies to produce a single estimate of global slavery in support of target 8.7 of the Millennium Development Goals, which calls on governments to "take immediate and effective measures to eradicate forced labor, end modern slavery and secure the prohibition and elimination of the worst forms of child labor, including recruitment and use of child soldiers, and by 2020 end child labor in all its forms." The single estimate is now about 40 million. See "ILO and Walk Free to Collaborate on Global Estimate of Modern Slavery," *International Labour Organization*, March 17, 2017, http://ilo.org/global/topics/forced-labour/news/WCMS_547316/lang--en/index.htm.

[18] Joel Quirk and Andre Broome, "The Politics of Numbers: The Global Slavery Index and the Marketplace of Activism," openDemocracy, *Beyond Trafficking and Slavery*, March 10, 2015, www.opendemocracy.net/beyondslavery/joel-quirk-andr%C3%A9-broome/politics-of-numbers-global-slavery-index-and-marketplace-of-ac; Anne Gallagher, "The Global Slavery Index: Seduction and Obfuscation," openDemocracy, *Beyond Trafficking and Slavery*, December 4, 2014, www.opendemocracy.net/5050/anne-gallagher/global-slavery-index-seduction-and-obfuscation.

too with its contemporary counterpart.[19] It follows that, despite scholars' caveats, ILO and GSI data in combination may offer a reasonable platform upon which to place contemporary slavery in historical perspective.

ILO and GSI broadly agree on five issues:

First, the proportion of the world's population estimated to be in slavery or forced labor is around or under 1 in 200 (or 0.5 percent). ILO 2012 estimates put it at 3 per 1,000; GSI 2016 at closer to 6 per 1,000.

Second, the time spent by people in bondage ranges from a few weeks to ten years, although according to the ILO, the mean was about eighteen to thirty months. Such estimates concur with suggestions by Bales, architect of GSI, regarding the "disposability" of modern-day slaves.[20]

Third, today's slaves are overwhelmingly employed in the private sector. The ILO claims nine out of ten (or 18.7 million) forced laborers in 2012 were "exploited by individuals or enterprises" in the private sector, with the remaining 2.2 million in state-sponsored activities. Within the private sector, 4.5 million or one in four, most of them female, worked in sex-related activities, with the rest, more gender balanced, in other areas. GSI 2016 suggests a similar pattern regarding the balance between private and state employment.

Fourth, slavery today exists worldwide; however, its distribution is uneven and heavily skewed toward Asia and Africa. The ILO estimated 11.7 million (or 56 percent) of forced laborers were in Asia and 3.7 million (18 percent) in Africa, with the remaining 5.5 million (26 percent) in the Americas, Europe, the Commonwealth of Independent States (CIS or former Soviet Union), and the Middle East. GSI 2016 provides different regional breakdowns, but largely confirms the ILO picture, with Asia–Pacific said to account for 66 percent of the world's slaves; sub-Saharan Africa, 14 percent; and the Middle East, North Africa, Russia-Asia, the Americas, and Europe combined, 20 percent.

And fifth, there is a correlation between global population and geographical distributions of coerced labor, but this general correlation disguises significant variations in prevalence of such labor within the geographical categories chosen. The ILO, for example, has prevalence estimates of 4 or more per 1,000 for Central and Eastern Europe and

---

[19] For an historic example, see Philip D. Curtin, *The Atlantic Slave Trade: A Census* (Madison, WI: University of Wisconsin Press, 1969), and David Eltis and David Richardson, *Atlas of the Transatlantic Slave Trade* (New Haven, CT: Yale University Press, 2010).

[20] The eighteen-month figure allows interruptions to enslavement through external intervention, whereas the thirty-month one assumes enslavement was "completed" without intervention (and is closer to the norm). On disposability, see Bales, *Disposable People*.

CIS, close to the same for Africa, but 1.5 or less per 1,000 for the world's industrialized areas. GSI again reveals similar patterns. Unlike the ILO, however, it also provides country-by-country breakdowns of the numbers and prevalence of people in slavery. These are not immune to criticism, but, if not wholly trustworthy, do shed some further light on the geography of global slavery.

According to GSI 2016, India alone accounted for 40 percent of the world's slaves in 2016. Adding a further nine countries in Asia and sub-Saharan Africa raises that figure to over two-thirds. Apart from India, others on the list include China, Pakistan, Bangladesh, Uzbekistan, Russia, North Korea, and Nigeria. India, Uzbekistan, and North Korea are also among those with the highest prevalence of modern-day slavery: India's is estimated at around 14 per 1,000, North Korea's and Uzbekistan's are each at over 40 per 1,000. Fourteen other countries, almost all in Africa, Asia, and the Middle East, each have an estimated prevalence of 10 or more per 1,000. That contrasts with advanced Western countries where prevalence is computed at 1 or under per 1,000, with transitional economies, many in CIS, noticeably higher but less than 10. Such data highlight the inverse relationship between levels of modern-day slavery and national economic development, while underscoring the pivotal position of sub-Saharan Africa and South Asia in sustaining such slavery.

Having considered the data from both ILO and GSI, then, how does the story revealed by these data compare to that of historical slavery? In pursuit of an answer, I analyze four issues in sequence. The first concerns the relative scale of slavery; specifically, suggestions that there are globally more slaves today than at any time in human history. Such comparisons assume that definitions of slavery by historians are identical to those of students of contemporary slavery, an assumption that is clearly questionable. It also rests on estimates of slavery historically that may be no more reliable in global terms than those for contemporary variants. One historian estimates, nonetheless, that worldwide perhaps 45 million were in chattel slavery, strictly defined, around 1800. That figure rises to 75 million if one uses a definition similar to that of the ILO or GSI.[21] The former is more or less identical to the GSI estimate of 2016, but more than double that of the ILO in 2012. A more sensible comparator, however,

---

[21] B. W. Higman, "Demographic Trends," in David Eltis, Stanley L. Engerman, Seymour Drescher, and David Richardson, eds., *Cambridge World History of Slavery* (hereafter *CWHS*), Volume 4: *AD 1804–AD 2016* (Cambridge: Cambridge University Press, 2017), 23–4. Higman suggests 37 million enslaved in Asia, 5 million in Africa, and 3 million in the Americas, with 30 million serfs worldwide around 1800.

is the higher figure for 1800, which at least embraces some of the types of forced labor used to estimate contemporary slavery. Assuming that the historical figure for 1800 is as reliable as those for 2012–16, then it seems highly improbable that in absolute numbers there are more slaves today than at any time in human history. On the contrary, slavery was more commonplace two centuries ago than today, and maybe even in earlier periods too. That does not imply that the problem of contemporary slavery has been exaggerated. But it does beg the wider question of why slavery's international standing has diminished in modern history.

The second concerns the geography of slavery. Like contemporary slavery, exact evidence of the historical geography of slavery is patchy, but as with its contemporary counterpart, few areas of the world were seemingly untouched by it during the last three millennia. That suggests that slavery in the past, like today, transcended age, creed, ethnicity, gender, and race. Historically, slavery's regional concentrations probably varied through time, although in the absence of global censuses, how much is impossible to say. Among the primary factors shaping its distribution were poverty and destitution, sometimes linked to environmental disasters, which likely drove some to accept bondage as a survival strategy. This may have been prevalent in societies around the Indian Ocean, although symptoms of it existed elsewhere.[22] The most important single factor, however, was almost certainly warfare, most commonly linked to imperialism. Herodotus was among the first to observe its effects, and slavery was an integral feature of all the ancient empires, with historian Keith Hopkins describing Rome as a "warrior state."[23] The pattern continued in the Abbasid, Byzantine, Carolingian, Mamluk, and Ottoman empires that emerged in the millennium following the fall of Rome. It was evident in China during the Tang dynasty (618–907) and later; in the Viking era in Europe; and in the Ghaznavid and Chola empires in South and Southeast Asia from the ninth century.[24] Slaves, or *kholopy*, were associated with Muscovy's expansion, while

---

[22] Gwyn Campbell and Alessandro Stanziani, "Slavery and Bondage in the Indian Ocean World, Nineteenth and Twentieth Centuries," and Stanziani, "Slavery in India," in Eltis et al., eds., *CWHS*, Volume 4, 226–45, 246–71.

[23] Herodotus, *The Histories* (London and New York: Penguin Classics, 1996), 419; Keith Hopkins, *Conquerors and Slaves: Sociological Studies in Roman History* (Cambridge: Cambridge University Press, 1978), 32, 37; Keith Bradley and Paul Cartledge, eds., *CWHS*, Volume 1: *The Ancient Mediterranean World* (Cambridge: Cambridge University Press, 2011).

[24] Craig Perry, David Eltis, Stanley L. Engerman, and David Richardson, eds., *CWHS*, Volume 2: *The Medieval Period, AD 500–AD 1420* (Cambridge: Cambridge University

imperial powers preyed on Russia for slaves.[25] One finds slaves in sub-Saharan Africa and among the Aztecs and Incas before Columbus's landfall in the Americas.[26] Their presence within indigenous American empires was quickly overshadowed after 1500 by the rise of transatlantic slavery, in tandem with European colonization of the continent.[27] Although incomplete, this brief survey underscores slavery's links historically with international conflict and colonialism, vestiges of which remain even in today's postcolonial world. Accordingly, contemporary slavery is not new but rather a modern manifestation of an institution as old as humanity itself. The precise origins of chattel slavery, its most extreme form, remain uncertain, but likely date from around the fourth century BCE.[28]

The third issue relates to human trafficking, thought by some as a defining characteristic of contemporary slavery and by one recent commentator as a "particularly cruel type of slavery because it removes the victim from all that is familiar," rendering her or him "isolated and alone."[29] Victims are estimated to range from 600,000 to 2 million or more per year; they account annually for perhaps 2–10 percent of the world's estimated total slave population; and they ensure that trafficking

---

Press, forthcoming); Ehud R. Toledano, "Enslavement in the Ottoman Empire in the Early Modern Period" and Kerry Ward, "Slavery in South-East Asia, 1420–1804," in David Eltis and Stanley L. Engerman, eds., *CWHS*, Volume 3: *AD 1420–AD 1804* (Cambridge: Cambridge University Press, 2011), 25–47, 163–86; Mark E Lewis, *China's Cosmopolitan Empire* (Cambridge, MA: Harvard University Press, 2012), 127; Marc Abramson, *Ethnic Identity in Tang China* (Philadelphia, PA: University of Pennsylvania Press, 2008), 118–37; Pamela Kyle Crossley, "Slavery in Early Modern China," in Eltis and Engerman, eds., *CWHS*, Volume 3, 186–216.

[25] Richard Hellie, *Slavery in Russia 1450–1725* (Chicago, IL: University of Chicago Press, 1984).

[26] Paul E. Lovejoy, *Transformations in Slavery: A History of Slavery in Africa* (1979; Cambridge: Cambridge University Press, 3rd edition, 2011); Camilla Townsend, "Slavery in the Pre-Contact Americas" and Paul Lane, "Slavery in Medieval Sub-Saharan Africa," in Perry et al, eds., *CWHS*, Volume 2, forthcoming.

[27] David Eltis, *The Rise of African Slavery in the Americas* (Cambridge: Cambridge University Press, 2000).

[28] Yvon Garlan, *Slavery in Ancient Greece* (1982, revised and translated, Ithaca, NY: Cornell University Press, 1988), 38–9, who suggests that early Greek slavery was not chattel slavery, but rather was developed in the context of defining freedom in Chios and Athens. On the latter, see Moses Finley, "Was Greek Civilization Based on Slave Labor?" *Historia* 8 (1959), 164; Pierre Vidal-Naquet, *The Black Hunter* (Baltimore, MA: Johns Hopkins University Press, 1998); Marek Wecowski, "Slavery, Freedom and the Historians: Review of Melina Tamiolaki, *Liberté et escalavage chez les historiens grecs classique*, Paris, 2010," *Histos* 8 (2014), xxxvii.

[29] "What is Human Trafficking?" *Soroptimist*, www.soroptimist.org/trafficking/faq.html.

is considered "one of the fastest growing and lucrative crimes" worldwide, with estimated annual earnings of some $32 billion.[30] Such numbers are all consistent with continuing strong demand today for new slaves across many destinations, but they indicate too that probably a majority of those in contemporary slavery remain in the region or country in which they were born and/or forced into servitude.[31] Although there have been no known attempts to construct global estimates of historic trafficking, partial data reveal trafficking to have been at times as substantial and consistent a companion of slavery in the past as it is today. It is estimated, for example, that some 100 million people in total – or around 100,000 a year – were taken into slavery in the millennium-long Roman Empire.[32] Not all were probably trafficked, but if true, that annual figure would have been equivalent to about 5 to 7 percent of Roman Italy's estimated slave population of 1.5 to 2 million in the first century BCE, or around 2 percent of the possible 5 million slaves throughout the whole empire at its height.[33] Another calculation has shown that new entrants from Africa into Caribbean and Brazilian slavery around 1790 were equivalent to around 5 percent of the two regions' enslaved populations.[34] We do not know how typical such ratios of trafficked to slave populations were across history, but it seems safe to say that few societies with slaves

---

[30] UN official Michelle Bachelet/www.humantrafficking.org (accessed November 29, 2015) on income earnings; on numbers trafficked, see www.OpenDemocracy/Slavery/ Estimates for first number (US Report 2005) and "UN: 2.4 Million Human Trafficking Victims" (Yuri Fedotov, UN Office on Drugs and Crime), *TimeWorld*, Time online edition, April 3, 2012. It is unclear whether Fedotov's estimate refers to the total number of people in slavery who had been trafficked or the annual flow of trafficked people. Using ILO estimates of mean times in slavery, the former implies around 1 million were being trafficked annually, compared with the 2.4 million headline figure. On contemporary trafficking generally see Shelley, *Human Trafficking*, chs. 3–4; Sally Engle Merry, "How Big Is the Trafficking Problem? The Mysteries of Quantification," *openDemocracy*, January 26, 2015, www.opendemocracy.net/beyondslavery/sally-engle-merry/how-big-is-trafficking-problem-mysteries-of-quantification.

[31] The ILO 2012 Report estimated that 56 percent of forced laborers remain in their place of origin.

[32] Walter Scheidel, "The Roman Slave Supply," in Bradley and Cartledge, eds., *CWHS*, Volume 1, 309.

[33] Hopkins, *Conquerors and Slaves*, 101; Kyle Harper, *Slavery in the Late Roman World, AD 275–425* (Cambridge: Cambridge University Press, 2011), 58–60.

[34] David Richardson, "Consuming Goods, Consuming People: Reflections on the Transatlantic Slave Trade," in Philip Misevich and Kristin Mann, eds., *The Rise and Demise of Slavery and the Slave Trade in the Atlantic World* (Rochester, NY: University of Rochester Press, 2016), 43.

did not have recourse to human traffickers.[35] Accordingly, trafficking and the motives, structures, and human misery that accompany it define both contemporary and historical slavery. Trafficking and slavery have been bedfellows from time immemorial.

The fourth issue concerns the relative importance of slavery and trafficking past and present. In absolute terms, the numbers in bondage and subject to trafficking remain high in long-run historical perspective, but their relative significance is low. We have seen that up to 6 in 1,000 of the world's population may currently be in modern-day slavery. At 2 million annually, trafficking directly affects perhaps 3 per 10,000; the reality is probably rather less and maybe as low as 1 per 10,000. Such figures are small relative to two centuries ago, when about 75 per 1,000 (using a broad definition) and 45 per 1,000 (using a narrower one) were likely in bondage worldwide. The former – more comparable – figure is twelve to forty times greater than the highest slave to population ratios of GSI and ILO. Ratios for trafficking globally around 1800 are unavailable, but estimates confined essentially to forced migration out of Africa and within or out of Russia at that time reveal totals equivalent to close to 2 per 10,000 of the world's population, and thus not dissimilar to ratios for the whole world today.

It may be objected that comparisons based on global statistics are misleading when such statistics disguise major regional or national variations in prevalence rates of slavery. It is true that, as in the contemporary world, so two centuries ago there were major geographical variations in prevalence of slavery. A comparison of historic and contemporary data on prevalence, however, only underscores the larger picture revealed by global data described above. Thus, whereas North Korea and Uzbekistan, with estimates of over 40 per 1,000, have reputedly the highest prevalence of slavery in 2016, at least 750 per 1,000 of the Caribbean population were chattel slaves on the eve of the Haitian uprising in 1790.[36] Admittedly, Caribbean ratios were exceptional then and even perhaps in human history, but ratios of around 300 per 1,000 existed around 1800 in Brazil and the U.S. South, while elsewhere ratios of 100 or more per 1,000 likely existed in the Ottoman Empire and across

[35] This includes internal trafficking, for one example of which see Michael Tadman, *Speculators and Slaves: Masters, Traders, and Slaves in the Old South* (Madison, WI: University of Wisconsin Press, 1996).

[36] John J. McCusker, *Rum and the American Revolution: The Rum Trade and the Balance of Payments of the Thirteen Continental Colonies* (New York: Garland, 1989), 548–768.

sub-Saharan Africa.[37] Furthermore, prevalence levels of slavery in Indian Ocean Asia and places further east were likely higher around 1800 than they are today. Lest it be thought, moreover, that the prevalence of slavery today nonetheless may be comparable to periods in human history before 1800, it is worth noting that, at times, slaves may well have comprised up to a quarter or more of the populations of ancient Athens and the Roman Empire. These were not far removed from those of colonial Brazil, the US antebellum South, or the nineteenth-century Sokoto Caliphate.[38] Whether ancient Greece and Rome should be categorized with Brazil, the US South, the Caribbean, and even the Sokoto Caliphate as "slave societies," as Moses Finley argued, remains an open issue and depends in any case on more than the proportions of people enslaved.[39] Be that as it may, on almost any reckoning the prevalence of slavery today, even if more broadly defined than is commonly the case historically, is likely at an historic low. That finding cannot diminish, of course, the continuing hardship of those in slavery or the moral imperative to free them.

The unprecedented growth of the world's population from 1 to 7 billion is a vital backdrop to slavery's sharply declining global prevalence since 1800. The demographic explosion, however, does not necessarily explain that decline. To the contrary, there are claims that rising levels of inequality, poverty, and debt that in some parts of the world appear to have accompanied demographic change do much to explain today's "new" slavery, especially its African and Asian concentrations.[40] In searching for explanations of slavery's declining significance, then, we have to look elsewhere, notably at changes in social values, perceptions of human rights, and contract labor law, all of which have evolved rapidly,

---

[37] Susan B. Carter, Scott Sigmund Gartner, Michael R. Haines, Alan L. Olmstead, Richard Sutch, and Gavin Wright, eds., *Historical Statistics of the United States: Millennial Edition Online, Part A, Population* (Cambridge: Cambridge University Press, 2006); Laird W. Bergad, *Slavery and the Demographic and Economic History of Minas Gerais, Brazil, 1720–1888* (Cambridge: Cambridge University Press, 1999); Francisco Vidal Luna and Herbert S. Klein, *Slavery and the Economy of São Paulo, 1750–1850* (Stanford, CA: Stanford University Press, 2003); Gareth Austin, 'Slavery in Africa 1804–1936," in Eltis et al., eds., *CWHS*, Volume 4, 174–96 (which notes that slaves were up to a third of the population in French West Africa, the Sokoto Caliphate, and the Great Lakes region, among other places).

[38] T. E Rihill, "Classical Athens," in Bradley and Cartledge, eds., *CWHS*, Volume 1, 49–51; Neville Morley, "Slavery under the Principate," in ibid, 284; Mary Beard, *SPQR: A History of Ancient Rome* (New York: Liveright Publishing Corporation, 2015), 359.

[39] Moses I. Finley, *Ancient Slavery and Modern Ideology* (Princeton, NJ: Markus Wiener Publisher, 1998); Keith Bradley, "Slavery in the Roman Republic," in Bradley and Cartledge, eds., *CWHS*, Volume 1, 244.

[40] Bales, *Disposable People*.

if geographically unevenly, in the last two centuries.[41] I return to this issue later.

Historicizing contemporary slavery is more than an exercise in revealing its absolute and relative importance in long-run perspective. It invites also investigation of the processes that have shaped slavery past and present, as well as the factors that contribute to its somewhat checkered decline in the modern world. I explore these issues in the next two sections: the first focuses on three aspects of slaves' lived experience: the work of enslaved people, peoples' vulnerability to enslavement, and the processes and mechanics of human trafficking. An underlying theme of this section is the shifting position of the state with respect to slave employment and recruitment through time. That theme also informs the following section, where I discuss the rise of antislavery from the 1780s, its historic successes, and the obstacles or challenges to its further success in the present era.

ENSLAVEMENT AS LIVED EXPERIENCE OVER
THE CENTURIES

The most iconic image of slaves historically depicts Africans toiling from sunup to sundown on American plantations producing sugar or cotton for external markets. First made famous by late eighteenth-century British and other abolitionists, it is an image that, notwithstanding its provenance, presented a realistic picture of the unrewarding drudgery, brutality, and dehumanized working lives of transatlantic slavery's victims.[42] It assumed added significance from the fact that plantation-style slavery existed in other times and places.[43] Nevertheless, the transatlantic model came to define what many imagined slavery to be

---

[41] Lynn Hunt, *Inventing Human Rights: A History* (New York: W.W. Norton, 2007); Seymour Drescher, "Liberty, Equality, Humanity: Antislavery and Civil Society in Britain and France," in Misevich and Mann, eds., *Rise and Demise of Slavery*, 171–95; Robert J. Steinfeld, *The Invention of Free Labor: The Employment Relation in English and American Law and Culture, 1350–1870* (Chapel Hill, NC: University of North Carolina Press, 1991); David Eltis, Stanley L. Engerman, Seymour Drescher, and David Richardson, "Introduction," in Eltis et al., eds., *CWHS*, Volume 4, 3–19.

[42] Ira Berlin and Philip D. Morgan, "Introduction," in Ira Berlin and Philip D. Morgan, eds., *Cultivation and Culture: Labor and the Shaping of Slave Life in the Americas* (Charlottesville, VA: University of Virginia Press, 1993); Philip D. Morgan, "The Poor: Slaves in Early America," in David Eltis, Frank D. Lewis, and Kenneth L. Sokoloff, eds., *Slavery in the Development of the Americas* (Cambridge: Cambridge University Press, 2004), 288–324.

[43] Richard B. Allen, *Slaves, Freedmen and Indentured Laborers in Colonial Mauritius* (Cambridge: Cambridge University Press, 2006); Frederick Cooper, *Plantation Slavery*

between the seventeenth and nineteenth centuries, thereby helping to create what historians of slavery elsewhere have called a tyranny of the Atlantic that fosters neglect of the extent and resilience of slavery outside it.

One cannot ignore both the real and symbolic importance of African slavery in defining Atlantic history and revolutionizing economic life and income and wealth distribution wherever the slave plantation model existed in 1500–1850. Its products and profits are said to have transformed economies in Western Europe while simultaneously impoverishing Africa.[44] Its racism is claimed to have defined the modern world.[45] Neither argument can be so readily made for slavery's effects in other contexts. Yet, at its height in 1750–1860, slave-based plantation-style agriculture barely employed more than 10 percent of the 45 million people estimated to be in slavery worldwide. For the remaining nine out of ten in that period, as indeed for the vast majority in earlier ones, work regimes were very different, although not necessarily less demeaning or cruel. Outside the plantation economies, fewer proportions of slaves were employed in specific sectors of agriculture. In the ancient world, the Ottoman Empire, and sub-Saharan Africa, slaves worked in a wide range of activities: household and sexual services, finance, artisan crafts, building, the military, and agricultural pursuits. Sizeable proportions lived in elite households where some assumed prominent positions and many integrated into kinship structures.[46] In those societies, too, many slaves worked alongside peasants or small farmers in the fields, or free labor in workshops or other places.

Proportionately fewer slaves in the ancient world and in societies other than those dominated by plantations were recruited to and employed

---

on the East Coast of Africa (New Haven, CT: Yale University Press, 1977); Paul E. Lovejoy, "Plantations in the Economy of the Sokoto Caliphate," *Journal of African History* 19, no. 3 (1978), 341–68.

[44] Eric Williams, *Capitalism and Slavery* (Chapel Hill, NC: University of North Carolina Press, 1944); Walter Rodney, *How Europe Underdeveloped Africa* (London: Bogle-L'Ouverture Publications, 1972); Joseph E. Inikori, *Africa and the Industrial Revolution in England* (Cambridge: Cambridge University Press, 2002); Darren Acemoglu, Simon Johnson, and James Robinson, "The Rise of Europe: Atlantic Trade, Institutional Change and Economic Growth," *American Economic Review* 95 (2005), 546–79.

[45] Paul Gilroy, *The Black Atlantic: Modernity and Double Consciousness* (London: Verso, 1993).

[46] Colin Wells, *The Roman Empire* (London: Fontana, London, 2nd ed., 1992), 197–9; Igor Kopytoff and Suzanne Miers, "African 'Slavery' as an Institution of Marginality," in Suzanne Miers and Igor Kopytoff, eds., *Slavery in Africa: Historical and Anthropological Perspectives* (Madison, WI: University of Wisconsin Press, 1979), 1–84.

primarily in market-orientated activities.[47] Historian Dimitris Kyrtatas argues that in antiquity, "the distinction between productive and unproductive servile labor had no appeal to masters caring only to know that using slaves meant spending less."[48] Diversity of employments and employment of enslaved people alongside other workers further implied, he argues, that "Greek economies were not made structurally any different by the presence of numerous slaves."[49] There were exceptions to this: "the entire Spartan political, military, social and economic edifice" is said to have rested upon agricultural allotments employing helots or war captives.[50] But overall, Kyrtatas's depiction of ancient slavery's limited structural impact economically seems valid. It is extendable, moreover, to medieval Europe, the later Middle East, and precolonial sub-Saharan Africa, among other places. Equally valid in all these cases, too, is John Bodel's view that, although Roman slaves were considered property, slavery itself "was grounded in ideological rather than economic considerations," with hired workmen rather than slaves being identified with "productive" work.[51] Herodotus held that view about ancient Greece, and it found support among much later writers on slavery, notably Adam Smith.[52] Even in Sparta, where helots were the economy's backbone, their function was as much ideological as economic.[53] Insofar as slaves were considered profit-making assets, returns from them in antiquity and probably in other times arose from low prices of slaves relative to hired workers' pay.[54] That is consistent with theories linking coerced

---

[47] Ibid., p. 65, where Kopytoff and Miers note among slaves in Africa the "noneconomic emphasis in terms of [their] use."

[48] Dimitris J. Kyrtatas, "Slavery and Economy in the Greek World," in Bradley and Cartledge, eds., *CWHS*, Volume 1, 109.

[49] Ibid.

[50] Paul Cartledge, *The Spartans: An Epic History* (London: London, 2013), 66.

[51] John Bodel, "Slave Labor and Roman Society," in Bradley and Cartledge, eds., *CWHS*, Volume 1, 313. Bodel's comments echo Miller's remarks on historicizing the totality of circumstances underlying slave ownership (Miller, *Problem of Slavery*) and remind one of Davis's observations on ancient views on slavery and human progress, ideas that inform later debates about slavery (David Brion Davis, *Slavery and Human Progress* (Oxford and New York: Oxford University Press, 1986)).

[52] Herodotus, *Histories*, 340. Herodotus asserts that in Athens when men won freedom, "every man amongst them was interested in his own cause," a claim anticipating Smith's (Adam Smith, *An Inquiry into the Nature and Causes of the Wealth of Nations*, new edition (1776; London: Routledge, 1900), 298).

[53] Cartledge, *Spartans*, 88–9.

[54] Daniel C. Snell, "Slavery in the Ancient Near East," in Bradley and Cartledge, eds., *CWHS*, Volume 1, 9; Scheidel, "Roman Slave Supply," 309; A. H. M. Jones, "Slavery in the Ancient World," *Economic History Review*, 2nd series, 9, no. 2 (1956), 8.

labor historically with high land to labor and capital ratios within aris-
tocratic social structures.[55] Slavery's attractiveness from ancient societies
onwards, therefore, was that slaves were controllable and expendable.
In that sense, history anticipated a major theme of contemporary slavery
studies.

State-sponsored forced labor exists in contemporary North Korea and
some other authoritarian regimes, but compared to the past, few slaves
today work in households of political elites.[56] In other respects, the work
of contemporary slaves is barely indistinguishable from the past in terms
of its range as well as its menial and degrading nature. Slaves today work
in agriculture, fishing, mining, construction, sweatshops, domestic service, and the sex industries. In conflict zones, they are forced to become
soldiers. Some antislavery activists focus primarily on the recruitment of
women and children into the vice industry as part of larger campaigns
concerning global female exploitation. Such emphases have parallels in
historical studies of enslaved concubines from antiquity onwards. But,
unlike their predecessors, who were visible but "socially dead," today's
slaves are largely invisible, existing in shadowy recesses, toiling without
protection or reward in organizations supplying goods and services
within local, national, and international markets. A significant proportion, too, work in establishments at the furthest extremes of supply chains
connecting local African and Asian producers to consumers in North
America and Western Europe. Such slaves are heirs of those Africans
forced into transatlantic slavery before 1870 to accommodate demand
for low-cost goods among consumers of European descent, reminding us
of slavery's historic and ongoing ties to globalization since 1500.[57]

Significantly, the ILO defines forced labor not by work itself but by the
relationship between persons doing the work and those exacting it. So
what makes people vulnerable today to slavery? Are the factors behind
it different from those that informed slavery in the past? The imperialist
activities that directly generated slavery in the past may no longer carry
the same weight, but the global inequalities of power and wealth left by
imperialism underlie explanations of contemporary slavery that revolve
around international poverty, debt, state corruption, and ecological

---

[55] Evsey Domar, "The Causes of Slavery and Serfdom: A Hypothesis," *Journal of Economic History* 30, no. 1 (1970), 18–32.

[56] Rhoda E. Howard-Hassmann, "State Enslavement in North Korea," in Annie Bunting and Joel Quirk, eds., *Contemporary Slavery and Human Rights* (Vancouver: University of British Columbia Press, forthcoming), available at genocidewatch.org/images/N.Korea.

[57] Richardson, "Consuming Goods, Consuming People."

crises under globalization.[58] Recent research has refined that approach, offering a vulnerability index of peoples' exposure to risks of enslavement. First proposed in GSI 2014 as a weighted composite of thirty-seven variables relating to states' capacities to protect citizens from slavery, the index was recalibrated in GSI 2016, using measures of civil and political protections, social health and economic rights, personal security, and conflict and refugees to produce state-by-state indices.

According to the index, vulnerability to enslavement is today up to seven times higher in some states than others. States in Western Europe, North America, and other regions of historic white settlement occupy the lowest rungs on the vulnerability ladder. Several states in Africa, some in the Middle East, former CIS states (including Russia), and India and Pakistan are on the middle and higher rungs. A correlation between prevalence of and vulnerability to slavery is evident. A critical element of states with the highest levels of vulnerability is their broken or failed condition, where the rule of law has collapsed, corruption is rife, and ethnic and other forms of violence are endemic, causing huge population displacements and increased poverty. Weak states thus promote vulnerability to enslavement, but other factors such as poor enforcement of antislavery laws or protection of human rights increase vulnerability – even in states otherwise considered strong. It follows that reducing national and international conflict and strengthening the rule of law are prerequisites for eradicating contemporary slavery. The burden of history, however, weighs more heavily in some countries than others in efforts to achieve such goals.[59]

GSI offers a prism through which to view similarities between present and historic patterns of vulnerability to enslavement. Slaves today are commonly considered cultural or social "outsiders," people who occupy the margins of the society in which they live or to which they have been taken. Moved illegally across international borders, trafficked people are sometimes considered criminals, not victims, reinforcing their outsider status. Historically, culture was also a mechanism used to distinguish those who might be enslaved from others. In classical Athens, freedom

[58] Bales, *Disposable People*; Kevin Bales, *Blood and Earth: Modern Slavery, Ecocide, and the Secret to Saving the World* (New York: Spiegal and Grau, 2016). On ecology and Asian historic slavery, see Campbell and Stanziani, "Slavery and Bondage"; Stanziani, "Slavery in India."

[59] For Africa, see Joel Quirk and Darshan Vigneswaran, "Historical Legacies and Present Innovations," in Joel Quirk and Darshan Vigneswaren, eds., *Slavery, Migration and Contemporary Bondage in Africa* (Trenton, NJ: Africa World Press, 2013), 1–35.

was defined in relation to the slavery of others: Aristotle observed that
the enslaved were "barbarians" or "brutish," culturally different from,
even intellectually or morally inferior to, citizens of Greek city states
who enslaved them.[60] Similar outlooks informed attitudes toward slavery
among rulers of the Roman Empire, and would continue to do so in
Western Europe, the Ottoman Empire, sub-Saharan Africa, and other
regions from the fall of Rome through the modern era.

In later periods, however, it was perceived differences based on
religion, ethnicity, or race that exposed people to risks of enslavement by others. States condemned their own citizens to slavery in
some circumstances, but in most instances historically, it appears that
enslaved people or their descendants were classified as "outsiders." In
turn, abolitionists would at times emphasize peoples' shared humanity
even while acknowledging their cultural differences, but slavery's
continuing existence, and more particularly its concentration and
prevalence in some countries, indicate it is a message yet to achieve
worldwide acceptance in practice. That reflects in part the power of
human greed to override human rights. It also reflects resistance to
concepts of shared humanity identified with Western values, which
in some countries challenge deeply embedded social values rooted in
long histories of coerced labor and discrimination. Such traditions
help explain peoples' continuing vulnerability to enslavement across
Eurasia and Africa. Indeed, GSI's index underlines how history shapes
contemporary slavery.

There are claims that three out of four slaves historically were born
outside the group of their captors. The remainder, by implication, were
"insiders," sharing their masters' ethnic or cultural attributes.[61] We cannot
say definitively whether such ratios, even if historically reliable, apply
to contemporary slavery, but, on the basis of estimated distributions of
such slavery, they likely understate by some margin its domestic origins
in South Asia, China, Africa, and even maybe Russia. In each of these
places, traditions of domestically sourced forced labor run deep and
endured longer than in Western Europe, where coerced labor was small

[60] Aristotle claimed that "barbarian and slave are by nature one and the same thing"
(Aristotle, *Politics*, 9). He also noted that "a brutish person is commonest among the non-
Greek races" (Aristotle, *The Nicomachean Ethics* (New York: Penguin Classics, 2004),
168). See also Robert Schlaifer, "Greek Theories of Slavery from Homer to Aristotle," in
M. I. Finley, ed., *Slavery in Classical Antiquity: Views and Controversies* (Cambridge: W.
Heffer & Sons, 1960), 122–5.

[61] Patterson, *Slavery and Social Death*, 179.

in scale in some countries long before 1750. A look at forced labor's history in Russia and parts of Asia underlines the point.

In a comparative study of US antebellum slavery and Russian serfdom, Peter Kolchin challenged the assumption, identified with Finley, that slaves "were brought into a new society violently and traumatically." Kolchin argued instead that while "American slaves were aliens" of African origin, in Russia, masters and serfs largely shared "the same nationality." Following historian Richard Hellie, who saw Russians as "accustomed to enslaving their own people," Kolchin linked Russian peasants' entry into forced labor to *kholopstvo*, or limited service contract slavery, a process that Hellie associated with "a fundamental lack of ethnic identity and cohesion among the inhabitants of Muscovy." Kolchin proposed a "gradual degeneration" as encouraging Russians to take "the step of enslaving their fellow countrymen," but acknowledged that as serfdom became fully developed in the eighteenth century, "noblemen and peasants seemed as different from each other as white and black, European and African," with the "social distance" between the two helping to sustain serfdom.[62] Other studies have equated Russian serfdom in practice to slavery. Insights into its harshness were supplied by novelist Fyodor Dostoyevsky's mid nineteenth-century depiction of *katorga* (political labor camps) in tsarist Russia.[63]

Kolchin's analysis may be extended, for relationships based on forced labor and poverty continued in Russia well beyond serfdom's formal ending in 1861. Russian peasants remained tied to the village (or *mir*) through collective responsibility for compensation payments for emancipation until around 1910. They were subsequently subjected to state control through Stalinist collectivization. Incarceration of political prisoners in gulags outlasted that. And the post-Soviet transition to markets resulted in collapsing social welfare and massive property redistributions that left many women and children destitute.[64] In the same way, therefore, that it has been argued that slave emancipation in the USA in 1865 did not effectively liberate the African American descendants of former slaves before the civil rights movement a century later, so one may argue that abolishing serfdom has not truly freed the

[62] Peter Kolchin, *Unfree Labor: American Slavery and Russian Serfdom* (Cambridge, MA: Belknap Press, 1987), 43–6; Hellie, *Slavery in Russia*, 390, 711.

[63] On recent interpretations, see Shane O'Rourke, "The Emancipation of the Serfs in Europe," in Eltis et al., eds., *CWHS*, Volume 4, 422–40. On prison camps, see Fyodor Dostoyevsky, *The House of the Dead* (1862; New York: Penguin Classics, 1986).

[64] Shelley, *Human Trafficking*, 29–30.

descendants of Russia's former serfs.[65] When in his semi-autobiographical novel *House of the Dead* Dostoyevsky saw tyranny as "a habit which may be developed until at last it becomes a disease," he foretold how age-old forms of Russian coercion akin to slavery might continue long beyond his lifetime.

Russia was not alone in creating domestic forms of coerced labor that continue to shape the present. In precolonial sub-Saharan Africa there existed private-order systems of debt-related human pawning, which could transform into heritable forms of bondage or dependency similar to chattel slavery.[66] Drought and civil disorder compounded the situation, prompting self-enslavement or the selling of children into slavery as survival strategies. Such processes continued into the colonial period when laws imposed by imperial authorities outlawing slavery's legal status failed to protect people from continuing enslavement. Similar patterns are discernible in China. In Tang China (618–907 CE), laws protected free people from enslavement, but foreigners and even some criminals could be enslaved, while free but destitute people could sell themselves into slavery. Later dynasties followed similar practices through the early twentieth century, after which Japanese external aggression and then the communist takeover from 1949 imposed new forms of servitude on the Chinese.

Further west, in South Asia, forms of bonded labor have had equally long histories, linked partly to changing imperial conditions but also to internal circumstances. Easton argues that poverty caused by famine and other factors forced people historically into slavery in parts of South Asia. As insiders indebted to "nearby patrons, chiefs, moneylenders, or tax farmers," many were unable to clear debts, and as a result fell into "a state of permanent, even inheritable, dependency, and hence slavery."[67] Others have reminded us that historically, debt bondage was quite common – but "only in South Asia," home to four-fifths of those globally in debt bondage today, "can one still find a truly systemic, archaic, feudal system of slave-labor exploitation of one class of individuals by another." Such bondage constitutes, it is argued, "a form of slavery ... perpetuated by custom, corruption, greed, and social apathy," linked among other things to caste, social hierarchy, illiteracy, and continuing income and

[65] Douglas A. Blackmon, *Slavery by Another Name: The Re-Enslavement of Black Americans from the Civil War to World War II* (New York: Anchor Books, 2009).

[66] Paul E. Lovejoy and Toyin Falola, eds., *Pawnship, Slavery and Colonialism in Africa* (Trenton, NJ: Africa World Press, 2003).

[67] Eaton, "Introduction," 5–6.

wealth inequality on a massive scale.[68] Despite claims that identify contemporary slavery as a new form of servitude linked to inequality and debt, its pattern and distribution continue to reflect the domestic traditions and histories of those societies where bondage has long been and remains deeply entrenched.

The insider status of many enslaved people does not undermine the importance of human trafficking in fostering slavery, both past and present. Even where forced labor was primarily internally generated, forced relocation was commonplace and remains the case today. It is estimated that 2.8 million Russian serfs were relocated to the country's border regions in 1718–95 to bolster national security.[69] It is estimated too that 1.5 million largely domestically born slaves of African descent were trafficked from the Old to the Deep South between 1815 and 1860.[70] Such internal relocations of coerced labor were far from exceptional historically, and in fact date from ancient times. They also continue today in South Asia.

It is cross-border human trafficking, however, that attracts most attention from students of comparative historic and contemporary slavery. Consistent with Finley's depiction of slaves as outsiders, taken violently and traumatically, interstate conflict, raiding, and warfare were historically key sources of such victims. The story was told by Herodotus and Thucydides and repeated by later historians of the ancient world, the post-Roman middle ages, the Ottoman Empire, the transatlantic slave trade, and Asante and Sokoto Caliphates in sub-Saharan Africa. Antislavery campaigners' initial targeting from the 1780s of the slave trade reflected trafficking's perceived importance to sustaining systems of slavery and its wider impact on the areas sourced for captives.

The scale of trafficking historically was determined in part by attitudes of slave owners toward chattels' usage, which affected their reproductive capacity, and to slave manumission.[71] Age and gender of victims, which

[68] Siddharth Kara, *Bonded Labor: Tackling the System of Slavery in South Asia* (New York: Columbia University Press, 2012), 5–10.

[69] Arcadius Kahan, *The Plow, the Hammer and the Knout: An Economic History of Eighteenth-Century Russia* (Chicago, IL: University of Chicago Press, 1985), 16.

[70] Tadman, *Speculators and Slaves.*

[71] For the changing balance between slave recruitment and slave reproduction, see Scheidel, "Roman Slave Supply"; David Richardson and Judith M. Spicksley, "Le Sexe, l'esclavage et la biopolitique: approche comparée," in Martine Spensky, ed., *Le Contrôle du corps des femmes dans les empires coloniaux: empires, genre et biopolitiques* (Paris: Editions Karthala, 2015), 83–106. On manumission and slave imports, see Toledano, "Enslavement in the Ottoman Empire," 25–46; Hopkins, *Conquerors and Slaves,* 115–32.

reflected potential owners' preferences for slaves, could also affect slave reproduction. Satisfying buyers' demands typically involved militarily stronger states or groups preying on weaker neighbors for human bounty. That usually involved raiding, but it could also include the weak paying tribute in people to more powerful neighbors. Whatever the mechanisms were, however, it was interstate or inter-group disparities of power, and the inability of the weaker to shield their members against external or even internal aggression, that particularly exposed people to slavery. Accordingly, there is nothing novel – as sometimes seems to be suggested by students of contemporary slavery – in the fact that enfeebled or failed states expose people to enslavement. The pattern has deep historical roots dating from the dawn of human civilization. Furthermore, it was typically compounded by inequalities of wealth and its companion, extreme poverty. Together, they help explain who, within failing states, were and remain most susceptible to enslavement.

If politics and power are pivotal to explaining vulnerabilities to enslavement of people today and in the past, the destinations of the victims were and remain largely dictated by traffickers' efforts to integrate supply with local and international demand for slaves. Its illegality makes today's trafficking shadowy and difficult to calculate. Equally, the erosion of evidence through time means we have highly imperfect knowledge of these phenomena in the ancient and medieval worlds as well. Nonetheless, with estimated numbers trafficked ranging from perhaps 100,000 annually in the ancient world to maybe 2 million today, and with growing evidence of slave prices, slave markets, and the traffickers involved from antiquity onwards, it is possible to shed some light on the efficiency and costs of trafficking, including the lived experience of those subject to it.

Our richest evidence of trafficking historically relates to the Ottoman Empire, the western Indian Ocean, and above all the Atlantic slave trade.[72] Each drew heavily on sub-Saharan Africa for its human captives. Each

---

[72] Ralph A. Austen, "The Trans-Saharan Slave Trade: A Tentative Census," in Henry A. Gemery and Jan S. Hogendorn, eds., *The Uncommon Market: Essays in the Economic History of the Atlantic Slave Trade* (New York: Academic Press, 1979), 23–76; Ralph A. Austen, "The 19th Century Islamic Slave Trade from East Africa (Swahili and Red Sea Coasts): A Tentative Census," *Slavery and Abolition* 9, no. 3 (1988), 21–44; Ralph A. Austen, "The Mediterranean Islamic Slave Trade out of Africa," *Slavery and Abolition* 13, no. 1 (1992), 214–48; Richard B. Allen, *European Slave Trading in the Indian Ocean, 1500–1850* (Athens, OH: Ohio University Press, 2015); David Richardson, "Involuntary Migration in the Early Modern World, 1500–1800," in Eltis and Engerman, eds., *CWHS*, Volume 3, 570; www.slavevoyages.org/estimates.

involved collaboration between indigenous African political and commercial elites and European or Arab merchants.[73] Each relied to a greater or lesser extent on water transport and involved moving victims over considerable distances, with resulting heavy losses of people in transit by most international standards. In many respects these forms of trafficking had their own peculiarities. Despite that, the practices involved in moving enslaved Africans to overseas markets in 1500–1900 offer important insights into how trafficking proved commercially sustainable and profitable in other places and times.

In particular, we know that enslaved Africans were one element within a set of commercial exchanges comprising other goods, including gold and silver. We know too that it was a high-risk, high-entry-cost industry, in which relatively small proportions of merchant investors handled a disproportionate share of slave transactions. And we know that such merchants probably enjoyed unusual levels of access to the capital, networking, and knowledge resources needed to expand commercial dealings involving enslaved Africans across extended geographical spaces.[74] Our evidence on such matters in earlier times and places, as well as in the contemporary world, is partial and opaque, but the little we have is consistent with our knowledge of transactions in enslaved Africans after 1500. That, together with its likely scale in other eras, leaves little room to doubt that ingenuity, adaptability, and flexibility in trafficking have helped ensure the continuing resilience of slavery as a global phenomenon through the present day. As long as there has been a willingness to possess other people, there has been a capacity to supply them for profit. In that respect, today's human trafficking is the latest manifestation of an organized commerce as old as human history.

Trafficking is, for some, the epitome of contemporary slavery, transforming people into objects removed from social environments that gave meaning to their lives. In that respect, trafficking is considered archetypical of slavery itself, initiating victims into a world where others dictate their life experiences. But focusing on the ways in which

---

[73] See, for example, Joel Quirk and David Richardson, "Europeans, Africans and the Atlantic World, c1450–1850," in Joel Quirk, Shogo Suzuki, and Yougjin Zhang, eds., *International Orders in the Early Modern World: Before the Rise of the West* (London and New York: Routledge, 2013), 138–58.

[74] David Richardson and Filipa Ribeiro da Silva, "Introduction: The South Atlantic Slave Trade in Historical Perspective," in David Richardson and Filipa Ribeiro da Silva, eds., *Networks and Trans-Cultural Exchange: Slave Trading in the South Atlantic, 1590–1867* (Leiden: Brill, 2014), 1–30.

slavery regenerates itself through the process of trafficking while simultaneously reshaping peoples' lives is not new. It features regularly in
studies of historical slavery, no more so than in transatlantic slavery, with
the iconic image in 1789 of enslaved Africans stowed sardine-like on
platforms between decks, on board the British ship *Brooks*.[75] That sketch
foreshadowed other images of emaciated captives on mid nineteenth-
century Indian Ocean dhows, anticipating modern-day stories of people
being moved (and dying) in containers by sea and by land.[76] Around one
in six Africans entering the Atlantic slave trade died in the Middle Passage
from Africa to the Americas. That equates to an annualized mortality rate
of about 250 per thousand, excluding deaths before embarkation and
after reaching the Americas.[77] Testimonies of survivors underlined the
cruelty implicit in such figures, revealing the confusion, desolation, and
despair lying behind them. But losses in transit across the Atlantic were
not necessarily uniquely high, and narratives of other captives, among
them people of Caucasian birth, provide similar testimony of the daily
trauma, abuses, and indignities suffered by the enslaved in other places
and times.[78] Echoes of the same exist in stories of modern-day escapees
from slavery, as noted in James Sidbury's essay in this volume. It seems
appropriate to suggest, therefore, that in the particulars of transatlantic
trafficking may be contained the experience of all trafficked people, past
and present.

CONTEMPORARY ANTISLAVERY IN HISTORICAL PERSPECTIVE

By challenging from 1787 onwards their nation's continuing participation
in slaving across the Atlantic, British abolitionists began to redefine the
ethical boundaries of British commerce. When, after overturning Britain's

---

[75] Marcus Rediker, *The Slave Ship: A Human History* (New York: Viking, 2007), 308–42.

[76] See, for example, Marcus Wood, *The Horrible Gift of Freedom: Atlantic Slavery and the Representation of Emancipation* (Atlanta, GA: University of Georgia Press, 2010).

[77] Simon J. Hogerzeil and David Richardson, "Slave Purchasing Strategies and Shipboard Mortality: Day to Day Evidence from the Dutch African Trade, 1751–1797," *Journal of Economic History* 67, no. 1 (2007), 160–90.

[78] See, for example, Ehud R. Toledano, *As if Silent and Absent: Bonds of Enslavement in the Islamic Middle East* (New Haven, CT: Yale University Press, 2007). For the ancient world, Bradley notes "the absence in extant classical texts of anything that can be called a slave literature," but uses other sources, including fables, to throw light on slaves' lives. K. R. Bradley, *Slaves and Masters in the Roman Empire: A Study in Social Control* (Oxford: Oxford University Press, 1987), 18, 150–3.

slave trade in 1807, they turned their fire on British colonial slavery, they succeeded in outlawing property rights in people among British subjects. And when from 1815 onward, as citizens of the world's superpower, they convinced their government to use naval power, diplomacy, and even bribery to end trafficking by other nations, they initiated an international antislavery crusade that in the following 150 years would achieve the formal outlawing of slavery worldwide and extend that ban to practices akin to slavery. Britain alone did not accomplish the last. But insofar as Britons and others united in its pursuit, it represented an achievement of collective political will unsurpassed in human history. Its formal success is all the more remarkable given slavery's long history and the rewards that powerful vested interests worldwide continued to earn from it even while abolitionism gain political traction. Such interests, together with the plasticity and durability of institutions of such longevity, have ensured that slavery and human trafficking have been difficult to eradicate. Still, despite seemingly large absolute numbers of slaves and trafficked people worldwide today, the positive achievements of antislavery as a force for ideological change and beneficial social outcomes deserve to be recognized.

Antislavery led the way in the dismantling of slavery in nineteenth-century Brazil, the Caribbean, and the US South. And as it spread its message into Africa and worlds beyond the Atlantic, it assuredly saved millions from enslavement, although at the cost of imposing forms of external domination on the societies in question. Precise calculation of the numbers saved is impossible, but projecting from the global population and proportions in slavery in 1800 to today, it is conceivable that, without antislavery, a third to a half billion people might now be enslaved, depending on the chosen definition of slavery. Those figures are up to twenty-five times higher than ILO and GSI estimates of contemporary slavery. Whatever the number saved, however, such calculations invite consideration of why antislavery emerged when and where it did, as well as of its checkered pattern of success globally in the last 230 years.

The roots of abolitionism and the timing of its political resonance in Britain from the 1780s have been subjects of much debate. Challenges to morality and economic efficacy of slave systems evidently emerged in the Anglocentric Atlantic before the 1780s. Part of Enlightenment thought and debate, such questioning helped to establish an intellectual case for abolitionism that assumed particular ideological resonance in Britain, where the rights and liberties of its subjects were a vital element in defining the nation's identity. Abolitionism allowed the paradox between

Britons' defense of personal liberty at home and their promotion of slavery overseas to be resolved.[79] For some, antislavery's transformation into a political movement from the mid 1780s was a response to the crisis arising from the nation's defeat in the War of American Independence and its subsequent reassessment of its global position.[80] For others, it reflected the political connections and skills of the religiously inspired "Clapham sect," whose involvement offered affirmation of Margaret Mead's dictum about how small and committed groups can effect social change.[81] While acknowledging British antislavery's political leadership, it was a movement too that attracted mass public support in 1787–1833 across British society.[82] That populism has yet to be fully explained, but it represents an example of sustained and peaceful mass antislavery protest unmatched in history.

Although debate continues about the politicizing of British antislavery, historians find it impossible to uncouple abolitionism from wider changes in British society in the age of revolutions. Over seventy years ago, Eric Williams famously identified abolition with the rise of British industrial capitalism and an associated shift in British policy toward laisser-faire. Others have since linked it to what Steven Pinker has recently labeled "the humanitarian revolution," based on rising literacy and an expanding publishing industry.[83] Yet others associate it with a growth in mass politics and reformism in an age of exceptional rates of urbanization and expanding religious nonconformity.[84] Exceptionally insightful historians such as David Brion Davis have sought to show how the "antislavery movement, like Smith's political economy, reflected the needs and values of the emerging capitalist order" in Britain, and how antislavery was committed to demonstrating the belief "that all classes and segments

---

[79] Eltis, *Rise of African Slavery*, 281–4.

[80] Christopher L. Brown, *Moral Capital: Foundations of British Abolitionism* (Chapel Hill, NC: University of North Carolina Press, 2006).

[81] Roger Anstey, *The Atlantic Slave Trade and British Abolition 1760–1810* (Atlantic Highlands, NJ: Humanities Press, 1975).

[82] Seymour Drescher, *Capitalism and Antislavery: British Mobilization in Comparative Perspective* (Oxford: Oxford University Press, 1987); John Oldfield, *Popular Politics and British Anti-Slavery: The Mobilisation of Public Opinion against the Slave Trade, 1787–1807* (Manchester: Manchester University Press, 1995).

[83] Steven Pinker, *The Better Angels of Our Nature: A History of Violence and Humanity* (New York: Penguin Books, 2012), 210.

[84] David Turley, *The Culture of British Antislavery, 1780–1860* (London and New York: Routledge, 1991); Joel Quirk and David Richardson, "Religion, Urbanisation and Anti-Slavery Mobilisation in Britain, 1787–1833," *European Journal of English Studies* 14, no. 3 (2010), 263–79.

of society share a natural identity of interest," even in the pursuit of humanitarianism.[85] Or, like Seymour Drescher, how it became increasingly a badge of "national honor" that transcended class status and to which the state was prepared to allocate huge levels of diplomatic, financial, and human resources.[86] Nuances in interpretation apart, however, the thrust of scholarship is clear: British abolitionism achieved its immediate objectives by developing from within and in harmony with the grain of wider contemporary change in British society. Linked to the Industrial Revolution and coinciding with the onset of the post-1815 Pax Britannica, it represented a national ideological and political *volte-face* of truly historic proportions and significance.

By any measure of achievement and sustained national commitment, British antislavery proved exceptional. Only in the United States was there an antislavery movement that came close to matching the British in enthusiasm.[87] But there, abolitionism failed to match Britain's international ambitions or to achieve its domestic goals peacefully, the freeing of USA's 4 million slaves coming about only through a divisive and bloody civil war. That itself was an event of seismic proportions that, together with the Haitian Revolution of 1791–1804, had ultimately as profound an impact on the course of emancipation in the Americas as the British abolition act of 1833. Elsewhere, however, formal endings of slavery during the last two centuries have proved much less bloodstained, primarily following Britain's legislative path but without the mass populism that accompanied it. For the most part, it involved top-down intervention, sometimes by colonial authorities, as in Africa following the Scramble, but also by independent states, as in nineteenth-century Western Europe and the Ottoman Empire or in states founded after 1945. The circumstances in which intervention occurred varied. They frequently involved external pressure, whether British in the Victorian era or from the League of Nations and later the United Nations from the 1920s. In such circumstances, one may assume that intervention sometimes reflected political expediency among governments seeking to enhance their international profiles, as much as a wholehearted acceptance of the

---

[85] David Brion Davis, *The Problem of Slavery in the Age of Revolution 1770–1823* (Ithaca, NY: Cornell University Press, 1975), 350.

[86] Seymour Drescher, *The Mighty Experiment: Free Labor versus Slavery in British Emancipation* (Oxford: Oxford University Press, 2004).

[87] James Brewer Stewart, "Antislavery and Abolitionism in the United States, 1776–1870," in Eltis et al., eds., *CWHS*, Volume 4, 399–421.

wider principles of personal liberty and human rights increasingly identified with antislavery.[88]

The implications of that conundrum were and remain profound for
both the historic enforcement of antislavery measures and antislavery
activism's prospective success. Historically, the passage of abolitionist
legislation often involved compromise, including gradualism in introduction and financial compensation to owners, although not to slaves.[89]
After passage, its implementation has sometimes proved difficult, notably
in non-Western societies, in the face of corruption, civil disorder, intransi-
gent and powerful vested interests, and deeply embedded social practices
and relationships. Looking forward, the prospects for full enforcement
of antislavery commitments looks bleak in states with poor records of
social order or defending civil liberties and human rights. Those records
assume wider significance when one considers the shifting balance of
global wealth and power from the north Atlantic, where antislavery and
human rights as we know them first took root, toward the south and the
east, where history shows that bondage of one's own people has been
longstanding and security of personal liberty often frustrated by ruling
elites.

"THEN" AND "NOW": IMPLICATIONS AND CONCLUSIONS

Challenging the right of one person to possess another, antislavery has
made huge advances in the last two centuries. Slavery and other forms of
human bondage are now illegal worldwide. And the relative and probably even absolute decline since 1800 of practices now considered slavery
are sometimes overlooked in our understandable preoccupation with
twenty-first-century global levels of slavery. The antislavery movement
alone does not, of course, explain those trends. As with historic slave
codes, where the gap between the formal rules governing slavery and
the realities of slaves' lived experiences were often large, so slavery's persistence today is a reminder that, however well intended and framed,
laws and protocols are in themselves insufficient to eradicate it. History
shows that equally important is the need to understand slavery's resilient,
chameleon-like nature; the underlying social conditions that help sustain

---

[88] Drescher, "Liberty, Equality, Humanity," 172–95; cf. Hunt, *Inventing Human Rights.*
[89] Stanley L. Engerman, "The Slow Pace of Slave Emancipation and Ex-Slave Equality," in
Misevich and Mann, eds., *Rise and Demise of Slavery*, 266–79.

it in practice; and the ideological shifts, not just changes in laws, required to transform attitudes toward slavery beyond the advanced industrial societies where antislavery first found political expression. In concluding, I comment briefly on these three issues.

Slavery's robustness and flexibility as an institution help explain its historical longevity as well as its profitably to those possessing slaves. Throughout history, enslaved people have been employed in a wide variety of tasks and in a range of sociocultural environments, with the balance of their employment differing in time and place. That truth applies also today. As now, so historically, human trafficking has been a constant adjunct to slavery, enabling enslaved populations to be replenished and allowing their relocation in response to changing patterns of market demand. Even when trafficking and slave ownership were outlawed, therefore, infrastructures that had previously supported them remained in place, allowing those eager to continue to profit from slavery to adjust to the new legal arrangements, particularly when demand for slave-produced goods and services continued or the enslaved did not possess the wherewithal to resist or escape their bondage.

Over 1 million enslaved Africans were transported across the Atlantic illegally in the three decades after 1836, despite international treaties to end trafficking and the British naval patrols intended to enforce them.[90] Only Britain's blockade of Brazilian ports helped stem that illegal tide. British moves to end the legal status of slavery in Nigeria and East Africa in the early twentieth century also failed immediately to eradicate slavery in practice, initiating instead its "slow death."[91] Even that call was perhaps premature; if the GSI is correct, slavery's funeral in Nigeria (and in most of sub-Saharan Africa) has yet to take place. What these historical examples underscore is the difficulty of effectively policing laws to outlaw slavery and human trafficking when the geographical arenas involved are large, profits remain attractive, legal sanctions against slavery are low, and high levels of dependency on former owners among those officially "liberated" continue. In effect, legal freedom commonly failed to translate into effective emancipation. History suggests that antislavery laws, although necessary, remove only one of the numerous barriers preventing people from becoming free.

---

[90] Eltis and Richardson, *Atlas*, 274.
[91] Paul E. Lovejoy and Jan S. Hogendorn, *Slow Death for Slavery: The Course of Abolition in Northern Nigeria, 1897–1936* (Cambridge: Cambridge University Press, 1993).

History reminds us too that – in varying combinations – autocracy or tyranny, prejudice, and violence have been elementary in exposing people to risks of trafficking and enslavement. Herodotus and Thucydides would doubtless have been unsurprised by GSI findings that the dissolution of modern-day Iraq, Syria, Somalia, and South Sudan into warring factions has raised vulnerability levels to enslavement of their people to among the highest worldwide. Religious or ethnic divisions, even fissures within such groups, unknown to Herodotus and Thucydides, compound those risks, as they did historically in contested Christian–Muslim borderlands of the medieval and early modern Mediterranean, or the twentieth-century German enslavement (and genocide) of Jews in the heart of Europe.

Such examples could be multiplied, underlining the point that, in the midst of disorder and struggles for territory – primary drivers of slave supply historically – antislavery legislation is unlikely to deter some from enslaving others. Perhaps what would have surprised Herodotus and Thucydides was the extent to which some states continue to fail to protect their citizens from being enslaved within their homelands. For ancient Greeks, slavery was for barbarian outsiders, but in South Asia and other parts of the world, domestic enslavement through debt bondage and other means has been and remains critical to slavery's existence, with caste and other social divisions, not alien status, demarcating those who might be enslaved from those who cannot. Where prejudice and conflict exist, there exists heightened vulnerability to enslavement, regardless of slavery's legal status.

Those attempting to eradicate slavery in the twenty-first century have formidable obstacles to overcome. Laws and international protocols are preconditions for that task, but more is needed. Military action is not a viable or cost-free option. On the other hand – if history is a guide – a more conflict-free, less culturally antagonistic world would help, but as factors unconnected with slavery are usually primary sources of human conflict and prejudice, antislavery activists themselves will likely carry little weight directly in reducing their incidence and their repercussions for human bondage. Adopting a more sharply focused lens, activist strategies to eradicate slavery that draw on historical precedents can be identified, even if their original efficacy is open to question. They include boycotting goods and services with an identifiable slave labor input; search and rescue missions for the enslaved; and buying people out of slavery by compensating their owners. Reflecting globalization, there are efforts to expose international labor exploitation, pressurizing transnational corporations to ensure ethical working practices in their supply chains.

Other than the last, all such strategies echo British antislavery in 1815–50, while compensation schemes invoke debates around thorny issues of reparations. In the end, the variety of antislavery strategies pursued by today's activists is a measure of both the complexity of the challenges they face and their dependence on the private sector and the state, among others, to resolve them. This last, in turn, focuses attention on state priorities and on the importance of moral and other commitments by non-activists to the antislavery cause.

Early British antislavery goes some way to affirming Margaret Mead's aphorism that social movements are "motivated and seen through by the passion of individuals." The genius of the movement's instigators, however, lay not only in the religiously inspired fervor with which they articulated their message, but also in their ability to mobilize public support for it, thereby making it a priority for British legislators. There is no consensus about how this was accomplished. Nonetheless, no other people embraced the antislavery cause so enthusiastically as the British did in 1787–1833. In no other country, either, did political leaders commit such a high proportion of the nation's resources to suppressing international slave trafficking as Britain in 1807–67, prompting the suggestion that "nineteenth-century costs of suppression were certainly bigger than the eighteenth-century benefits" from British slaving.[92] And nowhere was a nation so consistently involved diplomatically as Britain was in the same period to the signing of antislavery treaties around the world.[93] None of those things were possible without Britain's industrialization and the shift in political opinion that accompanied the rise of British antislavery.

Two hundred years on, efforts to rid the world of slavery remain unfulfilled. This does not reflect diminishing passion among activists for the cause, but rather a more fragile political commitment to it compared to the more determined variant that Davis considered pivotal to undermining slavery in the Americas by 1888.[94] Put another way, twenty-first-century governments seem unwilling or unable to prioritize and resource antislavery activities at levels and with a consistency needed effectively to challenge slavery's continuing existence. In some cases, national political

---

[92] C. D. Kaufman and R. A. Pape, "Explaining Costly Moral Action: Britain's Sixty-Year Campaign against the Atlantic Slave Trade," *International Organization* 53, no. 4 (1999), 636–7; David Eltis, *Economic Growth and the Ending of the Transatlantic Slave Trade* (Oxford: Oxford University Press, 1987), 97.

[93] Eltis and Richardson, *Atlas*, 272.

[94] Shelley, *Human Trafficking*, 12; David Brion Davis, *Inhuman Bondage: The Rise and Fall of Slavery in the New World* (Oxford: Oxford University Press, 2006), 11.

disorder denies government the mandate to determine its priorities and to allocate resources to deliver them. But even where there is political stability, allowing state priorities to be set, national appetites for resourcing antislavery action may simply be weak. That may be partly a question of scale, with the low incidence of slavery in most contemporary societies perhaps making it difficult for antislavery to compete with other causes for resources. In effect, perceptions of antislavery's historic success can be among modern-day activists' worst enemies. It may also be partly a question of power, where the enslaved are invisible socially and by definition lack political influence. Perhaps most importantly, it may be a question of competing values, where advocacy of antislavery on grounds of universal rights and freedoms – a common humanity – conflicts, especially in Asia and Africa, with more traditional communitarian beliefs and institutions based on ancient systems of social hierarchy and division. That, in turn, can provoke attacks on antislavery as threatening social cohesion and order by its challenge to cultural and moral relativism and its imposition from outside of what are perceived as postcolonial forms of neoimperialism.[95]

Stripped of their intellectual baggage, such claims echo those of early nineteenth-century Caribbean and Southern US planters faced by their own opponents. Like their predecessors, modern claims of that sort could well evaporate as countries in Africa and Asia industrialize and urbanize, with resultant expansions in higher value-added employment and in the middle class. But insofar as ideological hostility to antislavery rooted in traditional values continues to resonate socially in some parts of the world, notably in nations with the largest slave populations, it poses a formidable obstacle to immediate and future antislavery success. In the absence of a comprehensive shift in values similar to that which occurred in Britain and in other parts of the West, it is difficult to imagine proponents of antislavery in most countries in Africa and Asia commanding access to national resources sufficient to sustain a conclusive campaign against an institution as old as human history. If, as Oscar Wilde asserted, the "aim of life is self-development" and to "realize one's nature perfectly," then until the principles of human rights and social justice identified with antislavery become universally respected and practised, humanity's final march to freedom for all will remain a long and difficult one.[96]

---

95 Brown, *Moral Capital*, 58; Indrani Chatterjee, "British Abolitionism from the Vantage of Pre-Colonial South Asian Regimes," in Eltis et al., eds., *CWHS*, Volume 4, 441–65.

96 Oscar Wilde, *The Picture of Dorian Gray* (1891; New York: Penguin Classics, 2012), 17.

2

Slavery and Civic Death

Making Sense of Modern Slavery
in Historical Context

James Sidbury

What is slavery? As the struggle against human trafficking has come increasingly to be understood as a fight against modern slavery, activists and scholars have been forced to realize that "slavery" is much more difficult to define than one might think. There are statutes, constitutional provisions, international protocols, and treaties outlawing slavery throughout the world, and one can look to those provisions to compile a checklist of practices that are prohibited as slavery. The United Nations and the International Labour Organization have done that, and almost all of the world's nation states have accepted that list.[1] Such legal definitions are, of course, crucial weapons in the fight to suppress modern slavery. Nothing in this essay should be read as suggesting otherwise. There is something unsatisfactory, however, in defining something that all agree is a fundamental violation of universal human rights with a dry laundry list of prohibited practices.

Frustration about the ambiguous nature of contemporary slavery sometimes finds expression when modern-day abolitionists look back toward their nineteenth-century forebears. It's not that the original abolitionists had it easy. Those fighting chattel slavery in plantation America prior to abolition faced politically powerful, generously funded, and well-organized opposition. But at least the early abolitionists knew exactly what they were fighting. Prior to emancipation, slavery was a powerful institution; abolitionists had to fight to convince others that slavery was

---

[1] Legal definitions of human trafficking and modern slavery can be found in US Department of State, *2012 Trafficking in Persons Report* (Washington, DC, 2012), 8–9. They are discussed in more detail below.

worth ending, but they did not have to convince anyone that it existed, and they did not have to search the shadows of the world economy to find slaves. They simply had to travel to plantations in St. Domingue (until 1794), or Jamaica (until 1833), or South Carolina (until 1865), or Rio de Janeiro (until 1888). The target was visible, if well protected. That is not true today.

On one important level, this comparison is accurate. American slave societies had clearly established legal procedures through which they could decide who was or was not a slave, and they were neither ashamed nor hesitant to use them. As the United States Fugitive Slave Law of 1850 illustrates, those rules were not free of controversy, but they did provide clear-cut answers to individual cases.[2] Slavery was legal. If one wanted to determine whether a human being was someone else's property, one did, in essence, a title search. That is not true today when no one holds legitimate title to another human being. Instead, to determine whether someone is being held in slavery, one must ask whether they are subject to treatment that is equivalent to slavery.

But what does it mean for treatment to be equivalent to slavery? It cannot simply mean that one lives a life of indefensible deprivation that almost surely creates inescapable structures of dependence and oppression, or the numbers would escape any meaningful comparison to what we cordon off as slavery in earlier eras. After all, the World Bank estimates that roughly 1.4 billion people live on less than $1.25 a day.[3] But the problem is not simply one of unwieldy numbers: if slavery is simply to be used as a synonym for poverty, then it will lack any meaningful analytical utility. The fight against world poverty proceeds with the understanding that however much one might wish it were otherwise, various national and global legal systems accept as legitimate myriad labor and social relations that produce untold misery. Slavery may leave its victims destitute, but destitution cannot serve as the defining marker of slavery. Slavery must entail a form of exploitation that is different in kind from straightforward poverty.

The goal of this essay is to develop a normative definition of modern slavery that is separate from and can stand beside the laws and international agreements that are familiar to those working in the field. Such

---

[2] For a classic contemporary critique of the Fugitive Slave Act of 1850, see Frederick Douglass, "Oration, Delivered in Corinthian Hall, Rochester, N.Y., July 5th, 1852 [What to the Slave is the Fourth of July]," (Rochester, NY, 1852).

[3] www.globalissues.org/article/4/poverty-around-the-world (accessed April 5, 2015).

a definition must proceed from the realization that, notwithstanding the recent global consensus that slavery is a violation of fundamental and universal human rights, bondage is one of the oldest and most ubiquitous of human institutions. Though American plantation slavery has come to stand as the essence of "true" historical slavery, and thus as the assumed baseline for discussions of slavery today, using antebellum chattel slavery in that way is historically misleading and distorts attempts to understand slavery today.[4] Developing a definition of the nature of slavery in the world today involves attending both to the varieties of forms that human bondage has taken across time and space and to the often ignored (and always unappreciated) complexity with which those living in the age of Atlantic slavery approached questions about the nature of slavery (as opposed to its legal definition). A simple normative definition of slavery should help activists and scholars escape the parameters that states and multinational NGOs have set on our understanding of trafficking and slavery and thus clarify the forms of labor exploitation, some of which remain legal, that constitute and should be fought as modern slavery.

I

What are the distortions entailed in turning nineteenth-century Atlantic slavery into a norm in comparison to which "modern slavery" should be judged more or less equivalent to "real" slavery? As the historical sociologist Orlando Patterson has pointed out, slavery was among the most common and protean institutions in human societies from the dawn of recorded history until the very recent past. In searching for a principle to tie together the remarkably diverse systems of legally recognized bondage that evolved in different times and places – systems that ranged from what we now think of as classic plantation slavery in the Americas, to domestic slavery among many sub-Saharan African and indigenous American peoples, to military slavery in the early modern Islamic world, to slavery in classical Greece and Rome – Patterson developed an argument that dishonor and natal alienation or social death constituted the bright line separating the enslaved from the free. In his famous formulation, "*slavery is the permanent, violent domination of natally alienated and generally dishonored persons.*"[5] By breaking the bond that tied people

---

[4] Joseph C. Miller argues that historians' focus on Atlantic slavery as normative has distorted our understanding of slaving in global history.

[5] Orlando Patterson, *Slavery and Social Death: A Comparative Study* (Cambridge, MA, 1982), 12 (for quotation) and throughout. Emphasis in original.

to their ancestors and descendants, enslavement robbed victims of their social existence and turned them into nakedly autonomous beings. These unmoored beings lacked the physical and spiritual protections provided by kin groups, leaving their owners free to use them as tools.

Given the transnational and trans-temporal scope of Patterson's analysis, one might ask whether natal alienation offers a key to understanding modern slavery.[6] Unfortunately the fit is not good. On the one hand, most people living today view personal autonomy as a goal to be achieved rather than a fate to be feared, so natal alienation no longer signals social death as it once did. In addition, modern traffickers seem as inclined to use family connections to control their victims as they are to destroy the links across generations, a practice that directly violates the principle of natal alienation. Because trafficking rings can connect the regions from which victims originate with the regions where they are forced to work, the criminal organizations behind some trafficking often coerce their victims by threatening to hurt or kill their family members.[7] Maintaining rather than breaking kin connections across the moment of enslavement provides an important method of control at least in these forms of modern bondage, suggesting that "modern slavery" may be different in kind from historical slavery.[8]

But if so, how should we understand that difference? What makes certain exploitative labor practices stand out as different in kind from the myriad distressingly oppressive working conditions that are legal and accepted under global capitalism? If, as the International Labour Organization (ILO) insists, "forced labour cannot be equated simply with low wages or poor working conditions," how do we distinguish between what is deeply unjust and properly a part of the struggle against poverty and inequality, and what constitutes not simply an injustice that should be redressed, but "a severe violation of human rights and human freedom"?[9] One way to answer that question is by turning to the protocols passed

---

[6] Patterson, "Trafficking, Gender and Slavery: Past and Present," in Jean Allain, ed., *The Legal Understanding of Slavery: From the Historical to the Contemporary* (Oxford: Oxford University Press, 2012), 322–59, adapts his classic definition of slavery to modern trafficking.

[7] US Department of State, *2012 Trafficking in Persons Report*, 15.

[8] Many have criticized Patterson's celebrated book, but the critiques do not generally question the role of natal alienation in enslavement; they focus instead on the way the enslaved respond to alienation. See, for example, Vincent Brown, "Social Death and Political Life in the Study of Slavery," *American Historical Review* 114 (2009), 1231–49.

[9] International Labour Organization, *A Global Alliance against Forced Labour* (Geneva, Switzerland, 2005), 5.

by various international bodies to specify what practices are prohibited as trafficking.

In other words, one can turn to international law. A series of international accords and protocols reaching back to the 1920s have produced a list of prohibited practices that focuses especially on the presence of force, fraud, or coercion in the relationship between a worker and the person for whom she is working. The foundational definition in international law comes from a League of Nations Slavery Convention held in Geneva, Switzerland in 1926. It defined slavery as "the status or condition of a person over whom any or all of the powers attaching to the right of ownership are exercised." In 1956 a United Nations Conference offered a "Supplementary Convention on the Abolition of Slavery, the Slave Trade, and Institutions and Practices Similar to Slavery" that restated the 1926 definition and appended a list of institutions "similar to slavery" that should also be abolished: debt bondage, serfdom, forms of forced marriage, and the transferring of children for the purpose of labor. Finally, in 2000 a United Nations Protocol against Trans-National Organized Crime included a section on the trafficking of persons, which prohibited the forced migration of people for, among other things, "forced labour or services, slavery or practices similar to slavery."[10] These three agreements provide the legal foundation for official attempts to combat trafficking and slavery in the world today.

Those legal definitions open an avenue through which trafficking in persons and slavery have increasingly been collapsed. The ILO seeks to define the nature of forced labor through a checklist of nine conditions, the presence of any one of which creates the assumption that a worker lacks the ability to consent to the conditions under which she labors, and another list of thirteen forms of coercion, the presence of any one of which indicates that a worker is being retained through illegitimate force.[11] The US Department of State relies on the same international protocols to define "severe trafficking in persons." Sex trafficking occurs when "a commercial sex act is induced by force, fraud or coercion," or when someone younger than eighteen is "induced to perform" a sex act; labor trafficking occurs when the "recruitment,

[10] Appendices, in Allain, ed., *The Legal Understanding of Slavery*, 381–6 (1926 Convention), 386–91 (1956 Supplementary Convention); www.unodc.org/documents/treaties/UNTOC/Publications/TOC%20Convention/TOCebook-e.pdf (accessed April 28, 2013), p. 42 for quotation (Palermo Protocols).

[11] International Labour Organization, *A Global Alliance against Forced Labour*, Box 1.1, p. 6.

harboring, transportation, provision, or obtaining of a person for labor" occurs through "force, fraud, or coercion for the purpose of subjection to involuntary servitude, peonage, debt bondage, or slavery." This very broad rubric allows the US government to "view 'trafficking in persons' as the term through which all forms of modern slavery are criminalized."[12]

Notwithstanding the need to create fairly technical legal boundaries that mark off behavior that will be subject to punishment in a court from actions that will not, there are downsides to the way this set of legal sanctions has evolved. The protean nature of enslavement has meant that in coming to play such a central role in the battle against slavery, "trafficking in persons" has become a less than fully coherent category. According to the United States government, a victim need not be moved to be trafficked. Nor is it necessary for a victim of trafficking to change hands – to be sold or bartered to a trafficker: parents can and sometimes do "traffic" their children in the sex industries.[13] Nor do other victims of "trafficking," even those who are transported into forced labor, appear to belong in a single category. There is not an obvious equivalence between a person living in rural India who entered into an inescapable (and illegal) debt with a large landowner, consigning him or herself and family to a life of debt peonage on the one hand, and, on the other, a young girl from rural Nepal who was tricked by a labor broker into traveling with him to India, where he sold her to a brothel owner.[14] Each of these situations is horrible and unjust and illegal and deserving of redress. What is less clear is why they, but not other examples of oppressive and unjust labor that are legal, should be understood as part of an overarching common problem – as examples of modern slavery.[15]

This problem may appear more daunting than it is, because of the way that plantation slavery in the Americas dominates assumptions about what constitutes "real" historical slavery. It was the remarkable diversity in patterns of human bondage that first called forth Orlando Patterson's pathbreaking assertion that natal alienation and social death tied together the many different systems of slavery prior to the age of

---

[12] US Department of State, 2012 *Trafficking in Persons Report*, 8–9.

[13] Ibid., 11–14 discusses many of these issues.

[14] Ibid., 23 (Nepal to India); Bales, *Understanding Global Slavery*, 1–3 (families in debt bondge).

[15] The essays collected in Allain, ed., *The Legal Understanding of Slavery* are indispensable for thinking through this issue, especially those by Antony Honoré, John W. Cairns, Seymour Dresher, Allison Mileo Gorsuch, Rebecca J. Scott, William M. Carter, Jr., Jean Allain, Robin Hickey, J. E. Penner, Joel Quirk, Kevin Bales, and Orlando Patterson.

emancipation in a way that made them recognizable as related elements in a single overarching historical institution. But the ambiguity of historical slavery extends beyond the kinds of slavery that are unfamiliar to many modern readers – military slavery in the early modern Levant, or domestic slavery in precolonial Africa. Even in the eighteenth- and nineteenth-century Anglo-American world, when plantation slavery was at its height and slavery was a legal institution, jurists and scholars found slavery much more difficult to define than one might expect. John Millar, the eighteenth-century Scottish philosopher and teacher of Adam Smith, told his students that it was "impossible to define the precise degree of subjection which constitutes what is called Slavery," because the "idea" was "different in different countries."[16] It could also be very different in the same country, as illustrated by the ways that white settlers in the Illinois Territory during the 1810s circumvented the Northwest Ordinance's prohibitions on slavery in the territory through the legal shield of indentured servitude. This created a confusing situation in which, according to the scholar Allison Mileo Gorsuch, "the question of whether the black indentured person was a *slave* might in fact be different than whether the black indentured person was *held in slavery*."[17] The line separating the slave and the free is blurry today, but it was also blurry when plantation slavery reigned throughout much of the Atlantic world.

The ambiguities were not only about who was a slave and who was not. Some thinkers also understood chattel bondage – what we today are inclined to think of as "real" historical slavery – as only one of the several forms that slavery took in their societies. It is a commonplace of the historiography of the American Revolution that supporters of American independence accused King George and Parliament of seeking to impose slavery on the virtuous Britons living in mainland North America.[18] Contemporaries in America and England, like historians since then, have often pointed to the hypocrisy of slaveholders equating illegitimate tax policies with the brutal denial of liberty to which they subjected black

---

[16] Quoted in John W. Cairns, "The Definition of Slavery in Eighteenth-Century Thinking: Not the True Roman Slavery," in Allain, ed., *The Legal Understanding of Slavery*, 63–4. Millar was referring to definitions of slavery in classical Rome, but Cairns makes clear that the point extended to slavery in Millar and Smith's world.

[17] Allison Mileo Gorsuch, "To Indent Oneself: Ownership, Contracts, and Consent in Antebellum Illinois," in Allain, ed., *The Legal Understanding of Slavery*, 135–51 (p. 136 for quote).

[18] The classic analysis is Bernard Bailyn, *The Ideological Origins of the American Revolution* (Cambridge, MA: Harvard University Press, 1967), 233–5 and throughout.

people. In the often-quoted words of Samuel Johnson, "How is it that we hear the loudest yelps for liberty among the drivers of negroes?"[19] Such accusations of hypocrisy rest on the assumption that the Founders invoked slavery metaphorically to claim that they suffered the same denial of liberty as chattel slaves.

It is not an unfair charge; some certainly did. But others believed slavery took more than one form, a view that casts helpful light on the struggles to define modern slavery. In 1796 St. George Tucker, the most distinguished legal scholar in Jeffersonian Virginia, published a pamphlet calling for the gradual abolition of slavery in Virginia. In it he published substantial parts of the "Lectures on Law and Police" that he taught to a generation of the sons of Virginia's elite at William and Mary.[20] Tucker recited the standard evidence that the institution took different forms in different places, and then he chose to consider it "under a threefold aspect ... to give a just idea of its nature." On the one hand, he pointed toward the "state of *political slavery*" in which conquered countries and colonies found themselves. This was, in his eyes, "the state of united America before the revolution." He also recognized the "state of *domestic slavery*," in which "one man is subject to be directed by another in all his actions." Here he referred to what is familiar to us as chattel slavery. It is his third category that is more interesting for current discussions. There was, he thought, an intermediary form that he called "*civil slavery*." This occurred whenever natural "liberty [was] by the laws of the state, further restrained than is necessary and expedient for the general advantage." This, he thought, could be found when states demanded more of their citizens than was legitimate – the Venetian Republic was his specific example – or when it created "an inequality of rights, or privileges, between the subjects or citizens of the same state" that exceeded necessity. Free blacks in Virginia, on whom the Commonwealth's laws imposed "civil incapacities ... almost as numerous as the civil rights" of "free citizens," provided what was, for him, a contemporary example of civil slaves. Tucker went on to argue that slavery damaged Virginia and that the General Assembly of the state, to whom he dedicated the pamphlet,

---

[19] www.samueljohnson.com/slavery.html (accessed April 29, 2013).
[20] St. George Tucker, *A Dissertation on Slavery with a Proposal for the Gradual Abolition of It, in the State of Virginia* (San Bernadino, CA: Forgotten Books, 2012 [1796]). All quotations are from this facsimile edition, which is unpaginated. An online edition is available, so quotations can be located with a keyword search (go to: www.forgottenbooks .org/).

should institute a scheme of gradual emancipation. Defining slavery in Jeffersonian Virginia was not, then, a simple and straightforward matter.

At this point, one might be forgiven for contemplating surrendering the effort to define slavery. If the sharpest legal mind in a slave society struggling with the legitimacy of its most important institution was left without a unified understanding, perhaps searching for one is a fool's errand. But there is a more optimistic reading of Tucker's *Dissertation on Slavery*. His convoluted definitions did not, after all, stop him from advocating emancipation, at least in 1796, nor did it prevent more ardent antislavery contemporaries from pushing for more radical solutions than his very gradual plan.[21] That is in part because slavery in his society was, in fact, legal, and thus activists had an easier target to hit, however fuzzy definitions may have gotten at the edges. But the fact that slavery was legal had another effect. It meant that those fighting it did not have to reach for the legal specificity required of criminal law; they did not have to provide laundry lists of behaviors that prosecutors could pursue. Instead, they could, even though they were lawyers, offer normative rather than legal definitions of slavery. Their challenge was to clarify what was wrong, not what was illegal, precisely because they believed that what was legal was also wrong.

Can we do the same for modern slavery? Can we identify in clear normative terms what distinguishes the forms of labor exploitation that, to repeat the ILO's terms, constitute a "a severe violation of human rights and human freedom"?[22] And can we separate that from the legal definitions, offering a normative definition that will usually parallel the legal one, but offer an important perspective when legal systems permit labor and social relations that should be prohibited as slavery? To answer those questions, we need first to catalog the main forms of coerced labor that come together under the rubric of human trafficking, and then to search for a common element by analyzing representative examples of those forms. Modern slavery is not defined by the brutality visited upon its victims, or by the poverty that they suffer. Alas, many of the world's poor and dispossessed suffer unspeakable brutality and poverty. To the extent, however, that people suffer exploitation that rests on their inability to appeal to civil rights and authorities, they suffer something

---

[21] For Tucker's retreat from his opposition to slavery, see Alan Taylor, *The Internal Enemy: Slavery and War in Virginia, 1772–1832* (New York: W.W. Norton and Company, 2013), 215–43.

[22] International Labour Organization, *A Global Alliance against Forced Labour*, 5.

different in kind from the forms of market-based inequality that leave so many in the world impoverished. They suffer from civic death.

First, I will offer a brief and schematic examination of what leads the US State Department to judge that individuals have suffered severe trafficking and thus are victims of modern slavery by surveying the brief case studies of victims of trafficking provided in the *Trafficking in Persons Report* for 2012. These stories are designed to put a human face on the problem of modern slavery while conveying a sense of the range of practices monitored by the office of the Ambassador at Large to Monitor and Combat Trafficking in Persons. The report tells eleven stories of victims – twelve if we include the slightly longer biographical account of Vannak Anan Prum, a one-time victim who has become an activist and whom the Report honors as one of its ten anti-trafficking "Heroes." These cases are chosen, of course, to illustrate the brutality of the behaviors the report is designed to fight, and not surprisingly, they offer clear examples of civic death. After using them to highlight the concept, I will discuss more ambiguous examples.

The authors of the report have clearly sought balance in choosing the victims whose stories they have told. Five of the victims either came from, or were trafficked to, Asia (three from South Asia and two from Southeast Asia). Two of the stories involve Africa (one North Africa, one sub Saharan Africa), and one the Middle East. There are three cases involving Europe, three involving Latin America, and two involving the United States.[23] The authors also use the victim stories to suggest the range of coerced labor that comes under the rubric of trafficking, including five (or six) stories of sex work, three (or four) of domestic work, one of industrial work, one (or two) of agricultural work, and two of maritime labor.[24] The report does not pretend to illustrate all of the forms of bound labor that plague working people in different parts of the globe today. There are no accounts, for example, of victims of a number of highly publicized forms of modern slavery: no accounts of forced labor in the North Korean gulag, or of enslaved children working on the cocoa plantations in Côte d'Ivoire, or of unfree migrant workers picking produce on farms in the United States. Such cases are acknowledged in the "country reports" for each nation that comprise the bulk of the report – there is certainly

---

[23] US Department of State, *2012 Trafficking in Persons Report*, 8, 11, 14, 17, 21, 13, 24, 27, 28, 35, 38, 47. The total adds up to sixteen rather than twelve, the number of case studies, because several victims were trafficked from one region to another.

[24] Ibid. The additional cases alluded to in parentheses refer to three case studies in which two specific victims are discussed.

no cover up – but they are not represented among the victim stories.[25] The victims whose stories are told do not appear to have been chosen to make overt political points, or to foreground one form of trafficking over another, so an examination of the different cases can inform a preliminary inquiry into what is or is not shared across the range of experiences that characterizes modern bondage.

The five case studies involving sex trafficking include at least one victim who comes from or was trafficked to Africa, Asia, Europe, Latin America, and the United States. One case involved a young girl in New York who ran away after an argument with her mother and sought temporary refuge with the older brother of one of her friends. That was a tragic mistake, as he refused to let her leave his apartment, declared himself her pimp, "beat her daily, and advertised her for sex on websites."[26] She could look out the window and see her mother posting missing person flyers on the street below, but she was locked in her pimp's apartment and could not escape. A second case involved a young Mexican girl whose family was deceived into sending her to the United States with a labor contractor. Upon arriving in Texas, she was confined, gang raped, and then forced into uncompensated sex work in Florida.[27]

There are two other cases of young women from less economically developed countries who were promised good work in a wealthier country, only to be forced into commercial sex once they arrived. In one of them, a Nepalese girl was promised domestic work in Lebanon, but the broker took her to India, "confiscated her passport, and sold her to a brothel." Undocumented and confined, she was not allowed to contact her family, and the money she made was withheld to pay the debt she allegedly owed to cover her purchase price. The police raided the brothel, but that only led to her confinement in jail and subsequent return to the brothel owner. She finally ran away and found a shelter.[28] The other story involved a young nursing student from Cameroon who was deceived into traveling to Spain, supposedly for the chance to "complete her university degree in Europe." The young woman's father gave his life's savings to the person posing as her patron, but "instead of being sent to school," the student was "forced into prostitution on the streets." She finally worked up the courage to run from her trafficker and to risk contacting the police,

[25] Ibid., 208–9 (North Korea), 130–1 (Côte d'Ivoire), 359–66 (United States).
[26] Ibid., 27.
[27] Ibid., 8.
[28] Ibid., 23.

and was ultimately permitted to stay in Spain.[29] In both of these cases, as in the case of the Mexican girl trafficked to the United States, young and relatively naïve women could be controlled in foreign countries at least in part because they lacked the cultural resources to avail themselves of existing legal protection.

The final case of sexual slavery discussed in the *Trafficking in Persons Report* occurred in Peru. A young girl was lured away from domestic work with the promise of a better job, only to be "forced into prostitution in a bar in the Amazon." While there, she was "repeatedly restrained, raped and drugged." Desperate, she accepted the traffickers' offer of freedom for convincing her best friend to come to them. Her friend was then trapped in uncompensated sex work until she ran to the police. Rather than prosecuting her traffickers, the police put the young victim in a "center for juvenile offenders where she was detained for two years."[30] These cases of sex trafficking differ from one another in large and small ways. In each, however, it was not, as one might expect if modern slavery was identical to the forms of slavery analyzed by Orlando Patterson, natal alienation that defined the victims' status. The traffickers did not seek to cut off their victims' ability to invoke kinship networks that, in earlier times, were understood to reach backward to the ancestors and forward to their descendants. The traffickers sought instead to cut their victims off from the legal protections to which they were entitled by a generally accepted social contract; rather than denying them social existence, they sought to extinguish their civic existence.

The three cases of trafficking in domestic workers that are used as victims' stories in the *Trafficking in Persons Report* come, like those involving sex work, from different regions, and they illustrate different aspects of modern trafficking. One echoes the story of the young Nepalese girl who was promised domestic work in Lebanon but sold to an Indian brothel. In this case, a Bangladeshi woman was also promised domestic work in Lebanon. This time the broker did, indeed, take her to Lebanon, but once there, "she found herself" in the "hands of an abusive employer" who "tortured, molested, and confined" her for three years. She finally escaped and was returned to Bangladesh by the agency that had sent her to Lebanon, but they "confiscated her passport and job contract," so she could not "file a complaint with the authorities or receive compensation" for the three years that she worked in Lebanon, much less

[29] Ibid., 38.
[30] Ibid., 35.

for the abuse that she suffered.[31] In a similar story, a Romanian couple living in the United Kingdom recruited a very young girl from their home country to work in their household. Once they got her to England, they "physically and verbally abused her daily." According to the report, the horrific treatment meted out to this child – she was only seven years old – so enraged an older Romanian man who had been enslaved and sexually abused by the couple that he risked escape and summoned the police. The enslaving couple was arrested, convicted, and sentenced to prison.[32] The final and most prominent story involves an Ethiopian woman transported to Malta to work without pay as a nanny for a family member of Moammar Qadhafi. While there, she was confined and physically abused until she was filmed and helped by a camera crew for Cable News Network. No doubt the high profile of her enslaver helped ensure that she received help and a temporary visa from the government of Malta.[33]

On the one hand, these stories underscore the somewhat artificial distinctions between different forms of trafficking. In at least two of these cases – that of the young woman from Bangladesh, and that involving the Romanians in England – victims of trafficking for domestic labor were also being sexually abused. There may be an important analytic distinction between trafficking whose primary purpose is to supply uncompensated labor for sex industries, and trafficking whose primary purpose is to supply uncompensated domestic labor. It is less clear, however, whether the sexual abuse experienced by victims of domestic trafficking – and it's difficult to believe sexual exploitation is rare in cases of coerced and uncompensated domestic labor – might be better understood not as ancillary sexual abuse but as uncompensated and involuntary sex work.[34] On the other hand, in each of these cases the victims of trafficking for domestic labor could, as was the case for the victims of sex trafficking, only liberate themselves from bondage when and to the extent to which they were able to contact civic authorities who recognized their claims to what international law defines as universal human rights.

The *Trafficking in Persons Report*'s lone story of a victim trafficked for industrial labor involves less than competent traffickers. In this case, an adolescent boy from India who dropped out of school was promised "a

---

[31] Ibid., 11.
[32] Ibid., 17.
[33] Ibid., 24.
[34] Patterson, "Trafficking, Gender and Slavery," makes a similar point.

good job in the Jharsuguda district" in eastern India. Upon accepting, he found himself part of a group of boys who were "confined to a factory … given little food, severely beaten, branded, burned with cigarettes, and allowed only a few hours' sleep." The factory owners allowed the victim to talk to his parents, but, as they later learned, "the owners were always present" while their son was on the phone with them. The factory owners did release the boy after holding him for a year, and his parents initiated legal proceedings against his traffickers. The young victim had no way to appeal to the police or other authorities while he was working at the factory – and we might wonder whether the local police would have been sympathetic, or whether they might have been working with the factory owner – but upon returning home, he regained his civic personality and sought to punish those who had violated his rights.[35]

The *Trafficking in Persons Report* also provides only one story of maritime bondage, though, as noted earlier, it is supplemented by the biography of one of the activists it honors. The first victim's story involves a young migrant worker who traveled with a broker from Burma to Thailand to take up a promised job working in a restaurant or factory. Once in Thailand he was told that he owed a large "brokerage fee," and he was put to work on a fishing vessel to pay it off. Once on board the vessel he was not allowed to leave, nor was he paid wages, and one of his fellow crewmen was tortured and killed when caught trying to run away. "Each time the fishing boat docked, the workers were taken to a house and locked in a room so that they could not escape." He liberated himself by jumping overboard with a buoy, tying himself to it for flotation, and swimming for six hours to freedom.[36] The story of Vannak Anan Prum, honored as a TIP Report Hero, is similar. He too was lured to Thailand, in his case from Cambodia, by the promise of good work. Instead the labor broker put him on a fishing boat where he "was mistreated, starved, and tortured." He and one of his fellow bondsmen jumped off the boat and swam almost two and a half miles to Malaysian Borneo. Even then they remained at the mercy of those who could deny them equal access to the protections they were guaranteed under law.[37]

There may be no setting better suited for denying someone a civic personality than a ship at sea. In the age of sail, maritime labor was often described as something like a form of slavery, because the captain's word

[35] US Department of State, *2012 Trafficking in Persons Report*, 14.
[36] Ibid., 28.
[37] Ibid., 47.

was law, and those working beneath him had virtually no recourse should he prove to be abusive. In that sense, the treatment suffered by involuntary maritime workers that is described in the *Trafficking in Persons Report* is not unlike earlier forms of maritime labor, though free sailors in the eighteenth and nineteenth century were allowed to go ashore when their ships were in port.[38] Through that extra denial of liberty, those holding maritime workers in bondage prevent them from gaining access to authorities who would be responsible, at least in theory and law, to protect these maritime workers' rights.

Perhaps the most surprising fact about the victims' stories included in the State Department report is the paucity of stories of agricultural labor, though Vannak Anan Prum experienced both maritime and agricultural bondage. After swimming to Malaysian Borneo to seek help, the officials Prum contacted sold him to work on a palm oil plantation. While laboring without pay on the plantation, he got into a fight with another worker. Prum was then put in jail, where he was finally able to contact two human rights NGOs. They returned him to Cambodia where he began his career as an activist. The only story in the report that deals solely with agricultural labor involves two Brazilian men enslaved on a ranch for at least a decade. Only when the older of the two men hurt himself and became dangerously unhealthy did they conspire to escape. They fled their captors for 14 miles, "arriving at an NGO that helped shelter them and assisted with filing a legal action against their traffickers." Ultimately, they "obtained compensation from their traffickers and have restarted lives free from fear of those who held them captive for so many years."[39] In both of these cases NGOs, in league with sympathetic civil authorities, restored these victims' rights. But the victims could only make that happen by escaping from their enslavers. These two stories end well, as, to a greater or lesser extent, do all of the victim stories in the report. These are, after all, the accounts of victims who got away; otherwise we would not know their tales. But there is reason to think that the stories of agricultural labor, even more than the stories about victims of other forms of trafficking, may provide not just a partial picture – that is unavoidable – but a misleadingly partial picture.

---

[38] W. Jeffrey Bolster, *Black Jacks: African American Seamen in the Age of Sail* (Cambridge, MA: Harvard University Press, 1998), throughout for vivid descriptions of the hardships faced by eighteenth- and nineteenth-century seamen. The freedom represented by shore "liberty" was constrained by forcing sailors to leave their trunks, holding all their possessions, on board ship.

[39] US Department of State, 2012, *Trafficking in Persons Report*, 21.

The largest single category of victims of slavery-like conditions is comprised of those caught in debt bondage in South Asia. The ILO reports that South Asian countries are experiencing a "growing incidence" of bound labor "in a wide range of industries beyond the agricultural sector," but clearly the agricultural sector continues to dominate. This is important, because the stories of agricultural workers bound through debt in the subcontinent do not resemble the story of the Brazilian ranch hands or Prum's time on a palm oil plantation. According to Anti-Slavery International, 80 to 90 percent of the "millions of people ... who are trapped in debt bondage" in India, Pakistan, and Nepal "are from communities designated as 'untouchable' ... or from indigenous communities." The system of bound labor is founded on the caste system: "in the same way that caste status is inherited, so debts are passed on to the succeeding generations." Rather than an innovative and largely hidden practice, debt bondage in large parts of South Asia is open and considered by many locals to be sanctioned by tradition, regardless of the law. "The origin of debt bondage lies in" the requirement that Dalit and other Scheduled Caste people, provide community "service without payment," service that can include public sweeping and cleaning or removing human and animal waste. The sanction of tradition means that magistrates in some regions, even when presented with clear evidence of bound labor that violates national and international law, "refuse to take action."[40]

A case study illustrates the way this form of bondage works and provides a sharp contrast with earlier examples. A bonded laborer in northern India explained that his family had "always" lived in his village, though his specific genealogical knowledge reached only as far back as his grandfather. The informant's father and grandfather had both worked as plowmen (*halvaha*) for the same family of landlords. "They were both bonded by debt, my father by his father's debt, I don't know about my grandfather's debt. It's a regular thing. Kol people like us have always been bonded to Brahmins like my master." Sociologist Kevin Bales, who carried out this interview, reports that the family lived "constantly on

---

[40] Anti-Slavery International, "The Enslavement of Dalit and Indigenous Communities in India, Nepal and Pakistan through Debt Bondage," www.antislavery.org/wp-content/uploads/2017/01/goonesekere.pdf, 1 ("'untouchable'"), 4 ("service without payment"), 5 ("action"). Also see International Labour Organization, *A Global Alliance against Forced Labour*, 31–9; Krishna Prasad Upadhyaya, "Poverty, Discrimination and Slavery: The Reality of Bonded Labour in India, Nepal and Pakistan," www.antislavery.org/wp-content/uploads/2017/01/1-poverty-discrimination-slavery-final.pdf, 1 (South Asian bonded labor primarily agricultural).

the edge of starvation" and faced "violence if they" defied "the system." They were not, however, living in the shadows beyond the purview of civic authorities. The man whom the bonded laborer referred to as "my master" was a "minor government official" – he worked for the Labor Department no less – and also spoke to Bales. "'Of course I have bonded laborers,' he said. 'I'm a landlord ... When they aren't in the fields, I have them doing the household work: washing clothes, cooking, cleaning, making repairs, everything. After all, they are from the Kol caste; that's what they do, work for Vasyas.'" He thought of himself "like a father to these workers."[41] One defining feature of modern slavery is the fact that it is, technically, against the law – a violation of international law and of the law in every nation. The practices that violate national and international law do not, however, invariably violate local norms and practices, and any effort to understand modern slavery as a single institution must wrestle with the difference between bondage carried out in the open, and understood by many who live in its presence to be a part of the natural order, and bondage that exists in hiding, even if it sometimes hides in plain sight.

Does it make sense to think about these diverse practices as linked in an analytically meaningful way? What do victims of evil opportunists, like the pimp in New York, have in common with victims of well-oiled criminal gangs that are alleged to transport involuntary sex workers across state lines? Do either of them have anything in common with young men shanghaied into bondage on fishing vessels in the Pacific, or with South Asian boys and men bound through debt to a brick kiln operator? And what do any of them share with those caught in patterns of agricultural debt bondage that they and their creditors understand to be timeless and natural? Are we tilting at windmills when we seek to fight all of these products of global capitalism as modern slavery, rather than seeing them as manifestations of the structural inequalities that consign so much of the globe's population to poverty and insecurity? Does focusing on "modern slavery" have the unintended consequence of drawing attention away from broader systemic problems?[42]

---

[41] Bales, *Understanding Global Slavery*, 33.

[42] One can read this concern into the way Joel Quirk concludes the best study of anti-trafficking's historical context (*The Anti-Slavery Project*, 252): "anti-slavery does not exist as an isolated issue, but instead becomes part of larger challenges such as racism and discrimination, poverty and inequality, human rights and development, migration and citizenship, and ethical trading and corporate responsibility."

II

Can we define modern slavery, with an obvious debt to Orlando Patterson, as a state of civic death? Each of the victims whose stories have been included in this essay suffered illegal treatment, and each of them was exploited as a result. But what ties them together is that all were prevented from asserting their civic rights, from acting as public figures demanding that civic authorities recognize and protect their rights. There was and is no single mechanism through which enslavers rob their victims of their civic personalities. Undocumented immigrants and legal immigrants whose documents are seized by labor brokers or employers are cast into statelessness, unsure that they can approach authorities without risking incarceration or deportation. Young girls involved in sex work might find themselves either confined, and thus physically unable to appeal for help, or told, often accurately, that the police will arrest and mistreat them, and thus frightened out of appealing for help. In addition, or in other cases, they might be physically threatened, and thus intimidated out of appealing for help. In any of these cases, they can be understood to have found themselves confined to a state of involuntary labor as a result of effectively losing their civic personality. Agricultural workers in debt bondage to landlords in India might realize that their region's law enforcement community does not see anything illegitimate in their condition; others might believe their condition to be time honored and natural; still others might be intimidated by their landlords' threats of violence should they complain to authorities about their treatment. All find themselves bound to labor in a system that effectively denies them the chance to claim their legal rights in the public sphere. All effectively suffer civic death.

Civic death is, it should be repeated, a normative rather than a legal test. It is not designed to provide a bright line separating who is a victim of slavery or who is guilty of enslaving. As such, it is not intended as a replacement for the legal definitions that do that work. It is intended instead as a tool that helps us think about what has long been recognized to be a spectrum of free and unfree labor, of consensual and coerced social relations. It was perhaps easier in the age when slavery was not recognized to be a crime for thinkers like John Millar or St. George Tucker to acknowledge in unproblematic ways that slavery had many meanings in different settings. They did not seek to identify and prosecute enslavers. But if we have different needs in a post-emancipation world in which slavery has been outlawed across the globe, it is a mistake to allow those different needs within criminal justice systems to push us toward unhelpfully rigid thinking about the way slavery works and has worked in society and history.

The lines separating slavery and freedom have always been fuzzy. The goal of a clear normative definition is not to eliminate the difficult cases. It is to provide clear criteria that can be used to judge where individual cases fall along the spectrum of free and unfree labor. Civic death offers a valuable way to make that judgment. It highlights some cases, like guest worker programs in which "the threat of deportation" becomes "the world's new whip," that are clearly legal, but which create structures that effectively bind workers to private employers in ways that open the door to illegal exploitation.[43] Those people are enslaved whose labor or persons are exploited, when and to the extent to which that exploitation is facilitated by the denial of the victim's access to the civil resources their society provides to protect its citizen's rights.

---

[43] Cindy Hahamovich, *No Man's Land: Jamaican Guestworkers and the Global History of Deportable Labor* (Princeton, NJ: Princeton University Press, 2011), 238.

3

From Statute to Amendment and Back Again

The Evolution of American Slavery and Antislavery Law

Allison Mileo Gorsuch

American slavery law began as a series of state-level statutes written to support slavery, and now exists as a series of state- and federal-level statutes prohibiting slavery. In between these sets of statutes, the Thirteenth Amendment abolished chattel slavery as a matter of federal law. This Amendment paved the way for today's antislavery statutes. Today, the United States has an array of statutes – including the Trafficking Victims Protection Act (TVPA) – in its antislavery legal toolbox, all of which are increasingly used to combat human trafficking.[1]

That statutes first defined pro-slavery law and now define antislavery law is no accident: statutes allow legislatures to articulate common goals, whether in support of or opposition to slavery. But the mere existence of antislavery statutes does not eradicate the practice of slavery in the United States – statutes must be enforced against those who break the law.[2] In a common law system like the United States, those statutes are then routinely challenged and refined through lawsuits.

History has an important role to play in the ongoing dialogue about what antislavery statutes mean. The evolution of American antislavery law has time and again returned to history to define the law, as courts import ideas about slavery from the past in the process of interpreting

---

[1] 22 USC §7101 et seq.; see "US Laws on Trafficking in Persons" at the US Department of State website for the TVPA and its reauthorizations at www.state.gov/j/tip/laws/.

[2] This chapter specifically addresses only one of the three "Ps" of the United States' antislavery framework – prosecution – because it is the direct antithesis of state positive law establishing slavery prior to the Thirteenth Amendment. The other Ps (protection and prevention) are of course important facets of an antislavery legal system and are supported by statutes, but are not addressed here.

new legislation. As litigants challenge antislavery statutes in court, courts regularly look to historical practices of slavery to create upcoming, "modern" antislavery jurisprudence. Our work as historians matters in helping courts to identify slavery that manifests itself in new ways that may not be captured in the words of a statute.

However, antislavery jurisprudence is now much less closely tied to historical definitions of slavery. Currently, as federal prosecutors and private attorneys seek to enforce the TVPA through criminal prosecutions and civil lawsuits against traffickers, they are attempting to develop a new law and canon of jurisprudence that reflects the realities of modern slavery, rather than consistently trying to compare contemporary slavery practices to those of the antebellum or post-Reconstruction eras. In our common law system, this development of law can only occur through repeated enforcement, both civilly and criminally, bringing different cases before the courts for analysis of what is and is not slavery under the TVPA. The best way to achieve practical abolition through law is through increased enforcement of existing laws – which have the capacity to capture the nuance, flexibility, and evolution of practices of modern slavery – rather than continually trying to pass new statutes with increasingly complex definitions of slavery. A combination of historical research and increased legal enforcement can work together to give our current antislavery law staying power.

THE POSSIBILITIES AND LIMITS OF
ABOLITION LAW

As historians passionate about responsibly using the history of slavery to end modern slavery, we must refocus our efforts from the work of general abolitionism to embrace more practical and specific solutions. We cannot adopt the same strategies as nineteenth-century abolitionists for the simple reason that the Civil War and the Reconstruction Amendments forever changed the legal landscape of slavery law. The legal tools that allow slaveholders to profit from others have changed. Now, modern-day traffickers seek to exploit ambiguities in antislavery statutes such as the definition of "serious harm" or the meaning of consent. Yet, the law – and more importantly, proper enforcement – is as indispensable in the twenty-first century as it was in the nineteenth and twentieth centuries. We must understand both the possibilities and limitations of law in order to eliminate the practice of slavery in contemporary America, as well as around the world.

There are three relevant types of law in the American justice system: statutes, which are passed by legislative bodies; regulations, passed by administrative agencies; and case law, which is propounded by judges through a series of decisions. When American law is at its most dynamic, these three types of law work in dialogue with each other. Congress (or a state legislature) identifies a problem – say, human trafficking – and passes a law that attempts to put limits on the practice through requiring registration of workers, or criminalizing the practice of taking workers' passports. In a federal statute, if Congress wants private citizens to be able to sue another party for a violation of the law, it must create what is called a "private right of action."[3] Express private rights of action are not common in statutes,[4] although courts may interpret statutes to give litigants an implied right of action in limited circumstances.[5]

Federal law also provides ways for private citizens to sue state government personnel and entities for violations of Constitutional rights through the Civil Rights Act of 1871, or what is popularly known as "Section 1983" litigation. But this section may not be used against a private citizen, only against a government entity.[6] A federal agency, such as

---

[3] For example, here is a very clear private right of action given to victims of human trafficking through the TVPA's Reauthorization in 2008:

> An individual who is a victim of a violation of this chapter may bring a civil action against the perpetrator (or whoever knowingly benefits, financially or by receiving anything of value from participation in a venture which that person knew or should have known has engaged in an act in violation of this chapter) in an appropriate district court of the United States and may recover damages and reasonable attorneys' fees. 18 USC §1595.

[4] Examples of express causes of action include: "(1) anti-discrimination statutes, such as 42 USC §§1981 (contracts), 1982 (property), 1985 (conspiracy), 2000d-2 (federally assisted programs), 2000e-5 et seq. (employment), and 45 USC §3612 (housing), the Rehabilitation Act of 1973, 29 USC §794; the Individuals with Disabilities Education Act, 20 USC §§1400 et seq.; the minimum wage and maximum hours provisions of the Fair Labor Standards Act, 29 USC §216(b); and the Consumer Credit Protection Act provisions, such as 15 USC §§1640 (truth in lending), 1691e (equal credit opportunity), and 1692k (debt collection practices)." "Causes of Action," Federal Practice Manual for Legal Aid Attorneys, http://federalpracticemanual.org/chapter5.

[5] The Supreme Court has made it clear that "[i]f the statute itself does not displa[y] an intent" to create "a private remedy," then "a cause of action does not exist and courts may not create one, no matter how desirable that might be as a policy matter, or how compatible with the statute." *Ziglar v. Abbasi*, 137 S. Ct. 1843, 1855 (2017).

[6] "Every person who, under color of any statute, ordinance, regulation, custom, or usage, of any State or Territory or the District of Columbia, subjects, or causes to be subjected, any citizen of the United States or other person within the jurisdiction thereof to the deprivation of any rights, privileges, or immunities secured by the Constitution and laws,

the Department of Labor, may promulgate a regulation that the agency may enforce against a corporation or person, but in general individuals may not enforce regulations. In short, there are actually very few ways under federal law to sue a private person – such as a trafficker.

State law works similarly. Many states have anti-trafficking laws on the books that criminalize trafficking.[7] States also have a type of law, called tort law, that may be used against individuals. Torts are private wrongs caused by one person against another – like false imprisonment, assault, or fraud – that state common or statutory law recognizes. These state law torts have evolved from English common law torts, but as they are completely creatures of state law and the result of a particular legal culture in a state, the requirements for proving a certain type of tort may vary state to state.

In the United States, many courts are only allowed to hear certain types of cases and to provide certain remedies. In particular, federal courts enjoy limited jurisdiction. The law provides what are called "causes of action" and "remedies" that limit the types of cases a person or government can bring, and what sort of relief the plaintiff might get, what restitution a victim of crime might get, or what sort of punishment the court can dole out to a convicted criminal. The law also requires that plaintiffs in civil suits provide sufficient facts to prove that the defendant violated the law, and that the government establishes each element of the crime that the defendant supposedly committed. Marshaling this type of evidence, in a sufficient quantity and clarity, requires investigation, creativity, and diligence on the part of abolitionist attorneys.

Other legal doctrines limit the availability of lawsuits to victims of trafficking. A civil plaintiff must also have what the law calls "standing," which means that the person who is suing must be the one who suffered the harm, that the defendant plausibly caused the harm, and that the harm must be able to be remedied by the court.[8] An individual person cannot sue someone on behalf of someone else outside a very small set of

---

shall be liable to the party injured in an action at law, suit in equity, or other proper proceeding for redress …,"42 USC §1983.

[7] As of 2014, thirty-nine states have passed antislavery laws. See Polaris Project, "2014 State Ratings on Human Trafficking Laws," https://polarisproject.org/sites/default/files/2014-State-Ratings.pdf.

[8] *Friends of the Earth, Inc. v. Laidlaw Envtl. Servs. (TOC), Inc.*, 528 US 167, 181 (2000). For a basic explanation of the complicated issue of standing, see "Standing," *Federal Practice Manual for Legal Aid Attorneys*, http://federalpracticemanual.org/chapter3/section1.

circumstances. What this means is that we have many tools to use the law to end modern slavery, but the tools have specific times and places that they can be used. This necessarily limits law's effectiveness as a general matter, but makes it a powerful weapon when used correctly.

We know that as a historical matter, the law is not descriptive, but proscriptive, prescriptive, and aspirational – and the same is true today. We cannot assume that simply because we have laws against contemporary slavery the practice does not exist, that those laws are actively enforced, and that those laws are finely tuned to actually address the problems on the ground. In fact, the reality is that too much of modern anti-trafficking law is merely expressive and little of it is actually applied. When the law is not enforced, it does not grow and change to adapt to the continually evolving reality of modern-day slavery. Therefore, our strategies as antislavery advocates must change – and it is not surprising that the study of the past is still relevant even though the legal attack differs. It is not surprising because the structure and practice of slavery remains the same on an individual level: one person is still exploiting the labor and body of another person for profit.

SLAVERY LAW: LEGISLATION TO AMENDMENT TO LEGISLATION AGAIN

Slavery law began as a state-based statutory system before federal law abolished slavery through amendment and statute. Even from its colonial beginnings, the original United States lacked a positive federal law of slavery.[9] Unlike French and Spanish colonial authorities that put forth the *Code Noir* and *Siete Partidas*, England did not have a written slave code for its colonies.[10] England used a system of law that was based on judge-made law rather than positively enacted law – a form adopted by the United States and known as the "common law."[11] Early laws in the American colonies began to mention slaves in the seventeenth century, but the laws were piecemeal and responded to situations as they arose.[12]

---

[9] Jonathan A. Bush, "Free to Enslave: The Foundations of Colonial American Slave Law," *Yale Journal of Law and Humanities* 5, no. 2 (1991), 416; 418.

[10] For discussion of the French and Spanish slave codes, the *Code Noir* and the *Siete Partidas*, see Rebecca Scott, "Slavery and the Law in Atlantic Perspective: Jurisdiction, Jurisprudence, and Justice," *Law and History Review* 13, no. 1 (Spring 1995), 23–62.

[11] Bush, "Free to Enslave," 423.

[12] Thomas Morris, *Southern Slavery and the Law, 1619–1860* (Chapel Hill, NC: University of North Carolina Press, 1996), 38–49.

Virginia had the first statute that referenced a sort of slave status in 1662, which codified the rule that enslaved status was passed from mother to child.[13] The law recognized slavery, but it did not *create* slavery.

This form of lawmaking continued after the American Revolution. The Constitution of the United States of America did not explicitly address the stateside institution of slavery, but rather set in place a plan for allocating political representatives in the House of Representatives on the basis of population adjusted for slaves and allowed for the possibility of ending the importation of slaves in 1808 or later.[14] The newly formed states each formed constitutions, most of which allowed slavery but again did not positively create the ability for white men to own black and Native slaves.[15] That ability existed independent of the law, but was upheld and supported by a scaffold of laws that enforced the master's power over the slave.

The Southern states' slave codes declared slaves to be chattel property,[16] restricted the movement of slaves,[17] provided for severe physical punishment of slaves,[18] and as time went on, reflected in law the assumption that all black people were slaves unless shown otherwise.[19] State judicial

---

[13] Ibid., 43.

[14] See Art. 1, §9 of the US Constitution, which allowed Congress to prohibit "the importation of ... persons" only after 1808, and Art. 1, §2, Clause 3, that indirectly referenced enslaved people for purposes of allocating political representation and taxation. Whether or not the constitution is a pro- or antislavery document at its core is a longstanding debate – suffice to say that it established a positive law neither of slavery nor of abolition. Compare Sean Wilentz, "Constitutionally, Slavery Is No National Institution," *The New York Times* (September 16, 2015), www.nytimes.com/2015/09/16/opinion/constitutionally-slavery-is-no-national-institution.html, with Paul Finkelman, "How the Proslavery Constitution Led to the Civil War," *Rutgers Law Journal* 43 (2013).

[15] Morris, *Southern Slavery and the Law*, 340.

[16] See William Goodell, *The American Slave Code in Theory and Practice*, 23 (New York Foreign Anti-Slavery Society, 1853).

[17] "No slave shall go from the tenement of his master ... without a pass, or some letter or token, whereby it may appear that he is proceeding by authority from his master..." Excerpts from *A Digest of the Laws of the State of Alabama* (1833), compiled by John G. Akin., 391, http://digital.archives.alabama.gov/cdm/singleitem/collection/voices/id/3708.

[18] For example, the "[p]unishment of slaves for killing, marking, or branding cattle" was "whipping on the bare back, not exceeding thirty-nine lashes." William A. Hotchkiss, ed. *Codification of the State Law of Georgia* (1848), Art. 1, §2-22.

[19] An 1838 Arkansas law, for example, forbid "any white person, or free negro or mulatto" from meeting, drinking with, or playing games with any "slave," making clear that slaves were non-white. *Revised Statutes of the State of* Arkansas (1838), 730-733-736 at §27. This was not the case early in colonial history, where colonial slave laws did not assume race. Morris, *Southern Slavery and the Law*, 18–19.

systems upheld both the slave codes and articulated a common law of slavery through decisions such as North Carolina's infamous *State v. Mann*, which enshrined the phrase "The power of the master must be absolute, to render the submission of the slave perfect."[20]

These laws reinforced the non-legal limits of slavery; as one historian has shown in the Mississippi River valley, slaveholders relied on the "carceral landscape" to prevent runaways, knowing that vast distances between plantations, hunger, and lack of shoes would prevent runaway slaves from succeeding.[21] Slaveholders never relied *solely* on the law as the primary means for effectively holding human beings in bondage, but the law provided a backstop of authority that slaveholders could call on when necessary. The written slave codes and the proslavery court decisions reflected both the legal assumptions that undergirded the system (certain people could be owned as property) and the legal creations that stitched together gaps or solved conundrums in the assumptions (what happened if your property stole from another slaveholder?).

Many Northern states also allowed slavery to continue within their borders. New Jersey and New York both enacted law providing a gradual emancipation process for slaves held by New Yorkers, but continued to protect the slaveholding rights of Southern visitors.[22] In the newly formed states of Indiana and Illinois, slavery continued as long-term indentured servitude.[23] Illinois, although carved out of the free soil of the Northwest

---

[20] *State v. Mann*, 13 N.C. (1829), 263; 266. The opinion continued, making clear how the law of slavery seemed to arise from some undefined agreement: "But in the actual condition of things, it must be so. There is no remedy. This discipline belongs to the state of slavery. They cannot be disunited, without abrogating at once the rights of the master, and absolving the slave from his subjection. It constitutes the curse of slavery to both the bond and free portions of our population. But it is inherent in the relation of master and slave." Ibid., 266–7.

[21] Walter Johnson, *River of Dark Dreams: Slavery and Empire in the Cotton Kingdom* (Cambridge, MA: Harvard University Press, 2013), 209.

[22] Leslie M. Harris, *In the Shadow of Slavery: African Americans in New York City, 1626–1863* (Chicago, IL: University of Chicago Press, 2004), 5; Martha S. Jones, "Time, Space, and Jurisdiction in Atlantic World Slavery: The Volunbrun Household in Gradual Emancipation New York," *Law and History Review* 29, no. 4 (November 2011), 1031–60; James J. Gigantino II, *The Ragged Road to Abolition: Slavery and Freedom in New Jersey, 1775–1865* (Philadelphia, PA: University of Pennsylvania Press, 2015), 213. See generally Sarah Levine-Gronningsater, *Delivering Freedom: Gradual Emancipation, Black Legal Culture, and the Origins of Sectional Crisis in New York, 1759–1870* (University of Chicago, PhD dissertation, 2015).

[23] Allison Mileo Gorsuch, "To Indent Oneself: Ownership, Contracts, and Consent in Antebellum Illinois," in Jean Allain, ed., *The Legal Understanding of Slavery: From the Historical to the Contemporary* (Oxford: Oxford University Press, 2012), 135–51.

Territories, also tried to amend its constitution to permit slavery after they had been admitted to the Union.[24]

The federal government kept an arm's distance from slavery law, viewing it, with some limited exceptions, as the province of state government. When Congress did speak on slavery – such as in the Northwest Ordinance of 1787 or with the 1850 Fugitive Slave Act – it did so in the context of comity and state self-governance. The Northwest Ordinance forbade slavery in the territories, but allowed each state to determine at a later point whether or not to allow slavery.[25] The Fugitive Slave Clause of the US Constitution, and later, the Fugitive Slave Acts of 1793 and 1850, required Northern states to return runaway slaves to Southern states.[26] The Fugitive Slave Acts both included a private right of action that allowed slaveholders to use proslavery state law to effectively trump free state laws that recognized personal liberty.

This state-based approach to building a slave law system depended on federalism: the idea that the states were sovereigns over certain issues, including slavery.[27] The relative weakness of the federal government and the strength of state governments meant that slavery was a local legal creation. This localism reflected the economics of slavery as well. Different geographies and economies meant different uses of slave labor

[24] Legislative Reference Bureau, *Constitutional Conventions in Illinois* (Springfield, IL, 1918), 11–12.

[25] An Ordinance for the government of the Territory of the United States northwest of the River Ohio, 1. Stat. 50 Art. 6: "There shall be neither slavery nor involuntary servitude in the said territory, otherwise than in the punishment of crimes whereof the party shall have been duly convicted: Provided, always, That any person escaping into the same, from whom labor or service is lawfully claimed in any one of the original States, such fugitive may be lawfully reclaimed and conveyed to the person claiming his or her labor or service as aforesaid."

[26] US Constitution, Art. 4, Sec. 2; Fugitive Slave Act of 1793, codified at 1 Stat. 302; Fugitive Slave Act of 1850, codified at 9 Stat. 462. In 1842, the Supreme Court described the Fugitive Slave Clause this way: "It is historically well known, that the object of the clause in the constitution of the United States, relating to persons owing service and labor in one state, escaping into other states, was to secure to the citizens of the slave holding states the complete right and title of ownership in their slaves, as property, in every state in the Union, into which they might escape from the state where they were held in servitude." *Prigg v. Com. of Pennsylvania*, 41 US 539, 540 (1842).

[27] As Chief Justice Taney of the US Supreme Court explained in 1850, "Every state has an undoubted right to determine the *status*, or domestic and social condition, of the persons domiciled within its territory; except in so far as the powers of the states in this respect are restrained, or duties and obligations imposed upon them, by the Constitution of the United States. There is nothing in the Constitution of the United States that can in any degree control the law of Kentucky upon this subject." *Strader v. Graham*, 51 US 82, 93–4 (1850).

and different local market potentials for profiting from the reproduction and sale of slaves. For example, in Illinois, slaves were used to mine lead,[28] while masters in other geographies used slaves to grow the more well-known crops of tobacco, sugar, rice, or cotton.[29]

THE THIRTEENTH AMENDMENT AND SUBSEQUENT LEGISLATION

Compared to the mosaic of slave experiences and the net of slavery laws that covered the United States, the Thirteenth Amendment was a clean slate. The Thirteenth Amendment, passed in 1865, abolished slavery as a matter of federal law in every square foot of American soil:

> Section 1. Neither slavery nor involuntary servitude, except as a punishment for crime whereof the party shall have been duly convicted, shall exist within the United States, or any place subject to their jurisdiction.
> Section 2. Congress shall have power to enforce this article by appropriate legislation.[30]

The Amendment overpowered the existing state laws because of the Supremacy Clause, which makes any state law that violates a federal constitutional provision unenforceable.[31]

---

[28] Lucy Eldersvald Murphy, *A Gathering of Rivers: Indians, Metis, and Mining in the Western Great Lakes, 1737–1832* (Lincoln, NE: University of Nebraska Press, 2004), 109. Other sources show many black persons in Galena in the 1830s: "there were quite a number of colored people, who were slaves" when S. W. McMaster first arrived at Galena, in 1833. S. W. McMaster, *60 Years of the Upper Mississippi: My Life and Experiences* (Rock Island, IL, 1893), 173; 178. An example of a slave used to mine lead can be found here: *Dunky, a colored woman v. Andrew Hay*, July Term of Court, 1831, Case File Number 12, Page 7. Circuit Court Case Files, Office of the Circuit Clerk – St. Louis, Missouri State Archives – St. Louis, Office of the Secretary of State, http://stlcourtrecords.wustl.edu.

[29] See Ira Berlin, *Generations of Captivity* (Cambridge, MA: Harvard University Press, 2003), 8–10 and generally, for a discussion of the various geographies of slavery over time in the United States.

[30] US Const. amend. XIII. It is also important to note the "duly convicted" clause, which allowed, and allows, prisons to force inmates to work for no pay. See, e.g., Douglas A. Blackmon, *Slavery by Another Name: The Re-Enslavement of Black Americans from the Civil War to World War II* (New York: Anchor Books, 2008); Raja Raghunath, "A Promise the Nation Cannot Keep: What Prevents the Application of the Thirteenth Amendment in Prison?" *William and Mary Bill of Rights Journal* 18, no. 2 (2009), 395.

[31] US Const. Art. VI, Cl. 2.

However, the broad, sweeping abolition amendment also left little explanation of the wide variety of slaveries that existed in the United States. In 1865, what the word "slavery" meant in that Amendment may have been perfectly clear for much of the South: chattel slavery was abolished and former slaves were now free. In reality, the legal status of "slave" and "free" became meaningless. More complex was the involuntary servitude provision; as time went on, courts would struggle to determine who was considered an involuntary servant, or what conditions constituted involuntary servitude.

Southern states responded to the Thirteenth Amendment's abolition of slavery by enacting Black Codes, state laws that severely limited the rights of black people and allowed long terms of forced labor as punishment for small infractions.[32] In response, Congress enacted the Civil Rights Act of 1866, which provided the framework for the Fourteenth Amendment and promised black people "the full and equal benefit of all laws and proceedings for the security of person and property" as white people.[33]

The Supreme Court reviewed the application and meaning of the Thirteenth Amendment and the Civil Rights Act of 1866 in the years following the Civil War in two cases, *The Civil Rights Cases* and *The Slaughter-House Cases*. In both of those decisions, the Court examined the scope of the Thirteenth Amendment in relation to the Fourteenth and Fifteenth Amendments. These cases are known for limiting the Fourteenth Amendment's reach to a narrow class of cases, but are also important for seeing the Court's early thoughts about slavery in a post-Thirteenth Amendment world.

The *Civil Rights Cases* Court noted particularly that the Thirteenth Amendment is self-enforcing – that is, that "[b]y its own unaided force it abolished slavery, and established universal freedom" – but that Congress could also clearly enact legislation to further this goal if necessary.[34] However, the Court also distinguished the range of the Thirteenth Amendment from the Fourteenth:

We must not forget that the province and scope of the Thirteenth and Fourteenth Amendments are different: the former simply abolished slavery: the latter

---

[32] Bridgette Carr et al., eds., *Human Trafficking Law and Policy* (Durham, NC: Carolina Academic Press, 2014), 17.
[33] Civil Rights Act of 1866, 14 Stat. 27–30.
[34] *Civil Rights Cases*, 109 US 3, 20–1 (1883).

prohibited the States from abridging the privileges or immunities of citizens of the United States ... The amendments are different, and the powers of Congress under them are different. What Congress has power to do under one, it may not have power to do under the other. Under the Thirteenth Amendment, it has only to do with slavery and its incidents.[35]

The Court explained what it considered to be examples of the "incidents of slavery," claiming that "[t]he long existence of African slavery in this country gave us very distinct notions of what it was, and what were its necessary incidents."[36] Such incidents included

[c]ompulsory service of the slave for the benefit of the master, restraint of his movements except by the master's will, disability to hold property, to make contracts, to have a standing in court, to be a witness against a white person, and such like burdens and incapacities ... Severer punishments for crimes were imposed on the slave than on free persons guilty of the same offenses.[37]

The *Slaughter-House* Court recognized that the Amendment abolished both slavery and involuntary servitude, noting that "[t]he word servitude is of larger meaning than slavery, as the latter is popularly understood in this country, and the obvious purpose was to forbid all shades and conditions of African slavery."[38] The Court distinguished involuntary servitude from slavery by limiting the definition of slavery to "African slavery," but simultaneously expanded the potential definition of "involuntary servitude" to include types of labor that did not fall directly within the practice of "African slavery."

Legal scholars have noted that the Thirteenth Amendment may have been limited by the proximity of the Fourteenth Amendment – giving separate sources for an individual's freedom from slavery and citizenship rights – because "the Thirteenth Amendment contained the provision that emancipated enslaved persons, while the Fourteenth Amendment contained the provisions that protected the rights of newly freed slaves."[39] If, as these scholars contend, legislators and jurists did see these Amendments as dividing rights in this way, this perception may have had the effect of always bringing attention to the historical practice of chattel slavery.

---

[35] Ibid., 21–3.
[36] Ibid., 21–3.
[37] Ibid.
[38] *Slaughter-House Cases*, 83 US 36, 69 (1872).
[39] Mark A. Graber, "Subtraction by Addition? The Thirteenth and Fourteenth Amendments," *Columbia Law Review* (2012), 1501.

Some courts directly interpreted the meaning of the Thirteenth Amendment. For example, in 1905, the Ninth Circuit Court of Appeals heard an appeal from Ah Sou, a Chinese girl who was being deported after being brought to the United States illegally as a sex slave. The trial court had found that deportation would essentially cause her to be enslaved back in China and so entered an order vacating her deportation, because deportation would violate the Thirteenth Amendment. The trial court judge reasoned that the Thirteenth Amendment required "the exercise of all the force necessary for the protection of liberty of any and every individual whose right to liberty has not been forfeited by conviction of crime," and there was "no other way in which to emancipate her from actual slavery" than to stop her deportation.[40]

The Ninth Circuit disagreed with the trial court's interpretation of how far the Thirteenth Amendment extended. The Thirteenth Amendment did not "by its terms prohibit ... the deportation of [Ah Sou]; nor is it contended ... that by virtue of an order of deportation her condition as a slave would be recognized, or that she would be sent into slavery."[41] The Ninth Circuit did not agree that deportation to China would be equivalent to slavery. Even if it was, the appellate court was not sure that the Thirteenth Amendment applied to a condition of slavery that only started once the person was in another country.

Courts also interpreted statutes passed under the power of the Thirteenth Amendment. The Peonage Abolition Act, passed in 1867, was Congress's first attempt to legislate in support of the Thirteenth Amendment. The Act declared that the "holding of any person to service or labor under the system known as peonage is abolished and forever prohibited in any Territory or State of the United States."[42] As one early twentieth-century court put it, "[b]y these enactments Congress undertook to strike down all laws, regulations, and usages in the states and territories which attempted to maintain and enforce, directly or indirectly, the voluntary or involuntary service or labor of any persons as peons, in the liquidation of any debt or obligation."[43]

Despite the federal anti-peonage law, Southern whites continued the Black Codes system of forced labor into the early twentieth century, arresting black persons for petty crimes and sentencing them to fines they

---

[40] *US v. Ah Sou*, 138 F. 775, 777 (9th Cir. 1905).
[41] Ibid., 778.
[42] 42 USC §1994.
[43] *United States v. Reynolds*, 235 US 133, 143 (1914).

could not pay. A third party would then pay the debt, and the imprisoned black person had to sign a contract to work for the bailor until the debt was paid off. The debt would never be fully paid, though, trapping the black person in a cycle of work that strongly resembled slavery.[44]

The first federal indictment under the anti-peonage law was brought in 1905, nearly forty years after its enactment. This first prosecution came before the Supreme Court in the case of *Clyatt v. United States*, and the Court upheld the anti-peonage law as constitutional.[45] The Court upheld the constitutionality of the law again in *Bailey v. State of Alabama* in 1911, explaining that the Thirteenth Amendment's "plain intention was to abolish slavery of whatever name and form and all its badges and incidents; to render impossible any state of bondage; to make labor free, by prohibiting that control by which the personal service of one man is disposed of or coerced for another's benefit, which is the essence of involuntary servitude."[46]

The *Bailey* decision articulated that a state law could not throw out established standards of criminal law in order to coerce individuals to work. In *Bailey*, a man was found by the Alabama Supreme Court to be in violation of an Alabama law that made it a crime of fraud to refuse to perform service after accepting payment when the worker had agreed to a contract for the service. Such refusal was good evidence of intent to injury or defraud the employer, and the worker could then be convicted and sentenced to work.[47] The Supreme Court found the Alabama law to be unconstitutional, because a jury could convict based solely on the refusal and not on the actual intent of the worker to defraud. It was "a convenient instrument for the coercion which the Constitution and the act of Congress forbid."[48]

The Supreme Court had again looked to the intention of the Thirteenth Amendment and discussed, in broad terms, what the Amendment had intended to forbid: the "badges and incidents" of slavery, the "control" over a person "disposed of or coerced for another's benefit." But the essence of the ruling held firm not to the conditions of labor – not looking to "whatever name and form it took," but rather to the legal status of the person held in involuntary servitude. The Alabama law had made it a crime to breach a contract, which in turn made the breaching

---

[44] Blackmon, *Slavery by Another Name*, 205.
[45] 197 US 207 (1905).
[46] *Bailey v. State of Alabama*, 219 US 219, 240–2 (1911).
[47] Ibid.
[48] Ibid., 244–5.

worker subject to a changed legal status that could be subject to slavery. The law lowered the standard of proof that the worker had *intended* to defraud the employer; to be convicted for most crimes, a criminal must be shown to have the required intent. This is the difference, for example, between a driver who accidentally kills a pedestrian while texting (being criminally negligent) and a driver who purposefully runs down an enemy walking in the street. By recognizing that the Alabama law changed the well-established standard to make it easier for employers to trap workers into unpaid labor, the Supreme Court linked the Thirteenth Amendment to the new forms of control authorized by state courts and wielded by employers.

In 1948, Congress enacted another piece of Thirteenth Amendment legislation, recognizing that the anti-peonage act was insufficiently broad. This statute, codified at 18 USC §1584, criminalized involuntary servitude:

(a) Whoever knowingly and willfully holds to involuntary servitude or sells into any condition of involuntary servitude, any other person for any term, or brings within the United States any person so held, shall be fined under this title or imprisoned not more than 20 years, or both ...[49]

However, Congress still did not define involuntary servitude, leaving it up to the courts to parse the exact meaning. This resulted in a circuit split, with some courts reading the statute broadly to include psychological coercion, while other courts read it narrowly to mean only physical and legal means of coercion sufficed to prove involuntary servitude, keeping the definition much more closely linked to the historical practices of chattel slavery and peonage.[50]

The Second Circuit took the narrow approach in the 1964 case *US v. Shackney*, where Shackney, a Polish immigrant, had hired a Mexican family, the Oros, to work on his chicken farm in Connecticut.[51] Shackney lent the Oroses money for their immigration and travel costs to be worked off through labor on the farm. But all did not go well – conditions were bad, and Shackney threatened the Oroses with deportation if they left the farm. Despite these threats, the family snuck letters out with visitors to the farm and the authorities came to investigate.

---

[49] 18 USC §1584.
[50] Carr et al., *Human Trafficking Law and Policy*, 47.
[51] *United States v. Shackney*, 333 F.2d 475 (2d Cir. 1964).

Shackney was indicted and found guilty under 18 USC §1584, the indentured servitude statute discussed above.

On appeal, the Second Circuit found that there was not sufficient evidence to support a finding of guilty. The court's "endeavor to construe the statute had best begin with its history," and so the opinion discusses the origins of the anti-peonage statute and the forced labor statute, before returning to the Northwest Ordinance to parse the meaning of "involuntary servitude."[52] After revisiting many cases brought under the Thirteenth Amendment's involuntary servitude clause around the country, the Second Circuit reasoned that the statute must mean "to abolish all practices whereby subjection having some of the incidents of slavery was legally enforced, either directly, by a state's using its power to return the servant to the master, or indirectly, by subjecting persons who left the employer's service to criminal penalties."[53] Physical and legal violence sufficed to constitute involuntary servitude, but the court saw "no basis for concluding that because the statute can be satisfied by a credible threat of imprisonment, it should also be considered satisfied by a threat to have the employee sent back to the country of his origin, at least absent circumstances which would make such deportation equivalent to imprisonment or worse."[54] Again, as in *Bailey*, the Court reinforced the connection between legal status and the Thirteenth Amendment.

In 1988, the Supreme Court addressed the indentured servitude statute in *US v. Kozminski*.[55] In that case, the Kozminski family was prosecuted for holding two mentally disabled men in squalid conditions on their Michigan farm and forcing them to labor for no pay. A jury found the Kozminskis guilty, and they appealed their conviction on the grounds that the district court's definition of involuntary servitude was too broad, "which would bring cases involving general psychological coercion within the reach of … §1584."[56] The Sixth Circuit, sitting *en banc*, reversed the convictions and remanded the case for a new trial, holding that such an expansion of the definition was beyond what Congress intended. The government appealed.

The Supreme Court noted that the circuit courts disagreed on whether involuntary servitude could be construed to include psychological

[52] Ibid., 481.
[53] Ibid., 485.
[54] Ibid., 486.
[55] *United States v. Kozminski*, 487 US 931 (1988).
[56] Ibid., 937–8.

coercion, but found that it could not be so broad. The Court looked to legislative history to determine that Congress did not intend to broaden the meaning of involuntary servitude to include psychological coercion as well as legal coercion (such as peonage) or physical coercion (requiring victims to be "physically unable to leave").[57] The Court went further, noting that broadening the statute to consider the victim's point of view or subjective position in determining voluntariness would "appear to criminalize a broad range of day-to-day activity" that was both unreasonable and unconstitutional, because the statute could not provide fair notice of what conduct would be considered illegal. The Kozminskis' convictions were reversed and the case was remanded for a new trial.[58]

INCORPORATING HISTORY: THE TVPA

The *Kozminski* decision spurred Congress into action. Because the Supreme Court declared that the Thirteenth Amendment could only prohibit physical or legal coercion under the legal precedents, Congress set out to clarify what forms of coercion could be allowed.[59] In 2000, Congress passed the Trafficking Victims Protection Act (TVPA), a statute that created new federal crimes for labor and sex trafficking, the most comprehensive American legislation ever to combat human trafficking. States, too, have enacted laws prohibiting human trafficking.

The TVPA provides both criminal and civil methods of enforcement against human traffickers. The part of the Act codified at 18 USC §1589, known as the forced labor statute, authorizes the punishment of anyone who

provides or obtains the labor or services of a person by any one of, or by any combination of … (1) by means of force, threats of force, physical restraint, or threats of physical restraint to that person or another person;

> (2) by means of serious harm or threats of serious harm to that person or another person;
> (3) by means of the abuse or threatened abuse of law or legal process; or
> (4) by means of any scheme, plan, or pattern intended to cause the person to believe that, if that person did not perform such labor or services,

---

[57] Ibid., 948.
[58] Ibid., 953.
[59] Carr et al., *Human Trafficking Law and Policy*, 87–8; Kathleen Kim, "The Coercion of Trafficked Workers," *Iowa Law Review* 96 (2011), 409, 435–6.

that person or another person would suffer serious harm or physical restraint.[60]

This provision was intended to allow for prosecutions of persons who used psychological or other forms of coercion that would not be criminalized under the anti-peonage statute nor considered slavery or involuntary servitude under the Thirteenth Amendment.[61] Congressional documents noted that "[s]ection 1589 will provide federal prosecutors with the tools to combat severe forms of work exploitations that do not rise to the level of involuntary servitude as defined in Kozminski," namely the "physical harm or threats of force against victims."[62]

The TVPA thus greatly expanded the types of cases that can be prosecuted. Now, federal prosecutors may determine if a particular case calls for prosecution under the anti-peonage statute (§1994), the involuntary servitude statute (§1584), or the forced labor statute (§1589), depending on the type of coercion involved. In addition, in 2003, Congress added a civil remedy to the statute, authorizing individual victims to bring civil lawsuits against their traffickers in §1595:

> (a) An individual who is a victim of a violation of this chapter may bring a civil action against the perpetrator (or whoever knowingly benefits, financially or by receiving anything of value from participation in a venture which that person knew or should have known has engaged in an act in violation of this chapter) in an appropriate district court of the United States and may recover damages and reasonable attorneys' fees.[63]

Finally, the TVPA also added a specific criminal section regarding sex trafficking of both adults and children, allowing for the prosecution of anyone who recruits or obtains, or benefits from another person doing so, an adult for commercial sex acts through "force, threats of force, fraud, or coercion," in §1591. The section defined coercion as "threats of serious harm to or physical restraint" or a scheme or plan intended to threaten such serious harm, or abuse of the law or legal process. For prosecutions of those accused of sex trafficking children, prosecutors must only show that a child was recruited or obtained for commercial

---

[60] 18 USC §1589.

[61] Carr et al., *Human Trafficking Law and Policy*, 113; US Department of Justice, "Involuntary Servitude, Forced Labor, and Sex Trafficking Statutes Enforced," www .justice.gov/crt/involuntary-servitude-forced-labor-and-sex-trafficking-statutes-enforced.

[62] H.R. Rep. No. 106–939 at 101 (2000).

[63] 18 USC §1595.

sex. There is no requirement that the prosecution prove that the child was coerced, forced, or defrauded.

EXAMPLES OF CRIMINAL PROSECUTIONS UNDER
THE TVPA

Federal prosecutors soon pursued investigations and brought cases under the criminal section of the TVPA. In 2005, the Kaufmans, a married couple who owned a farm in Kansas, were prosecuted under §1589 for forced labor and under §1584 for involuntary servitude in the case *US v. Kaufman*.[64] Local law enforcement had observed two men working outside on the farm in the nude under the supervision of the husband, a social worker. The couple considered this work "treatment" for residents of an unlicensed group home for the mentally ill, and was billing the patients' families and Medicare for this "therapy." The couple also directed the residents to perform sex acts on tape. The Kaufmans were convicted after a jury trial and sentenced to years in prison.

On appeal, the couple challenged the way the district court had defined "labor" and "services" for their convictions under the forced labor and involuntary servitude statutes. They claimed that the sex acts could not be considered "labor or services" because those acts were not "compulsory labor akin to African slavery," as the Supreme Court in *Kozminski* had defined "involuntary servitude."[65] In *Kozminski*, the Supreme Court had discussed the *involuntary* aspect of "involuntary servitude," not the "servitude" definition. Looking to the legislative history and scholarship on slavery, the Tenth Circuit then determined that "labor or services" could be broader than simply "economic" work. In particular, the court noted that historical slavery was full of non-"economic" examples of the "badges and incidents of slavery" that the Thirteenth Amendment intended to abolish: "In our view, if an antebellum slave was relieved of the responsibility for harvesting cotton, brought into his master's house, directed to disrobe [and engage in sex acts], his or her condition could still fairly be described as one of involuntary servitude and forced labor."[66]

Not all circuits have upheld more expansive interpretations of §1584. In 2012, the Third Circuit declined to find that Walmart cleaning workers had properly alleged that they had been subject to involuntary servitude when

---

[64] *United States v. Kaufman*, 546 F.3d 1242 (10th Cir. 2008).
[65] Ibid., 1263.
[66] Ibid., 1264.

they were locked inside the building at night.[67] The Third Circuit cited *Kozminski*, stating that "[t]he phrase 'involuntary servitude' was intended … 'to cover those forms of compulsory labor akin to African slavery.' " The appellate court also relied on pre-TVPA cases that limited involuntary servitude to "labor camps, isolated religious sects, or forced confinement" or cases involving actual physical injury.[68] "Plaintiffs have presented evidence of some difficult working conditions, but they have demonstrated nothing 'akin to African slavery' or any modern analogue," noted the court, further declaring that "[a]ny such comparison is plainly frivolous."[69]

As historians, we can claim credit for the difference between the Tenth Circuit's broader definition of labor or services that included work that was not traditionally "economic" and the Third Circuit's position that involuntary servitude must resemble either "African slavery" or labor camps; this split is the result of the changing historiography of slavery, even if only two law professors are cited by the Tenth Circuit.[70] The Tenth Circuit takes a historically accurate approach to drawing on the history of slavery, recognizing that even "African slavery" included a variety of states of subjection that were not performed for "economic" value but rather in the service of performative power. The Third Circuit, on the other hand, invoked African slavery and labor camps as the only comparison worth making as a matter of law. The Third Circuit called up images of the physical restraints and punishment of some forms of American chattel slavery and the physical and geographical limitations of some ahistorical "labor camps." Historians have shown that the Third Circuit's understanding of slavery, and the resulting comparison, is inapt.

Courts are also now empowered to move beyond the historical image of slavery to parse the text of the new statute themselves. For example, the First Circuit addressed the definition of "serious harm" under §1589

---

[67] *Zavala v. Wal Mart Stores Inc.*, 691 F.3d 527 (3d Cir. 2012). The current legal standard is that a plaintiff's complaint must plausibly allege facts that would sustain their legal complaint; if a complaint does not contain what the court deems to be sufficient facts, it may be dismissed early in the proceedings of the case on what is called a "motion to dismiss." See *Ashcroft v. Iqbal*, 556 US 662 (2009) (defining the controlling legal standard for pleading in complaints).

[68] *Zavala v. Wal Mart Stores Inc.*, 691 F.3d at 540.

[69] Ibid.

[70] The Tenth Circuit in *US v. Kaufman* cites Akhil Reed Amar, "Remember the Thirteenth," Faculty Scholarship Series, Yale Law School Digital Commons (1993), 403; 405, http://digitalcommons.law.yale.edu/fss_papers/1043/; Neal Kumar Katyal, "Men Who Own Women: A Thirteenth Amendment Critique of Forced Prostitution," *103 Yale Law Journal* 103 (1993), 793; 796; 811.

in a case that turned on statutory interpretation of specific terms, not on a historical slavery analogy.[71] In *US v. Bradley*, federal prosecutors brought charges of forced labor against employees of a New Hampshire tree service company who had recruited Jamaican workers to work for them but then paid less than what was promised, housed workers in substandard conditions, withheld the men's passports, threatened to kill a worker who had returned to Jamaica, and treated the workers poorly. A jury found the defendants guilty, and they appealed based on the definition of "serious harm" in §1589.

The district court had instructed the jury that serious harm included "both physical and non-physical types of harm" so that the threat of serious harm could include "threats of any consequences ... that are sufficient under all of the surrounding circumstances to compelling or coerce a reasonable person in the same situation to provide or to continue providing labor or services."[72] Defendants claimed that the statute meant "dire consequences" not "any consequences"; for example, that a threat to not pay for passage home to Jamaica was a legitimate stance for the employer to take, not a coercive threat. The First Circuit upheld the district court's jury instructions, stating that "the defendants' arguable threats or coercion involved the taking of passports and mentions of violence" as well as limits on local travel. Finally, the defendants also appealed on the grounds that the jury was instructed improperly regarding the victims' opportunity to flee. Defendants claimed that "the opportunity to flee is determinative of forced labor" but the jury instructions stated that it was not. The First Circuit found no error with the instructions.

Essentially, the First Circuit recognized – without stating it explicitly – that the underlying purpose of the TVPA was to include non-physical and legal modes of compulsion. Again, historians recognize many familiar patterns of legal, chattel slavery in the descriptions of the ways in which the New Hampshire tree service controlled its immigrant workers: limiting their ability to leave, isolating them geographically, or threats of violence for leaving. The reasoning of the court rests on the statute's incorporation of that historical truth (via an expanded definition of threat and harm) rather than on the court's own volition or understanding of the purposes behind the Thirteenth Amendment.

There is another lesson to be drawn here: just as we could look to the early slave codes to ascertain what was important to slaveholders

---

[71] *United States v. Bradley*, 390 F.3d 145 (1st Cir. 2004), *cert. granted, judgment vacated on other grounds*, 545 US 1101 (2005).

[72] Ibid., 150.

in maintaining a system of race-based, chattel slavery, we can now look to challenges to the application of the TVPA to see where those accused of modern trafficking see the borders of slavery. For example, the New Hampshire tree service asked the First Circuit to view its threats as legitimate tools of employee control. Hidden in the defendant's argument about the difference between "dire consequences" and "any consequences" is the belief that trafficking requires threats completely outside the bounds of the legitimate employment relationship. Taken in isolation, any one of the consequences used by the tree service may have been a run-of-the-mill rule of employment – which any of us might be subject to – but the court rightly recognized that there a was a difference in circumstances here that pushed the restrictions over the edge of legitimate employment into coerced labor.

CIVIL CASES

The amended TVPA provides a civil remedy at 18 USC §1595, under which an individual who believes she has been subjected to trafficking may sue for civil compensation. Although this provision has been infrequently used,[73] a recent case provides an example. In 2012, Joy Guobadia, a domestic worker, filed suit against a couple, the Irowas, for luring her from Nigeria to the United States on false pretenses and forcing her to work as their domestic servant without pay.[74] Guobadia brought multiple claims, including violations of the peonage and forced labor statutes, as well as the Thirteenth Amendment. The Irowas were Guobadia's cousins; Guobadia had lived with and worked for her aunt in Nigeria since she was five years old. When the Irowas were visiting Nigeria in 2003, they told the plaintiff that she should come with them to the US where she would go to school as a reward for all of her hard work for her aunt. Once she accompanied the Irowas back to the US, however, she did not attend school, but instead worked as a domestic servant and nanny for a succession of relatives for no pay. The Irowas also later found the plaintiff outside work under false names and collected her paychecks.

---

[73] A WestLaw "citing references" search for 18 USC §1595, the private right of action in the TVPA, reveals that only twenty-five rulings cited that section in 2015. While almost certainly more than twenty-five cases were brought in 2016 under the private right of action of the TVPA, the section is still undoubtedly underused when compared with the number of criminal prosecutions brought.

[74] *Guobadia v. Irowa*, 103 F. Supp. 3d 325 (EDNY 2015).

The defendants moved for summary judgment before trial, arguing that the plaintiff had not alleged sufficient facts to satisfy the requirements of the TVPA that she suffered serious harm. The Irowas claimed that the plaintiff could leave the house and had often gone to church and the mall with them, and that the plaintiff never filed any complaints or reports with any authorities. The court found that there were sufficient facts alleged by the plaintiff that the case should go to trial and that it could not be dismissed – a victory for the plaintiff at that stage.[75] The district court judge noted that the threats of violence and deportation could satisfy the "serious harm" requirement under the TVPA, and recognized "the fact that the Plaintiff may have been able to come and go as she pleased from the home does not mean the Defendant[s] were not engaging her in unlawful forced labor."[76] Although this case did not ultimately receive a jury verdict that the defendants had trafficked the plaintiff, the district court's interpretation of the TVPA provides an example of the sorts of facts that might constitute a successful civil TVPA case.

CROSS-POLLINATION BETWEEN CIVIL AND CRIMINAL TVPA CASES

Because the civil cause of action in the TVPA relies on the other sections for definitions (requiring "a violation of one of these chapters"), many of the same issues are litigated in both types of cases. For example, as discussed above, the question of what constitutes "serious harm" is routinely challenged by defendants in both criminal and civil matters. Courts then look to both types of cases to see what the legal precedent is or for guidance. In the case of *US v. Kalu* – a criminal case involving a defendant who lured workers to the US to work in nursing homes and forced them to turn over their pay to him – the Tenth Circuit looked to both civil and criminal cases to determine whether it was sufficient for the defendant's threats of serious harm to *cause* a person to labor involuntarily or if those threats must *compel* the labor.[77] The court cited the Ninth Circuit's opinion in a criminal case,[78] a District of Oregon opinion

---

[75] It appears that the parties settled in October of 2015. Doc. #100. Docket Sheet in *Guobadia v. Irowa*, 2:12CV04042 12-cv-4042, EDNY District Court. Available on PACER.

[76] *Guobadia v. Irowa*, 103 F. Supp. 3d at 335.

[77] *United States v. Kalu*, 791 F.3d 1194, 1212 (10th Cir. 2015).

[78] *US v. Dann*, 652 F. 3d 1160, 1169–70 (9th Cir. 2011).

in a civil case,[79] and a famous Eastern District of Louisiana civil case opinion,[80] noting that the law was not on the defendant's side in any of these cases, and in fact, the Louisiana case specifically used causal language in its decision.[81]

This sort of cross-fertilization across civil and criminal areas of law is rare, because criminal law is what we consider "public law" relating to the relationship between individuals and government, while civil law is "private law" that relates to relationship between two individuals. But it illustrates what the slave codes and the Thirteenth Amendment both reveal: upholding or abolishing a system of slavery requires both individual and state action.[82] Chattel slavery depended on public, private, and quasi-public law; slave codes prescribed fines for whites who helped slaves run away, local laws fined masters who did not hire overseers on plantations of a certain size, and slaves who were hired out were subject to the regular rules of contract for rental of property.[83] Now, the TVPA uses civil penalties in the opposite way, allowing trafficked workers to recover damages from the traffickers who made illicit money from their forced labor. The private right of action under the TVPA provides trafficked individuals with the power of the state that was once available to slaveholders prior to the Civil War.

LESSONS FROM HISTORY: WHERE DO WE GO FROM HERE?

The law has now come full circle. From the line-by-line construction of slavery law through the slave codes to the wholesale abolition of the Thirteenth Amendment, Congress has enacted a statute that contains language that more accurately captures the essence of modern slavery by incorporating non-physical and non-legal coercion as a prescribed method of control. I have argued that rather than being historically ignorant by removing references to the Thirteenth Amendment, the TVPA returns to the roots of slavery by recognizing the importance of statutes in defining the boundaries of slavery. The Thirteenth Amendment

---

[79] *Garcia v. Curtright*, 2012 WL 1831865 (D. Or. 1012).

[80] *David v. Signal Int'l, LLC.*, 2012 WL 10759668 (E.D.La. 2012).

[81] *Kalu*, 791 F.3d at 1212.

[82] William M. Carter, Jr., "Race, Rights, and the Thirteenth Amendment: Defining the Badges and Incidents of Slavery," *University of California Davis Law Review* 40, no. 4 (2007), 1311, 1315; Akhil Reed Amar, *Remember the Thirteenth*.

[83] Morris, *Southern Slavery and the Law*, 132; 338; 341.

was a valuable political accomplishment and an essential declaration of freedom, but it also lost its force, and even undermined itself, as slavery adapted itself around the abolition of legal, chattel slavery. So now that we have a robust antislavery statute, what can historians do to keep the history of slavery playing a useful role in ending modern-day trafficking?

I have two suggestions along these lines. First, we need to put pressure on local, state, and federal executive branches to allocate more resources to the criminal prosecution of traffickers and to *pro bono* representation of workers who want to sue their traffickers civilly. Second, modern antislavery activists should avoid metaphors and symbols that equate modern trafficking with chattel slavery.

Increasing resources for trafficked persons to bring lawsuits against their traffickers, or for the state or federal government to pursue criminal penalties against traffickers, would help immensely in the fight against slavery, as the law is dramatically under-enforced. There have been very few civil lawsuits filed by plaintiffs who claim they were trafficked against their alleged traffickers. One non-profit organization reports that plaintiffs have filed only 152 civil lawsuits since the TVPA established this cause of action in 2003.[84] Many obstacles remain for potential plaintiffs: finding and paying for an attorney, other litigation costs, courts that are unfamiliar with these new claims, and the psychological stress of reliving a traumatic time in the plaintiff's life. Thankfully, there are non-profit organizations working to increase victims' ability to bring civil lawsuits under the TVPA.[85]

The Department of Justice (DOJ) the federal agency responsible for enforcing federal criminal laws – investigates and prosecutes individuals and gangs that engage in human trafficking.[86] The DOJ can seek an indictment and conviction of human traffickers under the laws discussed above, including the anti-peonage statute, the involuntary servitude statute, the Thirteenth Amendment, and the TVPA, each of which

---

[84] Martina E. Vandenberg, "Ending Impunity, Securing Justice: Using Strategic Litigation to Combat Human Trafficking and Modern-Day Slavery," *The Human Trafficking Pro Bono Legal Center and The Freedom Fund* (2016), 13, www.htprobono.org/wp-content/uploads/2015/12/FF_SL_AW02_WEB.pdf.

[85] See the work of the Human Trafficking Pro Bono Legal Center, which "link[s] trafficking victims with highly-skilled pro bono attorneys" to "obtain criminal convictions, criminal restitution, and civil judgment against traffickers," www.htprobono.org/.

[86] The Human Trafficking Prosecution Unit is based in the Civil Rights Division of the Department of Justice. The United States Department of Justice, *Human Trafficking Prosecution Unit*, www.justice.gov/crt/human-trafficking-prosecution-unit-htpu.

require the prosecutor to prove different facts for each law. Through two specialized offices based in Washington, DC, as well as the many United States Attorney Offices throughout the country, the DOJ now prosecutes hundreds of defendants per year under human trafficking laws. The DOJ did not always have such a robust enforcement record. In 2001, the DOJ prosecuted only ten cases of human trafficking.[87] In 2014, the DOJ prosecuted 208 federal human trafficking cases involving 335 defendants.[88] Of those cases, 184 ended with convictions.[89]

Most of these prosecutions are for sex trafficking crimes. Of the 253 defendants prosecuted by the DOJ, through the United States Attorney Offices for human trafficking in 2013, 222 were prosecuted for sex trafficking, while only 31 were prosecuted for labor trafficking.[90] The Civil Rights division prosecuted an additional 71 defendants, with 53 for sex trafficking and 18 for labor trafficking.[91] A federal prosecutor in the District of Connecticut indicated that there are a few reasons this disparity exists. First and most important is limited resources and the need to triage investigations and prosecutions. There are too few prosecutors, investigators, and victim advocates to undertake additional prosecutions. Because of this, the United States Attorney for a particular district must prioritize. Sex trafficking may take priority because it is connected with other crimes, like drug trafficking and gang violence, that the Office is prosecuting. Prosecuting sex trafficking of children also takes priority in that Office because of the horrific nature of the crime.[92] Finally, labor trafficking might be covered by other agencies, like state labor departments and the federal Department of Labor, which have their own investigative and law enforcement arms.[93]

Adding to the problem of lack of resources to enforce the law is a lack of clarity as to what the provisions of the antislavery statutes mean.

[87] Carr et al., *Human Trafficking Law and Policy*, 213.
[88] United States Department of State, *Trafficking in Persons Report* (2014), 353, www .state.gov/documents/organization/243562.pdf (hereinafter TIP Report).
[89] Ibid.
[90] TIP Report, 398.
[91] Ibid.
[92] Personal interview with David Novick, Assistant US Attorney for the District of Connecticut, November 25, 2015: "The United States should look to places like Brazil that are taking a forward approach to ending modern slavery by drastically increasing regulation and enforcement." See, e.g., "Brazil: History, Human Rights, and Contemporary Slavery Panel II," November 1, 2013, Ann Arbor, Michigan, http://web .law.umich.edu/flashmedia/public/Default.aspx?mediaid=3745.
[93] Carr et al., 221–2.

Of course, courts must look to the text of the statute, prior cases, and common sense about what particular language means. But this process occurs in the context of a factually specific case – the prosecutors must have already decided, based on prior court decisions and their reading of the statutes and the facts before them, to bring a criminal prosecution based on what they know about an alleged trafficker. In a criminal trial, the jury is instructed on the law based on the criminal statute and the case law interpreting that statute. The fewer cases that are brought and provoke a court to write some sort of decision, the less the law gets developed and the less likely it is that the jury will be instructed on the law in a way that is most analogous to a new type of case. Similarly, in a civil case, a lawyer seeking to prove a civil TVPA claim must survive a number of attempts by the defendant to dismiss the case, and may only survive if the facts of their case seem strong enough compared to prior similar cases. Again, the more diversity of cases that are brought and tried, the more the law will develop, and the clearer the statutes will become.

SYMBOLS

The path from early slavery law to these recent prosecutions and civil lawsuits was not predictable. From a hodgepodge of state laws upholding slavery – supported by an agnostic federal government – to a broad abolition constitutional Amendment, to three successive Congressional statutes criminalizing peonage (passed in 1867), involuntary servitude (1948), and forced labor (2000), the state of the law over time reflects the complexity of slavery. This dynamic complexity is what makes slavery so enduring: the ability to profit from the bodies of other people without paying them, using coercion to keep them working for you, is a proven business model. But this similarity can lead to problematic results, if not discussed carefully.

As many parallels as historians perceive between past and present – and there are many – it is important as a matter of legal strategy to avoid drawing comparisons too neatly. A quick review of the statutes and case law confirms why: the TVPA was enacted in response to the Supreme Court in the *late twentieth century*, looking to the practice of chattel slavery for the legal standard of what force and coercion was required for a person to be enslaved. Later, Congress specifically changed the law so that prosecutors and civil advocates did not have to prove the level of physical and legal coercion that corresponded with chattel slavery.

Continually drawing parallels between modern and chattel slavery is antithetical to the state of our current law because it reinforces the idea that slavery requires physical force. Such a comparison subtly undermines the great strides that we as a nation have taken in understanding the complexity of modern slavery.

That said, the legal advocates I spoke with were not concerned with the actual legal effect of importing ideas about chattel slavery into modern advocacy. Public perception of slavery actually has very little to do with the outcome of cases; that is, it is not as if someone's Uncle Fred or Aunt Beatrice sits on a jury and refuses to convict a trafficker because he or she believes a victim of trafficking must be picking cotton in chains. The fact is that many criminal cases never are presented to the public. Most criminal cases end with the defendant pleading guilty; the charges are never brought to trial and many are not even challenged through pretrial motions. A criminal defense attorney would advise a criminal defendant on the elements of the crime based on the existing law, and based on that standard of law and what the client understood his or her behavior to be, the client would decide whether or not to plead guilty or not guilty to the charges. If the defendant chose to plead guilty, the specific reasons why the defendant chose to do so, or any detailed information about the charged conduct of that defendant, would not become part of the law defining human trafficking. The advocates I spoke with did applaud efforts to educate law enforcement and other public servants, who are often in the best position to recognize trafficking and channel the information to the proper authorities. To a lesser degree, public awareness campaigns more generally have also proven helpful in generating leads for law enforcement to follow.

But overall, law enforcement and the civil and criminal justice system operate outside the world of public perception. What matters is case law, and prosecutors and judges have the greatest effect on what cases are brought and what decisions are written. Getting prosecutors and civil attorneys into court with cases seeking enforcement of the TVPA would be the most effective way to create change in the law to reflect the historical and modern reality of slavery. And in a world of limited resources, every dollar donated to "raising awareness" rather than funding law enforcement efforts or supporting civil attorneys' *pro bono* work is a dollar that is less effective than most antislavery advocates would imagine, if the ultimate goal is to have a functioning law enforcement system that supports our shared goal of abolition.

CONCLUSIONS: THE HISTORIANS AND THE
LAWYERS

As this review of slavery law from pro-slavery jurisprudence to the Thirteenth Amendment to modern trafficking legislation has shown, history and the work of historians has played an important role in the development of modern antislavery law by providing content to the meaning of "slavery" in the Thirteenth Amendment and subsequent legislation. In some instances, the work has been a direct boon to the progressive jurisprudence, helping courts recognize that even in the purest forms of chattel slavery, slaves performed non-economic work that was integral to their enslavement. If there is one thing that historians can do to further develop antislavery jurisprudence that captures the wide range of slaveries experienced in America today, it would be to continue the exploration of the wide range of slaveries experienced in America's past. While prosecutors may not be able to point out the similarities to a jury, and courts are not required to look at historical analysis when interpreting the TVPA, direct historical comparison may be useful in limited cases when – as in *US v. Kaufman* – the specific facts of a particular present-day case are closely related to a practice used in chattel slavery. Such a comparison would not be legally determinative, but could aid a court in interpreting the TVPA, and be useful to prosecutors in rebutting any defenses based on chattel slavery that a defendant might make. However, historians should avoid making sweeping analogies or comparisons between past and present that erase the important nuances of both forms of slavery.

Ultimately, abolishing modern slavery in practice will require a robust law enforcement regime, based on nuanced and historically informed statutory and case law, paired with zealous civil advocacy under the TVPA. Without state and private enforcement of the law that makes trafficking too expensive or incarcerates traffickers, traffickers will continue to profit off the forced labor of others. Raising awareness simply will not stop traffickers. And comparing modern slavery to historical chattel slavery can be legally counterproductive when cases do make it to court, if the comparison is not narrowly tailored. Everyone deserves to live in a world, and especially a nation, free from forced labor and the other practices of modern slavery – and we should demand that our state and federal governments ensure freedom for all as the law requires.

PART II

FORMS OF SLAVERY, PAST AND PRESENT

4

Kidnappers and Subcontractors

Historical Perspectives on Human Trafficking

John Donoghue*

The vast majority of the millions enslaved on the plantations of the Atlantic world descended from the African peoples of the Congo, the Gold Coast, and the Senegambia. But until the late 1650s, most of those who labored in chains in the English West Indies hailed from Britain and Ireland; the same would be true in the Chesapeake until the 1680s.[1] Classified in colonial law as "negroes" – a category that became synonymous with perpetual, hereditary bondage, Africans in the Atlantic world suffered systematic enslavement in the seventeenth century. In contrast, except in rare cases involving criminal punishment, English colonial courts did not sanction lifelong bondage for "Christian" workers

* The author would like to thank Historians Against Slavery (HAS), especially the editors of this series. He would also like to thank HAS's founder and series editor James Brewer Stewart for his tireless efforts to promote the cause of human freedom as a scholar and as an abolitionist. Jim's keen editorial eye also improved this article from its original, deficient state. The author also thanks Shamere McKenzie, Stacy Jewell Lewis, Kevin Bales, Kenneth Morris, and Robert Benz for their invaluable contributions to modern abolitionism and for their friendship and camaraderie. The author owes a debt of gratitude to the students of Hist 300: Slavery and Abolition Then and Now (Spring 2015, Loyola University Chicago) for helping to inspire this chapter, and then Loyola students (and now alums) Stephanie Tomazin and Natalie Fouty for reading and commenting on it, and for contributing to the vibrancy of the abolitionist movement at Loyola. Finally, and as always, my most important thanks go to Laura, Norah, and Meredith, who make everything possible.
[1] For colonial migration statistics, see David Galenson, *White Servitude in Colonial America: An Economic Analysis* (Cambridge: Cambridge University Press, 1984), 216–18, Tables H3 and H4. It has been estimated that a total of 125,271 people migrated out of England between 1651 and 1661. Besides the colonies, most left for Ireland or the European mainland. See E. A. Wrigley and R. S. Schofield, *The Population History of England, 1541–1871: A Reconstruction* (Cambridge: Cambridge University Press, 1981), 227.

from Europe.[2] But while colonial law limited their time as chattels, many European servants, most of them from Britain and Ireland, left this life in bondage; conservative assessments, both contemporary and historical, estimate that about a third or more of them died in term.[3] Moreover, most of these "indentured servants" did not voyage "beyond the seas" voluntarily. Tricked or forced aboard ships in British and Irish ports, they were trafficked to the Chesapeake and the West Indies to hoe tobacco and cut sugar cane.[4] Indeed, in the mid seventeenth century, the word "kidnap" entered the English language to describe how servant recruiters lured or strong-armed young people onto blue water ships, where they were sold into a future of chattel servitude. After crossing the Atlantic to be sold once again in the colonies, they were forced into labor that produced profitable cash crops for export around the Atlantic world and beyond. Other terms besides kidnap were minted – "spirit," "inveigle," "trepan," and even "Barbados" – all described the deceit and violence that had become endemic to the servant recruitment regime. The new language, as we now understand, became necessary to describe one of merchant capitalism's most sordid seventeenth-century innovations: a transatlantic human trafficking network that sent chattel labor from Europe to the colonies to produce commodities for a rapidly globalizing market.[5]

The invention of colonial servitude in seventeenth-century English colonies was a striking moment in the history of capitalism. It forged the first link in a transatlantic chain of human bondage, one that would lengthen through time, expanding from chattel servitude to racial slavery in what would become the world's largest slave-holding empire. But for many of those who endured it, plantation servitude was "slavery," a term

[2] Michael Guasco, *Slaves and Englishmen: Human Bondage in the Early Modern Atlantic World* (Philadelphia, PA: University of Pennsylvania Press, 2014), 157–8. In an earlier review of this book, I criticized Guasco's treatment of the slave trade in terms that I now recognize as overdrawn and unfair. Readers of *Slaves and Englishmen* will discover that Guasco has done more than any other scholar to uncover the roots of early modern English concepts of slavery.

[3] For servant mortality, see Theodore W. Allen, *The Invention of the White Race: The Origin of Racial Oppression in Anglo-America*, 2 vols. (New York: Verso, 1997), 2: 123, n. 41; 143, n. 180; George Gardnyer, *A Description of the New World; or, America Islands and Continent* (1651; Gale Sabine America, 2012), 99.

[4] For kidnapping's prevalence in the servant trade, see John Wareing, "'Violently Taken Away or Cheatingly Duckoyed': The Illicit Recruitment in London of Indentured Servants for the American Colonies, 1645–1718," *London Journal* 26, no. 2 (2001), 1–22; John Donoghue, "'Out of the Land of Bondage': The English Revolution and the Atlantic Origins of Abolition," *The American Historical Review* 115, no. 4 (October 2010), 960–1, 968–9, 970.

[5] The earliest use of "kidnap" dates to 1672. See Susan Amussen, *Caribbean Exchanges: Slavery and the Transformation of English Society, 1640–1700* (Chapel Hill, NC: University of North Carolina Press, 2007), 87.

contemporaries used with conceptual precision to describe the condition that resulted from being stolen and sold as chattel labor in the colonies. The use of "slavery" to describe plantation servitude was not, as some historians have argued, simply an exaggerated, rhetorical flourish borrowed from the lexicon of English political and popular culture to describe an oppressive situation.[6] Other historians have been more perceptive. As Eric Williams first argued over half a century ago in *Capitalism and Slavery*, chattel servitude laid the foundation for racialized slavery in the English Atlantic.[7] But the commodification of servants into chattel property did not begin, as Williams argued, in England's plantation colonies. Fashioned by merchants, planters, colonial governments, and the imperial state, the process by which servants were rendered into chattel property began in British and Irish ports, took shape aboard ships on the Atlantic itself, and came to completion in the colonies. Much like the transatlantic slave trade from Africa, human beings ensnared in the servant trade were sold and resold several times before being purchased by a colonial planter. Make no mistake, however; comparisons between the servant and slave trade should never conflate the two in terms of volume, profitability, duration, depth of human suffering, and lasting legacy. We should stress the crucial differences in these categories to emphasize the greater horrors and historical importance of the slave trade.[8] At the

[6] For contemporary references to servants/servitude as slaves/slavery, see John Cordy Jeafferson, ed., *Middlesex County Records*, Volume III (Middlesex County Records Society, 1888), 306; 336, available at *Hathi Trust Digital Library*, https://catalog.hathitrust.org/Record/000153663; Susan Myra Kingsbury, *Records of the Virginia Company of London* (Washington, DC: Government Printing Office, 1906), 4, available at *Library of Congress*, https://archive.org/details/recordsofvirginio2virguoft, 235; William Bullock, *Virginia Impartially Examined* (London: John Hammond, 1649), 13–14, 47, available at *Early English Books Online Text Creation Partnership*, http://quod.lib.umich.edu/cgi/t/text/text-idx?c=eebo;idno=A30076.0001.001; Charles Bayly, *A Faithful Testimony and Warning* (London, 1672), 8–9, available at *Early English Books Online Text Creation Partnership*, http://quod.lib.umich.edu/e/eebo2/A27126.0001.001?view=toc; Charles Bayly, *The Banner of Truth Displayed; or, A Testimony for Christ, and against Anti-Christ* (London, 1656), A2, 90; Lionel Gatford, *Publick Good without Private Interest* (London, 1657), 4–5; Ligon, *A True and Exact History of the Island of Barbados* (1657; Indianapolis, IN: Hackett Publishing, 2011), 43–4. Quotation from Susan Dwyer Amussen, *Caribbean Exchanges: Slavery and the Transformation of English Society, 1640–1700* (Chapel Hill, NC: The University of North Carolina Press, 2007), 129.

[7] Eric Williams, *Capitalism and Slavery* (Chapel Hill, NC: University of North Carolina Press, 1944); Simon Newman, *A New World of Labor: The Development of Plantation Slavery in the British Atlantic* (Philadelphia, PA: University of Pennsylvania Press, 2013); Hilary Beckles, *White Servitude and Black Slavery in Barbados, 1627–1715* (Knoxville, TN: University of Tennessee Press, 1989).

[8] Unfortunately, white supremacists have distorted the history of servitude's links with slavery, twisting the past beyond recognition to pursue their own racist, political ends. In sum, they argue that calls for racial justice today have no historical credibility, as both

same time, by looking at them together, we can see how multiple human trafficking networks wove circuits through Europe, Africa, and the colonies. These circuits for the trade in servants and slaves performed a historic task of lasting significance. They fused the *chattel* principle into the Atlantic economy as an *organizing* principle, one designed for the exploitation of multiple kinds of unfree labor in the English plantation complex. The design proved profitable, creating a lucrative catalyst that helped fuel the expansion of global capitalism in the early modern era.[9]

It is important to remember, however, that profits from human trafficking in the seventeenth century did not flow unopposed. The period witnessed the formation of abolitionist movements aimed at both the servant and slave trade, although it will be the servant trade that will detain us here. Popular outrage in Britain and Ireland, expressed through forms ranging from mob violence to Parliamentary petitions, made the imperial state aware of kidnapping's prevalence. The state launched several rounds of investigations into the servant trade in the mid seventeenth century but refused after a decade of Parliamentary bill readings and committee meetings to make the practice a felony. But despite this legislative failure, the resistance to kidnapping still matters historically, as it sheds light on evolving notions of freedom and slavery in the early modern Atlantic world. And as I will explain at the end of the chapter, studying kidnapping in the seventeenth century can provide us with historical perspectives on how human trafficking networks operate today.

whites and blacks suffered from slavery; many white supremacists even claim that whites, particularly the Irish, suffered worse than Africans.

On the other hand, in an article in the *New West Indian Guide* 91, no. 1 (Summer 2017), Jerome Handler and Matthew Reilly have attacked historians Hilary Beckles and Simon Newman (cited below) for arguing that the chattel principle of servitude made it a form of slavery (pp. 30, 26). Handler and Reilly believe that Beckles and Newman's scholarship works to the same end as the online ravings of white supremacists: to "minimize or discount the historical experiences and conditions of enslaved Africans," and to reject calls for reparations in the present. The charge is absurd on its face, but for the record, it should be noted that Hilary Beckles is a leader in the slavery reparations movement. See Beckles's book, *Britain's Black Debt: Reparations for Genocide: Reparations for Caribbean Slavery and Native Genocide* (Kingston, JM: University of West Indies Press, 2013).

[9] As Immanuel Wallerstein has written, it should be "questioned whether [wage labor] has been even the majority mode within historical capitalism ... It is surely not clear that in the history of the world there has been less slavery within the capitalist/'modern' historical system than in previous ones. One might perhaps make the opposite case." For the quotation, see Wallerstein's "The West, Capitalism, and the Modern World-System," *Review* 15 (Fall 1992), 561–95, esp. 575–6.

Tragically, comparisons between the past and present reveal that economic interests have consistently trumped popular outrage, perversely creating the political will to sustain rather than to end human trafficking.

Human trafficking took on many forms in the early modern Atlantic economy. Colonists and Amerindians in the Carolina Low Country carried on a brisk slave trade in the late seventeenth and early eighteenth centuries.[10] As Greg O'Malley has recently demonstrated, an inter-colonial slave trade connected the Caribbean to the eastern North American seaboard.[11] Although both of these forms of human trafficking were relatively expansive and lucrative, the transatlantic slave trade from Africa clearly mattered most when measured in terms of volume, profitability, and historical significance.[12] But the fact that racial slavery and slave trading in all of its forms served as a murderous yet legal linchpin of profitability begs the question as to why another, illicit form of human trafficking, the kidnapping of young British and Irish people into chattel servitude, persisted in the seventeenth-century English Atlantic.

An important part of the answer exists in the fierce competition between European states for profits in the African slave trade. Portugal and Spain dominated the Atlantic slave trade well into the seventeenth century. The Dutch emerged as a competitive slave trading empire by the mid seventeenth century, fueled by merchants from Amsterdam and other Dutch cities who acquired *asientos* (slave trading licenses) to conduct commerce in Iberian American markets. But such commercial inroads were not enough for the Dutch, who also turned to the forcible conquest of fortified Portuguese slave trading installations on the West African coast called "factories" or castles. Forces from the United Provinces conducted

---

[10] Allan Gallay, *The Indian Slave Trade: The Rise of the English Empire in the American South, 1670–1717* (New Haven, CT: Yale University Press, 2003).

[11] Greg O'Malley, *Final Passages: The Intercolonial Slave Trade of British America, 1619–1807* (Chapel Hill, NC: University of North Carolina Press, 2014).

[12] For the transatlantic slave trade, see Joseph C. Miller, *Way of Death: Merchant Capitalism and the Angolan Slave Trade, 1730–1830* (Madison, WI: University of Wisconsin Press, 1988); Marcus Rediker, *The Slave Ship: A Human History* (Boston, MA: Beacon Press, 2007); Stephanie Smallwood, *Saltwater Slavery: A Middle Passage from Africa to American Diaspora* (Cambridge, MA: Harvard University Press, 2007). For statistical research on the slave trade, see David Eltis, David Richardson, Stephen D. Behrendt, and Herbert Klein, eds., *The Atlantic Slave Trade: A Database on CD-ROM Set and Guide* (New York: Cambridge University Press, 1999, 2010, 2016).

these campaigns through the combined military might of the Dutch state and the Dutch West Indian Company. Indeed, the goal of persuading the Iberian empires to open a "free trade in slaves" by force of arms figured prominently among the causes that brought the Atlantic empires into a series of seemingly incessant, early modern imperial wars.[13] England, the European power that most concerns us here, eventually became the Atlantic's premier slave trading empire, but only after three costly mid-seventeenth-century wars with the Dutch (ca. 1652–76), decades of piratical pillaging on the Spanish Main, and a decisive victory in the War of Spanish Succession (1713) through which they gained the *asiento* for a free trade in slaves in Spanish America.

Besides lagging behind in the early slave trade, the English also faced other problems which impeded the rapid expansion of racialized slavery in their plantation colonies. In the Chesapeake, the enslaved population expanded slowly, as only a small number of elite Tidewater planters had accumulated enough capital by the 1650s to afford slaves, who were more expensive than servants since their labor could be exploited for a longer period. The market for slaves in the Chesapeake would not mature until the late seventeenth century, when the transatlantic trade surged in the 1690s, due in part to the end of the Royal African Company's monopoly.[14] Things were different in the West Indies, however, where English capital investment and profits from sugar were higher than what they were in the Chesapeake. Led by Barbados, England's Caribbean colonies enjoyed a profitable boom that commenced in the early 1640s. As early as 1643, there were six thousand black slaves on Barbados, most of them forced to work for planters who had or would soon transition from tobacco to sugar production.[15] For the next three decades, English

[13] Pepijn Brandon and Karwan Fatah Black, "'For the Reputation and Respectability of the State': Trade, the Imperial State, Unfree Labor, and Empire in the Dutch Atlantic," in John Donoghue and Evelyn Jennings, eds., *Building the Atlantic Empires: Unfree Labor and Imperial States in the Political Economy of Capitalism* (Leiden: Brill, 2015), 84–108.

[14] J. C. Coombs, "The Phases of Conversion: A New Chronology for the Rise of Slavery in Early Virginia," *William and Mary Quarterly* 68, no. 3 (2011), 332–60; L. S. Walsh, *Motives of Honor, Pleasure and Profit: Plantation Management in the Colonial Chesapeake, 1607–1763* (Chapel Hill, NC: University of North Carolina Press, 2010), chs. 2–4; Anthony Parent, *Foul Means: The Formation of a Slave Society in Virginia, 1660–1740* (Chapel Hill, NC: University of North Carolina Press, 2003), ch. 2; William Pettigrew, *Freedom's Debt: The Royal African Company and the Politics of the Politics of the Atlantic Slave Trade, 1672–1752* (Chapel Hill, NC: University of North Carolina, 2013).

[15] Russell Menard, *Sweet Negotiations: Sugar, Slavery and Plantation Agriculture in Barbados* (Charlottesville, VA: University of Virginia Press, 2006, 2014), 31.

pirates, private English traders, and the English Guinea Company began competing with the Dutch West India Company to supply English colonies with slaves, the demand for which only increased when England forcibly took Jamaica from the Spanish in 1655. England's Royal African Company (RAC), with heavy investment from the Crown, gained the largest share of the English slave trade for the rest of the century, although the RAC and its English and Dutch competitors rarely ventured as far north as the Chesapeake, a long, costly trip to a region where profits were less readily made.[16] Thus, throughout the seventeenth century, the demand for servants remained high in Virginia and Maryland. It did as well in the West Indies, where the hunger for unfree labor still outpaced the ever-growing supply provided by the transatlantic African slave trade due to the high mortality rates of both servants and slaves.[17]

How did English interests meet the trade gap between the supply and demand for unfree colonial labor? The state transported rebels, felons, and the poor to alleviate colonial labor shortages and to "vent," in the words of English social commentators, socially volatile, fiscally expensive, and politically seditious people out of the Three Kingdoms.[18] State transportation, however, could not close the colonial trade gap in unfree labor. The servant trade came much closer to doing so. Organized by merchants, planters, and colonial assemblies, those trafficking in servants shipped approximately 276,000 of the 345,000 European migrants (or about 80 percent of the total migrant population) who came to the West Indies and Chesapeake from Britain and Ireland during the seventeenth century.[19] That profit in the Chesapeake depended on servant labor

[16] Larry Gragg, "To Procure Negroes: The English Slave Trade to Barbados, 1627–1660," *Slavery and Abolition* 16, no. 1 (1995), 65–84; Nuala Zahedieh, "The Merchants of Port Royal, Jamaica, and the Spanish Contraband Trade, 1655–1692," *William and Mary Quarterly*, 3rd Series, 43, no. 4 (1996), 570–93; "Trade, Plunder, and Economic Development in Early English Jamaica, 1655–1689," *Economic History Review* 39, no. 2 (1986), 205–22; Pettigrew, *Freedom's Debt*.

[17] Newman, *A New World of Labor: The Development of Plantation Slavery in the British Atlantic* (Philadelphia, PA: University of Pennsylvania Press, 2013), ch. 4; Trevor Burnard, *Planters, Merchants, and Slaves: Plantation Societies in British America, 1650–1820* (Chicago, IL: University of Chicago Press, 2015), 62, 116, 123, 144.

[18] John Donoghue, "The Unfree Origins of English Empire-Building in the Seventeenth Century Atlantic," in Donoghue and Jennings, eds., *Building the Atlantic Empires*, 109–131; Gwenda Morgan and Peter Rushton, *Banishment in the Early Atlantic World: Convicts, Rebels, and Slaves* (New York: Bloomsbury, 2013), Part I.

[19] Christopher Tomlins, *Freedom Bound: Law, Labor, and Civic Identity in Colonizing English America, 1580–1865* (New York: Cambridge University Press, 2010), 32–8 (including FN 31–4), Appendix 1, 571–6; John McCusker and Russell Menard, *The Economy of British America* (Chapel Hill, NC: University of North Carolina Press, 1991),

registered as far back as 1619, the outset of the tobacco boom, when
Secretary John Pory informed the Virginia Company directors that "our
principal wealth ... consisteth in servants."[20] In the Caribbean, even as
slave imports soared, an English newcomer, Lt. Col. Francis Barrington,
observed in 1655 that the "livelihood" of Barbados' planters depended on
the labor of indentured workers: "their whole estates," Barrington wrote,
"lay in the good stock of servants."[21] The Barbados Assembly declared
in the preface to its servant code of 1661 that "much of the interest and
substance of this island consists in the servants brought to, and disposed
of in the same, and in their labour during the term."[22] But by 1668, in
the wake of England's increased share in the transatlantic slave trade
and the spoils of buccaneering raids on the Spanish Main, where pirates
carried away slaves to sell to Caribbean planters, the Barbados Assembly
could declare that "the wealth of this island consists in our negroe slaves,
without whose labour and service we should be utterly unable to manage
our plantations here."[23] The shifting demography of the unfree plantation workforce is telling. Before the terrible transformation to racialized
slavery, indentured servitude figured centrally in the interrelated set of
capitalist enterprises that made the early English plantation complex a
juggernaut of economic growth. But how did these migrants, most in their
adolescence or early twenties, get to the colonies? How, in other words,
was the transatlantic servant trade organized? Who was organizing it?
And for whose benefit? The answers to these questions lead us into the
parlors of colonial planters and the plush offices of wealthy merchants,
through the doors of lurid, reeking waterfront dives, and down the into
the cramped and creaking holds of the sloops, brigs, and ships riding at
anchor in maritime Britain and Ireland.

The servant trade relied upon kidnappers, or "spirits" and
"trepanners," as they were also known, who worked as free agents or on

---

136; Russell Menard, "British Migration to the Chesapeake Colonies in the Seventeenth
Century," in L. G. Carr, P. D. Morgan, and J. B. Russo, eds., *Colonial Chesapeake Society*
(Chapel Hill, NC: University of North Carolina Press, 1988), 99–132, esp. 100–3; H. A.
Gemery, "Emigration from the British Isles to the New World, 1630–1700: Inferences
from Colonial Populations," in P. Uselding, ed., *Research in Economic History: A
Research Annual*, Volume 5 (1980), 179–233, esp. 197.

[20] Pory quoted in Allen, *The Invention of the White Race*, 2: 95.
[21] British Library Egerton Mss 2648 fol. 245.
[22] *An Act for the Good Governing of Servants, and Ordering the Rights between Masters
and Servants* (September 27, 1661) in *Barbados Slave Laws*, 22.
[23] *An Act Declaring Negro Slaves of this Island to be Real Estate* (1668), in *Barbados Slave
Laws*, 63.

commission to procure and sell unwitting people, mostly teenagers and those in their early twenties, to merchants, planters, and sea captains. The methods through which they worked were unsavory to say the least; for example, the word kidnap is a corruption of the conjunction of "kid" and "nab" – a term to denote somebody who steals children. Although there were petitions against fraudulent recruiting for colonial laborers as early as 1618, the problem became urgent in the early 1640s, as voluntary migration across the Atlantic slowed due to the advent of the English Revolution and Civil Wars.[24] The military mobilization for these conflicts decreased the supply of unfree colonial labor, but at the same time, the demand for it increased in the colonies as the sugar boom exploded in the Caribbean and tobacco production expanded in the Chesapeake. The grasping hands of kidnappers, and not the alleged invisible hand of the market mechanism, recalibrated the balance between supply and demand in the transatlantic servant trade. Parliament began receiving petitions in the early 1640s about "divers lewd persons (who) go up and down the City of London and elsewhere and in a most barbarous and wicked manner steal away little children."[25] To "steal away young children," these "lewd persons" had to "intice (them) ... to convey them shipboard, to be conveyed to the plantations beyond the seas."[26] As Parliament noted in a 1647 discussion of this practice, "those that take up children in the streets ... are commonly called by the name spirits."[27] The word spirit in this case functioned as a noun. But spirit could also serve as a verb. To "spirit away" something is to carry it away. "Spirit" thus served in the lexicon of the servant trade to describe the shadowy and elusive means by which predators would take "up men and women and children and sells them a-ship to be conveyed beyond the sea," the quotation here deriving from an accusation made against Dorothy Perkins in 1655 for selling her captives to the captain of the *The Planter*, bound for Virginia.[28]

[24] W. N. Sainsbury, "Kidnapping Maidens, to be Sold in Virginia, 1618," *The Virginia Magazine of History and Biography* 6, no. 3 (1899), 228–30; Carla Pestana, *The English Atlantic in an Age of Revolution* (Cambridge, MA: Harvard University Press), 183.

[25] C. H. Firth and R. S. Rait, eds., *Acts and Ordinances of the Interregnum*, 2 vols. (London, 1911), 1: 681–2.

[26] John Cordy Jeafferson, ed., *Middlesex County Records*, Volumes III and IV: *1649–59* (London: Middlesex County Records Society, 1888), 3: 181 [hereafter *Middlesex County Records*, 3].

[27] *Middlesex County Records*, 3: 184.

[28] Ibid., 3: 239.

Spirits and kidnappers succeeded because they discovered how best to "betray" their prey with false but alluring promises.[29] With children, the betrayal could be especially poignant. In London locales such as Moorefields, Londoners gathered to cavort, play, wager, and roughhouse, indulging in wrestling matches and games of archery and lawn bowling. Kidnappers gathered there as well, since that's where the children were. In Moorefields, spirits "entice(d)" children "by promising them cakes" to gorge aboard ships riding on the Stepney waterfront in lavish feasts that would never come pass.[30] Teens and young adults could also be tempted with talk of high wages in the colonies. At Katherine's Stairs near the Tower of London, a kidnapper tried to lure young Katherine Penn into an Atlantic crossing with the lie that she would make £6 sterling per year as a colonial servant; Penn fortunately escaped her would-be captor either aboard the ship or within sight of it. Had she not freed herself, we most likely would never have heard of the fate of Katherine Penn.[31]

One can only speculate as to the exact nature of the "flattering and great promises" that the accused spirit William Stowne made to George Creek and Thomas Riddle. "He got them to yield and go with him to a ship, where he left them to be transported to Virginia."[32] While we can't be sure in this case, certainly "lewd" spirits, as they were often characterized, would have lured adolescent boys with spurious promises of alcohol and beautiful girls. Fantastical promises of merchant apprenticeships in the colonies proved attractive as well. Through artful questioning, spirits tried to discern the occupational interests of their targets; once they had, pledges to secure places for skilled and literate migrants tempted those of poor means but soaring aspirations. Moved by false spirits, young men seeking such work would take an often fatal plunge for a position "beyond the seas" that would never materialize.[33] Thomas Hellier's experience with indentured servitude in the Virginia Tidewater is instructive in this regard. In September of 1677, Hellier, a stationer by training, was in search of work having fallen into debt after

---

[29] Ibid., 3: 259.
[30] John Wareing, "'Violently Taken Away or Cheatingly Duckoyed': The Illicit Recruitment in London of Indentured Servants for the American Colonies, 1645–1718," *London Journal* 26, no. 2 (2001), 1–22, citation on p. 3.
[31] *Middlesex County Records*, 3: 99–100.
[32] Ibid., 3: 315.
[33] Wareing, "'Violently Taken Away or Cheatingly Duckoyed,'" 3, 7.

wasting his small inheritance. Repairing to the Eagle and Childe pub near the Tower of London, he

enquired if there were any Ship-Captain quartered there? one replied, There was no Ship-Captain quartered in that house, but that he himself was concern'd about Sea-faring matters. I enquired to what parts he was concerned? he answered, To Virginia: So asked withal, if I were minded for that Country; if I were, I should have Meat, Drink, and Apparel, with other Necessaries provided for me. I replied, I had heard so bad a character of that Country, that I dreaded going thither, in regard I abhorred the Ax and the Haw. He told me, he would promise I should be onely employ'd in Merchants Accompts, and such Employments to which I had been bred, if they were here used.

When Hellier was sold to a planter in Virginia, he did not sit down at a desk to work with ledgers. He was forced to take up the very tools he "abhorred[,] the Ax and the Haw" – to work in the steaming tobacco fields of the Tidewater.[34] Instead of sympathizing with them, patrician commentators harboring desultory views of the poor and vulnerable often blamed kidnapping on its victims. In 1649, the Virginia colonist William Bullock wrote that

a sort of men nicknamed spirits ... take up all the idle lazy simple people they can entice such as have professed idleness and would rather beg than work and are persuaded by these spirits that they shall go into a place where food will drop into their mouths: and being thus deluded, they take courage and are transported.[35]

But the runaway teenager Charles Baily was not lazy or idle; he was hungry and homeless and wandering the docks at Gravesend, the port town on the River Thames that served as the embarkation point for the English Channel and the Atlantic itself. There Baily "fell into a discourse" with a man named "Bradstreet ... commonly called a 'spirit,' for he was one of those who did entice children and people away for Virginia ... and I being in tender years, he did cunningly get me on board a ship, which was then there riding ready for to go to those parts, and I being once on board, could never get on shore."[36] When the colonial promoter George

---

[34] T. H. Breen, James H. Lewis, and Keith Schlesinger, "Motive for Murder: A Servant's Life in Virginia, 1678," *William and Mary Quarterly* 40, no. 1 (1983), 106–20, quotation on p. 111. See *The Vain Prodigal Life, and Tragical Penitent Death of Thomas Hellier* (London, 1680) for the source that gave rise to this article.

[35] William Bullock, *Virginia Impartially Examined and Left to Public View* (London, 1649), 14.

[36] Charles Baily, *A True and Faithful Warning unto the People and Inhabitants of Bristol* (London, 1663), 8.

Gardyner wrote in 1651 that those accosted by spirits were "barbarously stolen out of their own country," he was not exaggerating.[37]

Reaching the ship with those that they had "enticed" and "betrayed" meant success for the spirit, who either profited directly from selling his charges to ship captains or indirectly from merchant commissions. Ship captains, once they had purchased those who had been lured aboard ship, did not heed pleas for release as they stood to profit by selling servants through commissions from merchants and planters.[38] Mariners made it clear to those they had "inveigled" onto their ships that they were there to stay, revealing how the threat of force followed deception in the servant "recruitment" process. The seamen Edward Barlow encountered a "sperite" under the shadow of London Bridge in 1658. Fortunately for him, his uncle, who operated a nearby inn in Southwark, refused to bind him over to the smooth-talking operative. Barlow went on to describe the desperate plight of those spirited aboard a ship in his journal: "they cannot get away, not one out of a hundred of them; for they will always keep them onboard and will not let them land, nor send the least note to any of their friends to come and get them clear."[39] But force could also supersede deception in the initial stage of a kidnapping, as Judith Danie discovered in March 1656 when she was assaulted near Katherine's Stairs, on the East End London waterfront. Danie, as the court clerk noted, was to be "impresst" into servitude on "Jamego" (an early spelling of Jamaica).[40] Two years later, Katherine Wall accused Sarah Sharpe of being a spirit, having witnessed her commit violent assaults on children that involved "tearing and biting." Sharpe confessed to the magistrate that she had kidnapped four "young men and maidens," one aged only eleven, and sold them to ship captains bound for Virginia and Barbados.[41]

Although English ports such as London and Bristol became infamous for violent abductions, Ireland played host to the most systematic use of

---

[37] George Gardyner, *A Description of the New World, or America Islands and Continent* (1651), 9.

[38] Allen, *Invention of the White Race*, 2: 58–9. Captains also profited from the Chesapeake headright system, where those who transported servants to labor-starved Virginia and Maryland received 50 to 100 acres of land per "head," or the equivalent value in tobacco. Captains often sold these headrights for cash. For the headright system, see Edmund Morgan, "Headrights and Headcounts: A Review Article," *Virginia Magazine of History and Biography* 80, no. 3 (1972), 361–71. The headright system also marked the African slave trade to the Chesapeake. See Parent, *Foul Means*, Appendix 1.

[39] Basil Lubbock, ed., *Barlow's Journal of His Life at Sea in King's Ships, East and West Indiamen and Other Merchantmen from 1659 to 1703*, 2 vols. (London: Hurst and Blacket, 1934), 1: 26–8.

[40] *Middlesex County Records*, 3: 239.

[41] Ibid., 3: 259.

force in the servant trade. During the English Commonwealth's attempt to conquer Ireland (ca. 1649–58), Henry Cromwell, Lord Lieutenant of Ireland and son of Lord Protector Oliver Cromwell, lamented how the use of "force in taking them up" would be necessary to ship a thousand Irish (women, boys, and girls) into West Indian servitude, although his mood brightened when he mused that forced labor in the colonies might transform the savage Irish in the image of English civility.[42] The English issued several proclamations during the Irish conquest calling for the apprehension and colonial transportation of "tories" or Catholic rebels as well as the Catholic poor and homeless who flooded Irish roads and fields on the verge of starvation. Reports following the execution of these orders contained complaints that the imperial dragnet swept up Catholics of all descriptions, hardly just those identified in the transportation provisions. While orders went out to New Model Army commanders and ship captains to be more discriminate, Catholics "being once apprehended" could not be "discharged, but by special order in writing under the hand of the said Lord Broghill."[43] One wonders how many "special orders" Lord Broghill signed. The Irishman John King testified that in 1654 he

with divers others were stollen in Ireland, by some of ye English soldiers, in ye night out of theyr beds & brought to Mr Dills ship, where the boate lay ready to receaue them, & in the way as they went, some others they tooke with them against their Consents, & brought them aboard ye said ship, where there were divers others of their Country men, weeping and Crying, because they were stollen from theyr frends.[44]

The volume of Irish complaints against abuses of the transportation system, such as the one described above by King, signifies how kidnapping became an endemic feature of the Irish servant trade; it also conveys how cheaply English colonialism rendered Catholic life in Ireland.

Spiriting and kidnapping operated as the first phase of a system of forced migration where profits were made through the commodification of human labor and bodies. Spirits usually charged anywhere from 25 to 40 shilllings for their services, while merchants could expect ship captains to pay £4–£6 per servant; merchants might also consign the

---

[42] Thomas Birch, ed., *A Collection of the State Papers of John Thurloe*, 7 vols. (London, 1742), 4: 40.

[43] Ibid., 5: 243–58; Robert Dunlop, ed., *Ireland under the Commonwealth: Being a Selection of Documents Relating to the Government of Ireland from 1651 to 1659*, 2 vols. (Manchester: Manchester University Press, 1913), 1: 374–5, 467, 475, 528.

[44] Salem Quarterly Court, Salem, Massachusetts, June 25, 1661. *Records and Files of the Quarterly Courts of Essex County, Massachusetts*, Volume II: *1656–1662* (Salem: The Essex Institute, 1912).

captain to sell the servant in the colonies for a share of the profit.[45] Spirits often worked on their own, but just as often, they were employed by merchants to round up servants for sale through force or deception. As John Wareing discovered in his invaluable research into the seventeenth-century London servant trade,

> The evidence suggests that the structure of the spiriting trade consisted of a number of large agents who would have the resources to keep ... servants in confinement until a ship was available ... They actively encouraged other persons to bring them potential servants in return for money, many of whom earned a living in this way, and also operated spiriting gangs to ensure a supply for merchants seeking servants.[46]

As Wareing's work has demonstrated, the servant trade thrived through a transatlantic system of organized crime that profited allegedly reputable merchants. Profit-making from the sale of spirited captives started on the European side of the Atlantic in various venues, including the Royal Exchange, the heart of the English mercantile establishment. In 1698 Ned Ward described so-called labor recruiters as "those fine fellows who look like footmen upon a holiday, crept into cast suits of their masters, that want gentility in their deportment answerable to their apparel ... [they are the] ... kidnappers who walk the Change." According to Ward, a corner of the Exchange was known as "'Kidnappers Walk'; for a great many of these Jamaicans and Barbadian (merchants) ... are looking as sharp for servants as a gang of pickpockets for booty." The Exchange also housed "an Office of Intelligence pretending to help servants to places and masters to servants." Unwitting migrants would "loiter hereabouts ... till they are picked up by the Plantation Kidnappers and spirited away into a state of misery and whoredom,"[47] the last reference beckoning toward masters' expectation for sexual access to the bodies of their female servants. Spirits often deposited their captives in provisioning shops or "cooks houses" in the Katherine's Stairs neighborhood on the east London waterfront. These establishments functioned much in the way that barracoons did on the West African coast or as slave pens did in the antebellum United States. Merchants employing spirits paid the shopkeepers £3 for their services. Kidnapped captives languished in these shops, for up to five or six weeks according to contemporary sources,

[45] Wareing, "Violently Taken Away or Cheatingly Duckoyed,'" 4, 7, 8, and n. 67.
[46] Ibid., 8.
[47] Edward Ward, *The London Spy, Complete in Eighteen Parts* (1698–9, reprinted 1924), 55, 72–3. Also quoted in Wareing, "Violently Taken Away or Cheatingly Duckoyed,'" 8.

making them "prisoner until some master fetches them off." "Master" here did not signify an aspiring planter ready to set off for the colonies with a parcel of stolen servants in tow; master here meant ship master, or captain, who would visit these "cooks houses" to purchase both victuals for the voyage and a cargo of servants to sell in Barbados, Jamaica, Virginia, or other destinations across the Atlantic.[48] And as we have seen, when not relying on supplies of fresh bodies from the Royal Exchange and the victualling houses of the London waterfront, ship captains could simply wait for spirits to deliver captives straight to their ships.

Once the ships embarked, servants could expect a rough crossing, for as a Chesapeake planter remembered, the vessels were "extreme unhealthy" since captains "take so many (servants) ... that their ship is pestured and subject to disease." George Gardnyer likened the treatment kidnapped servants endured on the Atlantic voyage to "murder ... for when they have by spirits or lying tales, forced them aboard the ships, in their transportation only, there is yearly many starved to death."[49] William Bullock noted in 1649 that the weakened captives often died after arriving in Virginia, as they could not withstand the long march to the plantations where they had been sold into servitude.[50] Another Virginian, a minister, writing over two decades later, observed that conditions had hardly improved for servants trafficked to Virginia, crying out that

Men stealers, termed otherwise Spirits or Kidnappers' ... whole employ ... is to ... seduce indigent, ignorant Souls under fair pretences ... making Golden promises of things never likely to come to pass, drilling many distressed, desperate wretches on to their own speedy and unavoidable destruction.[51]

While barely comparable to the lethality of the transatlantic slave trade from Africa, the trafficking of servants into plantation bondage did lead to thousands of deaths on sea during the Atlantic passage and on land during the seasoning process. Taking a wider view, George Gardyner lamented, "'Tis dishonorable, in that we are upbraided by all other nations that know that trade for selling our own countrymen for the commodities of those places (colonies)." The infamy of the English servant trade, as Gardyner's remarks reveal, had spread beyond England

---

[48] Bullock, *Virginia Impartially Examined*, 12, 44.
[49] Gardnyer, *A Description of the New World*, 9.
[50] Bullock, *Virginia Impartially Examined*, 44.
[51] Paul Williams, *The Vain Prodigal Life, and Tragical Penitent Death of Thomas Hellier*, as quoted in Breen, Lewis, and Schlesinger, who identified the Anglican minister Paul Williams as the likely author of the pamphlet. See their "Motive for Murder: A Servant's Life in Virginia, 1678," 116.

itself and its colonies, drawing condemnation from competing Atlantic empires.[52]

Spiriting, although illegal, operated at the heart of the legal servant trade; its prevalence compelled its most impressive historian, John Wareing, to state that the majority of servants shipped to England's Atlantic colonies in the seventeenth century had fallen prey to spirits.[53] Contemporaries believed kidnapping formed an even bigger link in the transatlantic servant supply chain. The Londoner Christopher Jeafferson, corresponding with the steward of his plantation at St. Kitt's, reported that

> several eminent merchants who have dealt to Virginia, Barbados, and Jamaica are glad to compound with their old friends the kidnabbers, who finding the sweet advantage of turning informer Judas-like betray their masters. This is a great discouragement to the merchant, the procurerer, and the master of ships, who are very scrupulous of how they carry over servants.[54]

Jeafferson gave too much credit to the scruples of the "procurers" of the servant trade. The Virginian William Bullock's blunt statement comes closer to the truth: "the usual way for getting servants is by a sort of men nicknamed spirits."[55] Parliament had been aware of the problem since 1618 – the outset of the Virginia tobacco boom. A little less than two decades later, following a period of intense expansion of Chesapeake tobacco cultivation, the sugar boom in Barbados, and the outbreak of the English Revolution and English Civil Wars, working-class youths were being pressganged into Royalist and Parliamentary armies when earlier they might have chosen or been deceived into colonial servitude.[56] An acute chattel labor shortage for Caribbean and Chesapeake planters resulted, prompting spirits to redouble their efforts, but their "barbarous and wicked" ways sparked a popular backlash. Trafficking "freeborn Englishmen" to colonies outraged Londoners, who petitioned Parliament to crack down on the problem. In May 1645, Lords and Commons responded with seeming force, ordering that justices of the peace be

> hereby streightly charged and required, to be very diligent in apprehending all such Persons as are faulty in this Kind, either in stealing, selling, buying, inveigling,

---

[52] Gardnyer, *A Description of the New World*, 8.
[53] Wareing, "Violently Taken Away or Cheatingly Duckoyed,'" 5.
[54] Quoted by J. C. Jeafferson in *A Young Squire of the 17th C.* (London, 1878), 1: 317–18.
[55] Bullock, *Virginia Impartially Examined*, 14.
[56] Donoghue, "Unfree Origins of English Empire-Building," in Donoghue and Jennings, eds., *Building the Atlantic Empires*, 123–9.

purloining, conveying, or receiving Children so stolen, and to keep them in safe Imprisonment until they may be brought to severe and exemplary Punishment.

The ordinance, which was to be posted in every London parish, went on to call for

the Marshals of the Admiralty and the Cinque Ports do immediately make strict and diligent Search, in all Ships and Vessels upon the River, and at The Downes, for all such children; according to such Directions as they have or shall receive from the Committee of the Admiralty and Cinque Ports.[57]

Although it appeared to crack down on kidnapping, instead of proclaiming kidnapping as a new felony, the ordinance left it as a misdemeanor charge, provided no guidelines for sentencing, and called for no systematic search of Atlantic-bound ships – searches were left to the discretion of the Committee of the Admiralty and Cinque ports. The Lord Admiral of England at this time, Robert Rich, the Earl of Warwick, had little incentive to launch scrupulous searches. As the former treasurer of the Virginia Company, a director of the Bermuda Company, and the largest colonial proprietor in the House of Lords, Warwick only stood to profit by keeping the transatlantic servant supply chain intact, regardless of the criminal means that fastened its links.[58] Two years later, Parliament recognized that the Civil Wars and Revolution had led to "a great want of servants in the ... plantations" and called for more to undertake the journey to Virginia provided that they would be

first registered in customs house; and that neither force be used to take up any such servants, nor any apprentices enticed to desert their masters, nor any children under age admitted without express consent of their parents ... no such fraud be used to carry such persons to any other place.

No systematic servant registration regime materialized. Despite these tepid reforms, there were far-reaching calls for change in the 1647 bill. The House of Commons demanded that colonial assemblies send "certificate(s)" back to the home government proving "that no fraud be used to carry ... [servants] ... to any other place."[59] Unfortunately, since Parliament had no statutory authority over colonial assemblies, which

[57] Firth and Rait, eds., *Acts and Ordinances*, 1: 681–2.

[58] Sean Kelsey, "Rich, Robert, Second Earl of Warwick (1587–1658)," *DNB Online* (2008); Wesley Craven, "The Earl of Warwick, a Speculator in Piracy," *The Hispanic American Historical Review* 10, no. 4 (1930), 457–79.

[59] Leo Francis Stock, ed., *Proceedings and Debates of the British Parliaments Respecting North America, 1542–1688* (Washington, DC: Carnegie Institution of Washington, 1924), 185.

in any case were dominated by planter interests in the Chesapeake and Caribbean, Parliament's servant certification bill was worth as much as the parchment it was written upon. In the end, the Houses of Parliament passively sanctioned kidnapping and thus the enslavement of its own subjects in the colonies.

Across the Atlantic, colonial governments expressed dubious concern with the "delusive means and practices" by which spirits tricked young people onto West Indian bound ships. In 1661, Barbados collected and revised a series of earlier ordinances to codify a set of servant regulations. The Assembly debated the problem regarding servants who had arrived "without indenture, covenant, or contract for the same" and were so "disposed ... to serve according to the custom of the country."[60] "The custom of the country" referred to mid seventeenth-century colonial innovations in servant regulatory law, which both borrowed from and revised English labor law to suit the chattel labor regime planters had devised to control and often extend the labor time of their servants; these new legal customs governing servants also allowed masters to exert harsher discipline over them.[61] In the case of minors arriving without labor contracts, the Assemblymen of Barbados refined the custom of the country to declare that no servant under fourteen could be sold on the island without an indenture signed by "principal persons of the parish where the said child last lived, that it is done with their consent, or with the consent, or at the requests of the parents." They also called for imprisoning those who brought children under fourteen to Barbados without an indenture. If direct proof surfaced that the child had been kidnapped, the Assemblymen promised to send the children back home. No record exists (to my knowledge) of a spirit ever being prosecuted on Barbados or of a spirited child being returned to Britain or Ireland. One

---

[60] *An Act for the Good Governing of Servants, and Ordering the Rights between Masters and Servants*, reprinted in *Acts of Assembly, Passed in the Island of Barbadoes, from 1648 to 1718* (London, 1721), 22.

[61] For work on seventeenth-century servant law in the English Atlantic, see Newman, *A New World of Labor*, chs. 3 and 4; Warren Billings, "The Law of Servants and Slaves in Seventeenth Century Virginia," *The Virginia Magazine of History and Biography* 99, no. 1 (1991), 45–62; Hilary Beckles, "The Concept of 'White Slavery' in the English Caribbean during the Early Seventeenth Century," in John Brewer and Susan Staves, eds., *Early Modern Conceptions of Property* (London: Routledge, 1996), 572–84; Allen, *The Invention of the White Race*, 2: 125–42; Tomlins, *Freedom Bound*, Part II; Robert Steinfeld, *The Invention of Free Labor: The Employment Relation in English and American Law and Culture, 1350–1870* (Chapel Hill, NC: University of North Carolina Press, 1991), ch. 2.

possible explanation lies in the fact that the ordinance gave magistrates, who were either planters or merchants, the power to assess the child's age. Likewise, magistrates exercised the same prerogative when examining older youths who, having been spirited, arrived without indentures. On Barbados, those declared under eighteen would serve for seven years, and those over eighteen for five. As for the freedom dues for those who had been kidnapped, the plantocracy allowed for 400 pounds of "good muscavadoe sugar." The allotment was so meager that most servants, if they survived, had little stake in a future on Barbados, and so most left the island for other colonies around the English Atlantic.[62] Efforts to impose chattel terms on indenture-less servants became systematic in the English West Indies with the proclamation of Jamaica's servant code in 1683, which like Barbados's of 1661, included a collection of older laws that had been subjected to revision. Having been wrested from the Spanish only in 1655, Jamaica's new Assembly declared that where there was no contract, or indenture,

servants under eighteen years of age at their arrival in this island, shall serve seven years, and above eighteen years of age, shall serve four years, and all convicted felons, for the time of their banishment, and at the expiration of their terms aforesaid, shall receive from their master, mistress, or employer forty shillings, and a certificate of their freedom on demand.

The contracts imposed on kidnapped victims in Barbados and Jamaica thus mirrored each other, with the exception of Jamaica's even more miserly freedom dues.[63]

In the mid seventeenth-century Chesapeake, courts assumed the same power that their Caribbean counterparts had in imposing chattel labor contracts on migrants. Due to "diverse controversies" in Virginia about how long migrants without indentures would serve, the Assembly chose in 1643 to give those aged between twelve and twenty-five to seven-year terms while those over twenty would serve for four. Thirteen years later, the Assembly revised the precedent by ordering shorter terms for those over sixteen, who would labor for four years while those sixteen and younger would serve until they were twenty-one. Turning its attention to contract regulation once again in 1661, Virginia legislators diminished

---

[62] *An Act for the Good Governing of Servants* in *Acts of Assembly, Passed in the Island of Barbadoes*, 22, 26.

[63] *The Laws of Jamaica, Passed by the Assembly and Confirmed by His Majesty in Council, to Which is Added a Short Account of the Island and Government Thereof with an Exact Map of the Island* (London, 1683), 8.

terms for those over fifteen while lengthening them for new arrivals under that age, with the latter working as the chattel property of their masters until the age of twenty-four.[64] Maryland devised a similar statute in 1654, declaring that "all Servants Coming into this province without an Indenture or Covenant if they be above the age of twenty years shall serve four years, from sixteen years of age unto twenty six years, from twelve to sixteene, shall serve seven yeares, if they be under twelve, they shall serve until they come to the age of one & twenty years."[65] Taking an Atlantic-wide view of how colonial courts arbitrated age in relation to terms of servitude, a clear pattern emerges from the evidence presented above. Plantation colonies in the West Indies and the Chesapeake invested magistrates with the prerogative to determine the ages of young people, mainly teenagers, who arrived without contracts. Magistrates used their discretionary authority to regulate servant contracts in a way that forced the longest terms of service on the most vulnerable population of involuntary migrants, young teenagers, setting precedents that accumulated to form part of the "custom of the country," the colonial body of common law regarding servant regulation. Although these reforms drew upon English statutory and common law, they looked more to the future, helping to establish the chattel labor regime of English plantation capitalism. While the political will driving the creation of colonial legal custom advanced the economic interests of masters and merchants, no colony invested any political will in returning home the young people who had been stolen and sold into a future of chattel servitude. Colonial legislatures thus turned the tragedy of kidnapping to the profitable advantage of the seventeenth-century capitalists who dominated them.

While planters continued to demand fresh bodies, the people of Britain and Ireland demanded that action be taken against kidnappers, action they often took into their own hands. For example, due to the rising number of young people gone missing "beyond the seas," kidnappers became targets for street justice as administered by the London crowd. A 1664 petition from the Aldermen of London noted that mobs formed on city streets to accost both suspected spirits and those caught in the act. The ensuing street battles, as the Aldermen related, created "great tumults and uproars ... within the city to the breach of the peace and

---

[64] William Hening, ed., *The Statutes at Large: Being a Collection of All the Laws of Virginia, from the First Session of the Legislature, in 1619*, Volume 1 (New York, 1823), 257; Billings, "The Law of Servants and Slaves in Seventeenth Century Virginia," 48–9.

[65] William Hand Brown, ed., *Proceedings and Acts of the General Assembly January 1637/8–September 1664* (Baltimore, MA: Maryland History Society, 1883), 1: 436–8.

the hazard of men's lives ... being very dangerous ..."[66] One of these uproars involved Rebecah Allen, who accused Susan Jones of "raising a tumult against her" by calling her a spirit and saying she had caused her to be sent away "beyond the seas."[67] William Graunt and Thomas Faulkner were called to the bench "to answer for assaulting and pumping of Margarett Emmerson upon the false report of a spirit or an inticer or inveagler of children from their parents, there beinge noe charge or accusation laid against her."[68] The fact that no charge had been laid against Emmerson does not mean, of course, that Graunt and Faulkner assaulted her without just cause. The grocer Jonas Antherson was very sure that Nicholas Cooper was a kidnapper when he summoned a mob to corner him with the accusation that "thou art a spirit, thou has spirited a maid to the Barbados ... and I will call thee a spirit, till those lost vindicate thyself."[69] John Cole, a laborer from St. Giles in the Fields, appeared before a magistrate "to answer for reviling Captain William Staffe in the street, calling him spirit, which is so infamous a name that many have been wounded to death." It appears that the crowd Cole gathered against Staffe lived up to the violent reputation of anti-spirit mobs noted above by the court clerk, who observed that "the said captain is much beaten and bruised by the multitude, being a very aged man."[70] From these examples and others in the Middlesex County Records, we can conclude that working-class people organized direct, small-scale, collective action – often violent – to combat kidnapping, creating a tradition of ad hoc local resistance that unfolded in opposition to the establishment of a transatlantic human trafficking network in the seventeenth century. But the political impact of anti-kidnapping mobs transcended London's rookeries and waterfront, making street-fighting much more than a local affair. The mobs that raged on the streets of London – fighting for the life of freedom against the death of slavery – made their political influence felt in the highest legislative body in England, the Houses of Parliament. The Parliamentary debate that ensued, unfortunately, tells us as much about the class-based, political priorities of England's leading legislators, who advanced their own economic interests at the expense of the poorest and most vulnerable people in the Three Kingdoms.

---

[66] W. Noel Sainsbury, ed., *Calendar of State Papers, Colonial Series, America and West Indies, 1661–1668* (London, 1880), 220.
[67] *Middlesex County Records*, 3: 254–5.
[68] Ibid., 3: 181.
[69] Ibid., 3: 259.
[70] Ibid., 3: 278.

In July of 1661 MPs introduced a "A bill against stealing of children and servants, and carrying them beyond the seas," which, after finally having been read before the House of Commons in January 1662, did not pass in that session. Commons reintroduced the bill on April 10, 1662, and the MPs discussed it over the course of that month, attaching the issue of kidnapping to the plight of Royalist rebels who had been "transported and enslaved in any plantations, or parts beyond the seas." The bill died early that May, with no clear indication in the Parliamentary archives as to why.[71] The problem persisted, however, with Solicitor-General Heneage Finch informing Parliament in 1664 that "the mischiefs complained of ... are very frequent there being scarce any voyage to the Plantations but some persons are carried away against their wills or pretend to be so after they have contracted with the merchants and then run away."[72] Hoping to resolve three decades of legislative inertia concerning kidnapping, Parliament embarked on one last attempt to rein in the illegal servant trade in 1670. From March 10 through March 26, the House debated in committee and in chamber An Act to Prevent Stealing and Transporting Children, and other Persons, which they passed and sent to the House of Lords for their assent. After lengthy committee sessions the Lords sent the bill back to Commons in April 1671 with several amendments. It was not read again in Commons until February 1672. No further action was taken until November 1673, when the bill "to prevent stealing and transporting children, and other persons" was read before the House, "but the manner of it being disliked, the bill was withdrawn, upon question." MP Thomas Morris then

tendered a bill for preventing of stealing children and making it felony without clergy, but b/c it was thought there was an office in the belly, it being provided that all go over to plantations as servants shall enter their names somewhere, the house which always averse to any project of that nature, would not receive it.[73]

The mysterious, fearful reference to "an office in the belly" is telling. Centralized government, particularly through the creation of "offices" or bureaucracies, signaled tyranny to MPs vested in the tradition of the "free

[71] Stock, ed., *Proceedings and Debates of the British Parliaments Respecting North America*, 302–4, 306.

[72] Quoted in John Wareing, "Preventive and Punitive Regulation in Seventeenth-Century Social Policy: Conflicts of Interest and the Failure to Make 'Stealing and Transporting Children, and Other Persons' a Felony, 1645–73," *Social History* 27, no. 3 (2002), 288–308, 289.

[73] Stock, ed., *Proceedings and Debates of the British Parliaments Respecting North America*, 400.

born Englishmen." They feared that offices, such as the potential office to regulate the servant trade, would serve the interests of the Crown rather than Parliament, thus "enslaving" the body politic to the prerogative or unaccountable power of the monarchy. Rather than taking substantial action to prevent the term-bound enslavement of their own poor population in the colonies, MPs with means chose to fend off the political "slavery" of government bureaucracy. Class mattered in the failure to make kidnapping a felony in the seventeenth century.

The fear of bureaucratic "bondage" kept the British ruling class from taking effective action against kidnapping, but greed might have informed their indifference to the enslavement of British subjects in even more powerful ways. For instance, in September 1663, Lord Baltimore, the proprietor of colonial Maryland, petitioned the Privy Council to release servants for transport to his colony in the Chesapeake. The migrants were holed up in the English port of Plymouth, where they had complained to the Governor that they had been kidnapped. The Governor took decisive action and held Baltimore's ship at bay. But pecuniary interests won out over the plight of the poor below deck on the *Reserve*, the name of the vessel in question. Baltimore complained that the Governor's action had "much prejudiced the Adventurers" or investors in the voyage, prejudice here meaning financial loss. Taking note of this potential loss the Privy Council also took Baltimore's word on the matter, declaring "the assertion of the Parties [meaning the migrants] [was] no sufficient evidence that they were surprised and embarqued against their wills."[74] Clearly, in lieu of losing profits in the Atlantic plantation complex, the Crown did not want to peer too deeply into the holds of ships that carried unwilling migrants to labor in cash crop colonies like Maryland. Baltimore, it should be said, strengthened his case by arguing that customs officials had cleared the ship at Gravesend, finding no evidence of kidnapping. When placed in a larger context, however, the Chesapeake aristocrat's argument appears less persuasive. Local customs officials were notorious for entering into league with spirits. In the worst cases, they operated kidnapping rings themselves. One of London's most prolific servant recruiters, John Haveland, also served as the High Baliff of the Liberty of St Katherine's by the Tower, a neighborhood infamous in

---

[74] Wareing, "Violently Taken Away or Cheatingly Duckoyed,'" 12. Wareing found the case involving Lord Baltimore and the contested shipment of indentured servants in the Public Record Office (now the National Archives), Privy Council Minute Books, PC 2/57, 557.

London as the center of the spiriting trade. As High Baliff, Haveland's job included serving writs and conducting arrests of criminals and malefactors. Instead, Haveland became a malefactor himself and the subject of the largest prosecution effort against kidnapping in the seventeenth century, having helped to send over six thousand people into involuntary colonial servitude from 1658 to 1670.[75] Selling for approximately £6 per head, there was a great deal of money to be made on the supply side of the transatlantic servant trade, a fact that led law officers like Haveland into a life of crime.

While the commodification of servants through bodily theft made money for government officials, kidnappers, captains, and merchants, still more profit was to be made by planters in the colonies, where contracts allegedly protected servants from enslavement and other forms of exploitation. But far from protecting colonial migrants from abuse, contracts made the enslavement of kidnapped servants possible. First, most servants were illiterate and could hardly be expected to understand an indenture that rendered them into chattel property, that is if the agent recruiting them was even honest about the contractual terms on offer. We have also seen how many servants who arrived in the colonies without contracts were subjected to court-mandated indentures. The servants consent was also irrelevant in contracts between those who sold them and those who bought them. Moreover, servants could be sold again and again from master to master. But importantly, and in contrast to a staple of servant scholarship, servants themselves – body and soul – were being sold, and not simply their contracts. Simply put, contracts did not cut cane or pull tobacco, servants did, and they did so as the chattel property of their master for the duration of a contract to which they did not consent. There can be no question over the servant's chattel status in law and practice, despite the fact that many historians of servitude rarely discuss it. Servants were referred to with regularity in colonial estate law and labor, commercial, and financial contracts as the "goods and chattels" of their masters.[76] As term-bound chattel property, kidnapped servants, having been commodified through law, became capital assets of their masters in ways similar to enslaved Africans, with the crucial exception that servants escaped bondage if they survived their

---

[75] Ibid., 12.

[76] I have discussed the problem of buying and selling servants as opposed to their contracts at greater length in *Fire under the Ashes*, 244–6, 261–2; "Indentured Servitude in the Seventeenth Century English Atlantic," 893–902.

terms while their African counterparts and their children were bound for life. As capital assets, servants could be sold to relieve a master's encumbered estate. They could be sold to allow their masters to escape bankruptcy and to satisfy creditors. They could be sold to compensate for other contracts that their masters could not pay off. They could also be sold to liquidate an estate or even satisfy gambling debts.[77] The fact that servant labor and servants themselves became capital assets in colonial law helps explain why many were sold several times over; we have already met one such unfortunate figure, Thomas Hellier. After a spirit seduced him in a London pub with false promises of scrivener's work, Hellier crossed the Atlantic to Virginia, where he was bought and sold three times before he found himself working in a tobacco field on a plantation called Hard Labor for an abusive planter. Hellier lamented that he had become a "slave" in Virginia, a lamentation that can be found in the life testimony he gave shortly before being hanged by Virginia officials for murdering his master and mistress.[78] Other kidnapping victims such as Charles Baily, who was spirited at Gravesend around 1649, called themselves "bond slaves." Baily complained of frequent whippings, nakedness, and "hard labor" which he described as "beyond the common manner of slaves, for mine was often night and day." He concluded by saying he and his fellow servants would have "been better hanged" than subjected to the brutal work and disciplinary regime of the planation.[79]

Knowing that such fates awaited those spirited away to colonial plantations, plaintiffs accused kidnappers of "enslaving" their victims in the petitions they filed in England. In the Caribbean, contemporaries observing the treatment of servants on sugar plantations concluded that human beings were hardly able to endure "such slavery." Reflecting on his time in Jamaica in 1687, John Taylor wrote in his journal that

the English servants laboriously wear out their four years' servitude, or rather slavery, having sufficient cause to repent their adventures in coming from England, to be slaves in America, where many servants are never free; for by their master hard usage (which some do on purpose) they sometimes run away for a day, week, or month, etc., [by] which means their time of servitude is increased and many never become freemen all their days.[80]

[77] Allen, *The Invention of the White Race*, 2: 99.
[78] Breen, Lewis, and Schlesinger, "Motive for Murder," 106–20.
[79] Baily, *A True and Faithful Warning*, 8, 9.
[80] David Buisseret, *Jamaica in 1687: The Taylor Manuscript at the National Library of Jamaica* (Kingston, JM: University of the West Indies Press, 2008), 267.

The explanation for such viciousness lies not in some inherent sadism on the part of masters. Instead, the chief imperative of capitalism – the quest to exponentially maximize profits – drove them to wield the lash with such severity. The whip and other weapons became necessary instruments of terror in an unfree colonial labor system where planters imposed multiple forms of slavery on "Christian" Europeans and "negros" of African descent. Although colonial law rarely referred to white workers as slaves, this does not mean historically that whites were not enslaved, although by the latter seventeenth century, even unskilled white servants were granted increasing legal privileges that further separated their condition from black slaves. But there can be no equivocation here. While white servants were subjected to periods of enslavement, the racialized, perpetual slavery imposed upon Africans in the Atlantic world evolved into the most barbaric and profitable enterprise in the global history of slavery, the racist legacy of which still perpetuates massive injustices in our own time.

Beyond the light that it sheds on the history of the Atlantic plantation complex, why does the history of kidnapping and the enslavement of servants matter? More to the point in a volume organized by Historians Against Slavery, what can historical perspective on the servant trade tell us about human trafficking in the present? Comparing eras of human trafficking reveals some startling consistencies between the seventeenth and twenty-first centuries. These constants are even more striking as they have endured in the face of one of history's most profound experiences of change: the abolition of slavery. For example, the tactics deployed by human traffickers – fraud, force and deceit – have remained the same. Kidnapping is still "the usual way" – as William Bullock wrote long ago – that traffickers captivate their victims.[81] This remains particularly true in the so-called "commercial sex industry," into which a minority of women enter voluntarily, while most women and children are routinely tricked and/or coerced into sex slavery, which feeds an illicit industry with trafficking networks on local, regional, national, and international scales. Shamere McKenzie and Stacy Jewell Lewis – women who were tricked and forced into slavery by pimps – have demonstrated through their work as leaders in the modern abolition movement that prostitution is not the

---

[81] For what remains some of the best work on the dynamics of human trafficking, see Kevin Bales, *Understanding Global Slavery: A Reader* (Berkeley, CA: University of California Press, 2005), ch. 7.

world's oldest "profession."[82] It is, for the most part, a form of slavery hidden in plain sight, as much scholarly research and the abolitionist work of other survivors has verified.[83] But slavery in the twenty-first century exists well beyond the world of the "commercial sex industry." Like the early modern Atlantic plantation complex, today commercial fishing in the Pacific, textile manufacturing in South Asia and Central America, high-tech manufacturing in China, mining in central and western Africa, commercial agriculture in the United States, and military operations the world over all rely on kidnappers to traffic unfree laborers into their work forces.[84] Moreover, as the geographic range of the examples above attest, human trafficking then and now supplies unfree labor for a global economy organized by capitalist interests. And again, capitalists today, as they did during the seventeenth century, continue to undermine the political will that exists to end human trafficking.

Take, for instance, the Coalition of Immokalee Workers (CIW) in Florida. Beginning in 1993, they began organizing consumers and workers to force tomato growers to pay fair wages, improve working conditions, and stop the trafficking and enslavement of migrant laborers, most of whom came from Latin America. Their efforts have produced the Fair Food Program, described by the CIW as "a unique partnership among farmers, farmworkers, and retail food companies" founded on worker-to-worker education and worker-monitoring of living conditions and hiring, labor, and compensation practices. In 2015–16, the CIW has expanded its Fair Food Program from Florida to North and South

---

[82] For McKenzie's story, see Kevin Bales and Rod Soodalter, *The Slave Next Door: Human Trafficking and Slavery in America Today* (Berkeley, CA: University of California Press, 2009), 84–5; for more on her story and her work in the modern abolitionist movement as CEO of the Sungate Foundation, see www.sun-gate.org. For Jewell Lewis's story and work as a playwright/performer/activist, see the website for her award winning play, *7 Layers Captive*: www.7layerscaptive.com.

[83] *ILO Global Estimate of Forced Labor: Results and Methodology* (2012), 13–15, 26, 41, www.ilo.org/wcmsp5/groups/public/---ed_norm/---declaration/documents/publication/wcms_182004.pdf; Grainne Healy and Monica O'Connor, *The Links between Prostitution and Sex Trafficking: A Briefing Handbook* (Coalition Against Trafficking in Women, October 26, 2006), www.catwinternational.org/Home/Article/234-the-links-between-prostitution-and-sex-trafficking-a-briefing-handbook; Alison Phinney, *Trafficking of Women and Children for Sexual Exploitation in the Americas* (Women, Health and Development Program, Pan-American Health Organization, 2001), www.oas.org/en/cim/docs/Trafficking-Paper%5BEN%5D.pdf.

[84] *Trafficking in Persons Report* (Washington, DC: United States Department of State, 2015); *The Role of Recruitment Fees and Abusive and Fraudulent Recruitment Practices of Recruitment Agencies in Trafficking in Persons* (Vienna: United Nations Office on Drugs and Crime, 2015).

Carolina, Georgia, Virginia, Maryland, and New Jersey, where it has made great strides against forced labor and has improved the pay and working lives of migrant laborers. But since 1993, the CIW has had to fight corporate lobbying groups such as the Florida Tomato Growers Exchange (FTGE) and multinational corporations on the picket line and inside the halls of state legislatures for every inch of ground that they have gained for migrant workers. Case in point: in an April 2008 hearing conducted by Sen. Bernie Sanders, it came to light that the FTGE planned to fine any of its members $100,000 *per worker* for cooperating in the CIW's "penny per pound" plan. In the plan, for each pound of tomatoes they purchased, buyers like McDonalds or Yum, Inc. would contribute a penny to a collective fund designed to supplement workers' wages. The FTGE, which represents 90 percent of the growers in the Florida tomato industry, protested that the penny-per-pound contribution would bankrupt the growers and force the relocation of the industry to Mexico. It should be noted here that the Florida tomato industry generates $650 million in annual revenues. In November 2010, after enduring over two years of relentless political pressure and negative publicity generated by the CIW, the FTGE signed on to the Fair Food Program and the penny-per-pound plan that it included among its litany of reforms.[85] Thanks to the research and activism of the workers, volunteers, journalists, scholars, and especially the survivors of slavery who make up the modern abolitionist movement, we could cite numerous examples to bear out the relationship between the past and present of human trafficking, but one particularly revealing case study, researched by investigative reporter Cam Simpson, will detain us here.[86]

During the Iraqi War (2003–11), Kellog, Brown and Root (KBR), a subsidiary of the US multinational Haliburton, gained no-bid contracts to supply American military bases in Iraq with contract laborers to work mostly in food service, transportation, construction, and custodial roles. KBR then outsourced its role as a labor contractor, either in direct fashion or through additional subsidiaries, to over two hundred firms, mostly based in the Middle East and South Asia. These companies included firms such as Prime Projects International

---

[85] Katrina vanden Heuvel and Greg Kaufmann, "Ending Slavery for Pennies," *The Nation*, April 16, 2008. Kristofer Rios, "After Long Fight, Farmworkers in Florida Win a Raise," *The New York Times*, January 18, 2011; www.fairfoodprogram.org; www.ciw-online .org/slavery; www.ciw-online.org/blog/2011/02/call_to_action3.

[86] Much of the following section on modern human trafficking draws from Simpson's award-winning *exposé*, "Pipeline to Peril," published in the *Chicago Tribune* over the course of 2005 and 2006.

(United Arab Emirates), Moonlight Consultants (Nepal), Morning Star for Recruitment (Jordan), Manpower Supply (Jordan), and Daoud and Partners (Jordan). The tactics these firms used to recruit laborers for US military bases in Iraq, ultimately for the profit of US multinational corporation KBR, parallel those of the spirits employed by seventeenth-century English merchants, ship captains, and colonial planters.[87]

Working mainly among the poor of India and Nepal, the agents employed by KBR's subcontractors kidnapped their "recruits" with false promises about where they would work and the kind of work that they would do. For instance, many of the Nepalese who ended up sweating in the Iraqi sun under the American flag were told that they would be employed with excellent wages as domestic workers in five-star hotels in Amman, Jordan. But the jobs in Amman never materialized because they never existed, except as bait to lure the poor and vulnerable into laboring as effectual slaves in an operation the US government dubbed "Operation Enduring Freedom." Once the workers arrived in Iraq, they were charged by subcontractors for their passage and had their passports confiscated, a maneuver that effectively held the workers captive until they paid off their fraudulent debt, which was made doubly difficult when their salaries were halved. Profiting from the work of kidnappers, KBR reduced its labor recruits to debt slavery via a contractual process that resembled the one used by seventeenth-century English merchants and planters to traffic young people into bond slavery. The comparison reveals a key difference concerning fraudulent contracts, as the seventeenth-century variant reduced the kidnapped person to a particular, legal species of chattel property, a status not imposed upon human trafficking victims today due to the legal abolition (as opposed to the final end) of slavery. Following this global circuit of corporate sponsored human trafficking, KBR's contractors enslaved approximately four thousand workers per year over the course of the Iraqi War, which ended in 2011. US multinationals and their subsidiaries continue to profit from human trafficking and forced labor in Afghanistan, where an estimated forty thousand workers now find themselves in situations similar to those kidnapped and enslaved in Iraq.[88]

KBR's lucrative involvement in human trafficking and slave labor might have remained an untold story had not Cam Simpson, then a

---

[87] Cam Simpson and Aaemar Madhani, "US Cash Fuels Human Trade," *Chicago Tribune*, October 9, 2005.

[88] Cam Simpson, "Into a War Zone on a Deadly Road," *Chicago Tribune*, October 10, 2005.

reporter for the *Chicago Tribune*, investigated the circumstances that led
to the execution of twelve Nepalese, employed on Iraqi military bases, by
Al Qaeda operatives. Curious as to why Nepalese were working there in
the first place, Simpson's shrewd and determined digging uncovered the
human trafficking network largely responsible for filling the demand for
cheap labor on US military installations. When pressed to comment on
its entanglement with modern slavery, KBR deferred any responsibility,
issuing a statement that questions "regarding the recruitment practices
of subcontractors should be directed to the subcontractor."[89] In contrast
to KBR's indifference, the US military took action, as Gen. George Casey
ordered the return of all passports confiscated from foreign contract
workers on American bases in Iraq.[90]

While the Pentagon, following Casey's lead, tried to crackdown on the
human trafficking networks that supplied unfree workers for US military
operations, corporate interests that profited from modern slave trading
dampened the political will to support such efforts. Congress passed a
slew of anti-trafficking measures in the face of the firestorm created in
large part by Simpson's intrepid reporting. But multinationals such as
Halliburton, Blackwater, and Dyncorp, whose profits largely depended
on no-bid contracts with the Federal government, successfully lobbied
Congress to prevent the establishment of an anti-trafficking oversight
committee in the Pentagon. The oversight board, these corporations
claimed, was "unrealistic" given the need to satisfy the acute demand
for the cheap, privatized labor that undergirded the US war effort.[91] In
the name of "Enduring Freedom," Congress thus enabled modern slavery
to flourish at the taxpayers' expense and for the profit of interested
multinationals; the events here resonate historically with Parliament's
failure to make kidnapping a felony, fearing that an oversight committee
for migration would enslave the body politic and prevent the flow of
unfree labor that profited merchants and planters. In a more recent development, the Fifth Circuit of the Federal District Court invalidated a lawsuit against Haliburton/KBR filed by the families of the twelve Nepalese
workers killed by Al Qaeda in Iraq. Citing a Supreme Court decision
limiting the applicability of US law to US corporations for their actions
outside US borders, the Fifth Circuit's decision has adversely impacted

[89] Simpson and Aaemar Madhani, "US Cash Fuels Human Trade."
[90] Cam Simpson, "Iraq War Contractors Ordered to End Abuses," *Chicago Tribune*, April 24, 2006.
[91] Cam Simpson, "US Stalls on Human Trafficking," *Chicago Tribune*, December 27, 2005.

multiple human rights movements, including the struggle against human trafficking and modern slavery.[92]

Much like the English merchants who profited from trafficking servants into slavery across the Atlantic, multinational corporations based in the United States and other nations can operate with relative impunity when staffing their workforces abroad with slave labor. Popular protest against trafficking in the past and present has moved those at the highest levels of government to combat the practice, but capitalist concerns have succeeded time and again in neutralizing the political will that could make human trafficking history. Human trafficking persists today largely because of corporate mastery over local, national, and global political processes. Making modern slavery a thing of the past depends on the work of activists (particularly survivors), scholars, and NGOs. But as history shows, they cannot succeed on their own, because their power pales in comparison to that of their enemies. In the end, ending slavery in our own time may depend on whether or not modern abolitionists successfully link their own movement with others devoted to diminishing corporate influence over the political process.

[92] Bryan Koenig, "KBR, Chamber Tell 5th Circ. Not to Revive Trafficking Suit," *Law360*, December 3, 2015.

5

Maritime Bondage

Comparing Past and Present

Kerry Ward

In 2012, Cambodian citizen Vannak Anan Prum was honored by the US State Department as one of the Trafficking in Person Heroes whose stories accompany the release of the annual *Trafficking in Persons* (TIP) *Report*. The only victim/survivor of human trafficking among the ten honorees who were presented their awards by then Secretary of State Hillary Clinton, Prum was enslaved on a Thai fishing boat for three years before escaping and being subjected to a further period of forced labor on a Malaysian palm oil plantation. Prum's plight brought to the fore the largely hidden dimension of forced labor at sea, particularly in the fishing industry in the Asia-Pacific region.[1] His story became the focal point of *Journey to Freedom*, the film produced by Fair Trade Pictures, funded partly by the National Underground Railway Freedom Center and the US State Department. The publicity material for *Journey to Freedom* claims that the film "brings to life many of the startling similarities between the slave trade that occurred in the early history of the United States and today's human trafficking. Although the institution of slavery has been outlawed, human trafficking continues, in the US and around the world."

Two men, centuries apart, were promised a job and found themselves trafficked into slavery. Each of them took care to make their story known.

---

[1] The trafficking of boy children in the lacustrine regions of Africa, particularly Lake Volta, has been well documented. See for example the documentary film *Not My Life*, dir. Robert Bilheimer (2011; Bloomfield, NY: Worldwide Documentaries Inc.), www.notmylife.org; and Raggie Johansen, "Child Trafficking in Ghana" (2017), *United Nations Office on Drugs and Crime*, www.unodc.org/unodc/en/frontpage/child-trafficking-in-ghana.html.

The same methods and maneuvers used to free people like Cambodian man Vannak Prum were used by the Underground Railroad to free men like Solomon Northup, from upstate New York. *Journey to Freedom* tells the stories of Vannak Prum and Solomon Northup, and the stories of the advocates and defenders, caretakers and freedom fighters, and everyday people who, together, make up the networks that bring people to freedom.

While *Journey to Freedom* offers powerful testimony to the human spirit of endurance, justice, and creativity that characterizes both Prum's and Northup's life stories, I would suggest that the comparison between the two men's experiences obscures the essentially distinct element of Prum's enslavement at sea. Historical comparisons between bonded labor in the maritime realm from the nineteenth to the twenty-first centuries show that maritime labor is a special case in terms of the complexities of the workforce composition and the labor rights of those working within it. Before Emancipation in the United States, the east coast harbor and maritime labor force comprised black slave seafarers and freedmen mariners, as well as white bonded seafarers and free mariners. African American slaves were not a mainstay of the west coast maritime labor force. Chinese and local bonded seafarers were, however, not uncommon. Claims that maritime labor was analogous to conditions of slavery were rife in the nineteenth century and eventually prompted a series of reforms in both the United Kingdom and the United States that were supposed to protect the rights of both professional seafarers and men taken to sea against their will. Yet these reforms were applied inconsistently at best. Seafarers – whether naval seamen, merchant mariners, or fishermen – have always occupied an extremely vulnerable position with regards to individual and collective rights, freedoms, and protection. By its very nature, maritime labor is a special category, and one that has historically and contemporarily been open to extreme forms of exploitation.[2]

In a radio interview, Ambassador Luis CdeBaca, Director of the Office to Monitor and Combat Trafficking in Persons from 2009 to 2014, characterized contemporary human trafficking in the maritime fishing industry as "a perfect storm of slavery and environmental degradation."[3]

---

[2] For classic scholarship on maritime labor in the Atlantic World see W. Jeffrey Bolster, *Black Jacks: African American Seamen in the Age of Sail* (Cambridge, MA: Harvard University Press, 1997), and the work of Marcus Rediker, including his latest *Outlaws of the Atlantic: Sailors, Pirates, and Motely Crews in the Age of Sail* (Boston, MA: Beacon Press, 2015).

[3] Luis CdeBaca quoted in Becky Palmstrom, "Illegal Fishing, Molotov Cocktails, a Daring Escape," *NPR*, June 20, 2012, http://m.npr.org/story/155048186.

The combination of maritime human trafficking and illegal fishing is a particularly difficult challenge for both nations and the international community because by nature it deals with the ambiguous realm of the sea, where legal boundaries are literally and figuratively fluid. State and international resources already stretched by the challenges of human trafficking and illegal migration across land borders are even less able to cope with patrolling ports, coastlines, territorial waters, and international waters. It is not surprising, therefore, that the ruthless exploitation of maritime resources through illegal fishing has gone hand in hand with the ruthless exploitation of people trafficked onto fishing vessels to toil without rest in this clandestine sector of the global fishing industry.

It is difficult to find an exactly equivalent historical figure to compare with Vannak Prum's experience of enslavement at sea. Although juxtaposing his life with that of Solomon Northup highlights their shared reactions of terror and resignation upon recognizing their enslavement, significantly, the comparison ends there, because Northup was wrongfully enslaved in a region where slavery was legal. I believe a more interesting set of comparisons can be found by juxtaposing three cases. First, the escape of Frederick Douglass from slavery by disguising himself as a sailor; second, the case of the Africans enslaved on the *Amistad*; and third, an examination of "shanghaiing" as a recognized form of maritime bondage that critics claimed was analogous to slavery and sought to stamp out on those grounds.

AMBIGUITIES OF MARITIME LABOR AND BONDAGE IN THE USA, 1790–1915

Historians of slavery in the United States have focused on the terrestrial realm, with the plantation slave system being the central case study of the system of enslavement. After his capture, Solomon Northup was shipped by sea along the coastal slave trading route from Washington, DC to New Orleans, whence he was sold inland and spent twelve long years as a slave working on plantations in Louisiana.[4] The coastal slave trade along the southeastern seaboard of the United States was not only a slave trading route but also a realm of labor for enslaved men. David Cecelski records the shock of one young Bostonian documenting his journey to the South in 1830. Arriving by sea to the mouth of the

---

[4] Solomon Northup, *Twelve Years a Slave* (1853; Vancouver B.C.: Engage Books Limited, 2014).

Cape Fear River and awaiting a pilot boat to guide the ship to harbor he declared in surprise: "And what saw I? *Slaves!* – the first I ever saw."[5] Cecelski estimates that African Americans comprised nearly 60 percent of the total population of larger seaports in North Carolina, but because of the sometimes seasonal nature of fishing and maritime labor, it is impossible to quantify or categorize exactly the numbers of slaves and freedmen engaged in maritime occupations. In his study of maritime forced labor from the mid nineteenth century to the passing of the 1915 Seaman's Act, Mark Strecker claims that black mariners comprised approximately 20 percent of the over 100,000 sailors working along the Atlantic seaboard.[6] Enslaved African American watermen were ubiquitous in the coastal region and worked as stevedores, coalmen, carpenters, harbor pilots, rowers, crewmen, oystermen, fishermen, and as crew and fishermen on deep sea vessels.[7] Slaves labored alongside freedmen and white watermen and seafarers, but racial boundaries and the meaning of freedom in assessing seafaring labor was not at all straightforward because several forms of bondage were the norm in the maritime world during this period.

It is therefore not surprising that perhaps the most famous American story of the journey from slavery to freedom, that of Frederick Douglass, involved taking advantage of the ambiguous nature of seafaring labor as a means of escape. Douglass had negotiated an agreement with his master to live as a semi-autonomous hired-out day laborer, earning cash wages as a skilled caulker in the shipyards of Baltimore, when in September 1838 he decided to make his bid for freedom by impersonating a free African American sailor journeying northward in search of employment:

I had one friend – a sailor – who owned a sailor's protection, which answered somewhat the purpose of free papers – describing his person, and certifying to the fact that he was a free American sailor. The instrument had at its head the American eagle, which gave it the appearance at once of an authorized document … In choosing this plan upon which to act, I considered the jostle of the train, and the natural haste of the conductor, in a train crowded with passengers, and relied upon my skill and address in playing the sailor as described in my protection, to do the rest. One element in my favor was the kind feeling which prevailed in Baltimore and other seaports at the time, toward "those who go down to the sea

---

[5] David S. Cecelski, *The Waterman's Song: Slavery and Freedom in Maritime North Carolina* (Chapel Hill, NC: University of North Carolina Press, 2001), xi.

[6] Mark Strecker, *Shanghaiing Sailors: A Maritime History of Forced Labor, 1849–1915* (Jefferson, NC: McFarland and Company Publishers, 2014), 28.

[7] Cecelski, *The Waterman's Song*, 13–21.

in ships." "Free trade and sailors' rights" expressed the sentiment of the country just then.[8]

Douglass, dressed in the garb of a typical sailor, boarded a train and waited with at least outward calm for the conductor inspecting the papers of black passengers to reach him.

He was somewhat harsh in tone, and peremptory in manner until he reached me, when, strangely enough, and to my surprise and relief, his whole manner changed. Seeing that I did not readily produce my free papers, as the other colored persons in the car had done, he said to me, in a friendly contrast with that observed towards the others: "I suppose you have your free papers?" To which I answered: "No, sir; I never carry my free papers to sea with me." "But you have something to show that you are a free man, have you not?" "Yes, sir," I answered; "I have a paper with the American eagle on it, and that will carry me round the world." With this I drew from my deep sailor's pocket my seaman's protection, as before described. The merest glance at the paper satisfied him, and he took my fare and went on about his business.[9]

Frederick Douglass married his partner, Anne Murray, a free woman from Baltimore who joined him in New York after his escape. They established their life together in New England and Douglass began his journey to become a preacher and a prominent abolitionist. At the same time, the case of the enslaved Africans from the Spanish ship *Amistad* was working its way through the American court system.

The United States had banned the maritime international slave trade under what became known as the Slave Trade Act (2 Stat. 426, enacted March 2, 1807). Under this law it was illegal for

any person (citizen or foreigner) or any other person whatsoever, either as master, factor, or owner, to build, fit, equip, load or otherwise prepare any ship or vessel, in any port or place within the jurisdiction of the United States, nor shall cause any ship or vessel to sail from any port or place within the same for the purpose of procuring any negro, mulatto, or person of color, from any foreign kingdom, place or country, to be transported to any port or place whatsoever, within the jurisdiction of the United States, to be held, sold, or disposed of as slaves, or to be held to service or labor ...[10]

The 1807 Slave Trade Act created the conditions for the US Navy to intervene against the slave trade along the African coast, on the high

---

[8] Frederick Douglass, *The Life and Times of Frederick Douglass: From 1817–1882* (1881; London: Forgotten Books, 2017), 165–8.

[9] Ibid., 168–9.

[10] "Act of 1807," *Schomburg Center for Research in Black Culture*, http://abolition.nypl .org/content/docs/text/Act_of_1807.pdf (accessed January 14, 2016).

seas, and in American territorial waters. Nevertheless, the transportation of slaves along the US eastern seaboard remained legal until 1865. Laws against the slave trade were extended with the Act to Protect the Commerce of the United States and Punish the Crime of Piracy (3 Stat. 510, enacted March 3, 1819), which made the importation of slaves into the United States an act of piracy punishable by the death penalty. What is interesting about this latter act is the provision that to seize or "decoy" onto a ship "any negro or mulatto, not held to service or labor by the laws of either of the states or territories of the United States with the intent to make such a negro or mulatto a slave is also piracy and punishable by death."[11]

The 1839 rebellion of the enslaved Africans on board the *Amistad* during their voyage to Cuba after having been kidnapped and transported from the West African coast was a cause célèbre for abolitionists in New England and beyond. The case, as Marcus Rediker demonstrates, caused bitter debate among "all stations and several nations in fierce debate, propelling the *Amistad* rebels to the center of a massive controversy about slavery and the rights of unfree people to shape their own destiny. The rebellion became one of the most important events of its time."[12] It was also a test of the treaties and laws passed by the United States government to secure allies and to end the slave trade. Favoring a 1795 bilateral treaty with Spain for mutual protection of shipping and trade, the United States government sought in the Supreme Court to have the enslaved Africans of the *Amistad* returned to their Spanish claimants over and above the laws regarding the abolition of the slave trade and the 1819 law against piracy. As Justice Story pointed out in the opinion of the Court, if the rebellious Africans were slaves, then they could be tried as pirates under American law. Spain had abolished the slave trade in 1820, but if the Africans were slaves before boarding the *Amistad*, then they were pirates and mutineers after. The Court rejected the claim that they were *a priori* slaves and that therefore they had been illegally detained and restrained on the *Amistad* and could not "be deemed pirates or robbers in the sense of the law of nations or the treaty with Spain, or the laws of Spain itself." Interestingly, the Court further rejected that the case came under the jurisdiction of the 1819 Act or requirements under

---

[11] Act of March 3, 1819, 3 Stat. 510 (An Act to protect the commerce of the United States, and punish the crime of piracy), *The Abolition of Slavery, New York Public Library*, http://abolition.nypl.org/content/docs/text/Act_of_1820.pdf.

[12] Marcus Rediker, *The Amistad Rebellion: An Atlantic Odyssey of Slavery and Rebellion* (New York: Penguin Books, 2013), 2–3.

any anti-slave trade act that the United States was required to repatriate the illegally enslaved Africans on the basis that they had already liberated themselves. "When the *Amistad* arrived she was in possession of the negroes, asserting their freedom; and in no sense could they possibly intend to import themselves here, as slaves, or for sale as slaves."[13] The *Amistad* Africans were therefore obliged to repatriate themselves if they wanted to go home and, with the support of abolitionists, they went on a fundraising tour to raise the money to sail home, which they did in November 1841.

But the case had brought attention to the slave trade in a unique way by personalizing the plight of enslaved Africans and their desperate fight for freedom as they experienced the terrors of the Middle Passage. Other famous narratives of individuals, like Olaudah Equiano, who wrote about the experience of enslavement, the Middle Passage, and acculturation to a life of slavery before they were able to escape, told redemption stories of personal fortitude and salvation and Christian faith.[14] The *Amistad* Africans freed themselves during the Middle Passage and remained resolute in their determination to return to their African homelands, a determination that fortified claims by the antislavery movement that enslaved people had their own ideas about freedom.

Newspaper articles, pamphlets, plays, portraits, and even mass-produced souvenirs made the leader of the *Amistad* Africans, Cinqué, into a romantic hero who uttered the rallying cry "Death or Liberty!," thereby echoing romanticized ideas about the origins of America as a nation.[15] As the charismatic spokesperson for the group, Cinqué became a sought after speaker, attracting hundreds of people to hear him talk about the quest for liberation. Rediker traces the incredible popular reach of Cinqué's and the *Amistad* Africans' celebrity, made manifest in the thousands of dollars raised from a broad range of black and white social groups, churches, factories, as well as individuals, to provide funds for their expenses and repatriation. American abolitionists regarded the *Amistad* case as one of their greatest victories along the long road to freedom, he

---

[13] *The United States, Appellants, v. The Libellants and Claimants of the Schooner Amistad, her tackle, apparel, and furniture, together with her cargo, and the Africans mentioned and described in the several libels and claims, Appellees.* Supreme Court of the United States. 40. US 518. January, 1841 Term. http://law2.umkc.edu/faculty/projects/ftrials/amistad/htm (accessed December 8, 2015).

[14] Olaudah Equiano, *The Interesting Narrative of the Life of Olaudah Equiano or Gustavus Vassa, the African. Written by Himself* (New York: Penguin Classics, 2003).

[15] Rediker, *Amistad Rebellion*, 228–9.

argues, also asserting that the case made the abolitionist movement more militant, and inspired leaders including Frederick Douglass.[16]

As Douglass gained prominence in the antislavery movement in the United States, he became more vulnerable to being kidnapped and "recaptured" as a fugitive slave, as he wrote with a hint of irony: "It was thus I was led to seek a refuge in monarchical England from the dangers of republican slavery." Embarking on an antislavery tour of Great Britain and Ireland on board the *Cambria*, Douglass was invited by the captain to give a lecture to the passengers and crew on antislavery. He was later confronted by young male passengers from Georgia and New Orleans who felt his lecture (and his very presence) was an insult to their honor and who, as a result, threatened to throw him overboard. Douglass believed that it was only the captain's order to his crew to put the "salt-water mobocrats" in irons that prevented them from attempting to make good on their threat.[17] His vulnerability as an escaped slave had followed him into open waters.

Douglass returned to the United States only after his supporters arranged for his manumission for a sum of 100 dollars paid to his master. The payment was controversial in antislavery circles. "They thought it a violation of anti-slavery principles, conceding the right of property in man, and a wasteful expenditure of money. For myself, viewing it simply in the light of a ransom, or as money extorted by a robber, and my liberty of more value than one hundred and fifty pounds sterling, I could not see either a violation of the laws of morality or of economy."[18] Douglass returned to the United States a free man just as the winds of change were blowing in a new direction for global seafaring.

The end of the 1840s signaled the beginning of shifts in the global trade, with the United Kingdom repeal of the Navigation Acts opening up trading routes and markets to competitors, including the United States. The opening of the China trade after the First Opium War was followed by the Sino-American Treaty of Wanghia in 1844 that secured American access to treaty ports, especially Shanghai. Strecker argues that the California Gold Rush created a global shortage of maritime labor as crews jumped ship to head for the goldfields; as a result, maritime wages rose.

[16] Ibid., 230–8.
[17] Douglass, *Life and Times*, 289–91.
[18] Ibid., 315.

This situation exacerbated the lucrative "crimping" market, whereby men were kidnapped through fraud, force, and coercion and detained on ships as sailors. The well-established practice of crimping came to be known as "shanghaiing" in the second half of the nineteenth century. Men were tricked into debt bondage by unscrupulous boarding house keepers or "crimpers," who then sold them to ship owners or captains. Sometimes they were literally drugged or bludgeoned into submission and awoke to find themselves on board a ship, having "signed" articles that bonded them to a ship for a specific journey. Often their signatures were forged by shanghaiiers or captains. Seafarers had little recourse under the law to challenge their bondage. "No single factor caused shanghaiing to become a worldwide problem in the seafaring world between 1849 and 1915 – the Age of Shanghaiing. Rather, a variety of circumstances, some related, others not, created a conspiracy of events to make the seafarer's life one of the hardest and most dangerous in the world, exasperated by chronic debt, undermanned crews, and excessive ill-treatment by captains."[19]

The forcible recruitment or "impressment" of men against their will to be hauled on board ships to work as sailors was an old practice. During the colonial period, Strecker argues, "the effective enslavement of sailors by American and British Admiralty laws did not end when they came to shore. In South Carolina, deserting seamen were subject to being hunted as 'runaways.'" In Virginia, seafarers had to carry passes that restricted their ability to come ashore.[20] The first American maritime codes were actually based on British laws and provided for strict penalties for desertion, including imprisonment, forfeiture of wages, and forcible return to the ship. Provisions were also made for punishing those who harbored deserters. The 1790 US Seaman's Act therefore created quasi-military conditions of employment for seafarers who did not have equal rights under their contracts or "articles," and they were also subject to corporal punishment by captains for insubordination on board vessels.[21] Merchant seamen occupied a legal space between naval/military law and labor law that operated against their rights to freedom of choice and movement.[22] Seafarers were not free laborers. The impressment of American merchant sailors by the Royal Navy was the most popular

---

[19] Strecker, *Shanghaiing Sailors*, 24–5.
[20] Ibid., 183.
[21] Craig J. Forsyth, William B. Banston, and Carol Thompson, "The Merchant Marine Desertion Penalty: A Study in Legal Evolution," *International Review of Modern Sociology* 19, no. 1 (Spring 1989), 53–67.
[22] Ibid., 59–60.

cause of the Anglo-American War of 1812 for many American citizens who resented their sovereignty being impinged upon through the indignity of carrying off its men by force.

The United States Supreme Court determined in 1823 that seamen were not fully autonomous citizens. In *Harden v. Gordon* (1823), Justice Joseph Story, the very same justice who so eloquently determined that the *Amistad* Africans were not slaves, stated: "They [seamen] are emphatically the wards of the admiralty; and though not technically incapable of entering into a valid contract, they are treated in the same manner as courts of equity are accustomed to treat young heirs ... [or] wards with their guardians." Although Story sought to protect the rights of seamen from corporal punishment and abuse, including wage theft, his judgments made seamen into minors subject to the paternal control of the state.[23]

The shortage of maritime labor in the mid nineteenth century resulted in dozens of crimping gangs operating with apparent impunity in San Francisco from the 1850s onward. One of the most notorious areas in the city for crimpers was known as the "Barbary Coast," a center for boarding houses, saloons, and brothels. The allusion to the capture and ransoming of Americans by Barbary corsairs in the early nineteenth century was not lost on the locals. In port cities and harbors on both the west and east coasts sailors were susceptible to debt bondage through signing away their advanced wages in exchange for accommodation, food, and alcohol provided by boarding house owners. Sailors and landlubbers alike were vulnerable to being drugged and/or beaten, virtually sold for a bounty after crimpers forged the man's signature on ship's articles, and then forcibly carried on board rowing boats to be transported to ships in harbor in need of extra crew.[24] Once on board, whether voluntarily or not, they were subject to the harsh conditions, discipline, and legislation that governed seafarers. They were not free to leave, even if they had been shanghaiied. Even after the Civil War, when slave seafarers and fishermen became legally freemen, their freedom was mitigated by legislation governing maritime labor. Moreover, once at sea, mariners and fishermen were vulnerable to extreme forms of punishment, including being thrown overboard, either dead or alive, and disappearing without a trace. It was these extreme conditions of vulnerability and exploitation that

[23] R. Kent Newmyer, *Supreme Court Justice Joseph Story: Statesman of the Old Republic* (Chapel Hill, NC: University of North Carolina Press, 1985), 151–2.

[24] Lance S. Davidson, "Shanghaied! The Systematic Kidnapping of Sailors in Early San Francisco," *California History* 64, no. 1 (Winter 1985), 10–17.

bear comparison with the experiences of Vannak Prum in the twenty-first century.

Public commentators – whether pro- or antislavery – compared the conditions of soldiers and seafarers in the Atlantic world with slaves to make their respective cases. Both sides agreed that the paternalism embedded in maritime legislation mitigated against seafarers' fully exercising rights of free labor. Nevertheless, instead of protecting seafarers against crimping, the U.S Shipping Commissioners' Act of 1872 made provisions for the punishment by imprisonment for breach of contract by seafarers.[25] Bill Pickelhaupt has traced the political influence wielded by wealthy and socially well-connected crimpers and boarding house owners, basically gang lords, who were able in some cases to be elected to political office, gaining direct access to shaping legislation that protected their interests.[26]

The term "shanghaiing," of course, refers to maritime bondage linked to long-distance international trade. But shanghaiing existed in the vast array of American deep sea, coastal, riverine, and Great Lakes shipping – on merchant vessels, support vessels, whaling ships, and oyster vessels – wherever maritime laborers were in short supply.[27] Despite the establishment of a Marine Board in San Francisco to license boarding houses, little was done to change the business of crimping. Protests emerged on several fronts, however, not the least being the press, from which many of the most sensational stories emerged. In 1872, the Californian newspaper the *Daily Alta* reported the "Abuse of Seamen" outlining a case of shanghaiing, despite the existence of the Marine Board, where runners boarded a ship in harbor who beat sailors, including the captain's son, and removed them by force to a boarding house from where they were taken to another ship within twenty-four hours, with the shanghaiiers receiving $60 per man.[28]

---

[25] Leon Fink, *Sweatshops at Sea: Merchant Seamen in the World's First Globalized Industry, from 1812 to the Present* (Chapel Hill NC: University of North Carolina Press, 2011), 54.

[26] Bill Pickelhaupt, *Shanghaied in San Francisco* (San Francisco, CA: Flyblister Press, 1986).

[27] Denise, M. Alborn, "Crimping and Shanghaiing on the Columbia River," *Oregon Historical Quarterly* 93, no. 3 (Fall 1992), www/jstor.org/stable/20614468. For a dramatized account of the variety of forms that "shanghaiing" took, see Richard H. Dillon, *Shanghaiing Days: The Thrilling Account of 19th Century Hell-Ships, Bucko Mates and Masters, and Dangerous Ports of Call from San Francisco to Singapore* (Sanger, CA: The Write Thought Inc., 1961).

[28] *Daily Alta* 24, no. 1800, May 30, 1872, www.cdnc.ucr.edu.

The Dingley Act of 1884 again attempted to protect American mariners by making provisions that prohibited advances on wages and limited seamen's allotments to their close relatives. But in 1886 a loophole was created once again allowing boarding house owners to receive seamen's advanced wages. Attempts at organizing seamen's unions, marine hiring halls, savings banks, aid organizations, seamen's missions, and seamen's homes all aimed at improving conditions for seafarers and to end the practice of shanghaiing. The Coastal Seamen's Union started publishing its own newspaper, the *Coast Seamen's Journal*, which publicized cases of abuse against seafarers committed on ships and on land. But it was not until the passing of the Maguire Act of 1895 (28 Stat. 667, enacted February 18, 1895) that the imprisonment of seafarers deserting vessels was discontinued for coastal shipping but not for foreign trade.[29]

In 1895, another case of maritime abuse underlined how little had changed in over one hundred years. Four sailors on the ship *Argo* plying the waters of the west coast deserted ashore with the understanding they would be protected from imprisonment and forcible re-enlistment under the Maguire Act. Strecker describes how the sailors sued after their arrest, claiming protections under the provisions against indentured servitude under the Thirteenth Amendment. The case made its way to the US Supreme Court. The court decided authorities could indeed arrest seamen who refused to honor their contracts. More infamously, it ruled that the Thirteenth Amendment did not apply to military personnel, merchant mariners, or minors and those under guardianship, this last being a double strike against a seaman's liberty considering Judge Story had made all American sailors wards of the state with his 1823 ruling.[30]

It was not until 1906 that Congress addressed the issue of shanghaiing directly. President Theodore Roosevelt signed "An Act to prohibit shanghaiing in the United States" on June 28. The breadth of the Act demonstrates how widespread the practice had become. It was designed to protect "any person [who] shall perform service or labor of any kind on board any vessel of any kind engaged in trade and commerce among the several States or with foreign nations" against force, threats, untrue representations made under the influence of drugs and alcohol, and

---

[29] Forsyth, Bankston, and Thompson, "Merchant Marine Penalty," 60.
[30] Strecker, *Shanghaiing Sailors*, 190–1.

trickery. The Act was supplied to all American consular officials and the diplomatic representatives of maritime countries.[31] In draft, the bill had included the phrase "thereupon forcibly confine or detain such person on board such vessel with intent to make such person a slave ..." but it was decided that the term was "a little too severe."[32]

The headline from the *Oregon Journal* on December 6, 1908 declared in bold typeface that "Sailors Must Be Slaves No More."[33] Despite all previous measures, the power of boarding housekeepers and crimpers to entrap sailors in debt bondage endured. Ironically, it was the tragedy of the sinking of the *Titanic* that brought the issue of maritime safety and sailors' working conditions to global public awareness. Under the stewardship of Senator La Follette, the US Congress passed what has come to be known as the "Seamen's Act," which set health, safety, and conditions of employment regulations, including limiting the number of non-English-speaking and underqualified sailors. It also abolished imprisonment for desertion, reduced the punitive measures for insubordination, and established the seamen's right to quit. The Act provided for harsh penalties against captains and ship owners for breaking the provisions, especially for non-payment of wages. The immediate result, however, was that ship owners threatened to evade the law by using flags of convenience in order to evade the law and keep their operating costs low. As the author of the Act, Senator La Follette declared:

It is four days since the President signed the Seamen's Bill, and already the masters of the sea are beginning to threaten dire vengeance ... Already they are giving warning that they will cancel their American registry ... With the American flag at the masthead they now man their vessels with underpaid, underfed Chinese with whom the owners have displaced American seamen. The American sailor in his bondage has been forgotten for generations. At last his appeal has been heard. It was reserved for President Wilson ... to approve a measure which blots out the last vestige of slavery under the American flag. The Seamen's Bill is the second proclamation of freedom. The fourth of March, 1915, is the sailor's emancipation day.[34]

---

[31] *House Documents. Volume 1. Part 1.* 59th Congress. Second Session. December 3, 1906–March 4, 1907 (Washington, DC: Government Printing Office, 1909), 5.

[32] *Hearing on the Bill (H.R. 383) to Prohibit Shanghaiing and Peonage in the United States.* United States. Congress. House. Committee on Merchant Marine and Fisheries (Washington, DC: US Government Printing Office, 1906), 16.

[33] Alborn, "Crimping and Shanghaiing," 262.

[34] Philip B. Kennedy, "The Seamen's Act," *The Annals of the American Academy of Political and Social Science* 63 (January 1916), 232–3.

THE PAST IN THE PRESENT

The partial transition from sail to steamships during the late nineteenth century further complicated maritime labor regimes and organization. The implications of shifting skill sets had already undermined some forms of collective bargaining by seamen. In the aftermath of the First World War and the establishment of the League of Nations, there was an impetus for the internationalization of reform. The International Labour Organization (ILO) oversaw negotiations for international regulations, but these immediately highlighted the unequal conditions of seafarers in the British Empire and the particular plight of Chinese seamen hired on foreign vessels. As debates for an international maritime agreement continued, the United States and other nations continued to alter their own legal frameworks governing maritime labor.[35]

Robert La Follette's impassioned commentary on the aftermath of the American Seamen's Act proved to be prophetic. Flags of convenience have dominated global shipping since the early twentieth century and have mitigated against global reforms for seafarers. In a 2008 *Amicus Curiae* to the Supreme Court of the United States regarding seafarers' rights to compensation for injury, the organization Port Ministries International laid out their case:

The working conditions for seafarers remain largely unchanged since Justice Story's time. For thousands of today's international seafarers life at sea is modern slavery and their work place is a slave ship. Poor or unsafe living conditions, unpaid wages, long hours of work without breaks, abusive employers, abandonment of entire crews, little or no job security, the suppression of legitimate union activity and the blacklisting of seafarers that participate in union activities are all frequent occurrences on ships. Most seafarers work seven days a week with long hours each day for months on end.[36]

It is therefore not surprising that human trafficking has flourished in this already dangerous and insecure industry for seafarers and fishermen.

Human trafficking at sea is a global phenomenon. One of the most widespread cases involving slavery at sea is the Thai fishing industry – where Vannak Prum was enslaved as an illegal immigrant from Cambodia. A report produced by the Environmental Justice Foundation (EJF) about

---

[35] Fink, *Sweatshops at Sea*, 145–67.

[36] *Atlantic Sounding Co., Inc. and Weeks Marine, Inc. v. Edgar L Townsend.* On Writ of Certiorari to the United States Court of Appeals for the Eleventh Circuit. Brief of Port Ministries International as Amicus Curiae in Support of Respondent. Supreme Court of the United States. No. 08-214 (2008), 9.

maritime enslavement magnified the comments made about the vulnerability of legally employed international seafarers:

As a result of long hours, low and unpredictable pay, physically demanding work
and long periods at sea, the Thai fishing industry is suffering an acute labour
shortage, with a shortfall of labour for over 10,000 jobs in 2011. This labour
shortage is fuelling human trafficking to supply cheap labour for work on Thai
fishing boats. Multiple reports over the past five years have documented abuses of
trafficked boat workers in Thailand, including bonded labour, excessive working
hours, little or no pay, threats of violence, physical abuse and murder.[37]

The importance of the Thai fishing industry to the national economy
cannot be understated. Thailand is the third largest exporter of fish and
fish-based products in the world. The EJF report documents the collusion
of state officials, in particular the police, with human trafficking onto
fishing boats where migrants from surrounding countries including
Myanmar and Cambodia.[38]

The ILO's report *Caught at Sea: Forced Labour and Trafficking
in Fisheries* reiterates the vulnerability of men trafficked into the
fishing industry globally, particularly in areas where illegal fishing and
overfishing are rife. The collapse of regional fisheries aligned with the
ever-increasing consumption demand drive the impetus for both environmental and human exploitation. The reach of the illegal fishing industry
is global. An earlier EJF report stated that "Global Illegal, Unreported
and Unregulated (IUU) or 'pirate' fishing is plundering fish stocks, devastating marine environments and stealing from some of the poorest countries and people ... The abusive and often illegal treatment of workers
aboard IUU vessels ... meet the International Labour Organization definition of forced labor..."[39] Despite decades of the ILO, International
Maritime Organization (IMO) and United Nations, multilateral and
bilateral agreements, as well as international and national laws, the trend
is toward an expansion of slavery at sea.[40] The continued use of flags
of convenience, shell companies, and open registries obscures the jur-
isdictional boundaries of cases of enslavement, even if individual ships

[37] Environmental Justice Foundation (EJF), *Sold to the Sea: Human Trafficking in Thailand's
Fishing Industry* (London: EJF, 2013), 4.
[38] EJF, *Sold to the Sea*, 11.
[39] *All at Sea: The Abuse of Human Rights Aboard Illegal Fishing Vessels* (London: EJF,
2010), 4.
[40] *Caught at Sea: Forced Labour and Trafficking in Fisheries*, International Labour Office,
Special Action Programme to Combat Forced Labour (Geneva: International Labour
Organization, 2013).

are identified as having participated in human trafficking. Most of the thirty-two countries and international ship registries considered Flags of Convenience (FoC) by the International Transport Workers Federation are themselves poor countries, the majority being small island states. North Korea, Hong Kong, Cambodia, Myanmar, and Singapore are all FoC states. The United States territory of the Marshall Islands is one of the three major FoC countries, although it is not clear that all FoC states are linked to cases of human trafficking.[41] The 1982 United Nations Convention on the Law of the Sea appears to have had little effect and the Maritime Labour Convention (MLC) of 2006 did not enter into force until 2013.[42] "The challenge is to break this cycle of indeterminacy and ensure that all fishers – regardless of factors such as their status as migrant workers, the nationality of the fishing operator, the maritime zone in which the vessel is found or the flag State in which the vessel is registered – are protected from labour exploitation."[43] The proliferation of international agencies dealing with the issue, including the ILO, International Organization for Migration, Food and Agricultural Organization of the United Nations, INTERPOL, United Nations Office on Drugs and Crime, United Nations Inter-Agency Project on Human Trafficking, High Seas Task Force, and International Maritime Organization, to mention just a few of the organizations and initiatives, have had little effect.[44]

[41] EJF, *All at Sea*, 18–20.
[42] The Maritime Labour Convention (MLC) is considered the fourth pillar of modern international maritime law. The others are the International Convention for the Safety of Life at Sea (SOLAS), which was first passed in the wake of the *Titanic* sinking, with latest amendments coming into force in 2014; the International Convention on Standards of Training, Certification and Watchkeeping for Seafarers (STCW), with latest amendments coming into force in 2017; and the International Convention for the Prevention of Pollution from Ships (MARPOL), with latest amendments coming into force in 2014.
[43] ILO, *Caught at Sea*, 50.
[44] Department of State, United States of America, *Trafficking in Persons (TIP) Report*, July 2015. The 2015 *TIP Report* indicated the following states were involved in, or had cases of, human trafficking related to fishing and seafaring, including cases of sex trafficking of women and girls for tourist fishing boats and commercial fishing crews: Angola, Bangladesh, Belize, Brazil, Burma, Burundi, Cambodia, Cameroon, Comoros, Republic of Congo, Costa Rica, Fiji, Gabon, Ghana, Honduras, Hong Kong, India, Indonesia, Israel, Jamaica, Kenya, Democratic People's Republic of Korea, Kiribati, Republic of Korea, Laos, Madagascar, Malaysia, Malawi, Marshall Islands, Mauritius, Federated States of Micronesia, Mongolia, New Zealand, Namibia, Pakistan, Palau, Papua New Guinea, Peru, Philippines, Russia, Saudi Arabia, Seychelles, Sierra Leone, Singapore, Solomon Islands, South Africa, Sri Lanka, Suriname, Tanzania, Taiwan, Thailand, Timor-Leste, Trinidad and Tobago, Uganda, United Arab Emirates, United Kingdom, United States of America, and Uruguay.

Vannak Prum's journey as an illegal migrant from Cambodia seeking work in Thailand is emblematic of a much larger scale and enduring pattern of exploitation. In his case, it is clear that Thai and Malaysian officials were complicit in his being trafficked, first on board a fishing vessel and subsequently, after his escape, onto a plantation on the island of Borneo. "Male Cambodians are increasingly recruited in Thailand for work on fishing boats and subsequently subjected to forced labor on Thai-owned vessels in international waters. Cambodian victims escaping this form of exploitation have been identified in Malaysia, Indonesia, Mauritius, Fiji, Senegal, and South Africa."[45] Former Secretary of State, John Kerry, specifically mentioned the enslavement of men on board fishing vessels in Southeast Asia in his introduction to the 2015 Trafficking in Persons Report.[46]

One century after the passing of the LaFollette Act, modern "shanghaiing" is back in the news. Two major investigative reports in 2015 highlighted the plight of people enslaved at sea and the direct link between the cheap fish available for mass consumption in the United States and extreme forms of environmental and labor exploitation. Ian Urbina wrote a series of six articles under the title "Outlaw Ocean" for *The New York Times*, detailing the global spread of "scofflaw" ships which were not being identified nor prosecuted for breaking national and international laws, including cases of murder.[47] Part 3 of the series, "'Sea Slaves': The Human Misery that Feeds Pets and Livestock," details the story of men from Cambodia, like Vannak Prum, who were lured across the border to Thailand with promises of construction jobs in Bangkok, only to find themselves trafficked onto unregistered "ghost ships," which leave port for months or years at a time to catch fish in the South China Sea, docking with "mother ships" that process their catches to avoid going into port. Short-handed at the eleventh hour, captains sometimes take desperate measures. "They just snatch people," one captain explained, noting that some migrants are drugged or kidnapped and forced onto boats. "Brokers charge double."[48] Shanghaiing is alive and well in Southeast Asia.

[45] *TIP Report 2015*, 112.
[46] Ibid., 4.
[47] Ian Urbina, "Murder at Sea: Captured on Video, but Killers Go Free," *The New York Times*, July 20, 2015, www.nytimes.com/2015/07/20.
[48] Ian Urbina, "'Sea Slaves': The Human Misery That Feeds Pets and Livestock," *The New York Times*, July 27, 2015.

The International Organization for Migration documented an Associated Press investigation with ten stories revealing the vast extent of human trafficking in the Southeast Asian fishing industry.[49] In one case, more than a thousand potential victims of forced labor on fishing vessels were held on the Indonesian island of Bejina; some who tried to escape were kept in cages. Others were murdered for insubordination on the fishing trawlers or on land. The AP investigation linked the supply chain of fish processed by slave labor in Bejina and similar sites to pet food manufacturers in the USA, prompting legal action. "In the past month, three separate class-action lawsuits have been filed naming Mars Inc., IAMS Co., Proctor and Gamble, Nestle USA Inc., Nestle Purina Petcare Co., and Costco, accusing them of having seafood supply chains tainted with slave labor."[50]

One of the AP stories focused on Myint Naing, a Burmese man enslaved on Thai fishing trawlers on and off for twenty-two years. Myint was severely beaten and starved on numerous occasions, and also reported that "workers on some boats were killed for slowing down or trying to jump ship." The reporters followed his return home to a small southern Myanmar village in Mon state, where he was finally able to return to his family.[51] Most of the men rescued from slavery at sea go home injured and traumatized, many suffering from depression and PTSD, and remain for the most part mired in the poverty that lured them to risk seeking work away from home in the first place. Their stories have no happy ending. Vannak Anan Prum returned home and began to paint images about his experiences, at first to illustrate to his wife what his life had been like, and eventually to demonstrate to others the plight of modern sea slaves. A circuitous route led him to becoming a TIP Hero in 2012, after which he has continued to tell his story in order to inform others about the invisible slaves in our midst. His autobiography, *The Dead Eye and the Deep Blue Sea: The World of Slavery at Sea – A Graphic Memoir*, was published in

---

[49] Paul Dillon, "Over 500 New Human Trafficking Victims Identified in Indonesia since Benjina 'Slave Fisheries' Exposed," *International Organization for Migration Newsdesk*, August 3, 2015, https://weblog.ion.int/.

[50] Esther Htusan and Margie Mason, "More than 2000 Enslaved Fishermen Rescued in 6 Months," *Seafood from Slaves: An AP Investigation Helps Free Slaves in the 21st Century*, Associated Press, September 17, 2015, www.ap.org/seafood-from-slaves. Martha Mendoza, "Nestle Confirms Labor Abuse among its Thai Seafood Suppliers," *Seafood from Slaves*, November 23, 2015.

[51] Margie Mason, "Myanmar Fisherman Goes Home after 22 Years as a Slave," *Seafood from Slaves*, July 1, 2015.

2016.[52] 163 years after Solomon Northup published his memoir of illegal enslavement as a contribution to the abolition movement, Vannak Prum has become a neo-abolitionist, using his artistic talent to "paint the pain away," illustrating to the world the plight of modern slaves at sea.[53]

---

[52] Vannak Anan Prum, with Jocelyn Pederick and Ben Pederick, *The Dead Eye and the Deep Blue Sea: The World of Slavery at Sea – A Graphic Memoir* (New York: Seven Stories Press, 2016).

[53] Sarah Thrust, "Painting the Pain Away," *Southeast Asia Globe*, November 11, 2012, www.sea-globe.com/painting-the-pain-away.

6

"All Boys are Bound to Someone"

Reimagining Freedom in the History of Child Slavery

Anna Mae Duane

In his powerlessness, the slave became an extension of his master's power. He was a human surrogate, recreated by his master with god-like power in his behalf.

Orlando Patterson[1]

In the wake of the data gathered by the 1840 US Census, pundits asserted that freedom was a condition that one needed to grow into. The census's (soon disproven) statistics indicated that the further North black people lived, the more likely they were to become insane, or physically disabled, or both. Freedom, it seemed, made black people sick. The further South the census takers traveled, the healthier African Americans were reported to be. One startled physician, trying to account for the shocking figures, suggested that slavery must have had "a wonderful influence" by freeing its subjects of adult responsibilities which the free, self-thinking and self-acting enjoy and sustain." The enslaved actually enjoyed better health, the argument ran, precisely because they were denied "the liabilities and dangers of active self direction."[2] Another commentator agreed, adding that the census confirmed that black people simply had not grown into the necessary maturity for freedom. It would require "many successive generations," he argued, before people of African descent could handle

---

[1] Orlando Patterson, *Slavery and Social Death: A Comparative Study* (Cambridge, MA: Harvard University Press, 1982), 4.

[2] Edward Jarvis, "Statistics of Insanity in the United States," *Boston Medical and Surgical* 27 (1842), 116–21. To his credit, once he realized the figures were falsified, Jarvis worked strenuously to refute the assumptions based on this erroneous data.

the "difficult task of self-direction, amidst the dangerous temptations and ardent rivalries of civilized life."[3]

The idea that somehow racial characteristics could render one unfit for freedom – indeed, that freedom would actively harm minds not yet strengthened by "successive generations" of progress – became an important element in justifying slavery's continued hold in the United States. Proslavery proponents have made a variety of arguments that rendered all people of African descent perpetual children, too immature to cope with the demands of self-government. Although historians have illuminated and critiqued this infantilizing tactic, few disagree with its underlying premise: freedom is a privilege belonging solely to mature adults. Our objections arise at the act of rendering adults as children, not with act of disqualifying children for citizenship rights. This chapter suggests that scholars' and activists' approaches to historical and modern iterations of slavery are shaped by an investment in a particularly adult form of individuality, freedom, and citizenship. This independence-based model erases the perspectives and needs of children, even as evidence continues to accrue indicating that children have comprised a large proportion of enslaved people, both before and after Emancipation.[4]

Because the work of disentangling enslaved people from infantilizing narratives culled from the 1840 Census has been so arduous, it's not surprising that historians have been wary of putting children at the center of their inquiries into slavery and its legacies. But it is precisely within the facile comparisons between child and slave that we find one of slavery's most persistent, and pernicious, legacies: the seductive logic of paternalism, in which caretaking becomes a means of control, and "protection"

---

[3] "Reflections on the Census of 1840," *Southern Literary Messenger* 9 (1843), 340–52.

[4] It might seem a bold assertion that age is – and was – as vital a component of slavery as race, class, or gender, but even the most cursory look at the numbers provides remarkable verification of the claim. In the field of antebellum Atlantic slavery, the work of Wilma King, David Eltis, and others has revealed that perhaps as many as half the people who endured the Middle Passage were under the age of eighteen. Nineteenth-century census records indicate that the majority of people living in slavery in the US were minors. In our own era, figures from UNICEF indicate that 171 million children in the developing world are exposed to the worst forms of coerced and exploitative labor, including sex work and warfare. Wilma King, *Stolen Childhood: Slave Youth in Nineteenth Century America* (Bloomington, IN: Indiana University Press, 1997); David Eltis, The Transatlantic Slave Trade Database, www.slavevoyages.org/; Karen Sánchez-Eppler, "'Remember, Dear, when the Yankees came through here I was only ten years old': Valuing the Enslaved Child of the WPA Slave Narratives," in Anna Mae Duane, ed., *Child Slavery before and after Emancipation: An Argument for Child-Centered Slavery Studies* (Cambridge: Cambridge University Press, 2017).

provides cover for exploitation. It is largely assumed that children – like the allegedly suffering freed people cited in the 1840 Census – would be harmed by exercising the right to either give or refuse consent, by taking on the burden in the words of the 1840's commentator, of "self-thinking and self-acting." A broad investment in childhood innocence – that is, innocence of hardship, of the marketplace, of sexual relations – argues that children can only be harmed by exposure to, or action within, any of these dangerous realms. Young people must be kept from knowledge, kept from experience, and most of all, kept from making choices about work, sex, or other adult concerns. However, being "protected" from "self-thinking" actually denies children the ability to say no as well as yes. The work of paternalism naturalizes labor relations that would undoubtedly be considered exploitative when applied to adults. Children perform domestic or agricultural labor under extremely harsh conditions without pay; they are routinely subject to corporal punishment; and they are denied ability to legally protest or to leave conditions they find harmful or exploitative. All of these practices are largely accepted – even in the United States – within the normal experience of childhood. Further, these practices are held up as good for the child, who needs freedom curtailed for her own protection. In the wake of legal slavery's demise, an abiding attachment to an adult's "natural" proprietary and paternalistic claims toward children allows acts of exploitation to function as natural parts of the life cycle, in which coercion and oppression are benevolent correlates to the work of growing up.

I draw from Jean-Robert Cadet's twenty-first-century narrative of child slavery to suggest reading Frederick Douglass's 1845 *Narrative* – often interpreted as emblematic of a heroic fight for independence – as a site where we can engage slavery as a child's story, and where we can see freedom as a goal that children, past and present, have sought in courageous and creative ways. Considering childhood a central feature, rather than just the prelude to a triumphant ending, of both of Cadet's modern memoir and Douglass's antebellum autobiography asks us to rethink assumptions about the "natural" attributes of childhood. Centering children in these narratives illuminates how the legal and emotional investment we have in those attributes often exploits children's vulnerability to enslavement rather than protects them from it.

The 1845 *Narrative of the Life Frederick Douglass* is among the most famous, and thus the most widely taught, of pre-Emancipation slave narratives. It is, as many critics have asserted, a tale of manly valor that taps into Americans' admiration for heroic, rebellious independence.

Beginning as a helpless young boy deprived of maternal care, Douglass grows into awareness, rebellion, freedom, and eventual fame. In Douglass's words, his is a story that explains how a "slave was made a man." In doing so, his narrative conflates one act of transformation – a boy becoming a man – with another: a slave becoming free. Both childhood and enslavement are states that Douglass must grow out of and away from. In one of the most famous passages in the text, a teenage Douglass dreams longingly of freedom, but reminds himself that no child can lay claim to it. "Besides," he tells himself, "I am but a boy, and all boys are bound to some one." Freedom is something that children must wait for. While the misery of an enslaved childhood is galling, Douglass's youth encourages him to postpone his desire for freedom, to believe that "[t]here is a better day coming."[5]

That better day is hurried along by Douglass's decision to stand in open rebellion to the slave breaker Covey. The scene offers a satisfying David and Goliath story, in which the oppressed slave rises up and overpowers the man who seeks to dominate him. Douglass makes an explicit decision to refuse any further abuse, and to fight off anyone who might try to force him to change his mind. "I resolved to fight," Douglass relates, "and suiting my action to the resolution, I seized Covey hard by the throat; and as I did so, I rose." For Douglass, and for those who have read and studied his narrative, this moment of rising through resistance is a key point in his road to freedom:

This battle with Mr. Covey was the turning-point in my career as a slave. It rekindled the few expiring embers of freedom, and revived within me a sense of my own manhood. It recalled the departed self- confidence, and inspired me again with a determination to be free.

It's an incredibly gratifying moment – one in which the lines between oppressor and oppressed are remarkably clear, and resistance is forceful and decisive. By grabbing his tormentor by the throat, Douglass is finally able to rise.

In his rhetoric yoking freedom to empowered manhood, Douglass tapped into Enlightenment philosophies that had crafted rights and responsibilities in direct opposition to the attributes of childhood. John Locke and other Enlightenment thinkers made children's exclusion from political power not only necessary, but also natural, as they sought to

---

[5] *The Narrative of the Life of Frederick Douglass, an American Slave, Written by Himself* (New York: Simon and Brown, 2013), 52, 49. All further references to this text are from this edition.

imagine power that would reside in reason rather than heredity. Locke's *Second Treatise of Government* – undeniably influential to the foundation of liberal democratic rights – casts the young child's vulnerability as a valid (if temporary) exclusion from the rights Adam can claim. Only with the strength and reason of an adult can any subject lay claim to autonomy of citizenship.

Adam was created a perfect man, his body and mind in full possession of their strength and reason, and so was capable, from the first instant of his being to provide for his own support and preservation, and govern his actions according to the dictates of the law of reason which God had implanted in him. From him the world is peopled with his descendants, who are all born infants, weak and helpless, without knowledge or understanding: but to supply the defects of this imperfect state, till the improvement of growth and age hath removed them, Adam and Eve, and after them all parents were, by the law of nature, under an obligation to preserve, nourish, and educate the children they had begotten; not as their own workmanship, but the workmanship of their own maker, the Almighty, to whom they were to be accountable for them.[6]

The contract theory that shapes current legal conceptions of freedom – and the national and human rights that protect that freedom – rely on precisely the sort of "perfect man" Locke describes: an autonomous adult, able to proffer both assets and punishment at the bargaining table.[7]

Children have little to bargain with, and therefore cannot participate in a contract of equals. "In order to surrender rights and accept duties," Amy Dru Stanley reminds us, "parties to contract had to be sovereigns of themselves, possessive individuals entitled to their own persons, labor, and faculties."[8] As the opening anecdote about the 1840 Census illustrates, whites aligned African Americans with childhood and childishness in order to exclude them from the contract, an exclusion shared by women, indigenous people, the disabled, and others.[9] In short, adults

---

[6] John Locke, *Second Treatise of Government*, 6th ed. (London: A Millar et al., 1764), 6.56, www.gutenberg.org/files/7370/7370-h/7370-h.htm.

[7] Holly Brewer, *By Birth or by Consent: Children, Law and the Anglo-American Revolution in Authority* (Chapel Hill, NC: Omohundro Institute, 2007). For two different perspectives on how to realign our vision of rights and the social contract from which they are derived, see Martha Nussbaum, *Frontiers of Justice: Disability, Nationality, Species Membership* (Cambridge, MA: Harvard University Press, 2006) and Martha Fineman, "The Vulnerable Subject: Anchoring Equality in the Human Condition," *Yale Journal of Law and Feminism* 1 (2008–9), 1–23.

[8] Amy Dru Stanley, *From Bondage to Contract: Wage Labor, Marriage, and the Market in the Age of Slave Emancipation* (Cambridge: Cambridge University Press, 1998), 3.

[9] See "Introduction," in Anna Mae Duane, *Suffering Childhood in Early America: Violence, Race and the Making of the Child Victim* (Athens, GA: University of Georgia Press, 2010).

deserve freedom precisely because they are not children. Maintaining that freedom requires keeping all things childish at bay. "The child subject's exclusion," Lucia Hodgson argues, "is the foundation of the adult subject's inclusion."[10]

In the wake of legal slavery's demise in the US, home became the place where that adult freedom became defined in opposition to the dependent children in the household. In the introduction to Frederick Douglass's 1855 narrative, *My Bondage and My Freedom*, James McCune Smith argues that Douglass's move into freedom was only possible because he was unbound by the intensified slavery that emerges from the responsibility of heading a home he could neither control nor protect.

For his special mission, then, this was, considered in connection with his natural gifts, a good schooling; and, for his special mission, he doubtless "left school" just at the proper moment. Had he remained longer in slavery – had he fretted under bonds until the ripening of manhood and its passions, until the drear agony of slave-wife and slave-children had been piled upon his already bitter experiences – then, not only would his own history have had another termination, but the drama of American slavery would have been essentially varied.[11]

Douglass's freedom, and by extension the "drama of American slavery" – a drama that would end in freedom – was only possible because of Douglass's manly independence. Certainly he couldn't have achieved liberation as a child – the very presence of an imagined child in Douglass's life gives a dreary "termination" not only to Douglass's hopes for freedom, but for the trajectory of American slavery itself.[12] In McCune Smith's formulation, infantilization is a double-edged sword, enslaving adults by denying them the capacity to protect dependents, and diminishing children by denying them access to the care paternalism promises.

McCune Smith wasn't the only one figuring childhood as the antithesis of liberty: the ability to exert both protection and control over one's family was foundational to freedom as described both by those who supported slavery and by those who opposed it. Representative Chilton

---

[10] Lucia Hodgson, "Phillis Wheatley Peters: Infant Muse to Tragic Mulatta," *EAL* 49, no. 3 (2014), 663–82.

[11] James McCune Smith, "Introduction," in Frederick Douglass, *My Bondage and My Freedom* (Auburn, NY: Miller, Orton, and Mulligan, 1855), xix.

[12] For more on Frederick Douglass's masculinist vision of independence see: Karen Sánchez Eppler, Deborah Gray White, and Ben Slote, "Revising Freely: Frederick Douglass and the Politics of Disembodiment," *Auto/Biography Studies* 11, no. 1 (1996), 19–37; Deborah Gray White, *Ar'n't I a Woman?* (New York: W.W. Norton & Company, 1985); Karen Sanchez-Eppler, *Touching Liberty: Abolition, Feminism, and the Politics of the Body* (Berkeley, CA: University of California Press, 1993).

White of Ohio, arguing against abolition in 1865, made the case that the same property relations existed between master and slave as between parent and child – both were central to the freedom and rights of the householder. The parent, White argued, "has the right to the service of his child; he has a property in the service of that child … The master has a right of property in the service of his apprentice. All these rights rest upon the same basis as a man's right of property in the service of slaves. The relation is clearly and distinctly defined by the law, and as clearly and distinctly recognized by the Constitution of the United States." [13] In 1864, Representative Fernando Wood had made a similar argument, insisting that "the social and domestic relations are equally matters of individual ownership." For Wood, however, the householder owned not only the labor of household dependents, but also their love. "The affections of a man's wife and children," Wood insisted, "are among the dearest of his possessions." [14]

Antislavery activists were just as convinced that claiming ownership of both the love *and* the labor of children was part of the very definition of freedom. Arguing for the Civil Rights Act of 1866, Senator Jacob Howard asked, "Is a free man to be deprived of the right of having a family, a wife, children, home? What definition will you attach to the word 'freeman' that does not include those ideas!" As legal slavery waned in the US, children were repeatedly and explicitly exempted from conceptions of freedom. During debates surrounding the ratification of the Thirteenth Amendment to the US Constitution, *all* lawmakers agreed that repealing slavery had no bearing on the involuntary servitude of children. "The [Thirteenth] amendment, everybody knows and nobody dare deny," thundered Senator Edgar Cowen, "was simply made to liberate the negro slave from his master. Will anybody … undertake to say that it was to prevent the involuntary servitude of my child to me …? Certainly not." [15]

The assumption that adult freedom is based, at least in part, on a parent's proprietary rights to the affections and the labor of children continues to flourish in the twenty-first century. As a nation with out-sized influence on the United Nations' actions and humanitarian funding, the US remains the only nation that has refused to ratify the UN rights

[13] Lea S. VanderVelde, "The Labor Vision of the Thirteenth Amendment," *University of Pennsylvania Law Review* 138, no. 2 (December 1989), 454. I am grateful to Professor VanderVelde for drawing my attention to this debate. Cong. Globe. 38th Cong. 2d Session 215 (1865) (remarks of Rep. White).

[14] Cong. Globe. 38th Cong. 1st Session 2941 (1864) (remarks of Rep. F. Wood).

[15] Cong. Globe. 39th Congress. 1st Session 499 (1866) (remarks of Senator Cowen).

of the child, largely because of the perception that it attacks the "natural" freedom of parents. In 1995, Jesse Helms, senator for North Carolina, argued that the treaty's emphasis on children's right to consent contradicted the rights, freedom, and sovereignty guaranteed to parents by the US Constitution. Helms was particularly horrified by language in the treaty that stipulates that adults "shall assure to the child who is capable of forming his or her own views the right to express those views freely in all matters affecting the child." Not only that, the child's views should be "given due weight in accordance with the age and maturity of the child." "What on earth does this mean?" Helms asked, his incredulity echoing the shock congressmen expressed at the idea of a free child a century earlier. Helms found it unthinkable that the US would be censured if "a parent did not leave it to a child to choose which school to attend," if a parent "did not allow a child to decide whether to accompany the family to church," or "if a parent did not consult a child before requiring that he or she complete family chores."[16] According to Helms and his adherents, the freedoms enshrined in the US Constitution allow parents to compel children to work, believe, and learn according to adult demands without any consent on the part of the child. If parents cannot claim sovereignty over their own house and their own children, pre- and post-Emancipation arguments run, then they are not free. This argument still has enough weight to keep the US from ratifying the treaty – to date, the only nation not to do so.[17]

It's hardly surprising that twenty-first-century scholars and activists are unsure of how to define child slavery when both-pre and post definitions of slavery have cast control over home and children as a distinguishing line between slavery and freedom. As Amy Dru Stanley has demonstrated, in "postbellum America the promise of a home unscathed by the market

---

[16] June 14, 1995. Comments of Senator Jesse Helms (R-SC) on Senate Resolution 133 – Relative to the United Nations Convention on the Rights of the Child Congressional Record, http://pangaea.org/street_children/world/helms.htm.

[17] Until 2015, the United States was joined by South Sudan and Somalia in their failure to ratify this treaty. As of now, the USA remains the only holdout. The UN Human Rights webpage provides a full text of the Convention and its signatories: http://indicators .ohchr.org/. For one recent example of the persistence of Helm's perspective see: "Taking Kids to Church Violates Their Human Rights," *Charisma News*, June 29, 2016, www .charismanews.com/world/58109-taking-kids-to-church-violates-their-human-rights-says-un. For an explanation of the argument aligning parental power with American sovereignty, see "Why Won't America Ratify the UN Convention on Children's Rights?" *The Economist*, October 6, 2013, www.economist.com/blogs/economist-explains/2013/ 10/economist-explains-2.

distinguished the rewards of free contract and chattel slavery." Indeed, the rigors of the Industrial Revolution threatened to make little difference between the hireling and the slave in terms of quality of life, as wages often barely allowed for survival. The key distinction between slave and free labor, commentators argued, was not in living standards, but rather that such living could take place in a private home over which the residents had control. In response to worries that freed people would not work under harsh conditions for little pay, Henry Ward Beecher stipulated that Americans need only give the black man "the prospect of a home, a family that is not marketable, and he will work."[18]

That premise – that a home untouched by public predations of both the market and the government was the repository of a householder's liberty – was only amplified as the United States sought to create clear lines between slavery and freedom. Throughout the nineteenth century, children were increasingly cast as the embodiment of the household's sacred exclusion from the corruptive influences of money, and the sex and violence that often accompanied its exchange. As children became less important as laborers in white middle-class families, Viviana Zelizier has demonstrated, their value increased as repositories of a particular sort of innocence – an innocence that reinforced the power of adults who could, through their savvy negotiations with the public world, keep their children untouched by its hungers.[19] As the work of Robin Bernstein and others has made clear, children of color are often excluded from such protections, forced to shoulder adult burdens while still being denied adult privileges. Yet it is precisely this insistence that children occupy a space of innocent un-freedom protected by adults that creates a cruel double bind for vulnerable children like Haitian *restavec* Jean-Robert Cadet, whose slavery is built explicitly on the idea that children cannot, and should not, be free to refuse a householder's demands.[20]

While the laws that held Frederick Douglass captive were revoked in 1865, the idea that "all children must be bound to someone" remained firmly intact, as evidenced by the large number of children who, upon "emancipation," were immediately apprenticed, often to their old

---

[18] *National Freedman*, November 1865, 332. Qtd in Dru Stanley, *From Bondage to Contract*, 138.

[19] Viviana Zelizer, *Pricing the Priceless Child: The Changing Social Value of Children* (Princeton, NJ: Princeton University Press), 1985.

[20] Robin Bernstein, *Racial Innocence: Performing American Childhood from Slavery to Civil Rights* (New York: NYU Press, 2013); Erica Meiners, "Child's Play: Schools Not Jails," in Duane, ed., *Child Slavery before and after Emancipation*.

owners. To take just one example, 2,500 African American children were apprenticed to former slave owners in Maryland shortly after emancipation in 1865.[21] And the US was far from alone in its practice of drawing on logics of protection to keep children subject to adults who viewed them as property. As Audra Diptee has argued, Western conceptions of childhood actually helped to reinstate slave regimes in colonial Africa, even as colonizers claimed to be "freeing" their subjects from the barbarism of slavery. In particular, because so much antislavery rhetoric focused on the innocent vulnerability of children – and their attendant inability to consent – children were ineligible for meaningful freedom. Former slavemasters were given the new status of guardian, a change that did precious little to improve the lives of the children under their control. In the case of young girls, their masters would become their husbands, often over the protests of the children being thus "protected." The girls' protests were dismissed as the amusing recalcitrance of children, who so often resist what's "good for them."[22]

Both cultural and legal structures require that a slave be innocent of complicity in their situation, or of having consented to it. In the case of pre-Emancipation slavery, the legal transformation from person to chattel enforced such innocence – since one was legally unable to give consent to any aspect of their captivity, the line between villain and victim was clear. In post-Emancipation regimes, however, questions of consent are particularly difficult to parse, as people sometimes sign contracts, or even pay traffickers in the hopes of opportunity soon denied. In the complex world of "the free market," in which the poor must often choose exploitative work over starvation, the innocence demanded to demarcate the bounds of slavery is a nearly impossible standard for any human being to fulfill. Except, of course, when it comes to children, particularly when it comes to activities that fall outside the hallowed realm of private home – namely, sex and warfare. Overwhelmingly, the concept of child slavery – and the public outrage and substantial funding that follows that outrage – is generated by the specter of child sex trafficking. This practice is held up as particularly horrific because it represents the antithesis of

[21] See Barbara Bennett Woodhouse, *Hidden in Plain Sight: The Tragedy of Children's Rights from Ben Franklin to Lionel Tate* (Princeton, NJ: Princeton University Press, 2010), especially ch. 3; Peggy Cooper Davis, *Neglected Stories* (New York: Macmillan, 1998), especially 147; Steven Mintz, *Huck's Raft: A History of American Childhood* (Cambridge, MA: Harvard University Press, 2004), especially 115.

[22] Audra Diptee, "Childhood without Innocence in Colonial French West Africa," in Duane, ed., *Child Slavery before and after Emancipation*.

what we imagine the ideal childhood to be – an existence protected by loving parents, in a private home, kept innocent from adult desires and exchange.

This opposition between the exploited child in the marketplace and the free child produced by the constraints of adult supervision anchors much current rhetoric depicting child slavery, as children in commercial sex trafficking are almost always held up as the worthiest victims, with child soldiers coming in a close second. Advocates ranging from evangelical ministers to *The New York Times* columnists have made child sex trafficking an abuse equivalent to slavery, largely because it is directed at children, and because it violates deeply held beliefs that children should be kept innocent of both sex and the marketplace. Undoubtedly, the coercions forced on children both in the brothel and on the battlefield are horrific. But the harms suffered by such victims are not unique to those practices. The prolonged sexual abuse of children occurs in a host of situations, and young people are often caught in the midst of warfare, with few good choices available for their survival.[23] Yet again and again, the enslaved sex slave or child solider is cast as an anomaly – a violation of the most basic definitions of childhood.

The solution to these horrors is often figured as a return to home and family, whose protections can restore a child to an innocence of adult desires and abuses. Yet, as years of failed rescue attempts indicate, returning young people to private homes, far from solving the problem, may exacerbate it still further. There is ample evidence that abuses within the private home often lead children to sex work in the first place.[24] Even anti-child-sex trafficking advocates, who acknowledge that incest within the family is a common contributor to young girls' paths to prostitution, rarely mark this abuse as slavery. It is only sex outside of the family, for money, that elicits the term, although arguably the child's suffering is equal, if not greater, at home.[25] Further, girls often escape from their rescuers – like *The New York Times*'s Nicholas Kristof – laying bare the insufficiency of restoring children to places conducive to "innocence" to

[23] For more on child soldiers, see David M. Rosen, *Armies of the Young: Child Soldiers in War and Terrorism* (Camden, NJ: Rutgers University Press, 2005).

[24] For just a few examples see: Heather Montgomery, *Modern Babylon? Prostituting Children in Thailand* (New York: Berghahn, 2001); Laura María Agustin, *Sex at the Margins: Migration, Labour Markets and the Rescue Industry* (London: Zed, 2007); and Elizabeth Bernstein, *Temporarily Yours: Intimacy, Authenticity, and the Commerce of Sex* (Chicago, IL: University of Chicago Press, 2007).

[25] Bernstein, *Temporarily Yours*, 56.

solve the problem of exploitation.[26] Although it serves fantasies of adult rescue and benevolence to imagine that slavery looks like the opposite of a protected innocent childhood, for many children, slavery actually manifests as an amplification of what a "proper" childhood is supposed to be, as they find themselves "protected" from consent as private property of adults.

The unquestioned assertion that children are served by being dependents within a private household renders systems like the Haitian *restavec* system that enslaved Jean-Robert Cadet more as a difference of degree than of kind in its treatment of children. The term *restavec*, Creole for "stay-with," is a system of forced domestic servitude in which families "take in" vulnerable children who then, naturally, are expected to "help out" with household chores.[27] Notably, these children are often subject to physical and sexual abuses that rival the allegedly uniquely depraved environment of the brothels. As Jean-Robert Cadet notes in his narrative, girls are commonly "used as concubines for the teenage sons of their 'owners.' And if they become pregnant, they are thrown into the streets like garbage" (4).

Like other forms of coerced domestic labor, the *restavec* system enacts an extreme version of paternalism's exploitative bargain in which a child's need for care justifies the caretaker's complete control over that child. *Restavec* children are routinely denied basic education, medical care, or even sufficient food. They are subject to extremely long hours of arduous work often while suffering horrific physical, emotional, and sexual abuse at the hands of their "host families." And Haiti is far from the only place in which the private home functions as a site of slavery. As Jonathan Blagbrough and Gary Craig relate, current estimates identify more than 17 million children worldwide laboring in paid or unpaid domestic work in households other than their own. Many of these children live in the world's poorest regions.[28] Over two-thirds of these children are living in what are considered to be unacceptable

---

[26] See Nicholas D. Kristof, "Back to the Brothel," *The New York Times*, January 22, 2005; Gretchen Soderlund, "Running from the Rescuers: New US Crusades against Sex Trafficking and the Rhetoric of Abolition," *National Women's Studies Association Journal* 17, no. 3 (2005), 64–87.

[27] "Restavec" is the French spelling Cadet uses. Haitians often also spell the term restavek.

[28] Jonathan Blagbrough and Gary Craig, "Child Domestic Labor: 'When I play with the Master's Children, I must Always Let Them Win,'" in Duane, ed., *Child Slavery before and after Emancipation*; ILO, *Child Domestic Work: Global Estimates 2012* (factsheet) (Geneva: ILO, 2013).

conditions: they are younger than the country's legal minimum working age, or they are working in conditions so hazardous that they merit the term slavery. Despite growing public awareness of the practice, forced domestic labor remains an entrenched form of work that particularly exploits children.[29]

One reason why this form of coerced labor and enslavement remains hidden is that the logic of paternalism obscures the implementation of the "social death" that Patterson famously posited as one of the factors distinguishing slavery from other forms of dangerous labor. Coerced child domestic labor systems often claim to provide familial structure even as they deny enslaved people the community or protection that such structure promises. Children in particular are oppressed, not solely from being excluded from domestic and extended kinship networks, but also from the ways those very networks routinely claim all children as property. For example, the idea that adults have both the right and the duty to enforce childhood innocence – to shield them from knowledge that might be frightening or disturbing – becomes a means of denying children awareness of, or recourse from, their own oppression. Cadet begins his first book with a memory of realizing that his own kin were responsible for his enslavement. "A *blanc* [white person] is coming to visit today," he is told as a young child by his abusive mistress, whom he is compelled to call "mama." "He's your papa," she tells him, "but when you see him don't call him papa. Say 'Bonjour, monsieur' and disappear."[30] In a cruel mirroring of a loving household headed by a mama and a papa, in which children are told white lies "for their own good," Cadet learns that truth must not be spoken (his relationship to his white papa) and lies must be continually reinforced (his cruel mistress must be called mama). We soon learn that it was Cadet's white father who brought Jean-Robert to the home where he would spend his young life, enslaved.

Like Cadet, Frederick Douglass talks about the pain of being denied knowledge of his father, and of the likelihood that his father was responsible for his enslavement. He does know that his "father was a white man," because he was "admitted to be such by all I ever heard speak of my parentage." He also suspects that his master was his father, but cannot confirm this knowledge. "The means of knowing," he relates, "was

---

[29] Blagbrough and Craig, "Child Domestic Labor," 251–69.
[30] Jean-Robert Cadet, *Restavec: From Haitian Slave Child to Middle-Class American* (Austin, TX: University of Texas Press, 2009), 1.

withheld from me." Both Douglass and Cadet are kept from the knowledge of their own births: neither knows their birth date. Neither Cadet nor Douglass know their mothers in any meaningful sense: both women were likely raped by powerful white men. And like Cadet, Douglass spends much of his youth in the tenuous space as a child in a household that builds upon paternalism's promises of care and protection to extract labor from children.

While Frederick Douglass is never forced to call his mistress, Mrs. Auld, "mama," his palpable desire for a maternal connection emerges in the "rapture" he experiences at being met by the semblance of a welcoming family.

Mr. and Mrs. Auld were both at home, and met me at the door with their little son Thomas, to take care of whom I had been given. And here I saw what I had never seen before; it was a white face beaming with the most kindly emotions; it was the face of my new mistress, Sophia Auld. I wish I could describe the rapture that flashed through my soul as I beheld it. It was a new and strange sight to me, brightening up my pathway with the light of happiness. Little Thomas was told, there was his Freddy, – and I was told to take care of little Thomas; and thus I entered upon the duties of my new home with the most cheering prospect ahead.[31]

In a Victorian novel, being welcomed by a smiling woman and her small child would mark the resolution of a (white) orphan's long journey. Yet, Douglass's relationship with his new "family" evokes idealized notions of nurturing protection not for Douglass's own well-being, but rather to better control and exploit the child's labor and loyalty.

Just as Cadet's family situation reminds us that the divide between safe home and menacing world isn't – and never was – as clear as we might like, his journey also reveals how circuitous the path from childhood slavery to adult freedom truly is. Unlike Douglass, Cadet doesn't cross a neat line from slavery to emancipation. He comes to the US as the ward of the very family that has abused him since his early childhood. What's more, he does so at his own request. When his owner initially wants to "free" him by leaving him behind when she emigrates, Cadet chases after her departing car, crying, "Maman! Maman! Please don't leave me!" (57) For the enslaved child Cadet, this form of "freedom" is a terrible fate. It's not simply a version of Stockholm syndrome that fills Cadet with terror, but the very practical consideration that freedom without resources or

---

[31] Douglass, *Narrative*, 26.

education is not independence, but rather, a virtual death sentence. Cadet wisely "didn't want to be abandoned in the streets like other *restavecs* who were no longer wanted" (56). He willingly follows his enslavers to the US, because he has no other options. Once he's arrived in the US, Cadet's eventual success comes not from breaking ties, but by creating them, first through a public school, where a teacher helps him to arrange for social services, then through the armed forces, which provided present stability and, through the GI Bill, future mobility. Cadet's trajectory, in which he obtains freedom through participation in collective public institutions, seems starkly different from Douglass's story, which valorizes a stark individualism.

But reading Douglass's life through Cadet's perspective provides a decidedly different message than the one we often recite in histories of abolitionism: it's interdependence, rather than independence, that enables true freedom, for both children and adults. A child's need for community and support is not the exception, but a rule we often overlook in order to hold up the ideal of the autonomous freedman. Ten years after he first described the iconic fight scene with slave breaker Covey, Douglass relates that his victory was actually enabled by other enslaved people who refused Covey's orders. In his 1855 narrative *My Bondage, My Freedom*, Douglass relates that he, a sixteen-year-old boy, had been grappling with Covey for some time, when "Bill, the hiredman, came home ... [Covey] evidently was afraid to let me go, lest I should again make off to the woods; otherwise, he would probably have obtained arms from the house, to frighten me. Holding me, Covey called upon Bill for assistance." Bill pretends to misunderstand Covey and does nothing. When finally ordered to restrain Douglass, Bill responds spiritedly: "My master hired me here, to work, and not to help you whip Frederick." Even Covey's own slaves help Douglass to succeed by refusing to help Covey beat him. Shortly after Bill refuses to aid Covey in his violent intentions, Caroline, who was "a powerful woman, and could have mastered [Douglass] very easily, exhausted as [he] now was," also refuses to follow orders, at great peril to herself. "Poor Caroline," Douglass relates, "was at the mercy of the merciless Covey; nor did she escape the dire effects of her refusal."[32]

Like Cadet's movement to freedom, Douglass's escape was not the sole work of an autonomous man, but an endeavor that required the

---

[32] Frederick Douglass, *My Bondage and My Freedom* (Auburn, NY: Miller, Orton, and Mulligan, 1855), 245.

support of a larger community. Although Douglass was no longer a child – estimates put him at about twenty when he made the escape – he required the help of others. Anna Murray, whom Douglass would later marry, supplied both the disguise (a sailor's uniform she obtained through her work as a laundress) and money for the passage north. Without her emotional and material support, his escape would have been much more likely to fail. Once Douglass arrived in New York, his success was made possible in larger part by an extended support network, including the New York Committee of Vigilance.[33] Rather than reinforcing a narrative in which dependent children step into the clear light of adult autonomy, the stories of Douglass and Cadet actually make the case, not for deferring children's freedom, but for holding up a child as a model for creating a realistic portrait of the collective, communal nature of freedom itself.

Siddharth Kara and others argue that until we address the economic pressures that make slavery profitable, we'll never be able to abolish it.[34] I would add that until we address our own longings for heroic narratives and clear divisions between "innocence" and "complicity," both policy and funding will be distracted from larger systemic issues. As Robin D. G. Kelly has taught us, while Marxist analyses that view racism as a byproduct of capitalism have historical merit, reform of economic systems alone cannot undo the now-established beliefs and practices racism produces.[35] Similarly, capitalism's investment in individual assets was created in tandem with a model that rendered slaves, women, and children forms of property. The Western world has largely rejected the morality of the first two arrangements, but for the most part, children remain the exception. Until we come to terms with a long-standing attachment to the belief in an adult autonomy propped up on the naturalized subjugation of children, we perpetuate structures that facilitate slavery. Excavating the voices of enslaved children of the

---

[33] Dorothy B. Porter, "David Ruggles, an Apostle of Human Rights," *The Journal of Negro History* 28, no. 1 (1943), 23–50; Graham Russell Hodges, *David Ruggles: A Radical Black Abolitionist and the Underground Railroad in New York City* (Chapel Hill, NC: University of North Carolina Press, 2010); Julius Eric Thompson and James L. Conyers, *The Frederick Douglass Encyclopedia* (Santa Barbara, CA: Greenwood, 2009), 124.

[34] Siddharth Kara, *Sex Trafficking: Inside the Business of Modern Slavery* (New York: Columbia University Press, 2010).

[35] Robin D. G. Kelly, *Freedom Dreams: The Black Radical Imagination* (Boston, MA: Beacon, 2003).

past and creating spaces for twenty-first-century children to be heard is necessary both to address long-standing legacies of oppression and to forge a concept of freedom that can accommodate vulnerability as well as autonomy, that doesn't find dependence a disqualifier, but rather a fundamental aspect of liberty.[36]

---

[36] For more on vulnerability as a precondition we all share, see Martha Fineman, *The Vulnerable Subject: Anchoring Equality in the Human Condition* (Princeton, NJ: Princeton University Press, 2013), Karen Sánchez-Eppler, *Dependent States: The Child's Part in Nineteenth Century American Culture* (Chicago, IL: University of Chicago Press, 2005), and Lennard Davis, *Enforcing Normalcy: Disability, Deafness, and the Body* (London: Verso, 1995).

7

From White Slavery to Anti-Prostitution, the Long View

Law, Policy, and Sex Trafficking

Jessica R. Pliley

Stories of sexual slavery circulated the Atlantic World and beyond from the late nineteenth to early twentieth centuries. From the opening of the twentieth century to 1917, popular media and concerted campaigns waged by committed activists alerted Americans to the problem of "white slavery," defined at the time as the luring, deceiving, coercing, and forcing of women into sexual slavery in a brothel. The issue of sexual trafficking re-emerged at the end of the century as feminists inspired by Kathleen Barry's 1979 *Female Sexual Slavery* allied with Christian activists to publicize the sexual exploitation of sex trafficking after the fall of the Soviet states, which coalesced in 2000 to produce the United Nations' Palermo Protocol and the United States' Trafficking Victims Protection Act (TVPA).[1] Today, the anti-sex trafficking movement and the anti-modern-day slavery movement of which it is a part is one of the most dynamic human rights campaigns in the world. The parallels between the first anti-sex trafficking movement and today's anti-trafficking movement are striking: from the travelers' aid society pamphlets of the 1910s to the contemporary postings in airports that warn of sex trafficking, from arguments about the size of the traffic in women in the 1910s to today's fights about the reliability of the statistics produced by the International Labour Office and the Global Slavery Index, from the bitter denunciations

---

[1] Kathleen Barry, *Female Sexual Slavery* (New York: New York University Press, 1979); Hebah Farrag, Richard Flory, and Brie Loskota, "Evangelicals and Human Trafficking: Rescuing, Rehabilitating, and Releasing One Individual at a Time," in Kimberly Kay Hoang and Rhacel Salazar Parreñas, eds., *Human Trafficking Reconsidered: Rethinking the Problem, Envisioning New Solutions* (New York: Idebate Press, 2014), 116–22.

of the activist "parasites" of the earlier period to the critique of the "big business" and "rescue industry" of anti-trafficking activism today, echoes of the first anti-trafficking movement resonate.[2]

The focus of this essay is upon the ways that trafficking policies and laws have functioned to bolster state power and law enforcement while also criminalizing women's behavior under the guise of "protecting" them during the first anti-trafficking movement. Shifting attention away from the rhetoric of anti-sex trafficking activists and their reform campaigns and toward the enforcement of anti-trafficking policy raises important questions for historians and contemporary activists alike. This essay examines the emergence of the anti-trafficking movement in the later nineteenth century, paying close attention to the policies promoted at the international level. It then turns to the legislative response to the challenges raised by sex trafficking within the United States and the enforcement of these new laws prior to the Second World War. The essay concludes by shifting attention to the current-day situation, suggesting that the pre-Second World War era trends of erasing women's agency, treating "perpetrators" and "victims" as aliens from the community, and building border control regimes still shape the fight against sex trafficking.

Sex trafficking first emerged as a public scandal in Great Britain in 1879 when rumors reached the ears of Alfred Dyer in London that an English businessman had been offered the services of a nineteen-year-old English girl in a brothel in Brussels. Dyer and his colleagues in the Ladies National Association for the Repeal of the Contagious Disease Acts, an organization founded in the winter of 1869–70 by Josephine Butler that opposed the legislation that governed prostitution due to the ways these laws stigmatized poor women while implicitly protecting men's sexual privilege because police only held women responsible for prostitution, immediately set off to investigate. They discovered that Belgian

---

[2] For critiques about the reliability of numbers and denunciations of reformers as "parasites" during the first anti-sex trafficking movement see Mark Thomas Connelly, *The Response to Prostitution in the Progressive Era* (Chapel Hill, NC: University of North Carolina Press, 1980), 130–3; Emma Goldman, "Traffic in Women," *Hastings Women's Law Journal* 13, no. 9 (2002), 9–20. For contemporary critiques, see: Julia O'Connell Davidson and Bridget Anderson, "The Trouble with 'Trafficking,'" in Christien L. van den Anker and Joroen Doomernik, eds., *Trafficking and Women's Rights* (New York: Palgrave MacMillan, 2006), 11–26; Julia O'Connell Davidson, "New Slaveries, Old Binaries: Human Trafficking and the Borders of Freedom," *Global Networks* 10, no. 2 (2010), 244–61; Laura María Agustín, *Sex at the Margins: Migration, Labour Market and the Rescue Industry* (London: Zed Books, 2007).

brothel keepers imported English girls between the ages of thirteen and twenty-one to avoid strict rules governing the age of Belgian girls permitted to work in brothels. According to the investigation, the Belgian brothel keepers frequently lured the girls to Brussels with false promises of employment in domestic service. Once placed in the brothels, the girls faced rape, abuse, and sexual slavery.[3] Dyer declared, "The more childish and innocent the victims, the more profitable they are." He noted that "English speaking girls … are systematically sought after, entrapped, and sold into a slavery infinitely more cruel and revolting than negro servitude, because it is slavery not for labour but for lust; and more cowardly than negro slavery, because it falls on the young and helpless of one sex only." Comparisons like this one between forced prostitution and African American chattel slavery were quite common and are deeply problematic, contributing as they did both to obscuring any sexual component from understandings of chattel slavery, as well as racializing forced prostitution as a crime only when it occurred to white women.[4]

With his proclamations, published in 1880, Alfred Dyer gave birth to the basic narrative features of the first anti-sex trafficking movement. He framed the issue as one of national honor: the ability of English men to protect English girls from foreign exploitation.[5] For this argument to function best, the "victims" needed to be young, innocent (deceived), and English (white). The perpetrators of this international traffic were necessarily foreign (in this context, not English, but a type of racialized profligate Continental) with lesser morals, well organized in the shadow economy, who benefited from the practice of legal (and tolerated) prostitution. To address this outrage, Dyer called on Parliament to investigate,

---

[3] Jane Jordan and Ingrid Sharp, eds., *Josephine Butler and the Prostitution Campaigns: Diseases of the Body Politic*, Volume 4: *Child Prostitution and the Age of Consent* (London: Routledge, 2003), 1–3.

[4] Alfred Dyer, "The European Slave Trade in English Girls (1880)," in Jordan and Sharp, eds., *Josephine Butler and the Prostitution Campaigns*, 25–54 (27). See Jessica R. Pliley, "Protecting the Young and the Innocent: Age, Consent, and the Enforcement of the White Slave Traffic Act," in Anna Mae Duane, ed., *Childhood Slavery before and after Emancipation* (New York: Cambridge University Press, 2017); and Gunther Peck, "Feminizing White Slavery in the United States: Marcus Braun and the Transnational Traffic in White Bodies, 1890–1910," in Leon Fink, ed., *Workers across the Americas: The Transnational Turn in Labor History* (New York: Oxford University Press, 2011), 221–44 (224).

[5] Donna J. Guy, *White Slavery and Mothers Alive and Dead: The Troubled Meeting of Sex, Gender, Public Health and Progress in Latin America* (Lincoln, NE: University of Nebraska Press, 2000), 77.

which it did when it established a committee in the House of Lords to look into the issue.[6]

Dyer's hysterical proclamations about sex slavery received validation in W. T. Stead's bestselling exposé, "The Maiden Tribute to Modern Babylon" (1885), a six-part series detailing the grotesque underworld of child prostitution in London. The articles outraged readers, generated protests in Hyde Park, established Stead as one of the leading new journalists of the day, and put the issue of child prostitution (and age of consent) on the political agenda.[7] In the conclusion of the series, Stead expanded his focus beyond London, claiming that there existed an "international slave trade in girls."[8] Stead's exposé popularized the narrative put forth by Dyer, as newspapers through Europe and the anglophone world eagerly reprinted the entire series.[9]

Beyond its sensational revelations, one reason that Stead's exposé galvanized the reading public was because commercialized sex had become a visible and public aspect of nineteenth-century urban life. Though empirical evidence poses significant challenges for historians of sexual labor, thousands of women worked in sexual marketplaces in the mid nineteenth century. By the 1840s commentators in New York suggested that the city housed between 10,000 and 50,000 prostitutes.[10] By the Progressive Era, investigators predicted that between 300,000 to 1,633,050 women sold sex in America's cities.[11] Reformers and journalists vigorously debated the accuracy of these figures at the time, and almost all estimates pose their own interpretive challenges. For example, in 1870 London one social reformer estimated that 80,000 women sold sex in

[6] Judith R. Walkowitz, *Prostitution and Victorian Society: Women, Class, and the State* (Cambridge: Cambridge University Press, 1980), 248; Jean-Michel Chaumont and Christine Machiels, eds., *Du sordide au mythe: l'affaire de la traite des blanches (Bruxelles, 1880)* (Louvain: Presses Universitaires de Louvain, 2009); Rachel Attwood, "Lock up Your Daughters! Male Activists, 'Patriotic Domesticity' and the Fight against Sex Trafficking in England, 1880–1912," *Gender & History* 27, no. 3 (November 2015), 611–627; and Julia Laite, *Common Prostitutes and Ordinary Citizens: Commercial Sex in London, 1885–1960* (New York: Palgrave MacMillan, 2012), 104.

[7] Judith R. Walkowitz, *City of Dreadful Delight: Narratives of Sexual Danger in Late-Victorian London* (Chicago, IL: University of Chicago Press, 1992); Christopher A. Casey, "Common Misperceptions: The Press and Victorian Views of Crime," *The Journal of Interdisciplinary History* 41, no. 3 (Winter 2011), 367–91.

[8] W. T. Stead, "The Maiden Tribute to Modern Babylon" (July 6–10, 1885), in Jordan and Sharpe, eds., *Josephine Butler and the Prostitution Campaigns*, Volume 4, 115–234 (119).

[9] Walkowitz, *City of Dreadful Delight*, 82.

[10] Timothy J. Gilfoyle, *City of Eros: New York City, Prostitution, and the Commercialization of Sex, 1790–1920* (New York: W.W. Norton & Company, 1994), 57, 59.

[11] Connelly, *The Response to Prostitution*, 20.

that city; yet police routinely reported only 8,000 to 10,000 "known prostitutes" for the same period. Obviously, women selling sex would be adept at avoiding contact with police, even if the act of prostitution was legal, as it was in London.[12] Police records are notoriously unreliable in accurately depicting the number of women working in prostitution, yet the figures suggested by moral reformers are just as problematic because moral reformers had a vested interest in exaggerating the problem of commercial sex to gain support for their rescue operations. As historian Julia Laite reminds us: "It is an exercise in relative futility to belabor numbers when it comes to the history of prostitution"; yet she concludes, "One thing is for certain: the number of women selling sex and, even more so, the number of men buying it, has been very high throughout the modern period, and perhaps more consistent than has previously been allowed."[13] Yet, as Timothy Gilfoyle argues in the case of New York City, over the course of the nineteenth century sex became increasingly commercialized in a wide variety of public forms, including prostitution, but also including pornography, erotic literature, sporting culture, and erotic dancing.[14] By the end of the nineteenth century, commercial sex was stunningly conspicuous.

Adding to the visibility of commercial sex was the reality of a reliable pool of women who sold sex in response to the economic precarity that defined nineteenth-century economic life. Prostitution emerged as a survival strategy for women who were routinely paid very little in a sex-segregated labor market. In New York City, it is estimated that between 5 and 10 percent of all women between the ages of fifteen and thirty sold sex at one point or another.[15] For many women, selling sex could be a casual affair, an act engaged in only in times of economic stress. Other women choose a more "professional" path by working in brothels on a more permanent basis. In both London and New York City, women who sold sex routinely came from the working-class families, and many reported having fathers who worked in the lowest-paid occupations or who had abandoned their families altogether. Physician William W. Sanger, who questioned 2,000 prostitutes in New York in the mid nineteenth century, found that 513 stated they voluntarily chose to sell sex, while another 525 claimed to be driven to sexual labor by destitution (and another

---

[12] Laite, *Common Prostitutes and Ordinary Citizens*, 28.
[13] Ibid., 30.
[14] Gilfoyle, *City of Eros*. See also Helen Lefkowitz Horowitz, *Rereading Sex: Battles over Sexual Knowledge in Nineteenth-Century America* (New York: Knopf, 2002).
[15] Gilfoyle, *City of Eros*, 59.

473 claimed abandonment, abuse, rape, and seduction, all of which led them to have to provide for their own economic maintenance and caused them to leave home and enter prostitution). Sanger's analytic categories pose a number of problems, but taken as a whole, it is clear that the sexual double standard that condemned female sexual behavior outside of marriage combined with women's economic precarity made young women disconnected from family structures that provided economic support more likely to engage in selling sex. Furthermore, over half of Sanger's sample were orphans. Family disruption and the economic destitution that followed led many women into sexual labor.[16]

Women could turn to prostitution as a temporary or longer-term occupation because prostitution was generally legal or tolerated by police, depending on the particular locale. Some countries and cities regulated prostitution through the police by registering women, examining them periodically for venereal disease, and requiring them to live in particular brothels in specific neighborhoods. Registration emerged in Napoleonic France as a measure to combat high rates of venereal disease amongst the military. But it soon spread to other countries, including, but not limited to, Argentina (1875–1934), Belgium (1844–1947), Czechoslovakia (1918–22), Germany (1830–71, 1891–1927, 1933), Greece (1922–1955), Italy (1860–1958), Japan (1871–1946), Mexico (1872–1942/3), the Netherlands (1852–1913), Russia (1843–1917), and Sweden (1859–1919).[17] As European powers (and the US and Japan) established their empires, registration of sexual labor became a key feature of colonial regimes the world over.[18] It is important to point out that in cities

[16] Laite, *Common Prostitutes and Ordinary Citizens*, 30; Gilfoyle, *City of Eros*, 65–7; Ruth Rosen, *The Lost Sisterhood: Prostitution in America, 1900–1918* (Baltimore, MD: Johns Hopkins Press, 1983), 139; William W. Sanger, *The History of Prostitution: Its Extent, Causes, and Effects throughout the World* (New York: Harper & Brothers, 1858), 488, 539.

[17] Stephanie A. Limoncelli, "International Voluntary Associations, Local Social Movements and State Paths to the Abolition of Regulated Prostitution in Europe, 1875–1950," *International Sociology* 21, no. 1 (January 2006), 31–59 (35); Katherine Bliss, *Compromised Positions: Prostitution, Public Health, and Gender Politics in Revolutionary Mexico City* (University Park, PA: Pennsylvania State University Press, 2001), 27; and Stephanie A. Limoncelli, "The Politics of Humanitarianism: States, Reformers, and the International Movement to Combat the Traffic in Women, 1875–1960," PhD diss. (Los Angeles, CA: University of California at Los Angeles, 2006), 59.

[18] Ann Laura Stoler, *Carnal Knowledge and Imperial Power: Race and the Intimate in Colonial Rule* (Durham, NC: Duke University Press, 2010); Eileen J. Findlay, "Decency and Democracy: The Politics of Prostitution in Ponce, Puerto Rico, 1890–1900," *Feminist Studies* 23, no. 3 (Autumn 1997), 471–99; Philippa Levine, *Prostitution, Race, and Politics: Policing Venereal Disease in the British Empire* (New York: Routledge,

and countries that embraced prostitution through regulation, the vast majority of transactional sex occurred clandestinely, outside of the gaze of the state. In other areas, regulation was a hotly contested policy. Great Britain famously introduced a highly coercive form of regulation that empowered police to detain and forcibly examine suspected prostitutes in naval ports in 1864. British feminists and Christian activists led a pitched battle against the Contagious Disease Acts, as they were called, due to the way that these laws offered the state's sanctioning of male sexual licentiousness while targeting poor women for police harassment. Faced with a growing outcry Parliament repealed the Contagious Disease Acts in 1888. Prostitution was technically legal in Great Britain, though third-party profiting from prostitution via brothel keeping and procuring was criminalized. In the United States, local municipal laws governed prostitution and local police departments often informally regulated the sexual marketplace, though cities like St. Louis and El Paso experimented with more formal policies of regulation.[19] Regardless of the legal status of prostitution, women who sold sex remained vulnerable to police harassment, yet the profitability of sexual labor attracted many women.

Stead's sensational exposé tapped into existing anxieties about the reality of the easy availability of commercial sex. He effectively brought out into the light of day, and into respectable middle-class parlors,

2003); Elizabeth B. van Heyningen, "The Social Evil in the Cape Colony, 1868–1902: Prostitution and the Contagious Diseases Acts," *Journal of Southern African Studies* 10, no. 2 (April 1984), 170–97; Petra de Vries, "'White Slaves' in a Colonial Nation: The Dutch Campaign against the Traffic in Women in the Early Twentieth Century," *Social and Legal Studies* 14, no. 1 (2005), 39–60; Philip Howell, "Race, Space and Regulation of Prostitution in Colonial Hong Kong," *Urban History* 31, no. 2 (2004), 229–48; Laura Briggs, "Familiar Territory: Prostitution, Empires, and the Question of US Imperialism in Puerto Rico, 1849–1916," in Lynne Haney and Lisa Pollard, eds., *Families of a New World: Gender Politics and State Development in a Global Context* (New York: Routledge, 2003), 40–63 (50); Jessica R. Pliley, "The FBI's White Slave Division: The Creation of a National Regulatory Regime to Police Prostitutes in the United States, 1910–1918," in Jessica R. Pliley, Robert Kramm, and Harald Fischer-Tiné, eds., *Global Anti-Vice Activism: Fighting Drink, Drugs, & 'Imorality,' 1880–1950* (Cambridge: Cambridge University Press, 2016), 221–45 (233–5).

19 John C. Burnham, "Medical Inspection of Prostitutes in America in the Nineteenth Century: The St. Louis Experiment and its Sequel," *Bulletin of the History of Medicine* 45, no. 3 (1971), 203; Ann R. Gabbert, "Prostitution and Moral Reform in the Borderlands: El Paso, 1890–1920," *Journal of the History of Sexuality* 12, no. 4 (October 2003), 575–604. "New American Responsibilities and Dangers," *The Philanthropist* 14, no. 1 (January 1899), 13–14; "State Regulation of Vice in Ohio," *The Shield* 4, no. 48 (August 1901), 61; and "American Regulation," *The Philanthropist* 18, no. 4 (January 1904), 1–2.

descriptions of the vibrant world of commercial sex in London, even if his descriptions were overwrought, highly mediated, and reflective of his own psychosexual desires.[20] He broke through the "conspiracy of silence" surrounding public discussions of sex, and he did so by criticizing the sexual double standard that forgave male sexual indiscretions, but harshly condemned female sexual activity outside of marriage. By doing so he initiated what historian John C. Burham has called a revolution in attitudes toward sex.[21] In Stead's telling, women who sold sex were young and usually the prey of nefarious individuals – privileged and debauched aristocrats, venal brothel madams, and irresponsible and drunken working-class parents. Trapped by conditions outside of their control, Stead eradicated any agency women who sold sex possessed and converted them to objects of pity who were lost. The white slavery narrative that Dyer asserted and Stead expanded upon suggested that young women who sold sex had been permanently stained and had no other recourse but to turn to prostitution willingly. "These ideas of corruption and innocence," remarks Laite, "would remain entangled in discourses about white slavery well into the twentieth century," and they functioned to quell the possibility of women's volition.[22] Stead's melodramatic rendering of prostitution provided a template for middle-class readers to interpret prostitution and as basis for organizing for reform.[23]

Stead's series galvanized social purity activists in the United Kingdom and Europe who organized in a large number of anti-trafficking societies. In England, Josephine Butler and the Ladies National Association took up the issue of white slavery as a women's rights issue within its international branch, which in 1898 was renamed the International Abolitionist Federation.[24] Responding to Stead's articles and complementing, and

---

[20] Walkowitz, *City of Dreadful Delight*, 97–102.
[21] John Burnham, "The Progressive Era Revolution in American Attitudes toward Sex," *Journal of American History* 59, no. 4 (March 1973), 885–908.
[22] Laite, *Common Prostitutes and Ordinary Citizens*, 32.
[23] Josephine Butler had long framed women who sold sex in a more sympathetic light. But Stead built on her arguments, erased the feminist nuance, and spread the idea that a woman wouldn't willingly sell sex without some coercion to a much broader audience. See Josephine Butler, "The Moral Redeemability of Prostitutes" (May 1870), in Ingrid Sharp, ed., *Josephine Butler and the Prostitution Campaigns: Diseases of the Body Politic*, Volume 1 (London: Routledge, 2003), 121–7.
[24] The International branch of the LNA was established in 1875 and was called somewhat clumsily the "British, Continental and General Federation for the Abolition of the Government Regulation of Vice."

at times competing with, Butler, William Alexander Coote formed the National Vigilance Association in 1885, which also expanded internationally in 1899 as the International Bureau for the Suppression of the White Slave Traffic.[25] The year 1885 also saw Jewish Britons organizing against white slavery with the formation of the Jewish Ladies Society for the Preventative and Rescue Work, which by 1896 became the Jewish Association for the Protection of Girls and Women.[26] Activists in other European and North American countries quickly followed suit. The first international meeting on the white slave traffic was held in Geneva in 1877; it was followed with meetings in London in 1899, Paris in 1902, Madrid in 1910, and London in 1913.[27]

International conferences quickly paved the way for international cooperation in the fight against sex trafficking. This cooperation first existed on the civil society level, but soon gave way to official governmental cooperation embodied in the 1904 International Agreement for the Suppression of the White Slave Traffic – which sought to set out the parameters for countries to share information about cases of trafficking, established travelers' aid relief in railway stations and ports, set up protocols for the repatriation of foreign prostitutes, and regulated employment agencies that operated in more than one country. Over twenty countries, including the leading imperial powers, eventually

---

[25] Stephanie A. Limoncelli, *The Politics of Trafficking: The First International Movement to Combat the Sexual Exploitation of Women* (Stanford, CA: Stanford University Press, 2010), 56–7; Rachel Attwood, "Stopping the Traffic: The National Vigilance Association and the International Fight against the 'White Slave' Trade (1899–c.1909)," *Women's History Review* 24, no. 3 (2015), 325–50.

[26] Edward J. Bristow, *Prostitution and Prejudice: The Jewish Fight against White Slavery, 1870–1939* (New York: Schoken Books, 1982), 238–40.

[27] For Canada see Mariana Valverde, *The Age of Light, Soap, and Water: Moral Reform in English Canada, 1885–1925* (Toronto: University of Toronto Press, 2008), 92; for the US see David Pivar, *Purity Crusade: Sexual Morality and Social Control, 1868–1900* (Westport, CT: Praeger, 1973) and Jessica R. Pliley, *Policing Sexuality: The Mann Act and the Making of the FBI* (Cambridge, MA: Harvard University Press, 2014), 19–20; for France, see Karen Offen, "Madam Ghénia Avril de Sainte-Croix, the Josephine Butler of France," *Women's History Review* 17, no. 2 (April 2008), 239–55; for the Netherlands, see Petra De Vries, "Josephine Butler and the Making of Feminism: International Abolitionism in the Netherlands (1870–1914)," *Women's History Review* 17, no. 2 (April 2008), 257–77; and Limoncelli, "International Voluntary Associations"; Anne Summers, "Which Women? What Europe? Josephine Butler and the International Abolitionist Federation," *History Workshop Journal* 62, no. 1 (2006), 214–31 (216); League of Nations, *Report of the Special Body of Experts*, Volume 1 (Geneva: League of Nations Publications, 1927), 7–9.

signed the world's first international anti-trafficking treaty.[28] The 1910 International Congress for the Suppression of the White Slave Trade soon fortified the 1904 agreement. The 1910 agreement mandated state legislation to criminalize the prostitution of women by force or fraud and prohibited the prostitution of minors.[29]

The First World War interrupted the international coalition building around the issue of sex trafficking. But after the war, the League of Nations Covenant declared that the League would have "general supervision over the execution of all agreements with regard to the traffic in women and children."[30] To restore the momentum of the anti-trafficking coalition, the League held an international conference on sex trafficking in 1919, which produced the 1921 International Convention for the Suppression of the Traffic in Women and Children, as well as a permanent committee in the League's Social Section devoted to the issue. The 1921 Convention called for extended regulation of employment agencies, set out the rules for extraditing traffickers, and raised the age of consent to twenty-one.[31] The Committee on the Trafficking of Women and Children brought together state and civil society representatives from around the world to develop strategies to fight sex trafficking. By the 1920s, the first anti-sex trafficking movement had matured beyond the sensational stories of the sexual enslavement of young girls to become an international movement that conducted sophisticated studies into women's migration and economic vulnerability, brought together state actors and activists in the

---

[28] The original signatories of the 1904 agreement included: Belgium, Denmark, France, Germany, Italy, the Netherlands, Portugal, Russia, Spain, Sweden and Norway, Switzerland, and the United Kingdom. Later adherents included Australia, Austria, Brazil, Bulgaria, Canada, China, Cuba, Czechoslovakia, Finland, Hungary, India, Japan, Luxembourg, Monaco, New Zealand, Poland, Siam, Uruguay, and the United States.

[29] Limoncelli, *The Politics of Trafficking*, 9. The original signatories of the 1910 agreement included: Austria, Belgium, Denmark, France, Germany, Italy, the Netherlands, Portugal, Russia, Spain, Sweden, Switzerland, and the United Kingdom. Later adherents included Bulgaria, Canada, China, Cuba, Czechoslovakia, Finland, Japan, Monaco, New Zealand, Norway, Poland, Siam, South Africa, and Uruguay.

[30] See Article 23 (c) of the League of Nation's Covenant. League of Nations, *Records of the International Conference on the Traffic in Women and Children* (Geneva: League of Nations Publications, 1921), 9–10.

[31] Limoncelli, *The Politics of Trafficking*, 9. The original signatories of the 1921 agreement included: Albania, Australia, Austria, Belgium, Brazil, Canada, Chile, China, Colombia, Costa Rica, Cuba, Czechoslovakia, Estonia, Germany, Greece, Hungary, India, Italy, Japan, Latvia, Lithuania, the Netherlands, New Zealand, Norway, Persia, Poland, Portugal, Romania, Siam, South Africa, Sweden, Switzerland, and the United Kingdom. Later adherents included Bulgaria, Denmark, Finland, France, Panama, Peru, and Uruguay.

hallowed halls of the Palais des Nations in Geneva, and established international human rights norms.[32]

Yet for all of their sophistication and maturity, the activities of the League still emphasized the basic elements that Dyer had established. In 1927 the League published the *Report of the Special Body of Experts on the Traffic of Women and Children*, which examined the extent of trafficking throughout Europe, North Africa, and the Americas. To conduct the study the investigators visited 112 cities in 28 countries, interviewed 600 police and government officials, 250 reformers working for voluntary societies, and 5,000 people who earned money from the selling of sex.[33] The report generated effusive headlines around the world and was republished by H. Wilson Harris in London under the evocative title *Human Merchandise: A Study of the International Traffic in Women*. The 1927 League's *Report* (and *Human Merchandise*) erased the agency of women who sold sexual services by declaring: "Many of the foreign women were interrogated, and from their stories, which were corroborated by other evidence, it is clear that they were not free agents in the sense that they had travelled to foreign countries on their own initiative either as prostitutes or otherwise. We do not wish to give the impression that all or most of these were unsuspecting and defenseless women who have been decoyed to a foreign country in ignorance of the

---

[32] The literature on the League of Nations and trafficking continues to grow. Some of the most recent works include: Eileen Boris and Heather Berg, "Protecting Virtue, Erasing Labor: Historical Responses to Trafficking," in Hoang and Parreñas, eds., *Human Trafficking Reconsidered*, 19–29; Magalay Rodríguez García, "The League of Nations and the Moral Recruitment of Women," *International Review of Social History* 57 (2012), 97–128; Stephen Legg, "'The Life of Individuals as well as of Nations': International Law and the League of Nations' Anti-Trafficking Governmentalities," *Leiden Journal of International Law* 25 (2012), 647–64; Limoncelli, *The Politics of Trafficking*; Barbara Metzger, "Towards an International Human Rights Regime during the Interwar Years: The League of Nations' Combat of Traffic in Women and Children," in Kevin Grant, Philippa Levine and Frank Trentmann, eds., *Beyond Sovereignty: Britain, Empire and Transnationalism, c.1880–1950* (New York: Palgrave Macmillan, 2007), 54–79; Ashwini Tambe, "Climate, Race Science and the Age of Consent in the League of Nations," *Theory, Culture & Society* 28, no. 2 (2011), 109–30; Jessica Pliley, "Claims to Protection: The Rise and Fall of Feminist Abolitionism in the League of Nations' Committee on the Traffic in Women and Children, 1919–1937," *Journal of Women's History* 22, no. 4 (Winter 2010), 90–113; Jean-Michel Chaumont, *Le mythe de la traite des blanches: enquête sur la fabrication d'un fléau* (Paris: La Découverte, 2009); Stephen Wertheim, "The League of Nations: A Retreat from International Law," *Journal of Global History* 7, no. 2 (July 2012), 210–32; Paul Knepper, "International Criminals: The League of Nations, the Traffic in Women and the Press," *Media History* 20, no. 4 (2014), 400–15.

[33] Limoncelli, *The Politics of Trafficking*, 77.

real purpose of the journey ... [But t]echnically she might not have been brought to this condition by force or fraud, but actually she is deceived at every step."[34] For the authors of the 1927 report, exploitation from third parties such as pimps and brothel managers converted foreign women who sold sex into sex slaves regardless of their consent.[35]

Sex traffickers were consistently characterized as disaffected foreign threats of usually Jewish, Arab, or South American extraction, "who were thought to be of the more undesirable European races, were international and at the same time without citizenship, dark horses of the new globalizing economy and the era of mass migration."[36] Jewish names routinely were featured in public discussions of sex trafficking. In 1922, Samuel Cohen, the representative of the Jewish Association for the Protection of Girls and Women, persuaded the League not to publish the names of known traffickers because he feared "that such publication must include very many Jewish names, and so give a handle for anti-Semitic exaggeration."[37] But when the League published its 1927 study, even though it did not publish proper names, it relied on Yiddish slang and highlighted places that were commonly associated with large Jewish populations, like Warsaw and Czernowitz, which according to historian Edward J. Bristow gave the impression that Jewish traffickers dominated the trade.[38] Certainly, Jewish traffickers participated in commercial prostitution, yet sensational media coverage of trafficking often suggested that an international cabal of Jewish traffickers directed the traffic in women and these stories contributed to the general anti-Semitism of the period and the enthnocentric bias of the League's report.[39]

---

[34] League of Nations, *Report of the Special Body of Experts*, 18–19.

[35] In this essay I have chosen to avoid the term sex worker when writing about the early twentieth century so to avoid anachronism. Yet, as Julia Laite points out, women who sold sex in the past often thought of prostitution as a job. Consequently, following her lead, I prefer to use the terms "women who sold sex" and "sexual labor." Because I am attuned to the feminist debates over the terms "prostitute" and "prostituted women," yet have a vested interest in capturing women's historical agency, I too avoid those terms. See Julia Laite, "(Sexual) Labour Day," *Notches*, April 20, 2014, accessed at http://notchesblog.com/2014/04/30/sexual-labour-day/. Laite, *Common Prostitutes and Ordinary Citizens*, 26–7.

[36] Laite, *Common Prostitutes and Ordinary Citizens*, 102.

[37] Qtd in Bristow, *Prostitution and Prejudice*, 298.

[38] Ibid., 299.

[39] Mir Yarfitz, "Uprooting the Seeds of Evil: Ezras Noschim and Jewish Marriage Regulation, Morality Certificates, and Degenerate Prostitute Mothers in 1930s Buenos Aires," in Adriana Brodsky and Raanan Rein, eds., *The New Jewish Argentina: Facets of Jewish Experiences in the Southern Cone* (Boston, MA: Brill, 2012), 55–80; Mir H. Yarfitz, "Polacos, White Slaves, and Stille Chuppahs: Organized Prostitution and the

The League Committee's Uruguayan delegate Paulina Luisi echoed the concern over bias within the 1927 report. South America was the first geographic area reported on by the body of experts; additionally, it was in South America where the body of experts spent the most time.[40] The report claimed that Buenos Aires was a main destination for traffickers, although it allowed that traffickers maintained an active presence in Montevideo and Rio de Janeiro as well. It also claimed that the prostitutes in Argentine brothels were approximately 75 percent foreign-born.[41] This assessment failed to take into consideration that a majority of women who sold sex in Argentina (especially native-born *Porteños*) did not work in brothels, preferring to escape the high fees of police registration and the lengthy stays in the lock hospital by working in clandestine sites like bars and apartments.[42] The report also failed to contextualize the data in any meaningful way.[43] Buenos Aires was a city of migrants. In 1895, four out of five adults in the city had immigrated there, and these migrants were overwhelmingly male. Consequently, Buenos Aires represented a profitable sexual and labor marketplace, attracting women looking for work in domestic service or the more lucrative sex trade.[44] The high number of immigrant women working in registered brothels reflected the high levels of immigration to Buenos Aires more generally on the one hand, and the higher likelihood that new immigrants could find a place in brothels with ease, on the other.[45] Yet, the League report painted an image of Buenos Aires as a debauched city ripe with immorality, ignoring its diverse migrant demographics. Responding to the report, Luisi noted that the report could only be regarded as "incomplete." Chief among her complaints was that the body of experts had visited only two cities in Argentina, two in Uruguay, and one in Brazil, and therefore could

Jews of Buenos Aires, 1890–1939," PhD diss., UCLA, 2012; Charles Van Onselen, *The Fox and the Flies: The Secret Life of a Grotesque Master Criminal* (New York: Walker & Co., 2007); Bristow, *Prostitution and Prejudice*, 168; Pliley, *Policing Sexuality*, 52–3; and Victor A. Mirelman, "The Jewish Community versus Crime: The Case of White Slavery in Buenos Aires," *Jewish Social Studies* 46, no. 2 (1984), 145–68.

[40] Guy, *White Slavery and Mothers Alive and Dead*, 27.
[41] Ibid. Anti-white slavery activists had argued that Argentina was a supposed destination since the 1860s. See Donna J. Guy, *Sex and Danger in Buenos Aires: Prostitution, Family, and Nation in Argentina* (Lincoln, NE: University of Nebraska Press, 1991).
[42] Guy, *Sex and Danger in Buenos Aires*, 52–6.
[43] Guy, *White Slavery and Mothers Alive and Dead*, 27.
[44] Donna J. Guy, "Prostitución y suicidio en Buenos Aires, 1880–1900," in Dora Barrancos, J. Guy, and Adriana María Valobra, eds., *Moralidades y comportamientos sexuales: Argentina, 1880–2011* (Buenos Aires: Biblos, 2014).
[45] Guy, *Sex and Danger in Buenos Aires*, 16.

not be said to represent the whole of South America.[46] She objected to the notion that South America was "a sort of Golconda" for traffickers, when only a few cities had been visited.[47] Taken as a whole, the League's 1927 study reasserted preexisting tropes that traffickers were people thought to be alienated from civilized society by virtue of their imagined (racial) distance from the civilizing effects of Europe.

The momentum of League discussions led to policies of repatriation and border control. As early as 1924 calls came forth to ban foreign women from working in legal brothels. Luisi objected to the proposal, pointing out that it would limit the employment and mobility of all women, raised questions about jurisdiction and national sovereignty in countries where prostitution was legal, and introduced a whole set of issues related to repatriation and deportation. She contended: "I would like to know how my Government could expel women merely on the grounds that she is a foreign prostitute? Is prostitution a crime? In my country [of Uruguay] only people guilty of offenses against the law can be deported. The foreign women are not to be expelled because they commit a crime in leading a life of prostitution? In that case prostitution is a crime; then why should we allow our nationals to commit crimes?"[48] In the face of such critiques, the proposal was shelved, but soon it was followed by another proposal that sought to achieve the same end by eliminating the age demarcation in the 1921 Convention that had prohibited the employment by brothels of foreign-born women under the age of twenty-one.

After years of debate, including significant opposition from feminist civil society groups who were sensitive to efforts to restrict the freedom of travel of any and all women, the proposal became the basis for the 1933 Convention for the Suppression of the Traffic in Women of Full Age.[49] The goal of this treaty was to stop the international migration of women who sold sex (either on a forced or voluntary basis), while mandating their repatriation. In practice, the convention codified, on the international level, a trend toward increasing border

---

[46] League of Nations, *Advisory Commission for the Protection and Welfare of Children and Young People, Traffic in Women and Children Committee: Minutes of the Eighth Session (Geneva, April 19th to April 27th, 1929)*, C.294.M.97.1929.IV (Geneva: League of Nations Publications, 1929), 61.

[47] League of Nations, *Report of the Special Body of Experts on Traffic in Women and Children*, Part 2, 13. "Golconda" refers to a famed city in India known for its diamond mines. By the late nineteenth century the term came to be used to refer to a place of great wealth.

[48] Qtd in Guy, *White Slavery and Mothers Alive and Dead*, 80.

[49] Pliley, "Claims to Protection," 101–2; Rodríguez García, "The League of Nations," 117.

control and the construction of a border control regime built, in part, on the policing of women's morality.[50]

These elements are even more explicit in the case of the United States' response to sex trafficking, both in policy and implementation.[51] By the time the stories of sexual slavery hit American shores they joined discourses about the ever-increasing number of migrants who, immigration officials claimed, were flooding American shores in a deluge, bringing with them immoral practices that might endanger the United States. Daniel Keefe, the head of the Immigration Bureau, declared in 1909, "The most alarming feature of this traffic from the [immigration] bureau's point of view consists ... of the vastly increasing numbers of alien prostitutes flooding the country, finding in the existing immigration laws, with their present means of enforcement, only slight impediment to their passage back and forth."[52] For Keefe, white slavery was less a problem of sex trafficking that exploited endangered innocents than it was a problem of an influx of foreign-born prostitutes. Reflecting the reality that the United States was an immigrant-receiving country rather than an immigrant-sending country, in the US context concern about sex trafficking during the early twentieth century reflected anxieties about high levels of immigration and the quality of migrants entering the country, as opposed to anxieties about how to protect one's own nationals in foreign settings.[53]

---

[50] Pliley, *Policing Sexuality*, 186–7. For literature on the gendered, sexualized, and moralized border in the United States see Grace Peña Delgado, "Border Control and Sexual Policing: White Slavery and Prostitution along the US–Mexico Borderlands, 1903–1910," *Western Historical Quarterly* 43, no. 2 (Summer 2012), 157–78; Martha Gardner, *The Qualities of a Citizen: Women, Immigration, and Citizenship, 1870–1965* (Princeton, NJ: Princeton University Press, 2009); Eithne Luibhéid, *Entry Denied: Controlling Sexuality at the Border* (Minneapolis-St. Paul, MN: University of Minnesota Press, 2002).

[51] Julia Laite finds similar tendencies in the United Kingdom.

[52] "Message from the President of the United States transmitting, in further response to Senate Resolution No. 86, of December 7, 1909, Information Concerning the Repression of the Trade in White Women," Senate, 61st Cong., 2nd Sess., Doc. No. 214, Part 2 (Washington, DC: Government Printing Office, 1910), 13.

[53] Other immigrant-receiving countries, such as Canada, Argentina, Brazil, Uruguay, Australia, and New Zealand, also conceptualized the white slavery problem as a problem imported by potentially dangerous immigrants. See Valverde, *The Age of Light, Soap, and Water*; Guy, *Sex and Danger in Buenos Aires*; Donna J. Guy, "Medical Imperialism Gone Awry: The Campaign against Legalized Prostitution in Latin America," in *Science, Medicine and Cultural Imperialism* (London: Palgrave Macmillan, 1991), 75–94; Cynthia Jeffress Little, "Moral Reform and Feminism: A Case Study," *Journal of Interamerican Studies and World Affairs* 17, no. 4 (1975), 386–97; Marilyn Lake, "Colonised and Colonising: The White Australian Feminist Subject," *Women's History Review* 2, no. 3

Yet, at the same time, stories circulated in the American media suggested that native-born, white girls were vulnerable prey to sex traffickers. Edwin Sims, a US attorney in Illinois, declared, "literally thousands of innocent girls from the country districts are every year entrapped into a life of hopeless slavery and degradation ... [by] 'white slave' traders who have reduced the art of ruining young girls to a national and international system."[54] As more and more attention was devoted to the plight of American-born white slaves – and historian Barbara Meil Hobson estimates that from 1900 to 1920 over 1 billion pages of print were devoted to white slavery and prostitution – the distinction between innocent sex slaves and professional prostitutes collapsed.[55] One reformer opined in 1912, "As for White Slavery, the girls who are forced into this or into immorality through the physical violence or intimidation of the vice promoter, are not the only ones that need our sympathy and our help. The girls who are *enticed into vice by other means* are often as much helpless victims as though they were taken into nets by force. Both classes soon become hopeless human wrecks. They are somebody's daughters and, sensational as it might sound, somebody is slowly killing them for profit."[56] By reminding readers that every woman who sold sex was someone's daughter, and infantilizing them by referring to these women as "girls," this reformer turned all prostitutes into sex slaves deserving of protection.

In these narratives the traffickers were always framed as *un-American*, people who existed on the margins of true American citizenship, usually non-white or of immigrant stock.[57] One overwrought but typical example of the types of pamphlets published to raise awareness of the issue declared, "Open prostitution – White Slavery, as it exists to-day in Chicago, is almost entirely under *foreign* control."

(1993), 377–86; Bronwyn Dalley, "'Fresh Attractions': White Slavery and Feminism in New Zealand, 1885–1918," *Women's History Review* 9, no. 3 (2000), 585–606.

54 Ernest C. Ball, *Fighting the Trafficking in Young Girls or War on the White Slave Trade* (copyright E. S. Ball, 1901, no publisher), 108, see https://babel.hathitrust.org/cgi/pt?id=hvd.rslyjp;view=1up;seq=8.

55 Barbara Meil Hobson, *Uneasy Virtue: The Politics of Prostitution and the American Reform Tradition* (Chicago, IL: University of Chicago Press, 1990), 140.

56 Wirt W. Hallam, "The Reduction of Vice in Certain Western Cities through Law-Enforcement," *Social Diseases: Report of the Progress of the Movement for their Prevention* (published by the Society of Sanitary and Moral Prophylaxis), 3, no. 2 (April 1912), 27–48 (31).

57 Barbara Young Welke, *Law and the Borders of Belonging in the Long Nineteenth Century United States* (New York: Cambridge University Press, 2010).

The author expanded on her point, writing, in a passage that is worth quoting at length:

Please remember, as you read this, that America is becoming more and more un-American every day. Each ship, each train Westward or Eastward bound, is now daily dumping into our Land, so lately the goal of the home-seeker from Germany, Sweden, Ireland, etc., the real future citizen – thousands of scum and vice and criminal element of South Eastern Europe, Asia and the Orient, and remember too that a short five-years of residence converts the filthiest criminal from Turkey, Arabia, Syria, Italy, or of any place else where vice and brutality reign supreme, into an American citizen with the right to vote into office men who will and are sworn to protect and aid in every possible way the Jewish, Russian, French or Chinese whore-master as he rents a shanty and proceeds to fatten on the very life-blood of the young girlhood of this and other lands.[58]

Xenophobic proclamations such as this one constituted a common feature of white slavery narratives in the United States.[59] Similarly, anti-white slavery bromides were infused with the racial logics of the Jim Crow era. Historian Brian Donovan persuasively argues that in the United States, the campaigns against white slavery strengthened "racial hierarchies by emphasizing moral and sexual difference between Anglo-Saxon or native-born whites on one hand and new European immigrants, Chinese, and African Americans on the other."[60] These racial and xenophobic logics helped to structure the United States' anti-trafficking policies and their implementation in the early twentieth century, which ultimately sought to federally criminalize "foreign" prostitution, while also controlling the sexuality of native-born white women and leaving the policing of non-white women who sold sex to local white supremacist law enforcement.[61]

Immigration law emerged as one of the key sites for anti-trafficking legislation in the United States. Congress passed the first anti-trafficking law in 1875 to halt the trafficking of Chinese prostitutes to the United

---

[58] Jean Turner Zimmerman, *Chicago's Black Trade in White Girls* (Lexington, KY: Black Oyster Publishing Co., 2014 [Chicago, IL: Chicago Rescue Mission, 1911]), 9–10.
[59] Pliley, *Policing Sexuality*, 52–3.
[60] Brian Donovan, *White Slave Crusades: Race, Gender, and Anti-Vice Activism, 1887–1917* (Chicago, IL: University of Chicago Press, 2006), 129.
[61] Kevin J. Mumford, *Interzones: Black/White Sex Districts in Chicago and New York in the Early Twentieth Century* (New York: Columbia University Press, 1997); Cynthia Blair, *I've Got to Make My Livin': Black Women's Sex Work in Turn-of-the-Century Chicago* (Chicago, IL: University of Chicago Press, 2010); LaShawn Harris, *Sex Workers, Psychics, and Numbers Runners: Black Women in New York City's Underground Economy* (Urbana, IL: University of Illinois Press, 2016); Khahil Gibran Muhammed, *The Condemnation of Blackness: Race, Crime, and the Making of Urban America* (Cambridge, MA: Harvard University Press, 2011).

States as part of a broader effort to limit Chinese migration into the Western US[62] The 1875 Page Act prohibited the "importation into the United States of women for the purposes of prostitution." This law set an important precedent that Congress built upon: the 1903 Immigration Act excluded sex traffickers and the 1907 Immigration Act made the practice of prostitution within three years of entering the United States a deportable offense. From 1907 to 1910, the Immigration Bureau conducted several studies into white slavery, concluding that sex trafficking constituted a significant threat to the country. According to the Immigration Bureau, "practically no steps could be expected [from the European signatories of the 1904 treaty] to prevent the free passage from their country to this of the professional prostitute or procurer, who constitute the bulk of the 'white-slave traffic' in this country."[63] Equating sexual slavery with professional prostitution, as it did, the Immigration Bureau sought to respond to the white slavery crises by building a moral fence around the country. It succeeded in doing so by lobbying Congress to pass the 1910 Immigration Act, which removed the three-year prohibition and barred prostitution for all non-naturalized foreign-born women, and the 1917 Immigration Act that prohibited the practice of prostitution for *all* foreign-born women, regardless of citizenship status. By 1917, US immigration law discarded any debate about innocent sex slaves and hardened prostitutes by taking steps to exclude all foreign-born women who sold sex and people who profited from prostitution.[64]

US immigration policy has two related processes: deportation (for those already in the country illegally) and exclusion (for those trying to enter the country illegally). From 1910 to 1930, the Immigration Bureau deported 7,972 women and men connected to the sex trade and identified

---

[62] George Anthony Peffer, *If They Don't Bring Their Women Here: Chinese Female Immigration before Exclusion* (Chicago, IL: University of Illinois Press, 1999), 102; Stuart Creighton Miller, *Unwelcome Immigrant: American Image of the Chinese, 1785–1882* (Chicago, IL: University of Chicago Press, 1969), 67 and 79; Lucie Cheng Hirata, "Free, Indentured, Enslaved: Chinese Prostitutes in Nineteenth-Century America," *Signs* 5, no. 1 (Autumn 1979), 3–29 (24); and George Anthony Peffer, "Forgotten Families: The Development of the Chinese American Community in San Francisco, 1860–1880," in Sucheng Chan, ed., *Remapping Asian American History* (Walnut Creek, CA: Alta Mira Press, 2003), 49–67.

[63] "Message from the President of the United States Transmitting, in Further Response to Senate Resolution No. 86, of December 7, 1909, Information Concerning the Repression of the Trade in White Women," Senate, 61st Cong., 2nd Sess., Doc. No. 214, Part 2 (Washington, DC: Government Printing Office, 1910), 4.

[64] For more on the Immigration Bureau's ideology of white slavery, white slavery investigations, and efforts to construct a moral fence, see Pliley, *Policing Sexuality*, 32–59.

6,401 men and women as prostitutes or pimps and barred their entry to the United States. Yet, due to the difficulty of proving a person was a woman who sold sex or a person who profited from sexual commerce at the point to entry, the Immigration Bureau usually excluded women suspected of potentially selling sex under the heading of "likely to be public charges" – a designation with a much lower burden of proof and much higher exclusion numbers. The Immigration Bureau excluded 142,964 migrants under this designation for the period from 1910 to 1930.[65] As Martha Gardiner and Eithne Luibhéid's research has illustrated, (hetero) sexual respectability, understood along class and racial lines, became a key marker for admittance into the United States.[66]

Congress complemented the policy of excluding and deporting "immoral foreign" women with efforts to protect the "blue-eyed girl" of America, who might be vulnerable to sex traffickers.[67] In response to the growing outcry produced by the white slave stories, Congress passed the White Slave Traffic Act of 1910 (also known as the Mann Act), which made it illegal to take a woman or child over state lines for the purposes of prostitution, debauchery, or "any other immoral purpose," with or without hire, or in other words, with or without her consent. It fell to the young Bureau of Investigation (renamed the Federal Bureau of Investigation in 1935) to enforce this domestic trafficking law.

The most troubling aspect rested in the vague phrase that outlawed taking a woman or girl over state lines for "any other immoral purpose." The Bureau of Investigation initially tried to limit itself to "the class of cases at which the act was primarily directed," but which cases those actually were remained highly contested.[68] With no clear mandate when Congress passed the law in June 1910, the Bureau of Investigation's sixty-one special agents began to investigate reported violations of the new law

---

[65] United States, Department of Labor, *Annual Reports of the Commissioner General of Immigration to the Secretary of Labor, 1915* (Washington, DC: Government Printing Office, 1915), 126; United States, Department of Labor, *Annual Reports of the Commissioner General of Immigration to the Secretary of Labor, 1929* (Washington, DC: Government Printing Office, 1929), 222–4; United States, Department of Labor, *Annual Reports of the Commissioner General of Immigration to the Secretary of Labor, 1930* (Washington, DC: Government Printing Office, 1930), 239–44;. Pliley, *Policing Sexuality*, 40–1.

[66] Gardner, *The Qualities of a Citizen*; Luibhéid, *Entry Denied*; Jessica Pliley, "The Petticoat Inspectors: Women Boarding Inspectors and the Gendered Exercise of Federal Authority," *Journal of the Gilded Age and Progressive Era* 12, no. 1 (2013), 95–126.

[67] United States House, *Congressional Record* 45, January 19, 1910, 811.

[68] *Annual Report of the Attorney General of the United States for the Year 1912* (Washington, DC: Government Printing Office, 1912), 48.

with some uncertainty.[69] Within the first six months of the act's existence, the Bureau of Investigation investigated forty-seven cases (fifty-eight individuals) of alleged violations of the Mann Act. During this period the Bureau of Investigation showed a marked preference toward pursuing cases that focused on commercial vice. Of the twenty-one cases that went to trial, a majority of them involved elements of commercialized vice, meaning that the female victims of these cases had been women who sold sex.[70] Agents at the bureau clearly felt justified in pursuing cases that policed the interstate movement of prostitutes, a view that remained consistent with the policing of prostitutes by the Immigration Bureau.

One result of focusing on commercialized vice was that the Bureau of Investigation made women the subject of federal investigations. Of the cases conducted in the first six months after the law's passage, women were the focus of 28 percent of the investigations. Investigations into sex trafficking regularly had both female and male subjects because both men and women took part in the sex trade. Within two years of the law's passage, savvy brothel madams and women who sold sex learned that to avoid coming under the purview of the law they could claim that they traveled of their own volition for reasons unconnected to commercial sex. After the first six months the number of women prosecuted in white slave cases dropped to 13.9 percent from December 1910 to October 1912.[71] As historian Marlene D. Beckman commented, the "conception of female weakness and male domination [common in the white slavery narrative] left no room for the possibility that prostitutes might consciously or aggressively choose their activities," and that these women would learn to evade detection.[72]

---

[69] Record Group 65, Records of the Bureau of Investigation, Administrative Reports on Cases, 1908–1911, Box 10, Entry 22, Volume 29 (29 June 1910–6 July 1910), 43–7, National Archives, College Park, MD [hereafter cited as BOI Administrative Reports on Cases].

[70] I say "at least" because out of the twenty-one cases, in four of them the investigating agent failed to note the specific characteristics of the case, making them impossible to classify. "Records of the Bureau of Investigation: Administrative Reports on Cases," 1908–1911, Boxes 10–16, Volumes 29–48 (June 29, 1910–Mar 3, 1911), BOI Administrative Reports on Cases.

[71] Women made up 62 of the 529 defendants involved in prosecutions of the Mann Act. Of the 39 of these 62 cases that had gone to trial, 38 were found guilty. "List of Prosecutions Instituted under the White Slave Traffic Act of June 25, 1910, Showing Pending Cases and Cases Disposed of Prior to October 31, 1912," *Annual Report of the Attorney General for the Year of 1912*, 442–51.

[72] Marlene D. Beckman, "The White Slave Traffic Act: Historical Impact of a Federal Crime Policy on Women," in Claudine SchWeber and Clarice Feinman, eds., *Criminal Justice*

The increase in female prisoners within the federal penitentiary system due to the Mann Act caused some concern for observers. One moral reformer looked at the women imprisoned in the federal prison at Lansing, MI, to try to discern what type of woman became a "white slaver." She noted that of the fourteen women imprisoned for violation of the Mann Act, the average age was thirty-one years, most had little education, almost all claimed to be occupied in domestic service, all but two had been married, and they came from diverse religious backgrounds although all seemed "slow" to take up prison church work.[73] The reformer felt most frustrated by what she deemed the short length of time served; to her it was long enough only to improve these women's physical health, but not long enough to improve their moral health. She gloomily concluded, "hope lies in prevention rather than cure."[74]

In contrast to the Bureau of Investigation's view that the Mann Act was an anti-prostitution provision, private citizens asserted a broader view of the law. Of the cases investigated in the first six months of the act's existence, 27.6 percent could be classified as seduction cases initiated by parents or concerned family members.[75] For example, one distraught mother, whose sixteen-year-old daughter had run away from home with a young man who had promised her marriage, wrote that she hoped the Bureau of Investigation would launch a white slave investigation after one of her tenants – twenty-one-year-old Harry West – seduced her teenage daughter, Ethel. When Ethel became pregnant, the couple ran away to Kansas City where they tried to acquire an abortion, and where, ultimately, Harry deserted Ethel.[76] Ethel's mother asked "how can we protect our houses and Daughters if we have no home protection?"[77] Unfortunately for the mother, the agent in charge of the case concluded that it would be difficult to get a conviction, and the Bureau of Investigation dropped the case.

Politics and Women: The Aftermath of Legally Mandated Change (New York: The Haworth Press, 1985), 85–101 (86).

[73] Mrs. J. K. Codding, "Concerning Female White Slave Prisoners at Lansing," *The Light* 16, no. 90 (March 1913), 19–21.

[74] Ibid., 21.

[75] BOI Administrative Reports on Cases.

[76] Special Agent Arthur T. Bagley, 2799-7, 7 Nov 1911, Case 2799, Roll 136, RG 65, Federal Bureau of Investigation, Investigative Case Giles of the Bureau, 1908–1922, M1085, National Archives, College Park, MD [hereafter cited as BOI Microfilm Records].

[77] Mrs. E. H. Osborne to H. A. Thompson, Sept. 30, 1911, reprinted in Special Agent H. A. Thompson, 2799-1, Oct. 16, 1911, Case 2799, Roll 136, BOI Microfilm Records. Underline in original.

The year 1917 settled the question of the scope of the Mann Act when the Supreme Court ruled that "any other immoral purpose" truly meant *any* other immoral purpose. The broad mandate of the "any other immoral purpose" clause contributed to the growth of the Bureau as a national, federal criminal justice agency through the policing of women's sexuality. From 1921 to 1936, the Bureau investigated over 47,500 Mann Act violations, yet it achieved only 6,335 convictions during this time. The majority of these cases had no element of sex trafficking or even commercial prostitution, but rather were cases of seduction, runaway daughters, bigamy, adultery, and sexual assault that fell under the "any other immoral purpose" clause of the law.[78] Consequently, the goal in many of these investigations was not conviction, but rather restoring order to disorderly homes. The enforcement of the Mann Act propped up the traditional patriarchal family by policing women's sexuality; in many ways the United States' first anti-trafficking law functioned as a family values law.[79]

By 1917, the United States had passed comprehensive laws to address the perceived crisis in sex trafficking. It had shored up the moral borders of the country by constructing policies that paved the way for the deportation of foreign-born prostitutes, thousands of whom were deported over the years, and it had "protected" native-born women by passing a federal sex law that policed white women's heterosexuality. These laws remained in effect and enforced from the early twentieth century onward. Anti-trafficking activism of the early twentieth century, on both the national and international levels, erased women's capacity for consent, imagined traffickers as a dangerously dispossessed or racialized "other," and led to policies that emphasized border control regimes in a moment when nation states were dramatically expanding their administrative states in the face of global mass migration.

Sexual slavery re-emerged as a topic of concern on the global stage in the late 1990s. Many of the trends present in the first anti-trafficking movement that I have emphasized in this essay are present in the modern-day slavery movement, which is no surprise given, as acclaimed feminist historian Linda Gordon recently noted, "neglecting earlier social theory is practically a constant in social movements, which so often reinvent

---

[78] J. Edgar Hoover qtd in "White Slave Traffic Gains: Hoover Asks Public Aid in Drive to Wipe Out Violations," *Boston Evening Recorder*, August 17, 1936.

[79] For more on this argument see Pliley, *Policing Sexuality*.

rather than recover and improve older ideas."[80] Indeed, the purpose of this volume is to interrogate the ways that the study of the past can shed light on contemporary activism, reform, and policy. Here, I will briefly point to three ways that prior trends of ignoring women's volition, racializing discourses, and carceral and border control regimes have become entangled in the enforcement of anti-trafficking measures.

In 2000 the United States spearheaded negotiations to form a new anti-trafficking international law within the United Nations. These negotiations produced the UN Protocol to Prevent, Suppress, and Punish Trafficking in Persons, Especially Women and Children (hereto after referred to as the UN Trafficking Protocol). The Protocol defined trafficking as a process that included the "recruitment, transportation, transfer, harbouring or receipt of persons, by means of the threat or use of force or other forms of coercion, of abduction, of fraud, of deception, of the abuse of power or of a position of vulnerability or of the giving or receiving of payments or benefits to achieve the consent of a person having control over another person, for the purpose of exploitation."[81] This vague and broad definition encompasses a remarkable number of activities and leaves open considerable space for interpretation. The UN Trafficking Protocol does not define "exploitation," "coercion," or "vulnerability." Significantly, the UN Trafficking Protocol was placed under the umbrella of the UN Convention on Transnational Organized Crime, thereby placing it under a criminal justice frame rather than the human rights realm, and the "criminal justice approach could provide a politically convenient means for governments to justify immigration restrictions under the guise of protecting trafficked persons."[82]

The development of the UN Trafficking Protocol was accompanied by the passage of the US TVPA of 2000, which included provisions for enforcing the UN Trafficking Protocol through the US State Department. The State Department ranks countries according to their efforts in fighting trafficking and mandates economic sanctions

---

[80] Linda Gordon, "'Intersectionality,' Socialist Feminism and Contemporary Activism: Musings by a Second-Wave Socialist Feminist," *Gender & History* 28, no. 2 (August 2016), 340–57 (341).

[81] United Nations, "The Protocol to Prevent, Suppress and Punish Trafficking in Persons, especially Women and Children, Supplementing the United Nations Conventions against Transnational Organized Crime," *United Nations*, 2000, www.uncjin.org/Documents/ Conventions/dcatoc/final_documents_2/convention_%20traff_eng.pdf.

[82] Janie A. Chuang, "Rescuing Trafficking from Ideological Capture: Anti-Prostitution Reform and its Influence on US Anti-Trafficking Law and Policy," *University of Pennsylvania Law Review* 158, no. 6 (May 2010), 1655–1728 (1663).

against those countries that the US judges to be failing in the global fight against trafficking, and, as Janie Chuang contends, this sanctioning threat became one of the primary ways that the Bush administration promoted its anti-prostitution stance throughout the world (the other powerful way of promoting this agenda was its policies toward HIV/AIDS funding).[83] So, US domestic law became a powerful driver behind establishing a particular set of international norms under the cover of UN action.

Additionally, the TVPA provided protections for trafficked persons by offering a T visa, which allows for temporary residence in the US for three years, gives the right to work, and offers access to social services. Yet, initially to gain access to a T visa, applicants had to prove that they would suffer "extreme hardship involving unusual and severe harm" if they are removed from the US Demonstrating "extreme hardship" proved very difficult, and some critics have suggested that it may increase a trafficked person's risk.[84] Furthermore, access to the T visa was limited to those persons who are willing to aid in prosecutors' efforts. As Wendy Chapkis argues, "by making assistance to even 'deserving' victims contingent on their willingness to assist authorities in the prosecution of traffickers, the legislation further seals US borders against penetration by 'undeserving' economic migrants."[85] Most damning for the notion of "protection" is that anyone with a history of prostitution in the ten years prior to their application is excluded from the program under the assumption that she might be a foreign sex worker illegally exploiting the T visa loophole to gain residency in the US.[86] Though the TVPA attempts to strike a balance between the human rights of victims and the prosecutorial agenda of the state, as Jennifer K. Lobasz notes, "even polices that are meant to protect the human rights of trafficked persons still prioritize the interests of the state."[87]

---

[83] Chuang, "Rescuing Trafficking from Ideological Capture," 1680.

[84] Helga Konrad, "Trafficking in Human Beings: A Comparative Account of Legal Provisions in Belgium, Italy, the Netherlands, Sweden and the United States," in van der Anker and Doomernik, eds., *Trafficking and Women's Rights*, 118–37 (131).

[85] Wendy Chapkis, "Trafficking, Migration, and the Law: Protecting Innocents, Punishing Immigrants," *Gender & Society* 17, no. 6 (December 2003), 923–37 (925).

[86] Jennifer A. L. Sheldon-Sherman, "Missing P: Prosecution, Prevention, Protection, and Partnership in the Trafficking Victims Protection Act," *Pennsylvania State Law Review* 117 (2012), 443–501 (466).

[87] Jennifer K. Lobasz, "Beyond Border Security: Feminist Approaches to Human Trafficking," *Security Studies* 18, no. 2 (2009), 319–44 (333).

Under George W. Bush's administration, the US State Department routinely emphasized sex trafficking over all other forms of trafficking and often paired its anti-trafficking efforts with its broader anti-prostitution agenda.[88] Additionally, the US took the perspective that sex work was not a legitimate form of labor, nor was it an acceptable purpose for labor migration. Instead, the administration conceived of anti-trafficking work as rescuing exploited and naïve women from the clutches of controlling traffickers.[89] Though the Bush administration spent over $150 million to identify and aid victims of trafficking, which were believed to number 50,000 persons each year, it found only 1,362 victims between 2000 and 2007, most of whom were female sex workers.[90]

Throughout the 2000s (and indeed beyond) sensational stories of sex trafficking circulated. The narratives routinely erased the agency of the women being "rescued." Carole Vance, in her analysis of a series of television documentaries about sex trafficking, coined the useful term "melomentary" to describe the basic narrative features of most trafficking stories. She notes that "melomentaries present themselves as documentary reports, but the bits of empirical evidence (interviews, comments of experts, facts) are organized by a highly predetermined plot line and limited set of characters (or subject positions), all moving toward a triumphant endpoint that is highly overdetermined."[91] Inevitably, news accounts, documentaries, and magazine exposés feature "victims" who are young, men who are blurry and threatening, and invisible but ominous customers. Jo Doezema notes that in typical trafficking narratives the "sex worker who is a 'trafficking victim' is rendered innocent by the ritual invocation of her poverty and desperation."[92] This discursive charade is accompanied by the routine blurring of distinctions between the

---

[88] Janie A. Chuang, "Exploitation Creep and the Unmaking of Human Trafficking Law," *The American Journal of International Law* 108, no. 4 (October 2014), 609–49 (610 and 618).

[89] For the most detailed background on the UN Trafficking Protocol and the TVPA see: Jo Doezema, *Sex Slaves and Discourse Masters: The Construction of Trafficking* (London: Zed Books, 2010); Chuang, "Exploitation Creep"; and Chuang, "Rescuing Trafficking from Ideological Capture."

[90] Davidson, "New Slaveries, Old Binaries," 252.

[91] Carole S. Vance, "Innocence and Experience: Melodramatic Narratives of Sex Trafficking and Their Consequences for Law and Policy," *History of the Preset* 2, no. 2 (Fall 2012), 200–18 (204–5).

[92] Jo Doezema, "Loose Women or Lost Women? The Re-Emergence of the Myth of White Slavery in Contemporary Discourses of Trafficking in Women," *Gender Issues* 18, no. 1 (1999), 23–50 (34).

child and the adult, which aids in fixing "the image of the 'trafficking' victim as young and helpless."[93] These narratives evoke the protection of the trafficking victims due to their youth and helplessness, while, in contrast, women who migrate for sex work are rendered as deviant Others who deserve no protection.[94]

Although, sex work is a legal occupation in many countries that have signed the UN Trafficking Protocol, these countries have eagerly embraced anti-trafficking legislation and policies, even when the question of how to identify the trafficking victim and the migrating sex worker poses significant challenges. For example, scholars Sharon Pickering and Julie Ham conducted a study of the enforcement of Australia's anti-sex trafficking law as part of the country's border control procedures at two airports. Sex work is legal in Australia. Their research yielded some interesting, if predictable, results: First, sex trafficking predominated border control officers' agendas over other forms of labor trafficking; second, "The imagery of the Asian women being forced into sex work still dominates at Australian airport borders"; and third, in spite of the growth in surveillance technologies, the primary factor in determining risk assessment was border control officers' judgments of women's clothing combined with women's age and race.[95] They concluded, "Border crossing lies at the heart of the definition of trafficking, and yet is often largely irrelevant because trafficking is rarely identified at the border."[96]

Though border control regimes are not particularly effective at identifying trafficking, anxiety about trafficking continues to justify the introduction of prohibitions challenging free mobility.[97] Recently, concerns about the presence of migrant sex workers in England has produced a moral panic that has included calls for the UK to adopt the so-called Nordic model, which criminalizes the purchase of sex. Amid such a panic in the lead up to the 2012 London Olympics, police raided more than eighty brothels in Newham. Though widely celebrated as a successful

---

[93] Doezema, "Loose Women or Lost Women?," 35.

[94] Lobasz, "Beyond Border Security," 340, 341; Chapkis, "Trafficking, Migration, and the Law," 924.

[95] Sharon Pickering and Julie Ham, "Hot Pants at the Border: Sorting Sex Work from Trafficking," *British Journal of Criminology* 54 (2014), 2–19 (9).

[96] Ibid., 16.

[97] For sustained critiques into the way that trafficking discourses function to racialize and limit mobility see Agustín, *Sex at the Margins*; Julia O'Connell Davidson, *Modern Slavery: The Margins of Freedom* (London: Palgrave MacMillan, 2015), 130–2.

police action to prevent sex trafficking, Andrew Boff reported that these types of raids have less than a 1 percent rate of finding women who had been trafficked. Rather, these anti-trafficking raids targeted voluntary sex workers and, according to Open Doors, an outreach organization, significantly undermined the safety of sex workers.[98] Yet, anti-trafficking narratives continue to appear in UK newspapers and anti-trafficking initiatives call for limiting the free movement of peoples from Europe to the UK. They also may have contributed to the pro-Brexit vote. As Julia O'Connell Davidson and Bridget Anderson note, the "conflation of anti-immigration and anti-trafficking measures obscures the fact that policies designed to control irregular forms of migration are known to encourage, permit, or exacerbate violations of migrants' human rights, and policies that focus on the prevention of illegal movements of people do nothing to address the factors that make it possible for employers and others to engage in exploitative and slavery-like practices at the point of destination."[99]

As the example from the London Olympics demonstrates, anti-trafficking policies often contribute to an increase in the policing of sex workers and the further victimization of "victims" at the hands of the state. Evidence of this dynamic can be found throughout the world. In 2003 the state of Texas passed one of the first state-level anti-trafficking laws in the US The US Department of Justice identified the I-10 highway that connects Houston to El Paso as one of "the most intense trafficking jurisdictions in the country."[100] In 2009 the Texas Legislature established a Human Trafficking Prevention Taskforce, which was intended to bring together various stakeholders in the fight against trafficking, including law enforcement officials, representatives of victims' service providers, and trade associations. The bill also provided for $10 million a year to be allocated to nonprofit organizations and counties to help provide for victims' services. This money has never materialized.[101] Though

---

[98] Phil Hubbard, Jane Scoular, and Teela Sanders, "Prostitution Policy, Morality and the Precautionary Principle," *Drugs and Alcohol Today* 16, no. 3 (2016), 7–13.

[99] Davidson and Anderson, "The Trouble with 'Trafficking,'" 23.

[100] Texas Advisory Commission to the US Commission on Civil Rights, *Human Trafficking in Texas: More Resources and Resolve Needed to Stem Surge in Modern Day Slavery* (August 2011), 4, www.usccr.gov/pubs/TX_HT_Report--ver%2050--FINAL.pdf (accessed August 31, 2016).

[101] The Texas Human Trafficking Prevention Task Force, *The Texas Human Trafficking Prevention Task Force Report 2011*, Office of the Attorney General, January, 2011, 55, www.oag.state.tx.us/ag_publications/pdfs/human_trafficking.pdf.

subsequent trafficking laws in Texas continue to emphasize the centrality of victims' services, the state budget prioritizes prosecution over victims' needs, and increased criminalization over prevention.[102] Following the Trafficking in Persons Office policy shift that trafficking does not require movement as a matter of law (as of 2006 harboring alone was enough to satisfy US definitions of trafficking), Texas does not consider transport as a defining condition of trafficking.[103] In Texas, domestic minor trafficking (coded language that refers to the criminalization of the selling of sex by people under the age of eighteen) has emerged as a central feature of the anti-trafficking and anti-prostitution agenda. Yet, when minors encounter police, they are often held in disciplinary institutions because the state has not made available enough funds for victims' services.[104] This trend of favoring criminalization and allocating money to law enforcement over providing services to victims is endemic to the entire US, and elsewhere as well.[105]

The ways that trafficking narratives and policies erase women's (and girls') agency, introduce racialized understandings of trafficking, and increase the carceral and border control regimes have long roots. Although the US currently dominates global anti-trafficking policy, the development of understandings of trafficking in early twentieth-century international civil society and under the auspices of the creation of international norms in interstate organizations like the League of

---

[102] SB 24 HB 2014, introduced in the 2011–12 session of the Texas legislature, enhanced penalties of domestic minor trafficking, removed the statute of limitations for cases with child victims, and introduced the possibility of life sentences for traffickers of children (i.e., anyone prostituted under the age of eighteen); while SB 532 HB 8, introduced in the 2012–13 session, sought to offer victims the possibility of confidentiality.

[103] Chuang, "Exploitation Creep," 620.

[104] See Rachel C. Hughey, "High Modernism of Human Trafficking: Ideological Criticism of Texas' Human Trafficking Leglislation," Honor's Thesis, Texas State University, 2014.

[105] Kimberly Mahlman-Orozco, "What Happens after a Human Trafficking Victim is 'Rescued'?" *The Hill*, July 29, 2016, http://thehill.com/blogs/congress-blog/judicial/289709-what-happens-after-a-human-trafficking-victim-is-rescued; Kimberly Kotrla, "Domestic Minor Sex Trafficking in the United States," *Social Work* 55, no. 2 (2010), 181–7; Sheldon-Sherman, "Missing P," 467; Cathy Zimmerman, Mazeda Hossain, and Charlotte Watts, "Human Trafficking and Health: A Conceptual Model to Inform Policy, Intervention and Research," *Social Science & Medicine* 73, no. 2 (2011), 327–35 (330–1); Ronald Weitzer, "Sex Trafficking and the Sex Industry: The Need for Evidence-Based Theory and Legislation," *The Journal of Criminal Law and Criminology* 101, no. 4 (2011), 1337–69 (1344); Lobasz, "Beyond Border Security," 331.

Nations points to a longer consensus on the dangers that trafficking poses to nation states: migrating women who sell sex, racialized men who may compromise the body politic, the irregular and suspicious migration of undocumented people. Anti-trafficking policies emerged as a way for nation states to assert control of migration, morality, and women, and they continue to do just that.

PART III

THE LESSONS AND SOLUTIONS OF HISTORY FOR TODAY

8

All the Ships that Never Sailed

Lessons for the Modern Antislavery Movement from the British Naval Campaigns against the Atlantic Slave Trade

Dave Blair

Here we are, on the most miserable station in the wide world ... attempting an impossibility – the suppression of the Slave Trade. We look upon the whole affair out here as a complete humbug. You may make treaties in London, and send the whole combined squadrons of England and France to this coast, and then you will not have gained your object. So long as a slave, worth only a few dollars here, fetches 80*l* or 100*l* in America, men and means will be found to evade the strictest blockade. The absurdity of blockading a coast 2,000 miles in extent must be obvious to the meanest capacity. Even if successful you must be prepared to continue the force forever and a day, or your labour is lost; for the moment the ships are removed, the business recommences.

Anonymous Royal Navy officer, West Africa Squadron, 1845[1]

We do not believe, nor did we ever suppose it possible, that the Squadron will suppress the Slave-trade. The substitution of two letters makes all the difference. It is in the hope of re-pressing, not of suppressing the Slave-trade, that all reasonable men insist upon the blockade. What can be more absurd, on the face of it, than to suppose, that four-and-twenty cruisers can extinguish a smuggling trade where the profits are a thousand per cent? We entirely agree with our opponents, that, whether the line of coast to be blockaded be 4,000 or 400 miles, a naval force will never be able to extinguish an illegal trade of such enormous value. When we talk of extinction or suppression, we use large terms, implying an

---

[1] "The Slave-Trade," *The Liberator*, November 14, 1845. Reprinted from the London Non-Conformist, *National Archives*, www.nationalarchives.gov.uk/help-with-your-research/research-guides/nonconformists/.

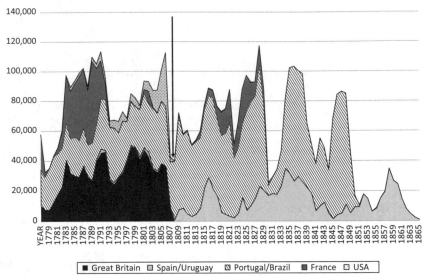

FIGURE 1 Captives moved through Middle Passage by year and nationality of sponsor (arrow represents abolition). Data from the Voyages Database, 2010.

object which cannot be achieved by any single means, however great or powerful.

George Stephen, Clapham-linked abolitionist, written
anonymously, 1850[2]

In thinking about slavery across time, the British suppression of the Atlantic slave trade serves as a dramatic example of a large-scale campaign against an international criminal enterprise across a commons. It is striking on a number of levels – first, the scale of the campaign, which cost thousands of British sailors, generated significant portions of the Foreign Office's correspondence for decades, and almost ended in failure four decades into its existence. This campaign demonstrates the promise and peril of state power against slavery, and illustrates many of the frustrations experienced by those on the leading edges of that power. It also illustrates the problem of unintended consequences.

[2] Written as "A Barrister," *Analysis of the Evidence Given before the Select Committee upon the Slave Trade* (Partridge and Oakey, 1850). Eltis identifies this author as Stephen. David Eltis, *Economic Growth and the Ending of the Transatlantic Slave Trade* (Oxford: Oxford University Press, 1987), 384.

Second, and most importantly, it is notable for its success, as the suppression effort played a major role in the nineteenth-century abolition of the Atlantic trade in persons. While trafficking took other forms and means, and found other routes, the collapse of this major mode of large-scale unfree labor traffic shaped the fates of many. Considering the increasing role of traffickers in the commons of our day – not least of which is the Internet – the magnitude, stubbornness, and ultimate success of the historical campaign should both ignite the modern abolitionist imagination while humbling any triumphalism about the scope of present efforts. It seems likely that a campaign of similar size, coordination, and tenacity will be required to eradicate the global, large-scale slave trade of our day. To that end, I introduce the nineteenth-century saga of British slave trade suppression, interpreted in light of its value as an example for those combating enslavement across national borders today.

On March 25, 1807, the British Empire shifted from serving as the primary backer of the Atlantic slave trade to become its most powerful, persistent adversary.[3] The ban on the slave trade removed the powerful ports of Liverpool, Bristol, and London from the trade. While undoubtedly a body blow to the trade, it was hardly a knockout blow – the coasts of West Africa and the Americas remained fertile ground for the trade. Within a few years, the British almost entirely stripped the Union Jack from the masts of slavers under the threat of increasingly dire penalties.[4] Other flags filled the vacated space, and the trade recovered quickly from the British exit. The British had taken the prerogative of unilaterally boarding slavers during the Napoleonic wars, but the onset of peace, increasing international resistance, and a series of court findings demanded a more overt and deliberate approach. By 1820,

---

[3] An Act for the Abolition of the Slave Trade, March 25, 1807, 47 Geo III Sess. 1 c. 36.

[4] It took longer to remove British subjects from participation in the trade, and multinational corporations with British holdings (especially the Zulueta Brothers) remained active for the duration. Christopher Lloyd, *The Navy and the Slave Trade: The Suppression of the African Slave Trade in the Nineteenth Century*, 1st ed. (London: Longmans, Green Co., 1949); Hugh Thomas, *The Slave Trade: The Story of the Atlantic Slave Trade: 1440–1870* (New York: Simon & Schuster, 2013); Marika Sherwood, *After Abolition: Britain and the Slave Trade since 1807* (New York: I. B. Tauris, 2007); Emma Christopher, Cassandra Pybus, and Marcus Rediker, eds., *Many Middle Passages: Forced Migration and the Making of the Modern World*, 1st ed. (Berkeley, CA: University of California Press, 2007). Zulueta also played a key role in opening the "Coolie Trade," by sending inquiries to China about bonded laborers. Evelyn Hu-Dehart, "Chinese Coolie Labour in Cuba in the Nineteenth Century: Free Labour or Neo-Slavery?," *Slavery and Abolition* 14, no. 1 (1993), 67–86.

the slave trade returned to its former strength under the Portuguese, Spanish, and French flags (Figure 1).

Freed of its own complicity in the international slave trade, in no figurative sense, Britain went to war against the slave trade. As with most wars against abstract concepts, this battle began in fits and starts with varying degrees of clarity and commitment; in contrast with most such wars, three decades in, the campaign was focused, aggressive, and effective. In September 1818, Commodore Sir George Collier sailed with a flotilla for the Gulf of Guinea under orders to "use every means in [our] power to prevent a continuance of the traffic in slaves and to give full effect to the Acts of Parliament in question."[5] With this, the Royal Navy West Africa Squadron began a formal naval suppression campaign against the trade's ships and later against its fortresses (Figure 2). Between that point and 1867, the year the last known Atlantic slave ship sailed, the British spent tens of millions of pounds and lost thousands of sailors in the course of this campaign. Their foreign office bribed and pressured European seagoing powers into an international treaty network against the trade, backed by Royal Navy cruisers. Royal Navy officers built a network of treaties with leaders on the West African coast, by way of a similar mix of economic incentives, pressure, and force.

This *volte-face* was an indispensable element of the eventual collapse of the trade,[6] but it was ethically fraught and highly contingent. The British were willing to act unilaterally, invading West African kingdoms, provoking the Portuguese, and assaulting Brazilian slave ships at their moorings in the Americas.[7] Questionably legal boarding procedures were commonplace, bloody assaults on resisting slave ships were well publicized, and by the later phases of the campaign, a number of captains took to marooning captured slave ship crewmen.[8] While the cruisers

---

[5] Lloyd, *The Navy and the Slave Trade*, 67.

[6] This point is highly debated by Atlantic history luminaries such as David Eltis, who contends that economic changes primarily extinguished the trade, and Seymour Drescher, who views suppression as a necessary element of the collapse. Eltis, *Economic Growth and the Ending of the Transatlantic Slave Trade*; Seymour Drescher, *Econocide: British Slavery in the Era of Abolition*, 2nd ed. (Chapel Hill, NC: The University of North Carolina Press, 2010).

[7] Lloyd, *The Navy and the Slave Trade*; Leslie Bethell, *The Abolition of the Brazilian Slave Trade: Britain, Brazil and the Slave Trade Question*, 1st ed. (Cambridge, MA: Cambridge University Press, 2009), 327–65.

[8] For an opposed boarding account, see Theodore Canot and Brantz Mayer, *Adventures of an African Slaver* (Mineola, NY: Dover Publications, 2002), 212. For a discussion of recommendations of marooning resistant crew members, see Lloyd, *The Navy and the Slave Trade*, 123.

FIGURE 2 "H. M. Brig 'Acorn' in Chase of the Piratical Slaver 'Gabriel,' " N. M. Condy, 1850. © National Maritime Museum, Greenwich, London.

added risk to the trade, the slavers transferred much of that risk to their captives, who might be thrown overboard to their deaths as a means of hiding evidence or as a distraction to a pursuing cruiser.[9] This was an ugly fight, and grew all the more ugly as the British grew more effective.

Amidst all of this, the perennially controversial effort faced vocal doubts as to its efficacy and social value, and was very nearly called off by Parliament and the Admiralty almost a half-century later amidst mounting weariness and political opposition.[10] In 1850, the British Prime Minister and Foreign Secretary staked their government on the continuance of the campaign; surviving this challenge, they doubled down on suppression. This renewed support propelled Royal Navy captains further ashore in West Africa in pursuit of the trade, which further entangled the British Empire in Yoruba civil wars.[11] Even as the British shut down all avenues

---

[9] Multiple accounts of these practices are recounted in Lloyd, *The Navy and the Slave Trade*.

[10] For a readable account of these debates, see Sian Rees, *Sweet Water and Bitter: The Ships That Stopped the Slave Trade* (Durham, NH: University of New Hampshire Press, 2011), 269–90.

[11] Paul Mmegha Mbaeyi, *British Military and Naval Forces in West African History, 1807–1874* (New York: NOK Publishers, 1978), 129.

to the trade on both sides of the Atlantic, and much of the force-based slave traffic from Africa was replaced by fraud-based human trafficking from South and East Asia, slavery continued in various forms.[12] Some of these forms were undone, some endured, and some even became excuses for imperial expansion.[13]

The naval suppression of the slave trade was a "savage war of peace,"[14] to borrow Kipling's phrase, with all of its connotations. Despite all of this, the cruisers prevailed and the Atlantic slave trade was no more. The British paid a high price over the course of this campaign. They made others pay a price as well, often against their will. But they accomplished their purpose. In Drescher's words:

The presence of British anti-slave trade policy meant that sooner or later the vital African source of New World expansion could be cut off, one sector at a time. It is easier to dismiss the impact of British persistence against the grain of economic interest than to imagine the relation of coercion to freedom without it. A nation with a less engrained commitment to antislavery as a matter of national honor might well have cut its losses in the midcentury crisis. It might well have called home its fleet in 1850, allowed the expanded flow of Africans to the Americas, and recognized the South in 1861 on impeccable grounds of political and economic self-interest ... All around us remains overwhelming evidence that abolition eliminated only one major network of human brutality and death. Yet it is hard to imagine a world that would have been far worse off without its elimination.[15]

For this reason alone, a deep understanding of the suppression campaign should figure strongly in our shared project to "use history to make slavery history." The great victory of 1807 was the end of the beginning, but it was hardly the beginning of the end.[16] The trials, travails, triumphs, and even the tactics of this campaign stand as lessons for the abolitionists of today. Given how often the analogy between Wilberforce's work and modern slavery is deployed, we do well to consider the difficulty of all that followed.

---

[12] Hu-Dehart, "Chinese Coolie Labour in Cuba in the Nineteenth Century"; Christopher, Pybus, and Rediker, *Many Middle Passages.*

[13] Richard Huzzey, *Freedom Burning: Anti-Slavery and Empire in Victorian Britain* (Ithaca, NY: Cornell University Press, 2012). Also the introduction to Adam Hochschild, *King Leopold's Ghost: A Story of Greed, Terror, and Heroism in Colonial Africa* (Boston, MA: Houghton Mifflin, 1999).

[14] A line from Rudyard Kipling's poem "White Man's Burden." Public Domain.

[15] Drescher in Derek Peterson, ed., *Abolitionism and Imperialism in Britain, Africa, and the Atlantic*, 1st ed. (Athens, OH: Ohio University Press, 2010), 236.

[16] Phrasing borrowed from Andy Crouch, "Tedium + Valor," *Books and Culture*, n.d., March/April 2012 edition, www.booksandculture.com/articles/2012/marapr/tedium .html.

The sheer magnitude of the task is humbling and impels us to increase the scope of our thinking; the contingency of its success should scare us a bit and drive us to build more durable foundations for modern abolitionist movements. The unintended consequences of intervention, the bitter consequences of faults in the suppressors' ideological frames, and the indirect cost of suppression paid by captives and bystanders should sober us to the nature of these enterprises and remind us to consider these consequences in our own choices. But ultimately, the imperfect success of the campaign should encourage modern-day abolitionists to believe that it is possible to defeat an evil on the order of the Atlantic slave trade.

In the essay "Abolishing Slavery in Lincoln's Time and Ours: Creating a New Antislavery Movement," James Brewer Stewart reminds us that "the first and most basic lesson we can take from the original abolitionists is this: Demand the impossible and know precisely that this is what you are doing. Nevertheless, mean it irrevocably and act on it absolutely."[17] In that spirit, we will recount the British struggle with an eye to lessons that might be applied today.

I begin by discussing the strengths and limitations of an analogy between the West Africa Squadron and efforts to combat modern-day slavery. Considering these events through the lens of naval history provides profitable parallels (and contrasts) with contemporary transnational efforts against illicit criminal slaving networks, such as the online exploitation and trafficking of minors. It provides less leverage against in-place or culturally accepted exploitation, such as bonded labor. Next, I introduce the campaign by presenting two core pillars of the British victory: efficiency, or the difficulty with which innovations and information flows through the suppressor's network vis-à-vis the illicit market; and support, the socially embedded normative demand for suppression relative to the continuing economic demand for the illicit trade. After that we narrate four major periods of the squadron's campaign with vignettes relevant to modern efforts, beginning with first steps from 1808 to 1820, continuing through the learning and growth period of 1820–40, proceeding through the interventionist and combative 1840s–50s, and culminating with the trade's last stand in the 1860s. We conclude by deriving lessons learned

---

[17] James Brewer Stewart, "Abolishing Slavery in Lincoln's Time and Ours: Creating a New Antislavery Movement" (16th Annual "Building Bridges" Conference, Gustavus Adolphus College, March 12, 2011), *Historians Against Slavery*, http://historiansagainstslavery.org/collaborate/wp-content/uploads/group-documents/1/1310008661-abolishingslavery_keynote.pdf.

from the Royal Navy experience, in order to apply them to modern anti-trafficking challenges.

Historical Assumptions. Acknowledging the rich historiographical debates surrounding this period, we require a few interpretative notes at the outset. First, the relationship between the slave trade and slavery itself was contested both during the time period and in our recollection. As a minimal interpretation, since suppression cut off the source of new captives, it eliminated the "buy" option from the planters' ghastly "buy vs. breed" equation.[18] As Kevin Bales argues about contemporary slavery, "disposable people" are subject to even more horrific treatment than were those who lived under generational models of slavery.[19] Across the Americas and with very few exceptions, suppression of the slave trade preceded the abolition of slavery itself. However, the relationship between the trade and the institution was complex; the end of the institution generally hinged on the demographics of servitude, into which the trade was only one input. I do not attempt to assess this relation further. Instead I assume that the suppression of the trade was a necessary but not sufficient condition for the eradication of the execrable institution, and I assert that the campaign's success checked the most lethal "disposable people" practices of exploitation.

Second, the West African Squadron's effectiveness in suppressing the trade is highly debated by historians such as David Eltis, who contends that economic changes, not the actions of the British navy, primarily extinguished the trade, and Seymour Drescher, who views suppression as a necessary element of the slave trade's collapse.[20] I tend toward Drescher's view, holding that changes in economic path dependency over time included calculations about the future cost of slave labor, which yielded appreciating impacts in economic shifts and at least accelerated these processes. I do find very helpful Eltis's thinking about the substantial indirect costs of the suppression campaign being paid primarily by Africans, and compare it to the effects on transit and producing countries in present Western Hemisphere counter-narcotics campaigns, similar to those described

[18] For an example of the latter, see Thomas Jackson, *Memoirs of the Life and Writings of the Rev. Richard Watson, Late Secretary to the Wesleyan Missionary Society* (New York: B. Waugh and T. Mason, 1817), 457.

[19] Kevin Bales, *Disposable People: New Slavery in the Global Economy*, 2nd ed. (Los Angeles, CA: University of California Press, 2004).

[20] Drescher, *Econocide*.

by Vanda Felbab-Brown's work on counterinsurgency and narcotics control.[21]

Finally, especially for American readers, I recommend divorcing the story of slave trade suppression from the larger arc of American slavery – by the early 1800s, the American institution of slavery was self-sustaining through birth rates alone, and the prohibition on the trade was one of the very few points of agreement between North and South on the issue. This was due to a complex cocktail of social norms (namely, a moral differentiation between the horrors of the trade and the evils of the established institution), general fears of slave revolt, and protectionism on the part of established slaveholders.[22] The major exception to this trend was a short-lived rash of Charleston yacht owners who participated in the slave trade in the run-up to the American Civil War, and who perversely imagined a patriotic logic in attempting to reinvigorate the trade.[23]

The American role in suppression was Janus-like: on one hand, United States Navy captains pushed the limits of their authority in order to suppress the trade, oftentimes to the consternation of their civilian leadership. On the other hand, American shipyards – largely Baltimore, New York, and New England – built the high-speed blockade runners that allowed slavers to run the British blockade, which were then laundered by way of forged paperwork and indifferent officials in contravention of American law.[24] This notwithstanding, these episodes involved primarily indifference and corruption rather than an ideological commitment to the trade, and the willingness to indirectly profit at the expense of African captives was not specific to regional views of the institution.[25] Therefore, I envision this participation more akin to a sanctuary or transit country in the contemporary drug wars than as an adjunct to sectional conflict. With these assumptions stated, we move to the core analogy.

---

[21] Vanda Felbab-Brown, *Aspiration and Ambivalence: Strategies and Realities of Counterinsurgency and State Building in Afghanistan* (Washington, DC: Brookings Institution Press, 2013); Felbab-Brown, *Shooting Up: Counterinsurgency and the War on Drugs* (Washington, DC: Brookings Institute Press, 2010).

[22] Don E. Fehrenbacher and Ward McAfee, *The Slaveholding Republic: An Account of the United States Government's Relations to Slavery* (New York: Oxford University Press, 2001); Warren S. Howard, *American Slavers and the Federal Law, 1837–1862* (Los Angeles, CA: University of California Press, 1963).

[23] Erik Calonius, *The Wanderer: The Last American Slave Ship and the Conspiracy That Set Its Sails* (New York; Godalming: St. Martin's, 2008).

[24] Anne Farrow, Joel Lang, and Jenifer Frank, *Complicity: How the North Promoted, Prolonged, and Profited from Slavery* (New York: Random House LLC, 2007); Howard, *American Slavers and the Federal Law, 1837–1862*.

[25] Calonius, *The Wanderer*.

THE ATLANTIC AND THE INTERNET: CALIBRATING
THE ANALOGY

James Brewer Stewart and Joel Quirk's works describe the promise and peril of analogizing from their time to ours, particularly the problems of ungrounded, rhetorically driven linkages.[26] Poor analogies make for poor conclusions, and the temptation to appropriate examples that suit one's organizational and ideological ends brings neither clarity nor analytical leverage to this cause, which so rightly commands our passions and energy.

Still, the history of slavery provides an essential foundation for understanding today's slavery. We can avoid these pitfalls by directly linking a historical trajectory to a contemporary problem. For instance, British suppression generated demand for alternate sources of unfree labor. This led to the "Coolie trade" of the mid 1800s, which shipped millions of forced laborers from South and East Asia to the Americas. This trade links certain types of modern slavery to the Atlantic model, as the use of fraudulent contracts and debt bondage resembles modern trafficking, while the forms of agricultural exploitation recall the historical African trade. Historical innovations and legal countermeasures employed against the historical trade might prove effective against contemporary manifestations.

Alternately, we can indirectly link the story of historical suppression to the challenge of modern slavery within the larger arc of slavery and freedom by identifying similarities in essential aspects of both. I take this latter approach. By the 1820s, the majority of transoceanic maritime powers had nominally declared themselves against the trade, though many of these worked at cross purposes to the suppression campaign, and most of the rest lacked the capacity or political will to enforce their commitments. Slave traffickers had the run of the Atlantic Commons, moving with near impunity through a leaky legal patchwork, with a better understanding of the local contours than their government pursuers.

The state of the Atlantic during this period resembles the current role of the Internet in some forms of modern slavery. Traffickers use major popular websites to conduct illegal activities – notably Backpage.com (whose creators were indicted in 2018 under new legislation), but also the hard-to-trace sites of the "deep web" – while government pursuers

---

[26] Stewart, "Abolishing Slavery in Lincoln's Time and Ours"; Joel Quirk, *The Anti-Slavery Project: From the Slave Trade to Human Trafficking* (Philadelphia, PA: University of Pennsylvania Press, 2011).

have not yet fully come to terms with the space.[27] Attempts to deny these spaces to traffickers meet many of the same frustrations as the historical suppression attempt, as illicit actors can call upon excellent hackers, and online spaces are easily remappable.[28] International law remains unclear and international coordination is imperfect, and, of course, traffickers make good use of the gaps. If the analogy holds, as improving legal regimes increasingly deny impunity to traffickers, the competition for this common space will become all the fiercer.

Furthering the analogy, both the Atlantic and the Internet are "technical commons" – made accessible to human enterprise only through technological mechanisms. Ships and navigation opened the waves of the Atlantic to commerce; protocols and routers make the same possible across the Internet using the electromagnetic spectrum. In both instances, these "unlocking technologies" have their own inherent strengths, weaknesses, and unrealized possibilities. As we will see through naval technology, harnessing or innovating changes in these technologies grants advantage during these contests. The slavers owned the fastest sailing ships during the opening bouts of the British campaign, but the tide turned in favor of the Royal Navy as steam technology matured and overtook sail.[29] We seem more in the former situation than the latter against the slavers of the Internet, so it is particularly important to understand how the suppressors harnessed these technological changes while denying them to their adversary.

As a note of caution, there is much that this analogy misses. Most importantly, the vast majority of today's slaves are held in bonded labor, which requires relatively little movement and is generally dependent on local social controls. These practices are more akin to the forms of African continental slavery left behind by the suppression attempt, and are generally unlike the Atlantic slave trade itself. Therefore, this parallel offers little analytical leverage for the problem of bonded labor.

However, it matches well with forms of slavery that require the movement of people, whether in real space or virtual spaces, such as sex slavery or transnational forced labor. Improvements in justice systems

---

[27] M. Latonero, "Human Trafficking Online: The Role of Social Networking Sites and Online Classifieds," available at *SSRN* 2045851, 2011, http://papers.ssrn.com/sol3/papers.cfm?abstract_id=2045851.

[28] Mark Latonero, "Technology and Human Trafficking: The Rise of Mobile and the Diffusion of Technology-Facilitated Trafficking," *SSRN eLibrary*, November 13, 2012, http://papers.ssrn.com/sol3/papers.cfm?abstract_id=2177556.

[29] Lloyd, *The Navy and the Slave Trade*.

and domestic legal structures are generally effective in countering bonded labor, so while cyber-facilitated trafficking is a smaller fraction of world slavery, it is resilient in ways that bonded labor generally is not.[30] Therefore, the whispers of well-considered and long-rehearsed strategies from long-dead captains provides a basis for thinking about fighting slavery on the cyber-oceans of our day: if "four-and-twenty cruisers" drove slavers out of their West African haunts, then perhaps a contemporary force of law enforcement professionals with strong social backing might drive today's slavers out of the "deep web." With this end in mind, we proceed.

TWO PILLARS: EFFICIENCY AND SUPPORT

Two themes run throughout the half-century battle to wrest control of the commons from slaver networks. First, both the British and the slavers took ground through rapid innovation, unconventional partnerships, and by harnessing rare events. Flat organizational structures make for easy conversations and, hence, easy partnerships, which accelerated these processes. I use the term *efficiency* as shorthand to refer to these sorts of "market-like" structures. As the campaign went on, the West African Squadron evolved from a standard bureaucracy of the Admiralty to an agile, adaptive unit resembling modern Special Operations Forces. The Foreign Office grew equally adept at seizing "fast transient" opportunities to build an international treaty network against the trade, including unorthodox partnerships with opponents of the slave trade who served in other governments.[31]

Second, the enduring strength of the British abolitionist movement provided these efforts with the resilience required to outlast the trade. To the great credit of Sharp, Equiano, Wilberforce, and Clarkson, the founders of the abolitionist movement passed the torch to an increasingly international movement led by Thomas Buxton and Thomas Denman in time to weather the trials of the mid 1800s.[32] These issues were ultimately

---

[30] For estimates of the magnitude of these problems, see the Appendix to Siddharth Kara, *Bonded Labor: Tackling the System of Slavery in South Asia* (New York: Columbia University Press, 2014).

[31] John Boyd, "Destruction and Creation," unpublished paper.

[32] David Turley, *The Culture of English Antislavery, 1780–1860* (New York: Routledge, 1991), 64; Davis, *Inhuman Bondage*, 237–8. This was in spite of a needless row between Clarkson and the children of William Wilberforce, who slighted the then-elderly campaigner in their biography of their father. Adam Hochschild, *Bury the Chains: Prophets*

reconciled, and the movement moved into the second half-century of its existence intact. These deeply embedded, politically and culturally cross-cutting ties, which I bundle as the concept of *support*, ultimately proved deeper than the demand for slaves across the Atlantic. The movement did more than simply provide voters and taxpayers – many of the most successful West Africa Squadron captains were themselves ardent abolitionists.[33]

While support "wrote the checks" for suppression, efficiency "cashed" them. At the outset of the campaign, support was plentiful, but the illicit networks of the slave trade easily outpaced the British cruisers on the seas. By the 1840s, support began to wane, but the British diplomatic effort had denied the slavers legal impunity. Simultaneously, a cadre of experienced captains learned to capture and reuse the best of the slaving fleet back against the slavers, while blunting the slavers' tactical and technological edge through innovations of their own. Not least of these was Joseph Denman, son of Lord Chief Justice Thomas Denman, who set the precedent of attacking slave fortresses ashore and defended the suppression effort on the floor of Parliament in contravention of his commander, Commodore Charles Hotham.[34]

Now on the offensive, the West Africa Squadron became markedly "market-like" as the slave trade ossified behind increasingly inflexible defensive structures. By the 1860s, the technological and tactical breaks went to the suppressors, reversing the situation of the 1820s. Despite a long and exhausting generational struggle, the abolitionist coalition held long enough to underwrite this effort – as time would tell, the abolitionists demanded the end of the slave trade more ardently than the slavers demanded slaves or profit.

Thus, the sailors and the social leaders together achieved this "impossibility." Ground was taken through short spurts of innovation, which lasted only as long as it took the adversary to devise a counter. This is a story about people and structures, about both humans and hardware,

---

and Rebels in the Fight to Free an Empire's Slaves, 1st ed. (Boston, MA: Houghton Mifflin Harcourt, 2005), 350–8.

[33] Denman was most notable amongst these during the height of suppression, but they included Fitzgerald, Matson, USN Captain Foote, and many others. Mary Wills, "The Royal Navy and the Suppression of the Atlantic Slave Trade c. 1807–1867: Anti-Slavery, Empire and Identity" (University of Hull, 2012), http://ethos.bl.uk/OrderDetails.do?uin=uk.bl.ethos.572212.

[34] Ibid., 104. Citing correspondence between Hotham and Captain Hamilton, November 1, 1848. *Analysis of the Evidence Given before the Select Committee upon the Slave Trade.*

but it is not a story about impersonal historical forces. Moreover, no one strategy or policy explains the outcome, as the slave trade shifted form and composition in order to outpace the plan *du jour*. This is a story about agency, about the human ability to capture and even force rare events,[35] and about the networks of human relationships that enacted, stabilized, and institutionalized that agency.

The key to British success was their ability to weave (and continually tighten) a regime that covered the whole of the space formerly occupied by the illicit market. The British began by targeting the most accessible nodes of the slave trade: the ships. Since ships were replaceable, this did not bring about their goal directly, but it at least channelized the trade, stressed the network, and forced costly countermeasures. Through trial and much error, they became willing to press the attack deeper into the supply chain with efforts ashore, rather than to abandon the effort. The suppression network that defeated the slave trade's network spanned the space previously occupied by its adversary: across the Atlantic, a maritime boarding regime included all major seagoing powers that had once been part of the trade. In West Africa, a lattice of treaties with African leaders displaced the slave trade's coastal stronghold. Finally, in the Americas, a framework for domestic enforcement of anti-slave trade laws backed by abolitionists attacked the enterprise at its destination.

This campaign was an emergent process, rather than the result of a deliberate, centralized strategy. This was not due to lack of trying; there was no shortage of pamphlets circulating from across the British foreign policy spectrum offering a plan for a quick end to the trade.[36] These strategies typically were not so much "wrong" as they were "fragile" – they might work for a time against a key vulnerability of the trade, but the trade would adapt and sidestep the plan. The same held for the slavers, but market structures allowed them to trade many small losses for a few big wins.

The slaver market was "anti-fragile," in that chaos refined its business models rather than eroding them, at least at the outset.[37] As time went on,

---

[35] Such as those described in Nassim Nicholas Taleb, *The Black Swan: The Impact of the Highly Improbable* (New York: Random House Trade Paperbacks, 2010).

[36] For a sample of these see: Thomas F. Buxton, *The African Slave Trade and Its Remedy* (RareBooksClub.com, 2012); Joseph Denham, *The African Squadron and Mr. Hutt's Committee* (J. Mortimer, 1850); Philadelphia Yearly Meeting of the Religious Society of Friends and Society of Friends Philadelphia Yearly Meeting, *A View of the Present State of the African Slave Trade* (Philadelphia: William Brown, printer, 1824).

[37] Nassim Nicholas Taleb, *Antifragile: Things That Gain from Disorder* (Harmondsworth: Penguin, 2014).

the West African Squadron became similarly "anti-fragile." The Foreign Office made good use of exogenous events in the world to improve the treaty regime – debt crises often provided leverage to tighten the ratchet, and these were in no short supply as Spain and Portugal struggled to repair what Napoleon left behind. As the Royal Navy slave trade suppression squadron grew more "market-like," especially in the 1840s, junior officers in command of the Royal Navy cruisers aggressively experimented with tactics and legal limits. Most importantly, when the British took ground, they rarely gave it back.

FIRST STEPS: 1808–20

At the outset of the campaign, the British learned through trial, experience, and frustration the magnitude of their task. On a positive note, the British were able to effectively police the actions of their own vessels. However, they learned that unilateral force was too imprecise and costly an instrument to effect the suppression of the trade. It would "take a network to defeat a network," and by the end of this period, the British laid the groundwork and took the first steps toward building that network.[38]

Modern anti-traffickers can take heart from this period. Despite groping in the dark with ineffective technologies and inadequate strategies, the British arrived at plausible ways forward through trial, error, and conversation. Most importantly, they came to terms with the fundamental nature of the contest: as soon as the British would identify and exploit a vulnerability of a slaver business model, the model would re-map itself around the threat. This resulted in a characteristic "sawtooth" shape, as an intervention would deeply impact the volume of the trade for a time, but the trade would recover if given enough time. To their credit, the suppression forces realized early in the campaign that the *speed* of successive interventions was as important as the *magnitude* of any given intervention. This realization should hold for the adaptive slaving models of our day.

This campaign began at wartime, in the waning era of the privateer, after the ban of 1808 and amidst the Napoleonic wars. During the age of sail, crews might become rich in the course of commerce raiding by

---

[38] John Arquilla and David Ronfeldt, *Networks and Netwars: The Future of Terror, Crime, and Militancy*, 1st ed. (New York: Rand Corporation, 2001). See also William McChrystal, Charles Fussell, and Tatum Collins, *A Team of Teams: New Rules of Engagement in a Complex World* (New York: Penguin Books, 2015).

seizing and claiming enemy vessels as "prizes." The initial British policy applied the same logic to slave ships – a slaver could be seized, and a bounty claimed for each captive rescued. These financial incentives for interdictors persisted throughout the 1800s, but the latitude given sea captains during wartime quickly faded with the advent of peace, and was no more by the end of the 1810s.[39]

Beyond sweeping the seas of the few remaining British-flagged slavers, Royal Navy captains applied privateer seizure rules liberally on the high seas.[40] Using the prerogatives of wartime, they seized both French and neutral slavers. These prizes were sent to British Vice-Admiralty Courts, who adjudicated seizures; by and large, these vessels were condemned.[41] Since these captures were not part of a deliberate framework, these gains generally did not translate into precedent and, therefore, were limited in their deterrent value. They injected friction into the slaver business model, thereby likely reducing throughput through the trade, but lacked a network to "lock in" any gains achieved.

This broad unilateral approach to maritime rules yielded unfortunate long-term consequences, especially against the backdrop of the War of 1812. While the United States tolerated British seizures of American-flagged slavers throughout the campaign, effectively passing the buck and the risk for enforcing the American ban on slaving along to British cruisers, the antipathies fostered by the prior conflict poisoned hopes of meaningful formal coordination between the two nations for decades.[42] Unfortunately, the American rhetoric of "free trade and sailors' rights" that emerged from this conflict left a glaring gap in the treaty network until very late in the campaign.[43]

---

[39] Lloyd, *The Navy and the Slave Trade*.

[40] Unilateralism was not a solely British approach. After the United States banned the trade, the cruiser USS *Alligator* seized a French-flagged slaver, *Jeune Eugenie*. Although an American judge found the trade contrary to natural law in the case, the practical-ities of enforcing a contested international norm were too costly and the vessel was delivered back to the French. Howard, *American Slavers and the Federal Law, 1837–1862*; David R. Murray, *Odious Commerce: Britain, Spain, and the Abolition of the Cuban Slave Trade* (Cambridge: Cambridge University Press, 2002); Donald L. Canney, *Africa Squadron: The US Navy and the Slave Trade, 1842–1861*, annotated edition (Washington, DC: Potomac Books Inc., 2006).

[41] However, condemnation rates for this period in the Vice-Admiralty Courts were lower than in the later unilateral phases of the 1840s. Voyages Database, 2010.

[42] Lloyd, *The Navy and the Slave Trade*; Canney, *Africa Squadron*.

[43] Paul A. Gilje, "'Free Trade and Sailors' Rights': The Rhetoric of the War of 1812," *Journal of the Early Republic* 30, no. 1 (2010), 1–23.

With the Treaty of Paris ushering in peace between Britain and France, the use of wartime powers against the slave trade came to a close. This was definitively marked by the 1817 *Louis* court case, which held that foreign slavers could be captured and condemned only if authorized by a treaty.[44] The problem could not be solved with the simple application of force, or at least not be solved at a diplomatically and socially acceptable price. As support for abolitionism was vibrant and deeply politically entrenched during this era, the British drew from the political well and updated their strategy. By crafting a boarding treaty network, they found a more efficient and pacific avenue for attacking the slave trade abroad. This network would provide the strategic foundation for the remainder of the campaign, and the means by which the British took ground in the wide open space of the sea.

By the end of this period, the British Foreign Office forcefully sought treaties with other seagoing states to ban the trade. By 1820, Spain, France, Denmark, Sweden, the Netherlands, and the United States agreed to ban the trade; Portugal agreed to geographic restrictions on the trade.[45] But a trade ban meant little two and a half thousand miles from Europe without enforcing cruisers, and the British were in the strongest position to provide such a force. Reciprocal right of search treaties allowed British cruisers to board suspected slavers from a partner nation, and vice versa; the Courts of Mixed Commission adjudicated these seizures with judges from the British and the partner nation.[46]

This improvement had immediate effect as Spanish-flagged slaving dropped by an order of magnitude between 1817 and 1822.[47] The French flag picked up the slack almost immediately.[48] The slave trade was remarkable in its ability to reroute around these obstacles, an aspect tragically shared with the current trade. Abstracting this pattern to the American, French, Spanish, and Portuguese flags reveals a "sawtooth"

[44] Siân Rees, *Sweet Water and Bitter: The Ships That Stopped the Slave Trade* (Durham, NH: University Press of New England, 2011). Jenny S. Martinez, *The Slave Trade and the Origins of International Human Rights Law*, 1st ed. (New York: Oxford University Press, 2012).

[45] Great Britain Admiralty, *Instructions for the Guidance of Her Majesty's Naval Officers: Employed in the Suppression of the Slave Trade* (San Bernardino, CA: Ulan Press, 2012).

[46] These courts involved three judges: one from each nation, and the third chosen randomly by lot. Martinez, *The Slave Trade and the Origins of International Human Rights Law*.

[47] Using Voyages Database.

[48] Ibid. There was a near equivalent upswing in French traffic to counterbalance Spanish losses.

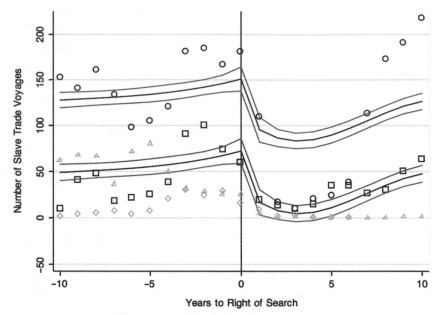

FIGURE 3 Interrupted time series, right of search regime vs. slave trade voyages –
ten-year bandwidths with 95 percent confidence intervals and scatterplots for
Portugal and Brazil (top, circles) and Spain (bottom, squares.) Scatterplot only for
United States (diamonds) and France (triangles). Data from Voyages Database,
2010.[50]

pattern (Figure 3) – the enactment of a Right of Search treaty correlated
with a dramatic drop in the number of slaving vessels making the journey
under a given flag – but these effects lasted for less than a decade.[49]

As expressed by the quote at the beginning of this chapter, the trade
was adept at finding "men and means"[51] to work around these imposed
costs. However, as the graph in Figure 3 demonstrates, these men and

[49] The finding of a reduction followed by an upswing can be established through interrupted
time series analysis. It is statistically robust down to a three-year bandwidth for a first-
order model, and to ten-year bandwidths for second- and third-order models.

[50] These data visualizations were developed in parallel with, but independently from, those
of Jenny Martinez in "Anti-Slavery Courts and the Dawn of International Human Rights
Law," *117 Yale L.J.* (Fall 2007, Draft.) Since Professor Martinez first had the idea of
juxtaposing captive flow with major events, she is the originator of this application of
data visualization to this case. My goal was to demonstrate network shock-response
effects, hers was to demonstrate the evolution of the boarding treaty regime. Since that
regime was a network, these visualizations seem to have reached equifinality. All data
from Voyages Database.

[51] "The Slave-Trade," *The Liberator.*

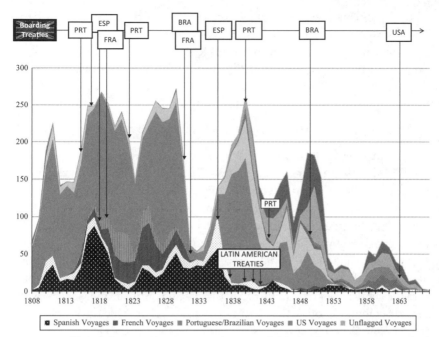

FIGURE 4 Treaty improvements over time vs. Atlantic slave voyages, stacked total. Striped areas indicate captured vessels from respective nations. Data from Voyages Database, 2010.

means came with non-trivial losses of fixed costs. The two sides were stalemated – the British could inflict dramatic costs, but the trade could recoup those costs given sufficient time. Therefore, the pivotal aspect of the fight was its tempo – if the British could slow adaptation, isolate and attack the slaving networks more quickly, or both, they could arc the "sawtooth" pattern downwards over time. They were successful in doing so, as demonstrated in Figure 4.

At the end of this period, the British embarked on a sustained campaign of treaty improvement. This effort resulted in increasing captures during the 1830s, and culminated during the 1840s, at which point all major seagoing European flags were incorporated into the treaty network. I refer to this as the "grey market" period, as the majority of slavers enjoyed some sort of legal cover during this time, and the British objective was to strip them of that cover. From 1835 onward, an increasing number of vessels have no registration noted in the Voyages Database. While it is difficult to interpret what this missing flag data actually means, qualitative sources during the period indicate that some large fraction of these were fraudulent flags or piratical vessels. I hold that this phase of the struggle was against a "black market," where slavers looked to secrecy and superior performance rather than legal maneuvering for protection. We turn next to this "grey market" fight to strip the trade of its remaining legal cover.

THE GREY MARKET: 1817–35

During this second phase, the British sought bilateral anti-slave trade treaties with all major seagoing powers. This was an evolutionary process; the slave trade would improvise workarounds each time the British would improve the regime. While this phase did not achieve its primary goal of disrupting the trade outright, it managed to channelize and constrain the trade and thereby increased its vulnerability to direct suppression. The British managed to achieve this at relatively low cost, due to their masterful ability to make use of the national crises of others in order to gain diplomatic leverage. Near the end of this phase, the British abolished slavery in their colonies, though they had extinguished large-scale slave trading to their colonies within a few years of their ban on the trade. Demand was primarily largely fueled by growth in Brazil and Cuban sugar plantations, and to a lesser extent from French holdings in the Americas.

Their ability to diffuse legal counters to slaver tactics, and to use a "ratchet" approach, which took and held incremental gains, mitigated the natural organizational advantages of the slavers' market. True to form, the illicit market was fast to innovate ways around the legal regime. The suppression regime countered this advantage by holding all the ground they took in countering these innovations. Eventually, this "ratchet" approach left no legal ground unclaimed and the illicit market was forced underground. Such an approach should be of obvious interest to modern antislavers seeking to corner, contain, and collapse the commons spaces available to the contemporary slave trade.

At the outset of this phase, the British found themselves at a strategic crossroads. Initial disorganized unilateral seizures had some suppressive effect on the slave enterprise, but they were clearly insufficient to disrupt the trade as such. Abolitionist political will supported an expansion of the struggle against the trade, which led to a question of strategy. On one hand, the British could double down on unilateralism – declaring a "war on slavery." New laws could declare the slave trade beyond the cover of any flag, and authorize cruisers to seize any and all slavers.[52] This approach would provide the British with a free hand on the high seas but offer little recourse ashore.

On the other extreme, the British could harness the nascent multilateralism of the Congress of Vienna and create a formal international institution to suppress the trade. Multilateral institutions provided comprehensiveness at the expense of speed and initiative, as each change to the regime required far more coordination than a bilateral treaty network. British efforts at the Congress of Vienna resulted in a vague condemnation of the slave trade, with a promise of extinguishing participation at some unspecified later date.[53]

Given the tepid results of multilateralism and the costs of unilateralism, the British plotted a course between the two. Bilateral treaties split the difference and provided British leaders with a position of dominant brokerage. Practical but slow, this effort minimized the cost of treaty building by using moments of host nation vulnerability in their negotiations. These negotiations were the heart of the "ratchet" strategy – while multilateral negotiations have any number of veto players, bilateral negotiations have only one. If a nation was unwilling to move forward to a stronger treaty, the British would await (or generate) a moment of vulnerability and then negotiate from an advantageous position. This tack minimized the cost of improving regime efficiency, allowing the effort to proceed for two and a half decades before triggering a public referendum on the strategy.

These treaties took three generally sequential forms. First, the British sought to construct an international norm against the trade through national bans on participation in the slave trade. It soon became apparent that, without effective enforcement, these were generally dead letters. Few powers other than the British had the forces or the political will to exert force in West Africa to police their countrymen in the absence of external pressure.

Second, the aforementioned reciprocal right of search treaties theoretically granted the British and their partners the right to search each other's vessels. Third, when slavers would invent legal loopholes around the treaties, the British would update the treaty network to close these

---

[52] This natural-law based unilateralism parallels Palmerston's Brazilian interventions, but by then he had (barely) marginal legal standing, an isolated trade, and an international framework by which the effects of the intervention could be stabilized.

[53] Martinez, *The Slave Trade and the Origins of International Human Rights Law*; Lloyd, *The Navy and the Slave Trade*.

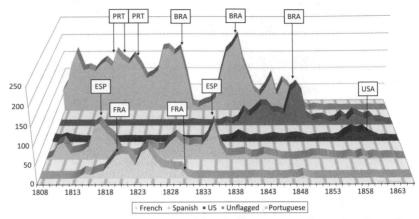

FIGURE 5 Treaty improvements vs. Atlantic slave voyages, by nation. Data from Voyages Database, 2010.

gaps. The most notable of these was the "equipment clause," though these also included rights of seizures for vessels that had previously carried slaves.[54] Once the British discovered and closed one of these loopholes, they incorporated the improvement into future treaties and tightened existing instruments whenever possible.

The channelizing effects of this "ratcheting" strategy are evident in Figure 5. An improvement in one flag shifts slave traffic to another flag, but the trade loses its maneuvering space over time. While the trade generally recovered most of its volume, at least initially, it progressively lost its capacity to innovate. Effectively, the suppression regime kept raising the diplomatic tide through low-level innovation with high-level partnerships – when the slavers invented a new model, West African Squadron officers would identify a legally exploitable weakness, and the Foreign Office would weave these improvements into the overall network.[55] This "immunized" the treaty regime to common forms of slaver legal maneuvering, and eventually drove the slavers generally out from under legal cover.

This strategy had flaws – by the late 1830s, Portuguese- and Brazilian-flagged slavers were working to break out of the "ratchet." Making matters worse, the slavers had performance, stealth, and thousands of miles of African coastline in their favor. Still, the diplomatic efforts of

---

[54] Martinez, *The Slave Trade and the Origins of International Human Rights Law*.
[55] For more on the Foreign Office, see Huzzey, *Freedom Burning*, 44.

this phase cleared much of the clutter from the strategic landscape. This made it possible to bring force to bear against diplomatic holdouts and the increasingly liable slavers, as the following instructive vignette clearly illustrates.

The squadron demonstrated initiative and efficiency in their circumscribed space of operations during this period. These qualities allowed them to turn fleeting opportunities into significant gains. Captain Fitzgerald of HMS *Buzzard* provided an excellent example.[56] In 1839, during its antislavery patrol the *Buzzard* captured three slavers, the *Wyoming*, the *Clara*, and the *Eagle*, with questionable paperwork.[57] After releasing the captives on board, the Mixed Commission court in Freetown, Sierra Leone decided that the vessels had American registration, and therefore could be tried only in an American court. Reasoning that slavery was illegal under American law, Fitzgerald decided to haul his would-be prizes to New York for adjudication.[58] To put the audacity of this choice in perspective, no British man-of-war had peacefully visited the United States with prizes since the American Revolution.[59] Fitzgerald handed the prizes to an American admiralty court, which rewarded his audacity by partially finding in his favor – the court decided that they would try any American citizens aboard.[60]

This remarkably aggressive act yielded two important second-order effects. First, the otherwise politically proslavery US President Martin Van Buren initially congratulated and thanked Captain Fitzgerald for his actions in apprehending American lawbreakers.[61] This led to a number of other attempts on the part of British captains to do the same. Realizing that he had invited *de facto* the right of search, Van Buren was

[56] This vignette can be found in Rees, *Sweet Water and Bitter*; Lloyd, *The Navy and the Slave Trade*; Marcus Rediker, *The Amistad Rebellion: An Atlantic Odyssey of Slavery and Freedom* (New York: Penguin Books, 2013).

[57] Rees, *Sweet Water and Bitter*. See also *Benton's Navy List Compilation, Online*. Entry for HMS *Buzzard*, www.pbenyon.plus.com/18–1900/B/00747.html.

[58] *Benton's Navy List Compilation, Online*. Entry for HMS *Buzzard*, www.pbenyon.plus .com/18–1900/B/00747.html.

[59] Rees, *Sweet Water and Bitter*, 196.

[60] Unfortunately for Fitzgerald, the ship itself remained in limbo, as the court ruled that the slaving vessels did not have legitimate American registration. While this meant that either the Mixed Commission or the Vice-Admiralty could try the vessel, as it had questionable Spanish registry, this was not to be. En route back to the Sierra Leone courts, his prize foundered. Rees, *Sweet Water and Bitter*; see also *Benton's Navy List Compilation, Online*, entry for HMS *Buzzard*, www.pbenyon.plus.com/18–1900/B/00747.html.

[61] Howard, *American Slavers and the Federal Law, 1837–1862*; Murray, *Odious Commerce*; Rees, *Sweet Water and Bitter*.

in a diplomatic fix – the British actions publically demonstrating that the Americans were failing to enforce their laws, but the Americans were still not wanting to formally authorize British searches. Ultimately, Van Buren was forced to dramatically increase United States naval antislavery patrols to West Africa patrols to placate the British.[62]

Secondly, Fitzgerald's presence in New York harbor serendipitously coincided with the highly publicized Amistad trial, which turned on the testimony of the once-enslaved African rebels who had risen in successful seaborne revolt and who spoke West African languages such as Mende. Finding a Mende translator familiar with the mechanics of the slave trade who could speak for the Amistad rebels would have been difficult anywhere on the eastern seaboard had it not been for the assistance of Yale Professor Josiah Gibbs, who had learned from the Amistad captives how to count in Mende. Seeking another Mende speaker, Gibbs walked the New York waterfront loudly counting these numbers aloud.[63] Improbably enough, he found one, a certain James Covey, who had been liberated from a slave ship years before by the British Navy and who now served as a member of Captain Fitzgerald's crew. Captain Fitzgerald's conspicuous prize quest put Covey on the New York docks as Gibbs was seeking a translator, where the two met. Fitzgerald was an abolitionist, and he gladly lent his crewman to the American abolitionist Lewis Tappan and the Amistad defense team.[64]

As for Fitzgerald himself, according to the Navy List, he testified on behalf of the prosecution against the purported captain of the *Eagle* in the case of the *US Government vs. Liggit*. Unfortunately for Captain Fitzgerald, the *Eagle* ran aground in the course of these travails; he was forced to find American legal counsel until he found the 1,200 dollars owed for repairs. In a case of "unilateralism-by-request," the American District Attorney's office ultimately decided that the three vessels had Spanish registry, and so the vessels were delivered to Fitzgerald and then sent on their way back to Sierra Leone. For all of these troubles, the

---

[62] Murray, *Odious Commerce*; Howard, *American Slavers and the Federal Law, 1837–1862*.
[63] David Brion Davis, *Inhuman Bondage: The Rise and Fall of Slavery in the New World* (Oxford: Oxford University Press, 2006). 23.
[64] John Warner Barber, *A History of the Amistad Captives: Being a Circumstantial Account of the Capture of the Spanish Schooner Amistad, by the Africans on Board; Their Voyage, and Capture Near Long Island, New York; with Biographical Sketches of Each of the Surviving Africans; Also, an Account of the Trials Had on Their Case, before the District and Circuit Courts of the United States, for the District of Connecticut* (E.L. & J.W. Barber, 1840). 15.

Clara and *Eagle* foundered en route back to Africa. After the Sierra Leone court delivered a condemnation-in-absentia, the captain and crew of the *Buzzard* were awarded their long-awaited prize money for the captures.[65] There is some dark humor in this, perhaps, for present-day law enforcement; the victories in this sort of work involve far more tedium than valor,[66] and it was ever thus.

THE BLACK MARKET: 1835–55

The treaty network left the slave trade channelized to Brazil and Cuba, and left the British with marginal standing to bring force to bear against these two now discrete problems. The trade had less room to maneuver, and the British had less ambiguity to navigate, and therefore the trade was now vulnerable to the direct application of force. Since the Spanish reached an accommodation concerning Cuba with the regime for the time being, Britain was able to isolate and strangle the Portuguese slave trade to Brazil using imperial gunboat diplomacy. For all their complications, these policies closed down the slave trade route from southwest Africa to Brazil.

During this period, the Royal Navy began a series of politically controversial amphibious assaults on the trade's infrastructure in West Africa. In order to secure a free hand to conduct these raids, British captains increasingly engaged with leaders ashore. This led to the development of a second treaty network – "engagements" with West African political leaders provided the cruisers' legal standing to seize and destroy European-owned slave fortresses ashore. On both sides of the Atlantic, the navy was the visible face and leading front of British policy. As opposed to the previous period of friendly treaty building, this phase was written primarily with powder rather than ink.

Modern anti-traffickers might take from this period a lesson about the increasing costs of these campaigns, and the importance of deep foundations. The abolitionist movement of 1850 had a less commanding hold of the political imagination of the empire than it had in the 1830s, but the task of suppression was far from done. Where the protracted diplomatic efforts of the previous decades took time but little political cost, strong-arming the remaining holdouts risked war. The prospect of a war,

[65] *Benton's Navy List Compilation, Online.* Entry for HMS *Buzzard*, www.pbenyon.plus .com/18–1900/B/00747.html.
[66] Crouch, "Tedium + Valor."

even an antislavery war, was not attractive to the Quaker elements of the abolitionist coalition. Meanwhile, a new faction of "radical free traders" desired the wholesale abandonment of the suppression campaign, seeing it an exercise in counterproductive moralistic folly.

This was a difficult time for the campaign – the abolitionists were caught between the risk of weariness eventually overtaking the stalled campaign, and the risk of political escalation leading to its immediate collapse. They "gambled for resurrection," and won their bet. Had their coalition been less resilient, the outcome of the campaign might have been drastically different.

Viscount Palmerston, the controversial British Foreign Secretary whose "gunboat diplomacy" embodied the contradictions of the British imperial mission, took the helm of British interventionism during this period. When negotiations for a renewed boarding treaty with the Portuguese stalled in the late 1830s, Palmerston unilaterally enforced his interpretation of Portuguese treaty commitments. When the Portuguese refused to sign a renewed treaty authorizing boarding across the whole Atlantic, Palmerston advanced a bill in Parliament that empowered Royal Navy cruisers to take these actions themselves. "Palmerston's Act," as it became known, gave sweeping powers to captains to seize vessels under the Portuguese flag and send them to the British-owned Vice-Admiralty courts. In later testimony to Parliament, Preventative Squadron leaders hailed this as "the first great blow," and "the first time when suppression became possible."[67]

While this stirred up a great deal of resentment in Portugal, the Portuguese government had little leverage. The climate of public opinion, both globally and in Portugal, warned against a defense of the slave trade, even on the grounds of national autonomy; the predominance of British power would have made any such effort futile. To remove this national embarrassment, the Portuguese gave the British their law – a comprehensive treaty, without geographic limits, with all contemporary improvements. Thus, in 1842, the Portuguese flag departed the trade.[68]

By this time, Lord Aberdeen had taken charge of the Foreign Ministry in a change of government. He openly questioned the legality of Palmerston's actions, but when the Brazilian-flagged trade continued

---

[67] Rees, *Sweet Water and Bitter*, 188. Also see Henry James Matson, *Remarks on the Slave Trade and African Squadron* (1848); Joseph Denman, *The Slave Trade, the African Squadron, and Mr. Hutt's Committee* (J. Mortimer, n.d.).

[68] Huzzey, *Freedom Burning*; Lloyd, *The Navy and the Slave Trade*.

unabated, he arrived at similar conclusions. "Aberdeen's Act" of 1845 presented an ultimatum to the Brazilian government similar to that presented to the Portuguese. If effective enforcement were not in place by 1850, the British would put enforcement to their liking in place on their own.

British domestic frustration with the seeming lack of progress had been mounting since the 1830s. Opponents of suppression argued, fairly accurately, that as many captives were moving in the late 1840s as they ever had during the legal trade.[69] The suppression regime faced a two-front political challenge during this period: on one hand, the more pacific elements of abolitionism were losing hope in suppression by force and increasingly saw the naval patrol as an ineffectual distraction, and even a source of increased suffering for captives. On the other hand, radical free traders held that the market itself would correct the slave trade, and the naval suppression efforts interfered with legitimate commerce.[70] The supporters of the diplomatic and naval campaign against the trade retained a slim majority against these challengers.

Palmerston's aggressive approach tripled the cost of suppression. While the previous stages of the "ratchet" strategy slowly expanded without sparking domestic counter-movements, this stage's more dramatic strategy was to break through blockages. The cost and aggressiveness of the policies of this period triggered a countervailing reaction that questioned the value of the effort – a faction of Parliament led by Mr. William Hutt, a radical free-trade advocate, assembled a select committee and began campaigning to end the campaign.

Captain Denman, former commander of the West Africa Squadron's Sierra Leone Division, publically answered these charges in a widely distributed pamphlet.[71] Denman's previous exploits in the squadron earned him public recognition and, therefore, legitimacy. Along with his comrade Captain Henry Matson, he argued for even more aggressive tactics, better ships, and more time. Denman's father, the Lord Chief Justice Denman, had common cause with Palmerston on the slave trade issue.[72]

Denman and Matson's previous commander, Commodore Charles Hotham, argued publically that suppression was futile. Regarding the

---

[69] Rees, *Sweet Water and Bitter*; Lloyd, *The Navy and the Slave Trade*.
[70] Mr. Hutt made such an argument in his Parliamentary select committee against the campaign. Lloyd, *The Navy and the Slave Trade*; Rees, *Sweet Water and Bitter*.
[71] Denman, *The Slave Trade, the African Squadron, and Mr. Hutt's Committee*.
[72] Lloyd, *The Navy and the Slave Trade*, 93.

junior officers' plans, he wrote that "almost every Politician and naval officer each naturally thinks that if his views were adopted success would be attainable ... You can no more stop the slave trade by y[ou]r present system than you can turn the course of the Danube."[73] For a time, it seemed that Hutt and Hotham would have the better of the argument. The Select Committee on the Slave Trade found broadly in support of his faction – suppression was ineffective, the trade outmatched the Royal Navy squadron, and it was difficult to identify actual progress from the campaign.[74] From an 1850 newspaper: "a negative opinion on the effectiveness of the squadron had taken such a hold of MPs, and, it must be presumed, of their constituents, that ... it was feared that there would be an absolute majority in favor of the motion, so apathetic and indifferent, if not opposed, have the people of England now become to a question that was wont to arouse their warmest sympathies or their strongest indignations."[75]

In Philip Curtin's phrase, this vote was "the last important stand of humanitarian politics."[76] Following a personally risky commitment on the part of Palmerston and the prime minister, senior Parliamentary leaders interpreted these findings as a reflection of inadequate forces rather than on the impossibility of the object.[77] The Whig government confronted Hutt's committee head on through party politics:

Now for the first time since the Whig defeat of 1841 over sugar duties, a government had to openly stake its survival on the outcome of a vote related to slavery. Prime Minister Russell and Foreign Secretary Palmerston gave intention of their intent to resign if Hutt's motion was supported by a parliamentary majority. Party loyalty and the prospect of an election comfortably carried the day, 232 votes to 154.[78]

Following the defeat of the motion, Palmerston doubled down on suppression. Denman's requests for increased forces, improved technology, and aggressive tactics were answered.[79] Palmerston eagerly seized this opportunity to take action against Brazil, and the Royal Navy commanders he dispatched to the Brazilian coast made use of all the

---

[73] Wills, "The Royal Navy and the Suppression of the Atlantic Slave Trade," 104, citing correspondence between Hotham and Captain Hamilton, November 1, 1848.

[74] Rees, *Sweet Water and Bitter*; Lloyd, *The Navy and the Slave Trade*.

[75] Drescher, *The Mighty Experiment*, 278.

[76] Ibid., 191.

[77] Rees, *Sweet Water and Bitter*.

[78] Drescher, *The Mighty Experiment*, 191.

[79] Rees, *Sweet Water and Bitter*; Lloyd, *The Navy and the Slave Trade*.

authority his laws granted them. By boarding, liberating, and burning slave ships at their moorings in Brazilian harbors,[80] the British intervention became an open and provocative challenge to the Brazilian government. This was a risky course – while open conflict was unlikely, backlash inside Brazil was a strong possibility. The situation resolved itself through internal reshuffling within the Brazilian government, as improved domestic enforcement staunched the trade to South America.[81]

Simultaneously during this period, the West African Squadron began to enter into treaties with West African leaders in order to assault slaver infrastructure ashore. In 1840, a local king in the Gallinas captured two British subjects from Sierra Leone.[82] Denman was sent on a mission to retrieve them. The slave fortresses located on the West African coast were a persistent frustration to the British cruisers – slavers would use the immunity of the land-based infrastructure for sanctuary. Denman used this opportunity to do something about it. In his negotiations for the release of the two captives, he asked the local leader for permission to attack the barracoons (slave fortresses or castles that were built as countermeasures to the British patrol efforts) on his territory and offered a treaty and the trade goods contained in the factories as spoils. Gaining this authorization, Denman assaulted the factories with Royal Marines, freed the captives contained therein, and destroyed the facilities with incendiary rockets.[83]

---

[80] Eltis, *Economic Growth and the Ending of the Transatlantic Slave Trade*; Bethell, *The Abolition of the Brazilian Slave Trade*; Huzzey, *Freedom Burning*; Lloyd, *The Navy and the Slave Trade*.

[81] This is also a subject of historical debate – I take Drescher's view here: "The overriding fact is the lack of any economic or demographic arguments against the trade, either in Britain or in Brazil at this climactic moment. In pleading for suppression before the Brazilian Chamber of Deputies, the conservative minister of Foreign Affairs, Paulino Jose Soares de Sousa, did not hide the fact that British naval action had precipitated the crisis. Brazil's economy still depended on importations of slaves, but Brazilian planters would have to adapt to abolition or face a ruinous war with Britain. A temporary slave glut, planters' indebtedness and mortgages to Portuguese slavers may have played their role in lowering planters' resistance at the moment of decision, but 'there is little evidence for thinking that in the years 1849–1850 the landed interest, or indeed any important section of the landed interest, was demanding the abolition of the African slave trade." Drescher, *The Mighty Experiment*.

[82] A region in modern Sierra Leone, near the Liberian border. See Davis's account in www .pdavis.nl/Gallinas.htm.

[83] Peter Davis, "Denman's Action at the Gallinas," www.pdavis.nl/Gallinas.htm. Derived from Christopher Lloyd, "The Navy and the Slave Trade," 93–9. W. L. Clowes, *The Royal Navy: A History from the Earliest Times to 1900*, Volume 6 (London: Chatham Publishing, 1997), 306. Annual Reports of her Majesty's Commissioners at Sierra Leone.

Denman, among others, had hoped that the bad blood from these attacks would sour relations between slave traders and local leaders and thereby "lock out" the trade from this area. This happened for a short time, but these barracoons would be rebuilt by 1844. The British would engage with local leaders once again and re-attack the barracoons in 1848; after this, the leaders expelled Spanish slave traders and the Gallinas remained out of the trade for the duration.[84]

Viscount Palmerston approved of the liberties Denman took with his mandate, commenting that "taking a wasp's nest ... is more effective than catching the wasps one by one."[85] Despite this approval, Denman faced legal trouble for these actions. The Spanish owners of these fortresses had prevailed upon Denman in their distress to return them to Europe during the assaults. They returned the favor by taking him to court; Denman eventually prevailed in 1848, and in the process set a crucially important precedent: Royal Navy captains could assault barracoons, provided local leaders signed treaties authorizing them to do so.[86] Therefore, cruiser captains created a treaty template and proceeded to recruit local leaders along the coast to sign with the promise of trade goods.[87] Matson testified before the 1849–50 Select Committee about the treaties:

[The Admiralty] gave orders that wherever we found slave barracoons erected we should endeavor to obtain the sanction of native chiefs to destroy them; failing

---

[84] Joseph C. Dorsey, *Slave Traffic in the Age of Abolition: Puerto Rico, West Africa, and the Non-Hispanic Caribbean, 1815–1859* (Gainesville, FL: University Press of Florida, 2003).

[85] Bethell, *The Abolition of the Brazilian Slave Trade*, 183.

[86] It took until 1848 for British courts to exonerate Denman using the same logic, though in the interim and afterwards the treaty-building and barracoon attacks continued. Rees, *Sweet Water and Bitter*; Lloyd, *The Navy and the Slave Trade*.

[87] Keene argues that this is an example of the creation of hierarchy in the international system; I hold that he neglects the institutional variable, and thereby does not understand the emergent innovation that led to the coastal treaty network. A cruiser-led treaty space versus a diplomat-led treaty space will look quite different. These two different path dependencies, rooted in two very different institutional experiences, fully explain this variation without presuming this sort of constructed project. Moreover, Palmerston displays contempt for Portuguese sovereignty and the British display remarkable thinking about sovereignty of the coastal chiefs, as displayed by Aberdeen's letter. The interesting problematic here is the British insistence on Westphalian territorial sovereignty for the coastal leaders, which causes difficulties for both the British and the coastal leaders as they attempt to make sense of the other through their own lenses. Edward Keene, "A Case Study of the Construction of International Hierarchy: British Treaty-Making against the Slave Trade in the Early Nineteenth Century," *International Organization* 61, no. 2 (2007), 311–39, doi:10.1017/S0020818307070117.

to obtain that consent we were in certain cases to do it without ... Most of the chiefs in Africa, in fact all the principal ones, entered into the treaties with us.[88]

This initiative led to a second treaty network with coastal leaders, which in turn led to complex results through deep entanglements in African politics. Legal uncertainties, the court troubles of Denman, and Aberdeen's less aggressive foreign policy slowed the growth of this treaty network, but it provided a coastal "ratchet" nonetheless. The coastal treaty network and the barracoon assaults deeply disrupted the trade.

By moving ashore, the British became embroiled in the complexities of African politics. This complexity often exceeded the British ability to make sense of it. An expedition to Lagos in the early part of the decade came to grief upon misunderstandings of the complexity of engagement.[89] Treaty commitments pulled the British into a later succession dispute in Lagos, which after several decades of follow-on disputes and a chronic inability to balance regional powers or stabilize British-backed powers, ultimately set the conditions that led to annexation and colonization in lieu of proxy influence.[90] During this period, the price for the campaign continued to climb, and the resulting entanglements became less manageable. Still, by the end of 1850, the trade was isolated to Cuba and confined to ever fewer West African haunts. The extinction of the trade, so recently barely imaginable, was now nearly inevitable.

ENDGAME: 1851–67

The last phase of the campaign attacked the one remaining channel of the illicit network: the largely American-flagged illicit trade to Cuba. The British had the overwhelming advantage of an expansive counter-network at this point. The treaty network was complete, with the glaring exception of the United States; the Royal Navy was driving the trade down the African coast with an increasingly airtight series of pacts with African leaders; the Brazilian trade had been crushed. There was little room for the slaver networks to reroute.

---

[88] William Ernest F. Ward, *The Royal Navy and the Slavers* (London: Allen & Unwin, 1969), 175.

[89] Robert Sydney Smith, *The Lagos Consulate, 1851–1861* (Berkeley, CA: University of California Press, 1979); Rees, *Sweet Water and Bitter*; Lloyd, *The Navy and the Slave Trade*; William Law Mathieson, *Great Britain and the Slave Trade, 1839–1865* (London: Longmans, Green and Company, 1929).

[90] Huzzey, *Freedom Burning*.

This phase, and with it the whole campaign, was brought to a favorable conclusion through three factors. First, sustained British pressure inflicted near 50 percent losses on the slavers, and those who made it paid high prices in bribes and countermeasures. Second, a series of Cuban captains-general put in place aggressive enforcement measures against the trade. Finally, the late entry of the United States into the boarding regime denied the slavers their last legal sanctuary.

In sum, the British built a network-of-networks, which contested and displaced the slave trade everywhere. They consumed the space previously occupied by their adversary – coastal treaty networks where there had been slave fortresses, the boarding treaty network where there had been national cover, and domestic enforcement where there had been slaving demand and slaver infrastructure. At the end of this half-century project, the British built an "anti-slave trade" – their suppression network ultimately mirror-imaged the network of the slave trade itself. These accomplishments surely confirm the counter-network axiom: "It takes a network to defeat a network."[91]

If that principle holds, then modern abolitionists should recalibrate their imagination to a much larger project capable of countering an illicit trade of millions of people worth billions of dollars.[92] As a first step, consider that the modern slave trade, just as its historical predecessor, naturally shares information and adapts by way of market mechanisms. While, as a whole, modern abolitionists have access to a tremendous amount of data about the workings and weaknesses of the modern slave trade, that knowledge is scattered between a thousand non-governmental organizations and governmental agencies. The British Foreign Office served as a clearing house of intelligence and coordinator for routing security, economic aid, and social services during the historical campaign. Perhaps we might imagine a commensurate effort, a data ecosystem founded on partnership between governments, NGOs, and private citizens toward ending modern slavery.

As prelude to this period, the Royal Navy sent out surveys to its captains of note with Africa Squadron experience in the late 1840s.[93] As part of the fallout of the Hotham–Denman–Matson fight, the Admiralty

---

[91] Arquilla and Ronfeldt, *Networks and Netwars*.

[92] For size estimates, see *2013 Global Slavery Index*, Sponsored by Walk Free, online, www .globalslaveryindex.org/findings/#overview. Also, Bales, *Disposable People*. Siddharth Kara, *Sex Trafficking: Inside the Business of Modern Slavery* (New York: Columbia University Press, 2010).

[93] Lloyd, *The Navy and the Slave Trade*.

polled the squadron for their opinions. After expressing sympathy for hanging or marooning slavers, these captains recommended a series of tactical and technological changes. The tactical preferences of this conclave of captains generally echoed those of Denman and Matson: a blockade close to the shore, independent ("detached") smaller ships, and decentralization in general were all strongly preferred.[94]

Technologically, the captains recommended small screw steamers that could chase a slaver in the unpredictable winds of the tropics yet still clear shoals and pursue slavers into inlets. Their recommendations included a number of tactical innovations as well – screw steamers with telescoping funnels could hide the nature of their propulsion system until the chase, and thereby surprise calculating slavers.[95] Pivot guns mediated between the broadsides of the previous age and anticipated the turrets of the next; it is itself intriguing how low-intensity conflict allowed the navy to adapt and begin to become accustomed to the technologies that would later prove pivotal to conventional war.

Arrayed against these adaptations and innovations was the remaining hard core of the slaving network. During these late phases of the trade, British pressure on the slaver supply chain drove the slave trade increasingly toward a cartel model, built around slave brokers. While the tide had turned, the remaining slavers were capable of strong resistance. After the collapse of the Brazilian trade, the trade took on its final defensive forms across the Atlantic. Increasingly organized criminal networks coordinated bribes, pickups, and drop-offs while pooling risk.[96] These firms attempted to swarm the blockade in hopes of making profit on those who got through. These firms increasingly gravitated toward the United States, with the Portuguese contractors (recently expelled from Brazil) providing the necessary expertise.[97] New York City increasingly became a hub of the trade: of 170 slaving voyages from 1859 to 1861, 74 were from New York, 43 from other US ports, 40 from Cuba,

---

[94] Mathieson, *Great Britain and the Slave Trade, 1839–1865*, 62, 66.

[95] There is some debate as to the value of these steamers – one account puts the average British steamer speed at 8 knots, and records a 15-knot slaver steamer. The latter vessel does not seem modal for the slaver fleet of this period, however. Since a large proportion of British captures were achieved with "sweeps" (essentially large oars) while both ships were becalmed, steam would excel against sail in these situations. Since the majority of the slaver fleet stayed with sail, steam as a whole favored the cruiser force against the slaver fleet. Ibid., 194.

[96] Ibid., 181.

[97] Ibid., 145.

and the rest from European ports.[98] The trade had become extremely speculative by this point, but the financial capital had no shortage of speculators. Along with these hardened traffickers, a handful of politically motivated "feral"[99] yachtsmen from the American South attempted the journey. Considering our present-day problem, this highly speculative market structure and risk pooling maps closely onto the use of organized crime by traffickers as a form of brokerage and insurance in high-threat environments.

Less adventurous criminal entrepreneurs attempted to relabel the trade as a form of contract labor. The British and the Dutch both attempted this scheme in West Africa in the 1840s, but the French system of *engagés* was the most prevalent and durable.[100] This provided a new form of immunity and was insidious due to its plausible origins. Recruiters initially attempted to recruit voluntary labor, but found it far easier to fill their rolls when they devolved back to purchasing people from local traders to send to the French West Indies.[101] This trade was dealt with diplomatically, as the British were on a poor footing to challenge this practice – they were doing much the same during this period from their colonies in India and Asia through the "Coolie Trade."[102] Eventually, the British coaxed the French away from African *engagés* by licensing them to recruit from British India in 1861.[103] In the light of today's problem, these late forms closely resemble forms of servitude with a legal façade, especially debt bondage. One model prevalent in Southwest Asia directly parallels this historical model: laborers will be enticed through fraudulent

---

[98] Ibid., 165. Between approximately 1859 and 1861, of 170 slaving voyages, 74+ were from from New York City, 43 from other US ports, 40 from Cuba, and the rest (13) from European ports. This broadly checks with the Voyages Database, which reports 167 voyages for this period, of which 69 percent come from the United States.

[99] Ross, *Sweet Water and Bitter*, 297.

[100] Ibid., 302.

[101] Howard, *American Slavers and the Federal Law, 1837–1862*, 150.

[102] This explains much of the demographics of Guyana, as the British switched labor flows during colonization. This is also one of the contradictions inherited from the early Wilberforce era of the abolitionist movement – leaders were mortally opposed to slavery, but they were not opposed to early workers' movements. Therefore, labor with a contract, provided it involved plausible assent, was not something against which they could bring force to bear.

[103] Mathieson, *Great Britain and the Slave Trade, 1839–1865*, 169. The French primarily conducted the *engagés* trade to Reunion and their holdings in the West Indies. The British negotiated with the French to end the trade in exchange for immigration "licenses" from British India. This occurred in 1861.

recruitment, but upon arrival will be denied an exit visa, and thereby forced into involuntary servitude.[104]

Cuba was the last major battle of the trade, and the primary focus of the last four commodores, from 1860 until 1869.[105] In addition to the strategic trends described in the previous section of this essay, operational patterns from this struggle support the network hypothesis. These commanders maintained effective liaison relationships with the Foreign Office's Slave Trade Department, which spearheaded the diplomatic effort.[106] Tactically, Denman's previously proposed patrolling tactics were in full effect – British ships bottled up the trade in the few remaining hotspots, paying close attention to likely slaver haunts, such as river inlets. These ships would anchor within signal distance of each other, creating a difficult-to-evade blockade network.[107]

The slavers created a glaring structural vulnerability by committing to the last remaining havens of the American flag and New York shipping infrastructure. The British did their best to exploit this vulnerability throughout this period, despite American reticence about cooperation. In 1858, the United States revoked the practical right of visit over a diplomatic slight.[108] The British were scrambling to patch this hole to little avail through paired cruising and an abortive 1860 international conference on suppression.[109] During this period, the remnants of the trade committed more fully to the use of the United States flag.

The Lincoln administration provided the British with the opportunity to attack these vulnerabilities in 1860. Compelled by the embarrassment of the Trent Affair into joining the treaty regime, Lincoln additionally aggressively enforced the anti-slave trade laws in New York, effectively disrupting the slavers' logistics network. The United States also invited

---

[104] US Department of State, *Trafficking in Persons Report 2016*, p. 325.

[105] These commanders were a remarkable cadre – Captain Edmonstone became a Member of Parliament; Captain Eardley-Wilmot, a previous veteran of the squadron, was the son of a prominent abolitionist judge; Captain Hornby became Admiral of the Fleet; Captain Dowell, the last commodore of the squadron, went on to command four more stations as an admiral.

[106] This office actually predated the Suppression Squadron, and was created during the early days of abolitionism. Eltis, *Economic Growth and the Ending of the Transatlantic Slave Trade*.

[107] Mathieson, *Great Britain and the Slave Trade, 1839–1865*, 183. Denman proposed a blockade where ships would remain within signal distance of each other.

[108] Ibid., 156. In 1858, there was a confrontation with the US over revival of Cuban trade. The US responded to British efforts and withdrew the practical right of visit.

[109] Ibid., 159.

British cruisers to Cuba, who had previously been steering cautiously away from the region for fear of igniting American paranoia.[110]

By 1862, the barracoons in Angola remained full, awaiting vessels that did not come; no slaving vessels departed from New York City that year. While eighty-eight vessels were still associated with the trade at this point,[111] fitting out for a voyage was now prohibitively expensive. As it had in 1850, when Portuguese slave trading experts departed Brazilian shores for New York, the trade attempted a final reboot. A few remnants of the New York market attempted to set up shop in Cadiz in 1864.[112] Between the increasing risks ashore in Cuba, the greater than 50 percent attrition afloat, the damage to the African slaving networks, the loss of fast American shipyards, and the complete removal of immunity, rebooting the trade required prohibitive costs. The cumulative network damage could not be overcome, and the collapse was permanent.

Interestingly, abolitionists were convinced up until the very end of the effort that the trade would reignite without continued suppression. In the words of the late-phase abolitionist leader Thomas Buxton, "it will avail us little that ninety-nine doors are closed, if one remains open. To that outlet the whole slave trade of Africa will rush."[113] It is difficult to adjudicate this claim, but to their credit, they maintained suppression and the trade did not reignite. Perhaps this is an artifact of organizational learning, from the many reversals that followed major victories – the 1830 death and resuscitation of the Brazilian trade, the multiple resurgences of the Caribbean trade, the collapse and recovery following the intervention of 1850, or even the initial regeneration of the trade following the British 1808 exit. This is a difficulty of fighting networks; it is hard to tell when they are actually destroyed. The British eased pressure off slowly, and the trade remained flatlined.

LESSONS FOR TODAY

I believe that the two main pillars of the British success would serve modern abolitionists well in large-scale campaigns against slavery in the technical commons of our day. At the outset, the illicit slave trade held

---

[110] Ibid. Lyons asked Seward for Joint Cruising, which Cass turned down, but the US withdrew the whole force for the Civil War blockade of the South.

[111] Ibid. No vessels from New York City in 1862; barracoons reported full awaiting ships. Eighty-eight vessels were still in the trade at this point.

[112] Ibid., 181.

[113] Ibid., 38.

strong advantages in ideation and innovation by way of the market itself. This allowed the slavers to recover from British interventions, as seen in the "sawtooth" pattern of shock and response. By the end of the historical campaign, the West African Squadron was in many ways more "market-like" than its adversary. Ideas moved more quickly, and were implemented more fully, among the suppressors than among the slavers. This allowed for remarkable agency on the part of British operators; while the resulting initiative entangled the British in new and complex foreign policy problems, it also allowed them to seize transient opportunities and thereby take ground in the campaign. Such approaches are harder to control and predict, but plodding bureaucratic approaches are predictably ineffective against adaptive dark networks in a wide open commons such as the Atlantic.

These lessons should apply today as well. In order to "arc the sawtooth down," flat networks, organizational spaces, and conversational structures should lower barriers of entry into the movement, while also accelerating ideation. Many of the best potential ideas of the modern anti-trafficking movement fail to navigate the labyrinthine maze of NGOs and governmental agencies in order to find a sympathetic ear. For instance, the US Agency for International Development sponsored a technology challenge for college students in 2013, resulting in "2,200 members from more than 100 countries" innovating projects such as "a web browser application that helps online shoppers make smart choices by alerting them to products that may have forced or exploited labor in their supply chains."[114]

If simply building a convening space allows collegiate activists to produce *pro bono* such powerful applications, then we must wonder how many effective solutions to slavery are lost to the tribalism and funding scrambles that have heretofore precluded a common space for the modern abolitionist movement. And we must ask whether traffickers or anti-traffickers hold the present innovation advantage. If the former, then we must ask how to shift that balance. It took the Royal Navy's use of "market-like" flat organizations to defeat the market structures of slavery in its day, and I hold that today, as well, it will take a robust marketplace of ideas and a vibrant conversation amongst modern abolitionists to riposte against the organizational advantages of today's slave markets. In short, it will "take a market to defeat a market." We have a long way

[114] "Campus Tech Challenge," *USAID*, www.usaid.gov/news-information/press-releases/usaid-announces-winners-campus-challenge-combat-human-trafficking.

to go toward this end, but fortunately the tides of technology facilitate these forms of collaboration, should we make use of them.

The second pillar – deeply embedded social support – is equally crucial to shared networks and convening spaces. To the historical abolitionists' credit, the coalition that produced the legal changes of 1807 held to see those changes through sixty years after. Given the magnitude of modern slavery, the number of power structures implicated in its practice, and the demonstrated ability of traffickers to employ emerging technology toward their ends,[115] we would do well to think likewise. Although I only briefly discussed the abolitionist movement itself during this work, the concepts behind crowd sourcing and viral messaging would have been quite familiar to British campaigners – pamphlets, petitions, and the ubiquitous "Am I Not a Man and a Brother" icon all speak to the significance of these methods.[116]

On this note, there is cause for optimism. The hard-won gains of anti-traffickers over the last two decades catapulted the issue of modern-day slavery from a niche humanitarian issue into a broad-based social movement. In many ways, the established figures who kindled this expansive social imagination for freedom are still coming to terms with these forces themselves. Many of the leading organizations still fit the mold of issue-based NGOs, and the requirements of a principal-agent model can conflict with the demands of serving as a standard-bearer for a movement.[117] Increasingly, though, there seems room for a more unified movement amidst and among the players in the anti-trafficking space. This is a good sign – the British abolitionists "out-demanded" freedom over the forces demanding slavery, which sustained the protracted campaign. So not only will it take a market, but it will take a movement to check and counter modern slavery.

In conclusion, I return to the parallel between cyberspace and the Atlantic. If the analogy holds, there are more reasons that modern

---

[115] Latonero, "Technology and Human Trafficking."

[116] Josiah Wedgwood, a marketing revolutionary, propagated the iconic image through his pottery and branding empire. Mark Dodgson, "Exploring New Combinations in Innovation and Entrepreneurship: Social Networks, Schumpeter, and the Case of Josiah Wedgwood (1730–1795)," *Industrial and Corporate Change* 20, no. 4 (2011), 1119–51; Neil McKendrick, "Josiah Wedgwood: An Eighteenth-Century Entrepreneur in Salesmanship and Marketing Techniques," *The Economic History Review* 12, no. 3 (1960), 408–33.

[117] For a theoretical exploration of this model, see Alexander Cooley and James Ron, "The NGO Scramble: Organizational Insecurity and the Political Economy of Transnational Action," *International Security* 27, no. 1 (n.d.), 5–39.

abolitionists should take notice of the online world that extends beyond cybercrime. Mastery of the seas was crucially important for the suppression of the Atlantic slave trade because the sea was the "fast road." That is to say, once a slaver made open water, they could travel to a wide range of places – and quickly. Since the British had the infrastructure and the expertise to contest the use of the "fast road," they could both complicate the slavers' tasks and simplify their own. Just as the water connected the slavers to their markets in the Americas, it connected captives aboard captured slavers to safety in Sierra Leone. The same waves that served slavers also served the Royal Navy, allowing the Africa Squadron to mass or disperse at will. Mastery of the commons provides a measure of control over these "fast roads."

In the same way, the aspects that make cyberspace increasingly attractive to modern slavers should make the space attractive to modern abolitionists as well. Slavers can use chatrooms and web boards to connect sellers to buyers, but abolitionists can use the same technologies to connect activists to allies. The free encryption software that insulates online exploiters can also guard secure collaboration amongst anti-trafficking players.

These ethereal "fast roads" have utility even against slavers who have no presence in cyberspace. For instance, consider an internal trafficking ring between two Indian states conducted solely through offline social trust networks. Law enforcement and NGOs in the ring's area of operation could still piece together the situation and develop responses to it quickly using online collaborative tools. Groups that can coordinate in both real space and cyberspace can envelop those that operate only in one or the other.

Coordination and rendezvous nodes are equally essential for cross-border trafficking, and in order to move beyond cloistered trust networks, traffickers need to access the world of data. Whether email, cell phones, or ATMs, networked electronic data is a ubiquitous element of modern international business. In this, cyberspace today parallels the Atlantic of the late slave trade era. Like the Atlantic, there are places to hide and ways to move quickly enough to avoid capture.

I predict that cyberspace will be a core domain for an expanded fight against trafficking – an effective suppression campaign should both deny (or at least contest) traffickers' use of these space, and use the space itself to facilitate communications and support. Policymakers are increasingly thinking along these lines – addressing the Clinton Global Initiative in 2012, President Barack Obama stated: "We're turning the tables on the traffickers. Just as they are now using technology and the Internet to exploit their victims, we're going to harness technology to stop them."[118] A slew of recent law review articles echo the British abolitionist strategy debates of the 1820s, imagining new international frameworks for excluding sexual exploitation from the cyber commons, learning early lessons from initial online trafficker countermeasures, and attempting to come to terms with what might be required to see the campaign through.[119]

In light of those strategy debates, I offer hope. As it turned out, no individual strategy proved the antidote to slavery, and more than any individual slaver business model proved the undoing of suppression. It is less important that we get these debates right than that we get them together. The captains of the West African Squadron innovated solutions faster than their commodores or the Admiralty. These solutions were generated through conversation and implemented through the same. Regarding support, it was similarly less important that abolitionists had an ideal legislative strategy, and more important that they continued to reinforce each other's convictions in community.

Those conversations, and that community, took place within commonplaces. The Royal Navy captains battled the slavers for the contested commons of West Africa. The abolitionists underwrote the naval captains from Clapham Common and its successor gathering places, while the slaving enterprise backed slave ship captains from the commonplaces in sundry harbors. To replicate the West African Squadron's results, we might imagine law enforcement professionals contesting the slavers on the "fast roads" of cyberspace, with abolitionist backers using online commons to coordinate, innovate, and strategize. This is one final encouraging sign – tech companies, private citizens, and

---

[118] Judge Herbert B. Dixon, Jr., "Human Trafficking and the Internet* (* and Other Technologies, Too)," *Judges' Journal* 52, no. 1 (2013), www.americanbar.org/content/dam/aba/publications/judges_journal/2013_win_jj_tech.pdf.

[119] For instance, Dixon, Jr., "Human Trafficking and the Internet* (* and Other Technologies, Too)"; Hao Wang et al., "Data Integration from Open Internet Sources to Combat Sex Trafficking of Minors," in *Proceedings of the 13th Annual International Conference on Digital Government Research*, Dg.o 2012 (New York: ACM, 2012), 246–52; K. Vitale, "Barricading the Information Superhighway to Stop the Flow of Traffic: Why International Regulation of the Internet Is Necessary to Prevent Sex Trafficking," *Am. U. Int'l L. Rev.* 27 (2012), 91–173; Erin I. Kunze, "Sex Trafficking via the Internet: How International Agreements Address the Problem and Fail to Go Far Enough," *J. High Tech. L.* 10 (2009), 241.

governments – including internet giant Google and the *enfant terrible* Palantir analytic engine, as well as the fascinating Freedom Collaborative online partnership – are increasingly engaging the problem of human trafficking with "big data" tools.[120] It seems the new fight for the fast roads is already underway.

[120] Joseph Marks, "Technology and Human Trafficking"; "Technology Is the Key to Combatting Child Sex Trade, White House Says," *Nextgov*, May 1, 2013, www.nextgov .com/emerging-tech/2013/05/technology-key-combatting-child-sex-trade-white-house-says/62917/.

9

Defending Slavery, Denying Slavery

Rhetorical Strategies of the Contemporary Sex Worker Rights Movement in Historical Context

Elizabeth Swanson and James Brewer Stewart

INTRODUCTION

As is amply demonstrated throughout this volume, people fighting for and against the idea and practice of slaving innovate using many tools to advance their positions: primarily legal, but also political, economic, military, cultural, and rhetorical. In this sense, it can be revelatory for contemporary readers to encounter antebellum proslavery tracts and speeches, inasmuch as those arguments often comprise sophisticated treatises grounded as much in philosophical and moral convictions as they are in the warrants of base commerce and profit. The arguments between those who favored the system of plantation slaving and could not imagine its demise (whether or not they themselves were slaveholders), and those who fought for the abolition of slavery and could not abide its existence, were vociferous and ongoing. Documentation of these arguments provides an important portal to the complexity of thought informing the historical origins, lifespan, and purported prohibition (or, as many of the essays in this volume have shown, the shape-shifting) of slaving in the US and globally.

While in the current moment no arguments (at least publicly) are put forth in favor of slaving in any form, abolitionists still face heavy critiques for their work (many of them worthy of close attention, as we show), and similarly forceful debates regarding the definitions, conditions, and responses to enslavement and exploitation abound. Perhaps nowhere are these debates as virulent as on the subject of the commercial sex trade, and it is here that we focus our attention in this essay. This issue has divided people and groups who otherwise appear to be natural allies, especially feminists who might be expected to find shared ground in struggles for women's rights, autonomy, and freedom from harm. It has also brought together people and groups – for instance, liberal and progressive secular feminists with conservative and far right-wing Christian politicians and activists – who might otherwise be natural antagonists. We bring history to bear as we explore how claims derived from one's particular historical orientation help to explain the seemingly endless contention between those seeking prostitution's abolition and those demanding its decriminalization or legalization. Might some "lessons of history" suggest how such contention can be minimized?

While the problem of contemporary sex trafficking is most often framed against the historical antecedent of the movement against "white slavery" in the late nineteenth and early twentieth centuries, we mine the contemporary and historical records for points of comparison between the rhetorical strategies of sex worker rights advocates in the contemporary US and proslavery ideologues in the antebellum South. Our goal emphatically is not to equate or even to compare contemporary advocates of decriminalizing sexual labor with antebellum defenders of plantation slavery, but rather to unearth similarities in rhetorical strategies and warrants that have shaped arguments about the commercial sex trade and antebellum slaving. As with most legal and ethical conflicts, so too these debates essentially boil down to competing rights claims and identifications: in the antebellum moment, between rights of slaveholders to their "property" and to an accompanying set of social and cultural norms and hierarchies versus the rights of enslaved persons to be emancipated and free from harm; in the current moment, between the rights of people who "choose" to enter the commercial sex industry and those who have been coerced and enslaved within it.[1] In each case, the arguments are infused with moral and ethical

[1] We place the term "choose" in scare quotes to signal the deep contestation around choice and consent and their limits in the context of the commercial sex industry. The literature on this subject is too vast to cover here, although many of the sources cited throughout this piece address it directly. In general, anti-trafficking advocates' position can be summed up as in this passage from the Soroptomist white paper "Prostitution Is Not a Choice": "Above all, prostitution is not a choice, as some claim. Survivors of prostitution have described it as 'the choice made by those who have no choice.' Women are forced into prostitution by gender discrimination, race discrimination, poverty, abandonment, debilitating sexual and verbal abuse, lack of formal education, or a job that does not pay a living wage," "Prostitution Is Not a Choice: Soroptomist White Paper" (Philadelphia, PA: Soroptomist International of the Americas, 2007), 1, www.soroptimist .org/whitepapers/whitepaperdocs/wpprostitution.pdf. For sex worker rights advocates, sex work is first and foremost work like any other, and so their focus is on rendering the

premises, deeply held philosophical convictions, and empirical evidence marshaled to support those convictions.

While the ground for such exploration is vast, we limit our examination to three rhetorical strategies used then and now: first, the denial or dismissal of abolitionists' claims as erroneous or false, and of abolitionists themselves as naïve moral crusaders; second, the assertion of the relative happiness or autonomy of enslaved or exploited persons; and third, the diversion of attention from the harm suffered by the enslaved or exploited person to the potential for greater harms they may suffer under other systems, or the acceptance of such harm as a condition of an unchangeable status quo. In addition to examining these warrants, we analyze what the rhetorics deployed by both groups suggest about their relation to those who are exploited, concluding with analysis of a human rights-based approach to the commercial sex industry that encompasses the rights of both those who choose to perform sexual labor and those who have been trafficked and exploited within the commercial sex industry.

MORAL PANIC

The literature generated by sex worker rights advocates is rooted in a specific understanding of history. Powerful convictions about the lessons of the past undergird indictments of the anti-trafficking movement by sex worker rights advocates, as well as their confidence that decriminalization protects not only the rights of sex workers, but those of sexually exploited persons as well.[2] Sex worker rights advocates, by and

conditions for that work as healthy and free from harm as possible and ensuring that stigma against such work(ers) be eliminated, while also advocating that criminal charges be upheld in actual cases of coercion or force. See, e.g., "World Charter for Prostitutes' Rights," *International Committee for Prostitutes' Rights* (1985), www.walnet.org/csis/groups/icpr_charter.html and "Consensus Statement on Sex Work, Human Rights and the Law," *Global Network of Sex Worker Projects* (2013), www.nswp.org/resource/nswp-consensus-statement-sex-work-human-rights-and-the-law.

[2] It is important to distinguish between legalization and decriminalization of commercial sex: while legalizing sex work would remove criminal statutes related to the purchase and sale of sex, it also could introduce new laws and regulations specific to commercial sex, such as mandatory STI testing, restrictions on where and when sex work can happen, and registration with local police departments. Decriminalization, on the other hand, would not require special regulations, but would simply demand the same compliance with standards around health, safety, taxes, zoning, and so forth by which other businesses must abide. Las Vegas, Nevada, is an example of a place where prostitution is legal, while in countries such as New Zealand and the Netherlands it is decriminalized. There is no consensus on which system is preferred among sex worker rights advocates; however, the World Charter for Prostitutes' Rights (1989) calls for decriminalization,

large, hold to a particular interpretation of the history of the "white slave trade" – a mass mobilization to suppress and abolish prostitution that swept much of the Western world during the late nineteenth and early twentieth centuries – as precedent for the twenty-first-century anti-trafficking movement, perceiving the current movement as revenant of the earlier sexual and moral "panic."[3]

As is well known, during the "white slavery" moment, influential sectors of public opinion in England, the United States, and in several other European nations became convinced that criminal gangs of enslavers were forcing vulnerable "white" women into prostitution. Prompting these specific fears were more general anxieties felt by those who embraced slowly fading Victorian moral codes. As they saw it, a rising tide of toxic "impurity" was eroding Christian values and the foundations of social order. These activists worried about gambling, drug addiction, alcoholism, pornography, and masturbation – as well as prostitution. Responding with what many historians have described as a "purity crusade" to suppress such "licentious" practices, this campaign included the goal of abolishing the then-legal sex trade. Christian responsibility and empathic feeling dictated not only the rescue of victims of sexual exploitation, but also the elimination of prostitution itself through stringent antislavery legislation. To "purity crusaders," the sex trade constituted enslavement, just as it once had in the British West Indies and the Southern United States.[4] It bothered them little that

as did the international human rights NGO Amnesty International in an August 2015 resolution recommending that "Amnesty International develop a policy that supports the full decriminalization of all aspects of consensual sex work. The policy will also call on states to ensure that sex workers enjoy full and equal legal protection from exploitation, trafficking and violence." "Global Movement Votes to Adopt Policy to Protect the Human Rights of Sex Workers," *Amnesty International News*, August 11, 2015, www.amnesty .org/en/latest/news/2015/08/global-movement-votes-to-adopt-policy-to-protect-human-rights-of-sex-workers/. See also "World Charter for Prostitutes' Rights," www.bayswan .org/ICPRChart.html; Gail Pheterson, ed., *A Vindication of the Rights of Whores* (Seattle, WA: Seal Press, 1989); Valerie Jeness, *Making It Work: The Prostitutes' Rights Movement in Perspective* (Piscataway, NJ: Aldine Transaction Publishers, 1993); Ronald Weitzer, *Legalizing Prostitution: From Illicit Vice to Lawful Business* (New York: New York University Press, 2012).

[3] For an approach to the movement that amplifies the one that follows, see Jessica Pliley's contribution to this volume.

[4] See David Pivar, *The Purity Crusade: Sexual Morality and Social Control, 1868–1890* (Westport, CT: Praeger, 1973); John S. and Robin Haller, *Primers for Prudery: The Physician and Sexuality in Victorian America* (New York, 1977); L. Hall, "Hauling Down the Double Standard: Feminism, Social Purity and Sexual Science in Late Nineteenth-Century Britain," *Gender & History* 16, no. 1 (2004), 36–56; John Tosh, *A Man's*

this understanding and its accompanying demands meant criminalizing otherwise legal employment for vulnerable women. This is the feature of the purity crusade against "white slavery" to which sex worker rights advocates object most strenuously.

With this historical analogy clearly in mind, activists in the early twentieth century condemned what befell women in the commercial sex trade in tones that echoed the indictments of their nineteenth-century British and American predecessors. At the same time, their antislavery appeals roundly disparaged immigrant women and women of lower socioeconomic class status for their "moral weaknesses" and cast their putative traffickers in highly racialized terms, particularly in the United States. Their descriptor of choice – "white slavery" – made their racist inclinations clear, as did their castigation of immigrants and ethnic minorities as carriers of corruption. Their demands for state surveillance and highly selective and restrictive immigration policies threatened basic human rights. Their lurid descriptions of sexual predation signaled their strong prurient interest in the very practices being condemned. In all these ways, a genuine solicitude for the plight of women engaged in sexual labor transmuted itself perversely into what historians refer to as "moral panic," an upwelling of anxiety laced with ethnocentrism, white supremacy, voyeurism, and chauvinism that imagined an inundation of prostitution that never really existed. The sex trade was simply continuing as it had always done, even as panicky purity crusaders were vastly exaggerating its dangers.[5]

This is the view of history that informs demands for the decriminalization of sexual labor today. Many sex worker rights advocates regard the twenty-first-century anti-trafficking movement as reprising the "moral panic" of their Victorian predecessors. As far as it goes, this account is substantially correct, which means that it reveals dangerous precedents and communicates urgent warnings that today's anti-trafficking activists would do well to heed. Just as in the past, according to this view, those demanding the abolition of the commercial sex trade today are perceived as puritanical moral censors chasing fear-driven phantoms and, in so doing, providing cover for racist and xenophobic government operations, particularly around border control. Anti-trafficking platforms threaten

---

Place: Masculinity and the Middle Class Home in Victorian England (New Haven, CT: Yale University Press, 1999).
[5] For an in-depth analysis of moral panic, consult Roger Lancaster, *Moral Panic and the Punitive State* (Berkeley, CA: University of California Press, 1999).

the livelihoods of women (including vulnerable migrants) who have embarked upon this line of work, while making it impossible to set professional and legal standards to prevent sexual exploitation, violence, and abuse. Now, as then, abolitionists demanding an end to the sex trade have twisted genuine concern for the sufferings of others into prurient fantasies and urgings for social control, with devastating effects upon those who choose to make their livings in the commercial sex trade or who use commercial sex as a pathway to mobility from intolerable situations marked by poverty and repression.[6]

At this juncture, enter the historian who observes, "it's more complicated," which, of course, it is. In addition to the negative description above, the movement against the commercial sex trade dubbed with the unfortunate moniker "white slavery" was much more than that. One problem with the analogy between the nineteenth-century campaign against "white slavery" and the twenty-first-century anti-trafficking movement is its inability to account for the fact that "purity crusading" also generated a compelling international program for women's emancipation. Crusading for social purity, to be specific, mobilized women's suffrage as never before and grounded revolutionary demands for birth control, at least on the British side of the Atlantic. It overthrew the hated Contagious Diseases Act, which had mandated invasive medical procedures for women suspected of carrying venereal diseases who were licensed to engage in the sex trade. It contributed mightily to the elimination of sexual double standards for women and men and changed the age of consent in England from thirteen to sixteen years. On the down side, some purity crusaders became fascinated with eugenics, a fact that surely bolsters modern sex worker rights advocates' indictment, despite its irrelevance for the issue of decriminalization versus abolition. Whatever one's estimate of moral panic, the accomplishments of the purity movement were undeniably substantial. In many respects, it left English women in a far better place than it found them.[7]

---

[6] See, for example, Kamala Kempadoo, *Trafficking and Prostitution Reconsidered: New Perspectives on Migration, Sex Work, and Human Rights* (Boulder, CO: Paradigm Publishers, 2005); Jo Doezema, *Sex Slaves and Discourse Masters: The Construction of Trafficking* (New York: Zed Books, 2010); Laura Maria Agustin, *Sex at the Margins: Migration, Labour Markets, and the Rescue Industry* (New York: Zed Books, 2007).

[7] Judith R. Walkowitz, *Prostitution and Victorian Society: Women, Class and the State* (Cambridge: Cambridge University Press, 1980) and Trevor Fisher, *Prostitution and the Victorians* (Stroud, UK: Sutton Publishing, 2001) well describe Victorian understandings

Then there's the hard-to-ignore fact that despite its legalized position, commercial sex in Victorian England produced at least as much oppression as free choice for women engaged in the trade. It is true, as advocates on both sides of the contentious debate observe, that poverty led many to elect commercial sex work, a survival strategy that paid better than the pittances offered by factory or domestic labor. In that narrow sense, women did enter prostitution as a personal preference, much as today's sex worker rights advocates claim – but then, as now, often under dire economic pressure that mocks the concept of authentically free choice. Although women likely found it easier to move in and out of the sex trade than is usually possible today (another valid anti-abolitionist claim), legalized prostitution itself was barely less fraught with peril and pain than had it been outlawed. Required state licensing and mandatory physical examinations invited incessant harassment and blackmail by sheriffs and police, as well as indictments (real and rigged) that could easily lead the offending party to debtor's prison. To avoid such travails, sex workers sometimes masqueraded as married women by living with men who often found ways to exploit them. As this process developed over the years, sex work became ever more dominated by profit-hungry men at the expense of once-autonomous women. Since licensing required enforcement of the notorious Contagious Diseases Act, sex workers underwent invasive cervical examinations. Enforcing this regime was a harsh double standard that encouraged Victorians to scorn sex workers as irredeemably "fallen women," to excuse the men exploiting them for "simply being men," and to dismiss the cruelties of the sex trade as the regrettable cost of doing business.[8]

In sum, the historical record demonstrates that there was much more substance to the "purity crusade" than a focus on moral panic allows, and much suffering involved in the Victorian sex trade (in England or as it manifested in the US) that makes it a questionable historical precedent for arguments in favor of legalization or decriminalization today. In spite of their damaging zealotry, purity crusaders developed a mass movement that generated powerful concern for others and that then led to substantial social reforms and a broad – if still limited by racism and classism – feminist vision of social justice.

---

of and policies related to the sex trade and form the basis for our treatment of it in these pages.

[8] Walkowitz, *Prostitution and Victorian Society*, 13–32, 69–90, 192–214.

It is proper now to put today's anti-trafficking abolitionists under the historian's microscope. What might be abolitionists' present understanding of the past? Where do they find historical precedents for their convictions? And how susceptible are they to the "moral panic" that characterized the response to "white slavery"? Here is a statement to start us off, taken from an evangelical Christian publication that embraces creationism, equates abortion with murder, and approvingly quotes politicized right-wing pastors. Of course, this statement in no way represents all or even the majority of contemporary abolitionists; however, it does provide a useful starting point for this inquiry into the tenor of the contemporary anti-trafficking movement, as well as an example of some of its most harmful tendencies:

In the early to mid-nineteenth century, New York City was at the center of the abolitionist movement to abolish slavery and Christianity was at its epicenter. Today, a new abolitionist movement is emerging in the city, this time to abolish the global trade of women and children for sex, and committed Christians are still deeply involved key players. Over 150 years ago, New Yorkers were motivated by outspoken religious leaders, religious groups, and organizations involved with the Underground Railroad. The fiery sermons of Brooklyn's antislavery preacher Henry Ward Beecher received international attention. His sister, Harriet Beecher Stowe, authored the best-selling novel, *Uncle Tom's Cabin*, which became the longest running play at the time ... Today, there are more slaves than at any time in history – an estimated 27 million worldwide are trafficked for sex, the majority of whom are women; 2 million are children. Every hour 34 children are forced into prostitution in America.[9]

Most importantly, statements such as these (and they are incessant and ubiquitous) go far to explain and even justify sex worker rights advocates' opposition to suppression of the commercial sex industry and studied disinterest in abolitionists' solidarity with the suffering of trafficked persons. What inspires such pronouncements surely is all too often moral panic and an unquenchable urge to "save" an all but geometrically multiplying population of "victims." Too often laced with paternalism, ethnocentrism, and lurid description, their messages truly do repeat the least attractive aspects of the moral purity crusade.

What often gets lost in the discussion, however, is that many anti-trafficking advocates would hasten to agree, and to dispel the idea that

[9] Bethany Blankley, "In 'The New Abolitionist Movement' to Stop Sex Trafficking, Christians Are Still Key Players," *The Christian Post*, June 17, 2013, www.christianpost .com/news/in-the-new-abolitionist-movement-to-stop-sex-trafficking-christians-are-still-key-players-97004/.

all such advocates are proselytizing, moralizing, prudish, racist, uncritical anti-sex crusaders operating only for their own narrow notions of the public good (not to mention for the large amounts of funding, federal and otherwise, raised by anti-trafficking NGOs).[10] For many anti-trafficking advocates (ourselves included), not all sex work is slavery by any means. Many sex workers enter the trade as adults and without the "force, fraud, or coercion" by which trafficking is defined in national and international law, driven by economic necessity or personal desire, just as was the case in England, and just as sex worker rights advocates contend. For them, it's much more about money and self-determination in a variety of contexts (even when such contexts are less than ideal) than it is about criminal enslavers. Further, violence against and exploitation of those who sell sexual services is undeniable, and provides fodder for arguments made both by sex worker rights advocates, who argue that decriminalization and reduction of stigma are solutions to this problem, and by anti-trafficking advocates, who promote the reduction of demand for and ultimately the end of the commercial sex trade as the best way to end such violence.

Recognizing these important nuances, our focus in this essay is upon the many within the commercial sex industry who labor under conditions that fit the most widely accepted definition of slavery, the one developed by the 2012 *Bellagio-Harvard Guidelines on the Legal Parameters of Slavery*, which defines slavery as follows:

… control over a person in such a way as to significantly deprive that person of his or her personal liberty, with the intent of exploitation through the use, management, transfer or disposal of that person. Usually this exercise will be supported by and obtained through means such as violent force, deception or coercion of enslavement.[11]

Some who make a "free will choice" to enter the sex trade subsequently find themselves in circumstances that match exactly this definition: being bought, sold, and coerced by pimps who often first claimed to love them and now claim to own them, or who first promised them legitimate

---

[10] For a critique of funding and anti-trafficking NGOs, see Anne Elizabeth Moore, "Special Report: Money and Lies in Anti-Trafficking NGOs," *Truthout*, January 7, 2015, www.truth-out.org/news/item/28763-special-report-money-and-lies-in-anti-human-trafficking-ngos.

[11] Jean Allain, ed., *The Legal Understanding of Slavery: From the Historical to the Contemporary* (Oxford and New York: Oxford University Press, 2012) explains the Harvard criteria and features scholarly essays that contextualize them historically.

employment and then claim ownership after kidnapping them. And then there is the problem of minors. Advocates from both camps would be quick (and correct) to remind us that young people found in the sex trade often come from families shattered by poverty, racism, addiction, sexual abuse, incarcerated parents, and dysfunctional state programs, and that determining age of entry is notoriously difficult.[12] Sustained efforts to reduce and prevent these drivers of sexual exploitation are much more effective than reactions driven by moral panic, as would be some of the protections described in the movement's proposed unionization of sex workers. But freely granting all these complications and exceptions, the plain fact remains that a great deal of sex work does come down to enslavement according to contemporary definitions.

These conditions are all too easy to witness, to document, and to describe, in spite of exhortations to the contrary from sex worker rights advocates.[13] Today, as in the antebellum era, opposition to such exploitation demands identification with those who suffer, whether at home or abroad – not from moral panic, but rather from global solidarity and partnership. In the twenty-first century, this connection across difference transcends the moral or sentimental bounds of empathy, having learned from transnational feminism that

[12] And under both national and international anti-trafficking law, a minor is by definition a trafficked person. For recent research on the correlation of abuse/neglect with child involvement in the commercial sex trade, see Debra Schilling Wolfe, "95% of Homeless Youth Who Experienced Sex Trafficking Say They Were Maltreated as Children," *Chronicle of Social Change*, September 14, 2017, https://chronicleofsocialchange.org/research-news/majority-of-homeless-youth-who-experienced-sex-trafficking-say-they-were-maltreated-as-children. For sex worker rights advocates' positions on such problems, see the *Global Network of Sex Work Projects*, www.nswp.org/, the *Desiree Alliance*, http://desireealliance.org/wordpress/about-us/, and the "Problems and Solutions" page of *COYOTE LA*, www.coyotela.org/what_is.html. See also the *Sex Workers Project* for an organization that provides legal and social services for both sex workers and persons trafficked for sexual labor, http://sexworkersproject.org/, and the *Red Umbrella Fund* for the first global fund by and for sex workers, www.redumbrellafund.org/.

[13] See, for instance, Laura Murphy, *Survivors of Slavery: Modern-Day Slave Narratives* (New York: Columbia University Press, 2014); Kevin Bales and Ron Soodalter, *The Slave Next Door: Human Trafficking and Slavery in America Today* (Berkeley, CA: University of California Press, 2010); Rachel Moran, *Paid For: My Journey Through Prostitution* (New York: W.W. Norton, 2015); Rachel Lloyd, *Girls Like Us: Fighting for a World Where Girls Are Not for Sale, an Activist Finds Her Calling and Heals Herself* (New York: HarperCollins, 2011); Siddarth Kara, *Sex Trafficking: Inside the Business of Modern Slavery* (New York: Columbia University Press, 2010). In addition to these volumes, an Internet search for "sexual slavery testimonies" yields thousands of results in journals, newspapers, magazines, websites, and blogs.

It would be impossible ... to advocate a transnational feminism as an improved or better or cleaned up kind of international or global feminism. Transnational feminism, for example, is not to be celebrated as free of these oppressive conditions. In fact, there *is no such thing* as a feminism free of asymmetrical power relations. Rather, transnational feminist *practices*, as we call them, involve forms of alliance, subversion, and complicity within which asymmetries and inequalities can be critiqued. [emphasis in original][14]

This quality of critical, reflexive solidarity is precisely what we believe a human rights-oriented approach to the problem of sex trafficking can achieve; but first, let us explore the rhetorical strategies and warrants undergirding some sex worker rights discourse in comparison with the discourses of those who defended the institution of slavery in the past.

DEFENDING AND DENYING SLAVERY, THEN AND NOW

From an historian's point of view, certain rhetorical elements of current sex worker rights arguments bear striking similarity with the rhetorical elements of antebellum planter class defenses of chattel slavery. To be clear, there is no suggestion in this analysis that advocates of legalizing sex work implicate themselves in slaving or slave systems, or that they would advocate such exploitation or abuse for anyone, least of all those engaged in the commercial sex trade they promote. Apart from rhetorical similarities, sex worker rights organization COYOTE and proslavery ideologue John C. Calhoun have absolutely nothing in common. Those who read this analysis otherwise will profoundly misunderstand its content and purpose. Instead, the argument is simply that both groups make claims that constitute a denial of some people's suffering at the expense of other people's protection, progress – and profit.

Both, for example, advance their interests with emphatic appeals to law: advocates for the institution of plantation slavery seek to protect the legality of human bondage, and sex worker rights advocates to decriminalize sex work. Whether by affirmation (slaveholders), or by denial (sex worker rights advocates), the effect of each is to continue slavery, the former as intention, and the latter as unintended consequence. Both,

---

[14] Inderpal Grewal and Caren Kaplan, "Postcolonial Studies and Transnational Feminist Practices," *Jouvert: A Journal of Postcolonial Studies* 5, no. 1 (Autumn 2000), https:// english.chass.ncsu.edu/jouvert/v5i1/con51.htm.

moreover, are challenged to defend themselves against abolitionists who deplore their ethical positioning, threaten their livelihoods, and claim to speak for the interests of the enslaved. Both are looking to their well-being first and foremost, which means dismissing competing concerns from other stakeholders in the conversation, and both prioritize their (or their constituencies') position in the capitalist marketplace. The ends they seek share no common ground (continued sanction of the institution of slavery for nineteenth-century slaveholders vs. free access to commercial sex markets for twenty-first-century sex workers); however, the arguments they employ are uncomfortably similar. We believe that mining those similarities, unnerving a project as it may be, holds potential for shifting from such shared rhetorical space to a common zone of struggle for the human rights of both sex workers and trafficking victims/survivors.

Antebellum planters built and proponents of legalization build their cases as do all capable attorneys: defending their claims by attempting to overcome evidence that undermines them. Whether the issue is defending or denying slavery, two distinct tactics serve this purpose. The first is to dismiss the opponent's evidence as fraudulently manufactured or misinformed, while contending that the enslaved are actually better off under the circumstances for which you are responsible, rather than those proposed by your opponent. *You* – and not those intrusive and moralizing abolitionists – speak for their best interests. The second involves characterizing the opponent's case as a distraction from a different, serious injustice that must be attended to instead. Let us compare both tactics, first as employed by antebellum apologists for slavery and then by advocates of sex trade legalization. The publication of Harriet Beecher Stowe's *Uncle Tom's Cabin* presents an ideal historical moment for initiating this analysis.

Consider first the tactic of dismissing abolitionists' evidence as fabricated or erroneous. By 1852, slaveholders had made themselves experts in this particular defense of their "peculiar institution." Well practiced in every rhetorical trope, legal rebuttal, and moral counter claim, they mobilized each of these resources in that year as Harriet Beecher Stowe's *Uncle Tom's Cabin* topped the bestseller list. This first charge, fundamental to their entire case, was that Stowe had made it all up, just as had all abolitionists from the very beginning. From the first, slaveholders had condemned them as "heedless fanatics," "religious zealots," and officious "busy-bodies" who were responding with what we might term "moral panic" to a normal form of social relations known as chattel slavery. As we have seen, this charge carries modern resonance when taken up by proponents of legalizing the sex trade.[15]

Because Stowe was seen as so perversely misrepresenting the facts, slaveholding novelists (at least twenty-seven in all, according to Thomas Gossett) rushed into print to set the record straight with titles such as Aunt Phyllis's Cabin and *Uncle Tom's Cabin as It Is* – the latter an obvious play on abolitionist Theodore Dwight Weld's *American Slavery as It Is*, referenced earlier.[16] Finding her veracity under ferocious attack, Stowe issued a minutely detailed rebuttal, the title of which conveyed her purpose perfectly: *Facts for the People: A Key to Uncle Tom's Cabin: Presenting the Original Facts and Documents upon Which the Story Is Founded Together with Corroborating Statements Proving the Truth of the Work.* No one since has found fault with her documentation. Defenders of slavery, Stowe insisted, were not entitled to make up their own facts or otherwise to deny the heavily documented sufferings of bondspeople.[17] Might the same be said of those today who deny the authenticity of sexual enslavement as a fiction or at least as a wildly overblown exaggeration created by the moral crusaders and NGO fundraisers of the anti-trafficking movement?

Not coincidentally, sex worker rights advocates often describe narratives of sex trafficking in the twenty-first century as "myth," or in other terms that imply that trafficking is simply the construction of a sensationalized media along with moral-crusading politicians, lawmakers, academics, and feminists. Consider these titles of recent articles: "Sex Work Is Work: Exploding the Sex Trafficking Myth"; "The Myth of Nepal to India Sex Trafficking"; "White Slavery as Political Myth"; "Myths about Human Trafficking"; "Debt Bondage and Trafficking: Don't Believe the Hype ..."[18]

---

[15] For an examination of slaveholders' indictments of abolitionism, consult Drew Faust, *The Ideology of Slavery: Proslavery Thought in the Antebellum South 1830–1860* (Baton Rouge, LA: Louisiana State University Press, 1982).

[16] Thomas F. Gossett, *Uncle Tom's Cabin and American Culture* (Dallas, TX: Southern Methodist University Press, 1985).

[17] Joan D. Headrick, *Harriet Beecher Stowe: A Life* (New York and Oxford: Oxford University Press, 1994), 218–53.

[18] Margaret Corvid, "Sex Work Is Work: Exploding the Myth of Sex Trafficking," *New Statesman*, July 7, 2014, www.newstatesman.com/economics/2014/07/sex-work-work-exploding-sex-trafficking-myth; Jo Doezema, "White Slavery as Political Myth," in *Sex Slaves and Discourse Masters: The Construction of Trafficking* (London: Zed Books, 2010), 41–62; Frederick John, "The Myth of Nepal to India Sex Trafficking: Its Creation, Its Maintenance, and Its Influence on Anti-Trafficking Interventions," in Kemala Kempadoo, ed., *Trafficking and Prostitution Reconsidered*, 127–48; Alison Murray, "Sex Trafficking and Debt Bondage: Don't Believe the Hype," in Kamala Kempadoo

What does it mean to summon the word/idea "myth," particularly in the title (headline) of an essay, when discussing sexual exploitation and trafficking in the current global landscape? Or to glibly invoke the "speak truth to power" vibe of rap group Public Enemy's famous "Don't Believe the Hype," anthem of Black Power politic and music, implying that those who oppose debt bondage and trafficking are equivalent to an oppressive police or media apparatus out to harass, silence, repress, and brutalize politicized young black youth? Or to put the words "Trafficked Women" in scare quotes, as if to call into question the existence of actual trafficked women, as Jacqueline Berman does in her essay "Biopolitical Management, Economic Calculation and 'Trafficked Women'"? We are interested here in how, to borrow from Theresa DeLauretis, the "rhetoric of violence is inseparable from the violence of rhetoric"; that is, the ways in which "some kind of discursive representation is at work not only in the concept of 'violence' but in the social practices of violence as well. The (semiotic) relation of the social to the discursive is thus posed from the start."[19] DeLauretis makes the case that language and representation inherently reproduce the violence of gender oppression, but her point about the relation of the social to the discursive is much more expansive in its application: in this case, the rhetorical violence done by dismissing the suffering of trafficked women and girls.[20] (Our reference to "suffering," we should note, is not meant to invoke victimhood, but rather, to witness bodies and selves damaged by coerced sexual labor and its accompanying violence.)

The literature of sex worker rights advocates is surprisingly redundant in its usage of such rhetorical tactics to call the empirical reality of sex trafficking into question. Some writers, such as UK sex worker Margaret Corvid, use the word precisely to argue that trafficking does not exist: "the very concept of 'sex trafficking ...' is a myth." Like many

and Jo Doezema, eds., *Global Sex Workers: Rights, Resistance and Redefinition* (New York: Taylor & Francis, 1998), 51–64; Ronald Weitzer, "Myths about Human Trafficking," *The World Post*, July 24, 2011, www.huffingtonpost.com/ronald-weitzer/human-trafficking-myths_b_935366.html.

[19] Teresa DeLauretis, "The Violence of Rhetoric: Considerations on Representation and Gender," *Technologies of Gender: Essays on Theory, Film, and Fiction* (Bloomington, IN: Indiana University Press, 1987), 31–50.

[20] We rely here on data from the International Labour Organization Global Estimate of Forced Labor (2012), which estimates that of the 20.9 million people currently trapped in forced labor, 4.5 million are victims of forced sexual exploitation; of these, 98 percent are women or girls. See www.ilo.org/global/about-the-ilo/newsroom/news/WCMS_181961/lang--it/index.htm. Gendering sexually exploited people female in this work is not meant to discount the experiences of male or transgender persons engaged in the commercial sex trade and/or experiencing commercial sexual exploitation.

who take this position, Corvid gestures toward concern for those who have been "coerced": "To say this is not to sideline the coerced; in dismantling this pernicious myth, we put their lived experiences front and centre. Coercion, force, and violence in sex work are very real, but they pertain generally to life as a member of the oppressed, not just to sex work."[21] Corvid's argument, then, seems to be that there are those who experience coercion, but always within the frame of *sex work* (implicitly, *voluntary* sex work) – a frame that functionally denies testimonies from all over the world of women who have neither entered nor remain in the sex trade voluntarily. Too, Corvid's construction displaces the violence from the specific experience of "sex work" to the more generalized experience of "oppression," another rhetorical sleight of hand that relies upon what Stanley Cohen has called the "sociology of denial": "It seems self-evident that a common reaction [to knowledge of the suffering of others] is to block out, shut off, or repress this information. People react as if they do not know what they know. Or else the information is registered – there is no attempt to deny the facts – but its implications are ignored."[22] The kind of denial that we explore in this essay manifests in both categories, but particularly the latter, in that sex worker rights advocates often give the nod to the existence of trafficking but, as Corvid does above, then proceed to downplay, deny, evade, and rationalize its impacts. Rather than triggering action or intervention, the admonition that "some are coerced" seems to be a necessary rhetorical device, empty of significance other than to bridge to the main argument about securing the rights of sex workers by legalizing or decriminalizing the trade and reducing stigma and violence against those engaged in it.

In addition to deflecting attention from the suffering of trafficked persons, the word "myth" also undermines or simply ignores the truth value of testimonials from survivors.[23] Some authors are careful to qualify their usage, indicating that they do not mean to imply "untruth," at least not solely or definitively; as John Frederick asserts in "The Myth of Nepal

---

[21] Corvid, "Sex Work Is Work."
[22] Stanley Cohen, *States of Denial: Knowing about Atrocities and Suffering* (Hoboken, NJ: Wiley and Sons, 2013).
[23] This charge of undermining or ignoring claims from trafficking survivors and sex workers respectively is made by both sides against the other; for an argument about abolitionists' refusal to acknowledge "sex positive" or other affirming accounts of participation in the sex industry, see, for instance, Alison Phipps, "'You're Not Representative': Identity Politics in Sex Industry Debates," *Genders, Bodies, Politics: Writings by Alison Phipps*, August 31, 2015, https://genderate.wordpress.com/2015/08/31/youre-not-representative/.

to India Sex Trafficking," he means myths "in the sense of typifying narratives" (128). In this way, such authors resurrect the classical and scholarly definition of *mythos*; that is, "speech, narrative, fiction, myth, plot" (OED). According to this definition, myth can be neutral in terms of content; that is, the word does not imply an untruth, per se, but indicates rather a speech act that depends upon rhetorical conventions, narrative principles, or formulae, rising from the neutral "speech" and "narrative" and encompassing the more charged "fiction, myth, plot."

Similarly, authors such as Jo Doezema conceptualize myth through the writings of postmodern critical theorists such as Terry Eagleton, Ernesto Laclau, Roland Barthes, and Louis Althusser as an exemplar of the classical ideological apparatus, that is, the repetition of formulaic elements in a predictable narrative pattern serving to interpolate subjects into a particular point of view that naturalizes its own assumptions and warrants while hiding its ideological underpinnings.[24] Doezema's analysis is theoretically sophisticated, worked out over a period of time in several essays and a book. In earlier work, based upon her dissertation and published as *Sex Slaves and Discourse Masters* (2004), Doezema notes, "My ... interpretation of trafficking discourses relied on a concept of myth which consisted of two elements: first, that of myth as a distortion of the truth (trafficking 'hid' what was really occurring in terms of migration of sex workers); and, second, that of myth as a metaphor, a way of explaining a complicated and threatening reality (trafficking narratives as stories that encoded, for example, fear of women's sexuality)."[25] In both cases, Doezema's use of the word myth deemphasizes the experience of those who are, in fact, unequivocally coerced/trafficked into systems of sexual exploitation.

Moving from *mythos* to *myth* in the Oxford English Dictionary yields this change in definition: "A traditional story, typically involving supernatural beings or forces, which embodies and provides an explanation,

---

[24] Interestingly, many of these theorists write from a Marxist perspective; for Marx, however, prostitution was the *sine qua non*, the exemplar, of the exploitative nature of labor within the capitalist system. While Marx shared none of the mural prurience around differentiating sexual labor from other forms of labor, he did not advocate equalizing and legitimizing sex work as just another form of work; rather, he called for wholesale revolution against the repressive economic base as a means of revolutionizing the superstructural social relations attached to it – the opposite of the arguments of writers such as Doezema, who works instead to normalize sex work and to empower sex workers through reduced stigmatization and better healthcare and working conditions.

[25] "Now You See Her, Now You Don't: Sex Workers at the UN Trafficking Protocol Negotiation," *Social and Legal Studies* 14, no. 61 (2005), 64.

aetiology, or justification for something such as the early history of a society, a religious belief or ritual, or a natural phenomenon" (OED online). This is the definition most heavily referenced by sex worker rights advocates, who identify shared elements of victimhood, sensationalization, and exploitation in media, NGO, and government/law enforcement "stories" of "innocent" girls and women kidnapped; brutalized; sold into the sex trade; "broken" by a series of gang rapes and abuses; plied with drugs in order to ensure compliance; and eventually habituated to a daily life of coerced sex (rape) with dozens of men per day. They contend that this story with its formulaic elements is not representative; rather, it has gained traction only because it holds the explanatory force necessary to contain and package as complex a moral, ethical, social, cultural, economic, and political phenomenon as the commercial sex trade, commercial sexual exploitation, trafficking, or, as these authors would have it, sex work. And because it appeals to the prurient interests of moral crusaders, as per the nineteenth-century movement against "white slavery" discussed above. Like Corvid, such writers often offer a *de rigueur* acknowledgment of violence and coercion in the sex trade, the legitimacy of which they go on to negate in the substance of their arguments. Rather than bearing witness to the atrocity of sex trafficking and commercial sexual exploitation for those who testify to having experienced it, the syntactical structure employed in such cursory acknowledgments does a further discursive violence to trafficked people through a shallowly instrumental "recognition" with no substance by way of address or amelioration.

Another common syntactical structure acknowledges the "truth" of some claims of sex trafficking followed by the conjunction "but ..." What lies after this "but" diminishes the significance of what comes before, such that the claims of women and girls who have survived commercial sexual exploitation are subordinated rhetorically to the arguments about how the "myth" of sex trafficking is produced and the impacts of this myth on women who choose to sell sex (with or without migrating to do so). To offer one example: In "The Social Construction of Sex Trafficking," Ronald Weitzer allows, "This [the construction of sex trafficking as a moral crusade through the rehearsal of the 'mythical narrative' of the trafficked woman] does not mean that coercive sex trafficking is fictional. Force and deception are realities in the sex trade, and the perpetrators deserve stiff punishment. *But* ..." (emphasis added).[26] Regardless of the

---

[26] The argument on the other side of the "but" in this case is that the anti-sex trafficking lobby, "instead of focusing on unfree labor ... has broadly targeted all migration if sex is sold at the destination" (467).

legitimacy of whatever lies on the other side of the "but," the ease with which the acknowledgment of the existence of "coercive sex trafficking" is made and dismissed in one swift rhetorical move is troubling from a human rights perspective. It is an acknowledgment that is not one, then, at least not in the sense required by the experience of having been trafficked for sex.[27] And the dismissal disavows the material violence, the physical and mental suffering that such experience entails. In an attempt to assert that the "mythical" narrative of the trafficked person is over-blown (which, as discussed above, in fact constitutes a legitimate critique), such arguments do rhetorical violence to the truths at the heart of the "myth"; that is, to the experiences of actual women and girls who have been trafficked for sex (and whatever one's take on the numbers, which researchers on both sides of the debate acknowledge are notoriously difficult to determine with any certainty, given the illicit nature of the sex trade and the migration/smuggling/trafficking of humans, there is no denying that there are hundreds of thousands of women and girls in this situation).

It is, we argue, impossible to employ the term myth in relation to sex trafficking without invoking the primary understanding of a myth as a story that is fundamentally untrue. This is precisely the judgment historians render on slaveholders' claims that the original abolitionists spun unfounded myths about their "peculiar institution." Moreover, evasions based on the preposition "but" are strongly reminiscent of slaveholding planters like James Madison and Thomas Jefferson who acknowledged slavery as a "necessary evil." Their slaves did indeed suffer, they admitted ... *but* ... such suffering, even though acknowledged, was not enough to prompt their emancipation.

HAPPINESS AND AGENCY: PERFORMANCES OF MERRY BONDS-PEOPLE

In the nineteenth century, the question of whether slavery was a benefit to society (a "positive good" in the parlance of slaveholders) or, as Stowe

---

[27] Significantly, Cohen asserts that the opposite of denial is "acknowledgment": "This is what 'should' happen when people are actively aroused – thinking, feeling, acting – by the information. They respond appropriately, in the psychological and moral senses, to what they know. They see a problem that needs their attention; they get upset or angry, and express sympathy or compassion; and they do something: intervene, help, become committed" (x). Cohen acknowledges that both "denial" and "acknowledgment" are "riddled with conceptual ambiguities," but that these are the best terms he has found in his research for these broad, complex states of mind and being.

would have it, a moral abomination, drove the larger debate over facts. It also drove the plots of the anti-Tom novels, as those proslavery literary polemics from slaveholders have come to be known. The trope, familiar to all, featured a benign, patriarchal master and his morally unblemished wife presiding together over childlike slaves in a benevolent extended-kinship version of the plantation. In the absence of kindly direction (and correction) from sagacious whites, it was argued, morally hapless, mentally feeble slaves would shamble their way into extinction, or close to it. Keeping this trope in mind, we turn now to consider the tactic of responding to abolitionists' criticisms by claiming to act in the best interests of the oppressed.

This strain of argument, which presented slaveholders as morally committed patriarchs by way of opposition to harshly exploitative, fundamentally racist capitalists in the North, was often combined with the story of the "happy slave" as another means of deflecting attention from the suffering of enslaved persons. This iconic trope circulated not only in proslavery tracts, but also in popular stereotypes of figures such as the "mammy" or "uncle" loyally and happily serving out their days in thrall on the plantation. Thomas Roderick Dew, one of the earliest and most prominent defenders of slavery, synthesized this position in remarks made in the only debate ever held in a Southern state legislature about the morality of slavery and the possibility of emancipation (this debate was prompted by Nat Turner's Virginia uprising, 1831, in which he and his men killed more than fifty white people, mostly women and children, before being captured and executed). In an article published in *The American Quarterly Review*, Dew famously disputed any just cause derived from the atrocities of slavery in Turner's actions, asserting that "In the debate [about slavery in the aftermath of Nat Turner's rebellion] in the Virginia legislature no speaker insinuated even, we believe, that the slaves in Virginia were not treated kindly; and all too agreed that they were most abundantly fed, and we have no doubt but that they form the happiest portion of our society. A merrier being does not exist on the face of the globe than the negro slave of the United States."[28]

In her authoritative account of the imbrication of terror and pleasure in the subjugation of enslaved people, Saidiya Hartman provides tools for analyzing this "merriment," showing how its apparent exhibition by

---

[28] Thomas Roderick Dew, "Abolition of Negro Slavery," in Drew Gilpin Faust, ed., *The Ideology of Slavery: Proslavery Thought in the Antebellum South, 1830–1860* (Baton Rouge, LA: Louisiana State University Press, 1981), 66.

enslaved people through dance and song, for instance, was actually either a "simulation of compliance for covert aims" or "the repressive construction of contented subjection."[29] In other words, enslaved people were often forced to perform the "merry" antics to which Dew testified before the Virginia legislature as a rebuttal to Nat Turner's categorical statement to the contrary; strategically performed such pleasure in order to stave off punishment from slaveholders; or experienced what limited joy might have been available to them as ambivalent shards of an otherwise atrocious life.

While sex worker rights activists in the present day do not try to repurpose the suffering of trafficked persons as "happiness" (despite the long shadow of the "happy hooker" imagery that originated in the 1976 film of the same name and that informs such dominant popular culture representations of the commercial sex industry as *Pretty Woman* [1997] and more recently the Starz Network series *GFE* [*Girlfriend Experience*]), their rhetoric has similar effects in that it diverts attention from the trafficked person to the sex worker (often cast as a voluntary migrant) who attains "agency" and "autonomy" via her decision to engage in sex work, and who experiences state or other interventions as disruptive to that "freedom." Returning to Corvid's argument about the negative impacts of "the trafficking myth," she repeats the argument of many others who write from this perspective: "Insidiously, the trafficking myth also deprives sex workers of agency and identity, as it sexualises and fetishises our lives and bodies."[30] Here, we might substitute "agency" for the "happiness" that was attributed to enslaved people in the antebellum South. In a similar rhetorical strategy, sex worker rights advocates assert that individual agency (sexual, economic, geographic) results from the freedom to pursue commercial sex as legitimate work while diverting attention from the many who, far from experiencing life within the commercial sex trade as autonomous, find it to be the source of coercion, pain, and suffering. By way of brief example, we cite the introduction to Kamala Kempadoo's anthology *Trafficking and Prostitution Reconsidered*, which reduces the anti-trafficking movement to a group of people from disparate quarters who share politically questionable alliances with the motive of "demand[ing] an end to women's rights to sexual self-determination and autonomy."[31]

[29] Saidiya Hartman, *Scenes of Subjection: Terror, Slavery, and Self-Making in Nineteenth Century America* (Oxford and New York: Oxford University Press, 1997), 8.
[30] Corvid, "Sex Work Is Work."
[31] Kamala Kempadoo, *Trafficking and Prostitution Reconsidered*, xxii.

Similarly, Jo Doezema asserts that the "myth" of human trafficking is "constructed around differing meanings of consent" (65), arguing that the dichotomy between consent/coercion must be overcome in order to understand the phenomenon of sex trafficking as a social construction based upon the power differentials at play in defining it and trapped within a liberal framework of rights that reifies women's lack of sexual and economic agency. While Doezema acknowledges her own investment in the liberal ideas of consent, autonomy, rights, and choice, she concludes her essay with a call to overturn the framework of consent in defining sex workers as opposed to trafficking victims, inviting feminists and sex worker rights activists to take on the "challenges ... encountered in attempts to replace, or reinscribe, the subject of the trafficking myth, the 'suffering body' of the female prostitute; to change the focus of our concern from the vulnerable subject needing protection to the desiring subject whose primary requirement is not passively confirmed 'rights' but a political arena conducive to the practice of freedom."[32] Doezema concludes: "This will necessarily involve overcoming the 'voluntary/ forced' dichotomy, and the concept of consent implicated in it, that the myth of trafficking both depends on and propagates."[33]

Doezema's attempt to undo the role of consent at the heart of the debate around trafficking is, ironically, still grounded in the idea of rights, which remain irrevocably anchored within the liberal framework she decries – just strictly focused upon the rights of the sex worker, not those of the trafficked person. As she notes, "In distinguishing between 'trafficking' and 'voluntary prostitution' through the qualifier of 'consent,' the Trafficking Protocol offers nothing to sex workers whose human rights are abused, but who fall outside of the narrowly constructed category of 'trafficking victim'" (80). Here, Douzema's commitments are made clear: they are to "sex workers whose human rights are abused," not to those who are trafficked – and the rhetorical claim does not allow room for *both* "the vulnerable subject needing protection" *and* "the desiring subject whose primary requirement is not passively confirmed 'rights' but a political arena conducive to the practice of freedom." It is the both/and framework that we strive toward in highlighting these discursive threads and their implications for the competing rights claims of trafficking victims and survivors and sex workers, rather than the binary "either/or" paradigm that dominates the discourse.

[32] Ibid., 81–2.
[33] Ibid., 82.

If Doezema's ultimate goal is to engender visibility and rights for sex workers, undoing the forced/consent dichotomy does not bode well as an auspicious means of achieving it. Arguing that abolitionist feminists have already undone the dichotomy by defining all prostitution as forced, Doezema expresses the desire to do the same but from the "other side," ensuring that all prostitutes are not constructed through the lens of the "suffering body" at the heart of the "sex trafficking myth." She does not articulate how this lifting of the line between coercion and consent would work from the perspective of sex workers, but if it is to be the inverse of the abolitionist argument, then the implication (intended or not) is that it would mean the erasure of the body and experience of the trafficked woman. And this, indeed, is precisely the (rhetorical, but complicit with material) violence done in the arguments by sex worker rights advocates who mobilize the term "myth" to describe the phenomenon of trafficking and who elide the experiences of those – migrants or not – who are not privileged to experience the liberal values of autonomy, mobility, and agency via their participation in the commercial sex trade.

The salient point for us is the claim of custodial empathy or solidarity on the part of slaveholders for their enslaved, or of sex worker rights advocates for their subjects, in spite of the sentimental racism and privilege pervading the entire tableaux. Influential historians have established that many slaveholders truly did feel that they were concerned for the well-being of those they enslaved, but in expressing such concern, were engaging in profound self-deception – some for emotional self-reassurance, others as a means for rationalizing displays of abusive power. In either case, slaveholders were usually dead certain that they knew what their bonds people needed, and were confident of their right to speak unbidden on their behalf.[34] The question today is whether sex worker rights advocates hold to similar assumptions when speaking for (and/or refusing to speak for or about) those engaged in (or exploited and enslaved by) the commercial sex industry. To what extent is their motive for claiming to uphold the best interests of others genuine, self-deceived, or rooted in interest in freedom of commerce and access to markets in a decriminalized global sex trade?

[34] Eugene Genovese, *Roll, Jordan, Roll: The World the Slaves Made* (New York: Random House, 1972), 1–112; Walter Johnson, *Soul by Soul: A History of the New Orleans Slave Market* (Cambridge, MA: Harvard University Press), 107–12.

JUST THE WAY IT IS: STATUS QUO ARGUMENTS
FOR DENYING SUFFERING

By way of response, we invite you to consider the tactic of dismissing an abolitionist's critique of slavery and its incumbent sufferings by drawing attention to more generalized injustices. Thanks to its clumsy title, one particular anti-Tom novel perfectly telegraphs this slaveholders' gambit: *Uncle Robin, in His Cabin in Virginia, and Tom, without One in Boston*.[35] According to this familiar telling, Robin lived far more comfortably in his enslaved condition than he would have as a free person struggling for survival in the urban North. Thanks to his owner's benevolence, he and his family were guaranteed food, clothing, medical care, housing, and so forth. Were Robin instead to find himself a member of the North's urban working class, coarsely bigoted capitalist employers would make brutally quick work of him and his family. Body-killing labor would eventually destroy him and his loved ones even as they battled starvation wages, frequent unemployment, Northern racism, the allure of urban vice, and impending destitution. Enslavement, not emancipation, guaranteed Robin an inestimably better life.[36]

The slaveholders' concern, however, extended far beyond the slave's comparative well-being. In addition, they insisted, the truly overwhelming problem was not about black people at all. Instead, the issue was the ever more wretched condition of the North's *white* working class. In the end, whiteness trumped all else, and the grim conditions slaveholders described as the lot of white workers in the North, though overdrawn, were far too often correct. The perverse purpose to which they put this insight, however, was to fortify their defenses of slavery, not to champion the cause of oppressed white laborers. To explain: By the 1820's, industrialization had begun making a visible impact in major northern cities as small-scale artisan manufacture gave way to factory labor and neighborhoods increasingly segregated day-to-day wage workers from an emerging middle class. By the 1850's, as *Uncle Tom's Cabin* piled up record sales, a flood of Irish immigrants provided a huge new source of unskilled labor, ethnic tension, class conflict, unemployment, crime, and impoverishment. Meantime,

---

[35] J. W. Page, *Uncle Robin, in His Cabin in Virginia, and Tom, without One in Boston* (Richmond, VA: J.W. Randolph, 1852), https://babel.hathitrust.org/cgi/pt?id=miun.abx8 680.0001.001;view=1up;seq=5.

[36] For a sophisticated exponent of this line of argument, see George Fitzhugh, *Cannibals All or Slaves without Masters*, C. Vann Woodward, ed. (Cambridge, MA: Belknap Press of Harvard University, 1988).

in England, the excruciating human consequences of rapid industrialization had grown into a grim international scandal. Working class activists on both sides of the Atlantic bitterly condemned their situation as "wage slavery," a charge to which abolitionist luminary William Lloyd Garrison once cavalierly replied, "They go in rags, it is true. Still, they have their freedom." For many abolitionists, but certainly not all, that "poverty is not slavery" was axiomatic, leading those who so believed to studied indifference to the suffering of industrial workers.[37]

This gaping moral blind spot gave slaveholders the easiest of opportunities to defend slavery by changing the subject. In addition to accusing them of promoting slave insurrection, race mixing, disunion, and moral infidelity, planters now charged abolitionists with colluding with rapacious Yankee capitalists to crush the white working class while "elevating" the positions of inferior blacks. Secure under his master's tutelage, Uncle Tom meanwhile remained protected from class oppression, happy, and well-fed down on the plantation. It was a line of defense that slavery's most perceptive defenders elaborated so impressively that one of them, John C. Calhoun, earned from historian Richard Hofstadter the sobriquet "the Marx of the master class."[38]

Hofstadter's point is that Calhoun took the ravages of industrialization utterly seriously, much as had Marx. But at the same time, he was changing the subject away from slavery: unlike the author of *Capital*, Calhoun wove this understanding into an attack on abolitionists, not an argument for worker's liberation. His choice, in turn, prompts challenging questions for proponents of sex trade decriminalization and their abolitionist critics.

Indeed, such diversion of attention away from the harm suffered by enslaved people and toward a pragmatic acceptance of the more general reality of inequality (and, indeed, of slavery as fundamental to the human condition and human societies from time immemorial) was widespread across the antebellum era, wielded as a rhetorical weapon against those who would fight for change in specific systems or institutions. In his *Memoir on Slavery* (1838), for instance, South Carolina jurist and politician William Harper dismissed abolitionists' claims that "man has a right to himself, and man cannot have a property in man" by asking, "Is it

[37] Sean Wilentz, *Chants Democratic: New York City and the Rise of the Working Class, 1788–1850* (New York and Oxford: Oxford University Press, 1984).

[38] "John C. Calhoun: The Marx of the Master Class," in Richard Hofstadter, *The American Political Tradition and the Men Who Made It* (New York: Random House, 1948), 69–92.

not palpably nearer the truth to say that no man was ever born free, and that no two men were ever born equal?"[39] He continues: "So when the greatest progress in civil liberty has been made, the enlightened lover of liberty will know that there must remain much inequality, much injustice, much *Slavery*, which no human wisdom or virtue will ever be able wholly to prevent or redress."[40]

At the time, such language was couched in racist biological terms that depended upon natural law to render the suffering of some people morally permissible. For instance, regarding abolitionist claims of the suffering of enslaved people, Harper asked, "How are we to weigh the pains and enjoyments of one man highly cultivated and of great sens-ibility, against those of many men of blunter capacity for enjoyment or suffering?" (90). Interestingly, Harper mobilizes the category of the indi-vidual, with its ideological apparatus of inherent rights and freedoms, to stand for the racist scientific "fact" of white men's greater capacity to feel pain by comparison with black men, here reduced to an undifferen-tiated mass whose ability to feel pleasure or to suffer is, by virtue of their race, intrinsically "blunted" (this argument was also used to reinforce the myth of the merry slave, discussed above). In the twenty-first century, such racist justifications for an unjust, unequal quotidian have given way to an acceptance of a similarly inequitable status quo in the context of neoliberal global capitalism – this time, impacting both gendered and racialized subjects.

For example, Corvid's rhetorical displacement of suffering from the specific problem of "sex trafficking" to the more general "oppression," above, is solidified when she claims that the "myth" of sex trafficking not only does not aid the general struggle against oppression, but actually impedes it by "obscure[ing] the fact that many types of workers, from caterers to builders, suffer force, violence and exploitation." A common complaint of sex worker rights advocates is, indeed, that anti-trafficking advocates pay far more attention to sex trafficking because of their prurient moral imperialism and the sensationalized marketability of the "myth" of the trafficking victim, ignoring the arguably larger population of persons trafficked not for sex but for labor – a much less, well, *sexy* cause around which to raise funds (NGOs) or garner attention (media). A legitimate argument in and of itself, when it is coupled with a defense of the right of some to engage in sex work, it echoes the common red

[39] William Harper, "Memoir on Slavery," in Faust, ed., *Ideology of Slavery*, 83.
[40] Ibid., 85.

herring employed by proslavery ideologues in the era leading up to the Civil War: that Northern abolitionists had no right to address the ills of Southern plantation slavery when workers in Northern US states and in Europe were so poorly treated.

Consider the argument made by US Representative, Governor of South Carolina, and plantation owner James Henry Hammond in his "Letter to an English Abolitionist" (addressed to British abolitionist Thomas Clarkson, 1845): "When you look around you, how dare you talk to us before the world of Slavery? For the condition of your wretched laborers, you, and every Briton who is not one of them, are responsible before God and man. If you are really humane, philanthropic, and charitable, here are objects for you. Relieve them. Emancipate them. Raise them from the condition of brutes, to the level of human beings – of American slaves, at least."[41] Such an approach does not explicitly dismiss claims of the suffering of enslaved people, but rather diverts attention from them by articulating outrage at the "moralists'" *lack of attention* to other forms of suffering, which may or may not implicate the moralists themselves in their perpetration – just as today, anti-trafficking and sex worker rights advocates alike are surely implicated for their participation in a neoliberal economy rife with slave and bonded labor – and worse, for their potential exploitation of that neoliberal economy by fundraising on the backs of "trafficked girls and women."[42] Easier to point fingers at the horrors of sex trafficking than to identify one's own participation in a fundamentally exploitative economy and political program.

In a similar vein, while Ronald Weitzer, prolific scholar of the commercial sex industry, acknowledges that that industry, especially the part that involves transporting people across borders, is not restricted to voluntary sex workers, his argument accepts debt bondage as a condition of everyday labor migration, a kind of status quo that again, elides a world's worth of violence and unfreedom in the process: "It would be mistaken to assume that coercion and deception are myths or that facilitators are necessarily benign agents even when they employ no force or fraud. Some women do not understand the terms of the contract or fully appreciate the impact of debt bondage or how difficult it can be to pay off the debt. Some facilitators alter the terms of the agreement after transit or renege

---

[41] James Henry Hammond, *Governor Hammond's Letters on Slavery Addressed to Thomas Clarkson* (Charleston, SC: Walter & Burke Printers, 1845), 18.

[42] See n. 11 for more on critiques of fundraising by anti-trafficking organizations.

on specific promises."[43] In this statement, Weitzer replaces "traffickers" with "facilitators," a euphemism that connotes help, assistance, promotion, ease, and guidance, and advances as legitimate, even *normative*, the devastating human rights violation that is debt bondage. Orlando Patterson, one of the leading experts on slavery past and present, calls modern forms of debt bondage "neo-bondage," and follows Basile and Mukhopadhyay in articulating that, "While bondage in pre-capitalist economy is a form of interpersonal and permanent link, 'neo-bondage' refers to a form of 'less personalized, more contractual and monetised' bondage that does not provide, as in the past, 'protection' and a 'subsistence guarantee' to bonded workers." Instead, it is "rooted in the asymmetry of power relations between capital and labour" resulting in "a form that is intermediate between the autonomous commoditization of wage labour and the heteronomous commoditization of slavery."[44] A generous reading of Weitzer would identify a deep pragmatism in his acceptance of debt bondage as a condition less worthy of note in his writings than the putative harm done to voluntary sex workers by the socially constructed "myth" of trafficking. A less charitable reading would discern the rhetorical violence that DeLauretis recognizes as irrevocably implicated in the material violence of gender oppression, delivered via the state of denial theorized by Cohen.

Further euphemisms related to participation (rather than coercion) in the neoliberal market abound in Weitzer's article. In one instance, Weitzer addresses the distinction between sex work and trafficking as follows: "[P]rostitution and trafficking differ substantively; the former is a type of work, and the latter is a means of accessing a new market."[45] Unpacking the rhetorical maneuver here takes some doing. Weitzer negates the claim that the differences between "sex work" and trafficking are "substantive" when he defines one (sex work) as *work*, and one as a seemingly voluntary attempt to gain employment (the euphemism "accessing a new market"). While he does not identify the agent who accesses the "new market" (presumably by crossing borders with a "facilitator"), the reader must assume that he means the "migrant" or trafficked person, the (statistically likely) woman who can now "access" the new

---

[43] Ronald Weitzer, "The Social Construction of Sex Trafficking: Ideology and Institutionalization of a Moral Crusade," *Politics and Society* 35, no. 3 (2007), 455.

[44] Orlando Patterson, "Trafficking, Gender, and Slavery: Past and Present," in *Legal Parameters of Slavery: Historical to Contemporary* (Harvard Law School: The Houston Institute, 2011), 4–5.

[45] Weitzer, "The Social Construction of Sex Trafficking," 455.

market that will commoditize her body and person. It is either a stunning naiveté or a willed ignorance cultivated by a misplaced postmodern theoretical stance that renders the "trafficked woman" such a slippery signifier. Weitzer's argument requires a corrective note indicating that the most likely agent capable of "accessing new markets" in the trafficking scenario is *the trafficker* him or herself, by selling the commodity of the trafficked person.

In another instance, Weitzer claims that, "Internationally, it is clear that sex trafficking has increased in some parts of the world, especially from the former Soviet Union and Eastern Europe. The breakup of the Soviet empire and declining living standards for many of its inhabitants has made such migration both much easier and more compelling than in the past."[46] Conceding that "sex trafficking has increased in some parts of the world," Weitzer replaces "sex trafficking" with "migration" (and the adjective "such" modifying "migration" cements its reference to "sex trafficking" in the first part of the sentence), arguing that it is now "easier" (which resonates with the term "facilitator" as euphemism for "trafficker") and "more compelling" than in the past. The literature on sex trafficking from the former Soviet republics and Eastern Europe to destinations all over the world is vast and wide; indeed, the term "Natasha" has been coined to capture the prevalence of women from these regions in the global sex industry.[47] Given the devastated economies of these regions in the post-Soviet era, many women are indeed in desperate straits, and many accept offers for employment or marriage opportunities abroad in an attempt to survive. These may be the women Weitzer describes as being "surprised" by the conditions of the contracts they have entered into: some surely are aware that sex work is part of the bargain, but many surely are not. The construction of "migration" from these republics as easier and more compelling (than during the Iron Curtain Soviet era?) gives the lie to the deep complexity and deeper material impacts of this phenomenon. More importantly for our purposes, "more compelling" implies that being trafficked is somehow "desirable," although not insignificantly, the verb "compel" means to constrain; to force. It's just that for Weitzer, the force implied is the gravitational pull of attraction to "new markets" for "migrant" women, as opposed to the force of the trafficker, or push factors such as poverty and lack of opportunity, "compelling" a woman into the commercial sex trade.

---

[46] Ibid., 456.
[47] Victor Malarek, *The Natashas: Inside the New Global Sex Trade* (New York: Arcade Publishing, 2014).

Ultimately, applying deconstruction as a theoretical framework for the case of trafficking, or any such grave violation of human rights, is problematic not only for the way its discursive machinations enable the material violence of the trafficking scenario, but also because such arguments often call for precisely the kind of concrete empirical analysis – albeit in service of different ends – that they decry from others. Weitzer offers a case in point:

> Any discussion [of policy in relation to trafficking] must take into account differences between types of prostitution. In other words, policies should be sector-specific. Some workers, concentrated in the upscale echelon (call girls, escorts), are not interested in leaving the trade, and their biggest concern is being arrested. Other workers, both internationally and domestically, whether trafficked or not, want to leave the sex industry, yet resources to facilitate exit are woefully lacking ... Interventions focused on persons who are unequivocally victims and perpetrators of coercive trafficking (involving force and fraud) would be a superior strategy to the undifferentiated and often counterproductive practices of many faith-based rescue organizations, whose practices are driven by this moral crusade's broad goal of abolishing the entire sex industry worldwide.[48]

Aside from the lack of recognition of economic and racial privilege on the continuum that starts with the "upscale echelon" of call girls and escorts who just want to avoid getting arrested, and ends with the trafficked, often underage girl trapped in a brothel, how does Weitzer's call to organizations to focus on "persons who are *unequivocally* victims and perpetrators of coercive trafficking (involving force and fraud)" (emphasis added) square with his emphasis upon the constructed nature of the trafficking "myth"? If his claims about the complexity and nuance, the difficulty of identifying "true" trafficking victims as opposed to migrants asserting varying degrees of agency and consent, are to be taken seriously, how then must we read the call for such "unequivocal" knowledge in his recommendation for policy change? There is certainly nothing constructivist in Weitzer's warrant that victims and perpetrators can be identified and differentiated with certainty, or that policy could be made to match such identification once it has been made. And the danger of a properly constructivist approach – that is, of a refusal to engage in a search for empirical facts in favor of an analysis of power relations at play in constructing the trafficking scenario – is that unless one wants quite simply to replace a focus on the rights of trafficked persons with a

---

[48] Weitzer, "The Social Construction of Sex Trafficking," 468.

focus on the rights of sex workers, then one *cannot not* look for the distinction between the two.

TOWARD A HUMAN RIGHTS-CENTERED APPROACH
TO THE COMMERCIAL SEX INDUSTRY

A more productive approach utilizes both tools: a deconstructive analysis of the ways in which representations of the trafficking scenario reflect ideological power relations *and* a search for facts upon which policy and action can be grounded to protect the rights of both trafficked people *and* voluntary sex workers (who may or may not also be migrants). An example of this approach can be found in Dina Francesca Haynes's analysis of the implementation of the Palermo Protocol and its Trafficking Victim Protection Act (TVPA) (2000). Her title –"(Not) Found Chained to a Bed in a Brothel: Conceptual, Legal, and Procedural Failures of the Trafficking Victim Protection Act" – reveals her awareness and critique of the dominant narrative of the innocent trafficking victim enslaved in a brothel, but not in the service of drawing attention and resources away from that scenario, or denying that it does in fact exist, but rather in order to better assist a range of trafficking victims and migrants by showing how law enforcement and government officials can be negatively conditioned by that dominant narrative to identify a victim of trafficking *only* if her story follows the same plotline. Haynes's article seeks to strengthen the application of the Trafficking Victims Protection Act; as she notes in her abstract, "The article presents an alternate view of trafficking, which involves reframing the trafficking issue through the lens of migration, and which would require US government personnel to approach trafficking with the understanding that being victimized by traffickers and yet still demonstrating personal agency are not only not mutually exclusive, but tantamount to surviving the crime."[49] Rather than deploying her analysis to show how the narrative identified by Doezema, Weitzer, and others disadvantages migrant/sex workers in the unhealthy debate between sex worker rights and anti-trafficking advocates, thereby reifying the distinction between the two, Haynes instead acknowledges the pervasiveness of the dominant narrative of innocent victimhood in relation to the trafficking scenario, but does so as part of a larger argument about how it

---

[49] Dina Francesca Haynes. "(Not) Found Chained to a Bed in a Brothel: Conceptual, Legal, and Procedural Failures to Fulfill the Promise of the Trafficking Victims Protection Act," *Georgetown Immigration Law Journal* 21 (2007), 337.

reduces the ability to "fulfill the promise" of the TVPA. The TVPA stands as a kind of empirical ground for the framework of rights applied to the problem of trafficking, and Haynes builds upon that empirical ground, taking as a desirable "good" the fact that an international and national US legal framework exists for addressing this crime, and utilizing her critique of the narrative in service of strengthening this "good." In this way, Haynes supports the rights of migrant/sex workers (by "set[ting] forth the ways in which the root causes of trafficking have been obscured, in service to a preferred focus on sex and victimhood") while also seeking to strengthen the application of the TVPA and to facilitate a "hardnosed and honest look at the problem of causation in trafficking."[50]

Equally important to the existing legislation, asserts Haynes, are efforts to cultivate a human rights-based approach to trafficking and migration. At their best, such approaches take a longer view of the problem: less a matter of strengthening state borders and security than understanding the economic and social conditions that contribute to trafficking, improving social services to at-risk communities, increasing access to essential documents such as birth certificates, creating a missing persons database, and improving coordination between government and NGO groups that address trafficking at different stages and through medical, legal, and social areas of concern that extend beyond the moment of "rescue."

And this brings us back to the debate between anti-trafficking and sex worker rights advocates, respectively. To what degree are the proponents of sex work genuinely concerned that their abolitionist critics direct their attention to larger problems of poverty, statelessness, governmental surveillance, and human rights? To what degree, conversely, do they emulate proslavery arguments by shifting the subject away from slavery in order to assert and protect a position in the capitalist marketplace? To what extent, to offer a third alternative, might such a shift in focus suggest points of agreement between advocates of decriminalization and their abolitionist critics? Might seriously engaged abolitionists, immune to moral panic, be wise to welcome challenges that test them for moral and ethical blindness? Are there not already seriously engaged abolitionists who critique mightily the sensationalized (and often salacious narrative) of sex slavery with its emphasis upon "innocent victims" as destructive and exploitative, rather than as helpful to the cause of ending the trafficking of humans for commercial sex? Might not advocates of legalization and decriminalization welcome these same rhetorical and representational

[50] Ibid., 337.

challenges, particularly since many of their abolitionist critics grant that some sex work is, in fact, a freely chosen occupation while also rejecting "moral panic abolitionism"? In the end, might not the proper questions be, do abolitionists and advocates of decriminalization actually share significant social and political concerns? Or are the two groups forever at loggerheads because denying slavery, like defending slavery, finally boils down to tending to one's self-interest?

We conclude our argument with a vigorous plea to identify shared terrain from which to address the significant social and political concerns attending evolving global markets for commercial sex.

10

The Power of the Past in the Present

The Capital of the Confederacy as an Antislavery City

Monti Narayan Datta and James Brewer Stewart

MAYHEM OVER MONUMENTS

Sad to see the history and culture of our great country being ripped apart by the removal of our beautiful statues and monuments. You can't change history but you can learn from it. Robert E. Lee, Stonewall Jackson, who's next? Washington, Jefferson? So foolish! Also the beauty that is being taken out of our cities, towns and parks will be greatly missed and never able to be comparably replaced.

> President Donald J. Trump's August 8, 2017 Twitter response to the growing demand by black activists and their white supporters for the removal of memorial statues of Confederate military figures and political leaders

Our sitting President expressed the foregoing sentiments four days prior to the murder of Heather Heyer in Charlottesville, Virginia on August 12, 2017, when a car plowed through a crowd protesting a gathering of white nationalists who had marched after sunset across the campus of the University of Virginia, torches alight and faces shrouded, chanting racist and anti-Semitic slogans. They claimed that they were defending the "sacred honor" of the Confederacy and celebrating the heroic leadership of its glorious "lost cause." Their immediate objection was to the city government's decision to remove an equestrian statue of Robert E. Lee from a prominent public space. Their fundamental complaint, however, was against the city council's conviction that such statues deserved removal because, instead of memorializing high moral purpose, they actually symbolize traitorous secessionists who were defending African American enslavement and systems of white racial tyranny. And because such memorials constitute a continuing outrage to African American people and to all those who abhor the history and legacies of slavery, and symbolize the widespread complicity that affects so much of today's political culture.

But when complaining about "the beauty being taken out of our cites," the President likely had little appreciation of the enormity he faced. *The New York Times* reported on August 18, 2017 that there are (or once were) perhaps a thousand statues, markers, and memorials to the Confederacy located in public spaces across the nation, and that in dozens of towns and cities in the North as well as the South they have either been taken down or were ripe targets for removal, sometimes voluntarily, sometimes through legislation, sometimes after peaceful demonstrating, sometimes from disfiguration by those critics called "vandals," and sometimes in the face of hostile "neo-Confederates," police barricades, tear gas, and batons. A partial list of cities witnessing such activism as of late August 2017 included:

Charlottesville, VA (Statues of Robert E. Lee and Jefferson Davis draped with plastic sheeting as debates about their future continue), **Annapolis, MD** (Proslavery jurist Roger B. Taney statue removed), **Austin TX** (Generals Robert E. Lee and Albert Sidney Johnson removed from the University of Texas campus), **Baltimore, MD** (Four monuments to the era of the Confederacy removed), **Brooklyn, NY** (two plaques honoring Robert E. Lee removed), **Durham, NC** (One Confederate soldier statue pulled down by demonstrators, a Robert E. Lee statue removed from the Duke University chapel), **Gainesville, FL** (Monument to Confederate soldiers removed), **New Orleans, LA** (Four Confederate monuments removed by city government), **Boston, MA** (Confederate memorial statue removed from Georges Island, Boston Harbor), **Jacksonville, FL** (Proposal pending to remove four Confederate monuments), **Lexington, KY** (City council approved removal of two Confederate statues), **Memphis, TN** (Statue of General Nathan Bedford Forrest proposed for removal by city council), **San Antonio, TX** (Proposal to relocate statues memorializing Confederate soldiers), **Nashville, TN** (Governor recommended removal from the capital of a statue honoring General Nathan Bedford), **Tampa, FL** (Monument to be removed if paid for by private money. The City's three major sports teams have volunteered to contribute), **The Bronx, NY** (Bronx Community College removed busts of Stonewall Jackson and Robert E. Lee from its Hall of Fame for Great Americans), **Washington, DC** (Democratic Party leaders introduce a bill to remove a dozen statues and busts in the National Statuary Hall), **Birmingham, AL** (Memorial to Confederate soldiers and sailors covered by a wooden crate in order to evade state laws against removal).

Other completed removals include: **Elliot City, MD; Franklin, OH; Los Angeles, CA; Louisville, KY; Orlando, FL; San Diego, CA; St Louis, MO; St Petersburg, FL; Daytona Beach, FL; Frederick, MD; Helena, MT; Madison, WI; Rockville, MD; Worthington, OH.**

Additional proposed removals include: **Chapel Hill, NC; Kansas City, MO; Portsmouth, VA; Alexandria, VA; Dallas, TX; Frankfort, KY; Pensacola, FL; and Seattle, WA.**[1]

The long-term significance of this burgeoning activism cannot be predicted, and such is not our goal. Instead, the purpose of this essay is to demonstrate how deep historical knowledge and understanding of the African American past enriches our power to resist and ultimately to undermine what these monuments to the Confederacy perpetuate, that is, myths about skin color and false suppositions about the antebellum South that have dire consequences for today's African American people – trauma, privation, marginalization, surveillance, and mass incarceration. We also contend that this same deep past-mindedness is vital for combating the scourge of slavery as we encounter today our very own moral equivalent of the old plantation system – the buying and selling of human beings for sex and for manual labor. The same statues that urge us to venerate slavery and defend the Confederacy – to excuse racism and to evade the brutal realities of African American bondage – render us silent in the face of the slavery practiced throughout our nation today in which human beings (the great preponderance immigrants of color, young people, and American citizens of color) are enslaved for sex and for work in America's restaurants, factories, fields, and households.[2] In short, we insist that overcoming the pernicious legacies of pre-Civil War slavery as embodied in the Confederate statuary and combating human bondage as practiced today are, together, a single, enormous problem. Historical knowledge and perspective, deeply grounded and equitably applied, can do much, we believe, to shrink this otherwise outsized challenge to human-sized proportions.

In support of these conclusions, our essay focuses on the City of Richmond, the former Capital of the Confederacy and, as of this writing, site of one of the deepest divisions over Confederate statuary and the meaning of antebellum slavery as can be found in the South today. The city, like others in the United States, is also site of forced labor in the form of sex trafficking and other hidden forms of modern slavery, including domestic servitude. Disagreements over the legacies

---

[1] "Confederate Monuments are Coming Down Across the United States. Here's a Full List," *The New York Times*, August 18, 2017, www.nytimes.com/interactive/2017/08/16/us/confederate-monuments-removed.html.

[2] See, for example, Alex Tizon, "My Family's Slave," www.theatlantic.com/magazine/archive/2017/06/lolas-story/524490, and Benjamin Skinner, *A Crime So Monstrous: Face to Face with Modern Day Slavery.*

of the "old" slavery coexist uneasily with deepening concerns about the causes and implications of the "new." Our essay's mission, given these circumstances, is to build a case for how increased historical literacy can support the remaking of the Capital of the Confederacy as an antislavery city, and through this example to suggest, even encourage, other such investigations and considerations in other urban locations

THE CHALLENGE OF 2017 RICHMOND

Richmond, predictably, is replete with compelling landmarks that commemorate its proslavery past. Since the 1960s, however, as will be discussed further, the city has developed impressive museums and other educational sites that present this history contextually, multiracially, and via multiple conflicting perspectives. Despite these gains the fact remains that one of the city's most famous, frequently visited tourist attractions, Monument Avenue, features a wide, verdant boulevard dominated by three enormous statues of Jefferson Davis (Figure 8), Robert E. Lee (67 feet in height), and Stonewall Jackson. Long before the Charlottesville explosion, these outsized representations of Confederate leadership had fomented bitter conflict between African American activists, neo-Confederates, and a city government committed to raising revenue by preserving civility, attracting investment, and generating new development projects. As of this writing, however, in the aftermath of the Charlottesville disaster, that conflict, ever more heated, prompted Richmond Mayor Levar Stoney to end his support for maintaining the status quo, calling for the statues' removal and remarking, "I wish they had never been built."[3] What to do next, however, if anything, is up to a divided city council in response to recommendations of a Citizens Advisory Committee. In late August 2017, the city was at an impasse. The question this essay addresses is how might historical understanding have been helpful to the city in moving beyond it?

The answer, we submit, is to offer an account of Richmond's slavery-entangled, racially divisive past which is more comprehensive, historically grounded, and supportive of social justice than the version usually absorbed by most of its white citizens, that is, the narrative of the "lost cause." The task of one co-author of this essay, historian James Brewer

---

[3] Daniella Silva, "Richmond Could Be Next Confederate Monument Battleground," *NBC News*, August 20, 2017, www.nbcnews.com/news/us-news/richmond-could-be-next-confederate-monument-battleground-n793741.

Stewart, is to counter these distorted views with a history more faithful to Richmond's past and more pertinent to its current struggles for social justices. A second objective, closely related, is to build on this revised history with proposals for public policies that combat enslavement as practiced today and the legacies of the original slavery that help to sustain it – structural racism and economic marginalization. This task is taken up by the article's other co-author, Monti Narayan Datta, a political scientist. Only after the city embraces a well-informed understanding of its past and begins acting on what that understanding reveals will Richmond be prepared to diminish its divisions between races and classes and direct itself toward a more democratic future.

HISTORY UP FOR GRABS

Casual walking tours of Richmond can lead to jolting encounters with conflicting views of the past. Take a stroll past those enormous statues that dominate the grassy boulevard of Monument Avenue, bordered by mansions that exude turn-of-the-twentieth-century opulence (Figures 6–8). In the late 1890s and early 1900s, Virginia's Daughters of the Confederacy bankrolled the construction of these colossal evocations of slavery's pre-eminent defenders as part of their ambitious programs to memorialize the "Lost Cause." At just that same time (no accident, as these "Southern ladies" understood), Virginia's state government was advancing new regimes of racial segregation, black exploitation, and racial terrorism – a bitter history with which Richmond's African American citizens are all too familiar.[4] How many white citizens, one wonders – or perhaps better, how few – appreciate the majority of African Americans' perspective that these statues symbolize white supremacist propaganda, not reverential memorials? How many instead respond to the nostalgia of the "lost cause"?

Continue strolling the Avenue, encounter one last statue, and racial provocation multiplies. Furthest from downtown and facing away from it, well apart from its Confederate counterparts, is a much smaller statue of local black hero and tennis champion Arthur Ashe, designed by an acclaimed local sculptor and installed in 1996 (Figure 9). Reflecting an undeniably post-civil rights sensibility, Ashe's statute stands in stark contrast to the outsized Confederate equestrians as he is presented as

---

[4] Sarah Shield Diggs, Richard Guy Wilson, and Robert Winthrop, *Richmond's Monument Avenue* (Chapel Hill, NC: University of North Carolina Press, 2001).

FIGURE 6 Stonewall Jackson. Getty Images, 165663481.

a life-sized figure, standing on his own two feet, holding a book and a tennis racket while the children clustered below, with faces alight, reach up to him.

Disquieting questions arise. Is this statue an ironic dissent against the triumphal pretentiousness of the Confederate memorials? Might it offer a tragic reflection of the power of white supremacy? Might it represent Ashe's and the children's uncompromised humanity shining forth against the Confederate statues? Might it register a spirit of racial submission that militants demanding equality find offensive?[5] Who knows? All that's clear is that every possible meaning of Arthur Ashe's statue amounts to a rejection of the Confederates as heroes, the monuments memorializing them as such, and the partial view of history they represent. For good or ill, up and down Monument Avenue the disruptive power of a racialized past is incontestable. How best to unpack such an entrenched and volatile a problem? Accurate, reliable history, accessibly presented, we believe, offers answers. As the following summaries of newspaper stories documenting only two months of racial contention in the city

[5] "Race Furor Stalls Arthur Ashe Memorial," *The New York Times*, July 9, 1995, www.nytimes.com/1995/07/09/us/race-tinged-furor-stalls-arthur-ashe-memorial.html.

FIGURE 7 J. E. B. Stuart. Getty Images, 672154111.

make clear, such answers are sorely needed if social justice is to advance in Richmond.

When reading these summaries, note references to a locale referred to as Shockoe Bottom – the racially mixed and ethnically varied center of industry and commerce in Richmond before and after the Civil War. Also note an African American-led activist organization named the Defenders for Freedom, Justice and Equality (DFJE), a group "working for the survival of our community through educational and social justice activities." Acting on "the imperative that contemporary Black Richmonders understand their history as integral contributors to the city's development and as slavery resistance fighters and self-emancipators," the DFJE, in 2004, launched its Sacred Ground Historical Reclamation Project, and more recently facilitated a community-centered process to craft a plan to develop a Memorial Park in Shockoe Bottom that would honor, protect, and present the African American past about "the unique history of Richmond from the 1690s through the Civil War." The date of the DFJE's

FIGURE 8 Jefferson Davis. Getty Images, 93477308.

emergence, 2004, is a blunt reminder that African American struggles to erase racism from urban landscapes hardly began in 2017 with the confrontations in Charlottesville and elsewhere. They were no passing fad, but instead, as the examples below will confirm, well-tested tactics deployed in a much more deeply rooted historical struggle.

June 25, 2015

"The VA [Virginia] Flaggers have announced a $1,500 reward for information that leads to the arrest and conviction of the vandal who painted 'BLACK LIVES MATTER' on the Jefferson Davis monument … The vandalism came following a petition to remove the statues from Monument Avenue after the fatal shooting of nine African Americans at a church in Columbia South Carolina." The web page of the VA Flaggers carries these slogans: "Return the [Confederate] Flags – Restore the Honor – Rise Up Southerner! This Is Our Hour!" Richmond's Mayor, Dwight Jones, U.S Senator Mark Warner, and Governor Terry McAuliffe publicly reject the removal petition (Figure 10).

July 4, 2015

Headline: "Richmond Split over Confederate History: In the Capital of the Confederacy Calls are Rising to Properly Memorialize the Slave Trade." Following is a lengthy article that reprints photos of the Monument Avenue statues and then describes what has befallen historic sites that document Richmond and slavery. What was once Lumpkin's Slave Jail, where tens of

FIGURE 9 Arthur Ashe. Getty Images, 95512631.

thousands of enslaved people were sold and driven in chains into the Deep South, is now buried fourteen feet below a grassy lawn surrounded by asphalt. Shockoe Bottom, the site of a significant African American burial ground, a gallows from which innumerable blacks and whites were hanged, and much else of rare historical import has been covered by a parking lot. A site immediately adjacent, equally historical, has been proposed as a site for a baseball stadium and shopping complex. An organization of historical preservationists, the Defenders for Freedom, Justice and Equality, has proposed a comprehensive Memorial Park for Shockoe Bottom that the city refuses to support.

September 14, 2015

The Defenders for Freedom, Justice and Equality rally at the foot of the Jefferson Davis monument to protest plans by Union Cycliste Internationale to use the statue as the half-way turning point for its Road World Championship

FIGURE 10 "Black Lives Matter" spray painted on a monument to Jefferson Davis. Associated Press/Steve Helber.

Bicycle race. Said Ana Edwards, Chair of the Defenders Sacred Ground Historical Reclamation Project, "At a time when cities across the South are removing these symbols of oppression of black people, it is an embarrassment that our city, the former capital of the Confederacy, would choose to highlight these statues to a world audience."

September 21, 2015

A pro-Confederate veterans group responded to a protest held on Monument Avenue by the Defenders for Freedom and Equality and Black Lives Matter by arranging a plane to fly overhead carrying a banner reading CONFEDERATE HEROS (sic) MATTER. The plane circled during the entire demonstration with the misspelled slogan.

And so forth.[6]

Finally, add to this review the image of President Barack Obama reproduced in Figure 12. For close to a year it covered two stories of an exterior wall of a strip club located nearby Richmond's black

---

[6] For the June 25, 2015 controversy over the Ashe statue see *The New York Times*, July 9, 1996, www.nytimes.com/1995/07/09/us/race-tinged-furor-stalls-arthur-ashe-memorial .html. For the neo-Confederate banner protest see the Michael Martz and Graham Moomaw, "Confederate Flag Is Flown over Protests of Rebels' Monument," *Richmond Times-Dispatch*, September 21, 2015, www.richmond.com/news/local/city-of-richmond/ article_9f6b0ece-9f28-5917-ba48-0e73f501dd5a.html.

(A)

(B)

FIGURE 11A AND 11B Memorial Park proposal to protect and preserve Shockoe Bottom. Courtesy of Ana Edwards, Sacred Ground Historical Reclamation Project.

neighborhoods. The strip club itself remains a controversial site for its past links to prostitution.[7] Taken in total, this tableau – the neighborhood, the banner, and the strip club – captures some of the most controversial

---

[7] Michael Martz, "Club Velvet Events Lead to Owner's Arrest," *Richmond Times-Dispatch*, February 26, 2008, www.richmond.com/news/club-velvet-events-lead-to-owner-s-arrest/article_85e6a67f-8fc9-517e-9431-adf5c4f063e2.html.

FIGURE 12 Barack Obama "Socialist Joker" poster. Courtesy of Phil Wilayto, editor, *The Virginia Defender*.

impacts of historical memory in Richmond today, a mixture of historically rooted racism with the fact that within the city and surrounding it, human exploitation persists.[8]

As already noted, Richmond's museums, particularly its American Civil War Museum, have helped educate and inform the public, making their exhibits more racially inclusive and emphasizing the fundamental importance of the African American past. In addition, the Black History Museum and Cultural Center of Virginia, founded in 1981, has made

[8] Philip Kennicott, "Impact of 'Socialist Joker' Obama Image," *Washington Post*, August 6, 2009, www.washingtonpost.com/wp-dyn/content/discussion/2009/08/05/DI2009080503252.html.

itself into a center for sustained engagement with Richmond's African American heritage. But as our news synopsis and the images accompanying it illuminate, museum exhibits, no matter how artful and inclusive, struggle to diminish the power of deep-seated historical memories shot full with racism and erroneous notions regarding the "lost cause."[9]

HISTORY HARNESSED

So what kind of history might accomplish this? That would be an account of African Americans' experience more complete and grounded than the history normally offered Richmond's citizens today. Despite all it reveals about the depth of white supremacy, this history is also one in which all Richmonders can take pride because it documents interracial collaboration and accomplishment even within the larger context of black/white estrangement.[10] It begins in the 1820s, with the evolution of slavery in the city of Richmond and slavery in the southern countryside into two contrasting systems. That difference opened for Richmond's African Americans more possibilities to shape their own lives than those laboring in the countryside. In pre-Civil War Richmond, African Americans faced a city built upon their exploitation, but also a city which provided them opportunities to develop resilience and to resist enslavement, build occupational skills, form viable communities, maintain an informal economy, organize secret societies, and create sustainable institutions. After Emancipation, these accomplishments prepared Richmond's black citizens to lead struggles that extended to the end of the nineteenth century, re-emerged in the civil rights years, and endure in Richmond today. It is a history rich with precedents for opposing injustice today and for

---

[9] For the American Civil War Museum's African American exhibits, see https://acwm .org/collection and for the Black History Museum and Cultural Center, see http:// blackhistorymuseum.org/.

[10] For detailed treatments of Richmond's history of racial struggle prior to the twentieth century see Benjamin Campbell, *Richmond's Unhealed History* (Richmond, VA: Brandylane Publishers, 2012); Jake Trammell, *The Richmond Slave Trade: The Economic Backbone of the Old Dominion* (Charleston, SC: The History Press, 2012); Midori Takagi, *"Rearing Wolves of Our Own Destruction": Slavery in Richmond, 1782–1865* (Charlottesville, VA: University Press of Virginia, 1999); Mary Tyler McGraw and Greg D. Kimball, *In Bondage and Freedom: Antebellum Black Life in Richmond* (Chapel Hill, NC: University of North Carolina Press, 1988); Peter Rachleff, *Black Richmond and the Knights of Labor in Richmond* (Champaign-Urbana, IL: University of Illinois Press, 1989); Charles Dew, *Iron Maker to the Confederacy: Joseph R. Anderson and the Tredegar Iron Works* (New Haven, CT: Yale University Press, 1966).

balancing the presence of Monument Avenue with a landscape featuring a park that memorializes Richmond's enslaved.

HIRING OUT

Enslaved in Baltimore before escaping North, Frederick Douglass observed, "A city slave is almost a free citizen ... compared to a slave on [a] plantation. He is much better fed and clothed, is less dejected in his appearance, and enjoys privileges altogether unknown to the whip-driven slave on the plantation."[11] Douglass's observation fit Richmond exactly. To be sure, slavery in Richmond paid off for its white citizens. It stimulated growth, spurred economic diversification, generated handsome profits, and transformed the city into the industrial engine that drove the upper South's economy. It also subjected not only the enslaved, but also free blacks in Richmond, to many restrictions reinforced with unvarnished terror, the worst being the prospect of being sold, chained, and whipped into the deep South via the city's intimacy in the interstate slave trade. Yet for all that, the circumstances of the enslaved gave them unusual opportunity to resist their owners' control, exercise a surprisingly wide variety of choices, and, with their free black neighbors, to sustain almost autonomous communities. All this came to pass as a result of profound changes overtaking the Virginia countryside beginning in the early 1800s that transformed Richmond into a unique center of skilled black labor.

In rural Virginia, tobacco always ruled, but at a severe price – soil exhaustion. To address this problem, numerous planters diversified into wheat and corn, products that, like tobacco, required numerous laborers to convert into products for the retail market, but unlike tobacco, entailed much less sustained labor to plant and cultivate. This transformation and the market demanding it came together in Richmond, creating an expanding need for labor – enslaved labor included. Raw tobacco needed manual laborers to clean, boil, dry, press, and flavor it, and then to hand-shape it into plugs and cigars. Wheat and corn production required baggers, cleaners, graders, weighers, and loaders. Spin-offs from these industries created jobs: barrel makers, box makers, textile workers, tool makers, clothiers, and blacksmiths. Building contractors recruited loaders, transporters and carpenters. To move an ever-expanding volume of goods, Richmond increasingly depended on dock workers, cart men, and boatmen. When the city plunged into iron manufacturing in 1837,

[11] Frederick Douglass, *My Bondage and My Freedom* (1855; New York: Penguin, 2003).

the pressure to secure laborers further intensified as canals, rivers, and, finally, railroads connected the city to the ore-rich regions in the north-west parts of the state. As the tightening employment market drove up labor costs, Richmond's employers turned to rural planters by signing contracts to "hire out" their slaves. Those enslaved people, now also leased laborers, became essential to Richmond's economy.[12]

How did Richmond's white employers end up hiring the enslaved? The answer takes us back to soil exhaustion, because as planters decreased their tobacco acreage and shifted to hard grain crops, their need for slave labor sharply declined. Meantime, the enslaved and the white populations kept expanding at identical rates, producing many more bonded laborers than planters could use. What to do with these "surplus" human beings? One alternative offered a quick cash return: Rip them away from their loved ones, dispatch them to Lumpkin's Slave Jail or any other of Richmond's numerous auction houses, and sell them off for purchase in the deep South's cotton belt. In 1850, a single slave-dealing firm, Templeton and Goodwin, netted well over $325,000 in 2015 dollars on the buying and selling of 130 enslaved persons. The second alternative, "hiring out," offered planters steady income by leasing some of their enslaved workers to Richmond employers where they lived beyond their masters' control. To prevent these slaves from escaping, planters kept their family members close at hand. Holding such dear ones hostage to the threat of the interstate slave trade greatly discouraged their "hired out" relatives from fleeing.[13]

Although cruelly manipulative, these tactics opened unique opportunities for "hired out" slaves who took up residence in Richmond. Gone were their days as field hands, household helps, and personal attendants. Now they turned themselves into skilled craftsmen, millers, blacksmiths, coopers, tailors, boat men, carpenters, and specialized iron workers. Those less skilled hauled cartage, loaded warehouses, shoveled coal, stacked wood, braided rope, and, of course, processed grain and tobacco. Though these were largely men's jobs, women also found outside employment. But whatever their gender and occupation, Richmond's enslaved moved through its streets at will during off-hours. Slaves lived together far from white surveillance in rigidly segregated quarters in places such as Shockoe Bottom.

---

[12] Takagi, "*Rearing Wolves of Our Own Destruction*," 17–36.

[13] John J. Zaborney, *Slaves for Hire: Renting Enslaved Laborers in Antebellum Virginia* (Baton Rouge, LA: Louisiana State University Press, 2012); Jonathan Martin, *Slave Hiring in the American South* (Cambridge, MA: Harvard University Press, 2004).

But these were only some of the jarring contradictions of urban slavery. In the face of laws that white authorities enforced reluctantly, if at all, those "hired out" circumvented their own enslavement by mingling intimately with Richmond's free blacks. As Midori Takagi's study of Richmond's slave community documents, these two groups were soon worshiping, partying, and creating families together. Together they developed an informal economy that trafficked in stolen property, traded services, bartered food and clothing, and generated cash exchanges involving the earnings both of free black people and of those enslaved.

Richmond's enslaved retained some of the cash paid to others for their labor by getting their masters' permission to choose their own employers and to negotiate the cost of their labor, which frequently included small personal maintenance payments. Some far-removed planters depended on this arrangement to keep their enslaved workers motivated while others saw it as a way to maximize their income. Since short-term labor needs fluctuated constantly, local businesses run by whites also found that these flexible arrangements met their changing requirements. In short, enslaved blacks found themselves able to renegotiate the terms of their bondage with the people who owned them and the people for whom they proposed to work.[14]

By 1860, as Richmond expanded into a major urban center with a population of 37,910, such arrangements had long been routine and were deeply entrenched. Of this number, 23,635 (62 percent) were white, 14,275 (38 percent) were black, most enslaved. In spite of the contradictions, or better perhaps because they stimulated black people's ambitions and rewarded innovation, Richmond became the engine that drove the economy of the upper South. But as the enslaved renegotiated their terms of labor, they came to understand themselves not only as an oppressed race, but also as part of an exploited working class.[15]

Indeed, for all its self-sufficiency, the menace of white supremacy and labor oppression hung heavily over Richmond's enslaved community. The manacled clusters shuffling out of the slave pens and heading south hammered enslaved residents with this truth. Even more so did the gallows close by Shockoe Bottom and its African American cemetery. Hiring out and a busy informal economy did little to buffer the enslaved against grinding privation and violent oppression. No matter how far

[14] Takagi, "*Rearing Wolves to Our Destruction*," 36–70.
[15] Richard D. Wade, *Slavery in the Cities: The South, 1820–1860* (Oxford and New York, 1964), 327, citing the US Census of 1860.

slavery in Richmond varied from plantation norms, it will never do to put a reassuring gloss over its inherent brutality. This understood, however, what black Richmonders accomplished thanks to those variances was truly consequential.[16]

IMPROVISING

Between 1852 and 1857, Richmond authorities decreed that those enslaved were banned from smoking in public, carrying canes (symbols of aggressiveness), preaching on street corners, driving or riding in carriages without their owners' consent, cohabiting with free blacks, hiring themselves out, failing to observe an 11 p.m. curfew, and living unsupervised, apart from their owners and/or employers. Though for reasons already mentioned these measures were quickly made dead-letter, they nicely convey the autonomy achieved by Richmond's blacks and the worries of the whites observing them. Equally revealing is what these prohibitions omitted. No legislation could alter the fact that many of the slaves who negotiated their own contracts had become skilled workers, traded in an informal economy, and had learned to read and write. No injunction could displace the literate leaders of Richmond's many Bible-believing African Americans or suppress the vital services they improvised.[17]

Before the 1840s, whites had admitted blacks to segregated seating in the galleries of their churches so that in 1821, African American Baptists petitioned to start an independent church. Many petitions later, in 1841, authorities relented but insisted upon significant restrictions. The head minister must be white, State law required. A whites-only superintending committee had to oversee the African Americans responsible for day-to-day administration. Stipulations agreed to, the petitioners raised $4,500, much of it donated by three white philanthropists and the balance by Richmond's wealthier free blacks, of whom, in 1860, there were roughly two hundred. Thus Richmond's First African Baptist Church was established, led by white head ministers who allowed the membership notably wide latitude to manage their own affairs.

Day-to-day authority resided heavily with black elected deacons, black standing committees, and assisting black pastors who did much of the preaching. By 1859, church membership had reached upwards

---

[16] Takagi, "*Rearing Wolves to Our Destruction*," 89–95: Trammell, *The Richmond Slave Trade*, 68–79.

[17] Takagi, "*Rearing Wolves to Our Destruction*," 115–17.

of three thousand and a Second and Third Baptist Church had been established. Justice became the specific responsibility of the deacons who were vested with authority to discipline wayward members, adjudicate private disputes of many types, and, most sensitive of all, determine the sanctity of marriages involving the enslaved.[18]

By exercising these judicial functions, the church was supplanting the authority of slaveholders, employers, and city officials. Church-dispensed verdicts were cost free, but far more important, they rendered decisions consistent with the values of the community. Uncowed by white authority, litigants spoke honestly and deacons rendered judgments that reflected justice as blacks themselves defined it. All involved found themselves held accountable to one another, a principle of mutual responsibility that also undergirded the many church-based organizations that black believers developed to the benefit of the larger community. Because city laws prohibited blacks from unauthorized congregating, these organizations did everything possible to guarantee their invisibility to whites.[19] Consequently, very few specifics are known about these secret societies until they revealed themselves in the immediate aftermath of the Civil War. Even less is known about how those escaping to freedom relied on hidden networks improvised by their community. Announcements of rewards for their return, however, littered local newspapers.[20]

Like the deacons' courts and the black churches themselves, these secret societies constituted a vital part of what is best described as antebellum black Richmond's underground government. Over a span of six decades, Richmond's system of slavery had enabled enslaved workers to join with their free counterparts to fashion an informal economy, practice their own politics, build spiritual sanctuaries, and invent their own methods of governance. All this inculcated powerful race pride and allegiance to working-class values. Finally, in 1865, having weathered the traumas of the Civil War, Richmond's newly emancipated black community jettisoned secrecy and presented itself to the nation:

We represent a population ... who have ever been distinguished for their good behavior as slaves and as freemen as well as for their high morals and Christian character; more than 6,000 of our people are members in good standing of Christian churches, and nearly the whole of our population attend divine services ... None of our people are in the almshouse, and when we were slaves the aged and

[18] Ibid., 102–12.
[19] Ibid., 102–12.
[20] Ibid., 106–23.

infirm who were turned away from the homes of hard masters, who had been enriched by their toil, our benevolent societies supported while they lived, and buried when they died ... The law of slavery severely punished those who taught us to read or write, but, notwithstanding this, 3000 of us can read, and at least 2000 can read and write, and a large number of us are engaged in useful and profitable employment on our own account.[21]

This statement closed with a condemnation of "unrepentant Rebels" and their collusion with racist Yankee soldiers then occupying the city. Thus did black Richmonders enter the struggles of the post-Civil War era politically seasoned, and committed to securing equality.

From 1865 to 1890 what had once been an improvised underground government evolved into a political network that drew its strength from a profusion of civic organizations built by black Richmonders throughout this era. The following listing offers a telling glimpse of their scope and variety:

Black Richmond Voluntary Associations (aka "Secret Societies"), 1865–90: Acme Literary Association, Bailey Factory Hands, Baptist Helping Society, Benevolent Daughters of Weeping Mary, Benevolent Daughters of the Young Army Shining, Benevolent Star, Building Aid Society, Cadets of Temperance, Chautauqua Literary and Scientific Circle, Children of Emmanuel, Christian Union Aid Society, Colored Mercantile Society, Combination No.14, Daughters of Elijah, Daughters of the Golden Band, Daughters of the Golden Rod, Daughters of Jerusalem, Daughters of Zion, Eureka Savings Society, Female Soldiers of the Cross, Female Star of Jacob, Friendly Sons of Temperance, Golden Rule Society, Good Samaritans, Grand Fountain United Order of True Redeemers, Humble Christian Benevolents, Independent Order of the Messiah, Knights of King Solomon, Knights Templar, Laborers' Organization Number 55, Liberty Lodge 104, Lincoln Lodge No. 20, Lincoln Mounted Guard, Lincoln Union Shoemakers, Society, Loving Charities Christian Tabernacle, Loving Christian Society, Loving Daughters of the Independent National Blues, Loving Daughters of Ruth, Loving Sons and Daughters of Bethlehem, Loving Sons and Daughters of Revelation, Loving Sons of Galilee, Manchester Band of Hope, Masons, Morning Pilgrims, Mechanics Union Society, Mutual Benevolent Society, National Laboring Club, Odd Fellows, Palmetto Club, Pilgrim Travelers, Railroad Helpers' Society, Richmond Radical Association, Rising Daughters of Liberty, Rising Sons and Daughters of the East, Rising Sons and Daughters of the New Testament, Rising Sons of America, Rising Sons of Elijah, Rising Sons of Liberty, Savings Club, Secret Sons of Love, Sisters of Emmanuel, Soldiers of the Cross, Sons and Daughters of Noah, Sons of the Union, Star Union Daughters, Star Union Sons, Stevedores' Society, Sylvester Evening Star Society, Teamsters Benevolent Society-Star of the East, Travelling Companions, True Laboring Class, Union Aid Society, Union Association of

---

[21] *New York Tribune*, June 17, 1867, quoted in Rachleff, *Black Richmond and the Knights of Labor in Richmond*, 13–14.

Richmond, Union Benevolent Star, Union Bengal Aid, Union Branch of the First District, Union Laboring Branch, Union Laboring Class, Union Liberty Protective Society, United Daughters of Ham, United Daughters of the Holy Temple, United Daughters of Liberty, United Daughters of Love, United Laboring Men's Society of Coalfield, United Sons and Daughters of Love, United Sons of Adam, United Sons of Ham, United Sons of Liberty, Virginia Home Building and Loan Association, Warehouse Combined Industrial Society, Young Brothers of Friendship, Young Home Secret Daughters, Young Female Hope, Young Lambs, Young Men of Liberty, Young Men's Gold Key of Richmond, Young Men's Self Interest, Young Men's Richmond Blues, Young Rising Sons and Daughters of the New Testament, Young Sons and Daughters of the Valley, Young Sons of Jerusalem, Young Twisters Aid of Shiloh

Black Richmond's Participation in Labor Organizations, 1865–90: Amalgamated Association of Iron and Steel Workers, Richmond Lodge No. 2, Amalgamated Association of Iron and Steel Workers, Sumner Lodge No. 3, Bakers Union, Colored National Labor Union, Consolidated Moulders Union, Coopers Union, Grand Lodge of Quarrymen, Hod-Carriers Union, Industrial Brotherhood Industrial Congress, Knights of Labor, Lincoln Union of Shoemakers, National Labor Union, Stevedores' Society, Tobacco Laborers Association, New Light Lodge[22]

How big or important were these organizations? What were their life spans? Who belonged? For most, documents yield little beyond names and brief notices, although, as will be seen, some developed high profiles. But whether prominent or obscure, when weighed in their entirety, their capacity to empower was substantial. All these organizations clustered and grew together, much like a coral reef. As with coral, the inert undergird the living and together sustain a complex ecology through which the reef itself is also nourished.

Historians such as Peter Rachleff and Lawrence Goodwyn describe what this ecology produced as a "movement culture," a highly democratic form of insurgent politics in which: 1) ordinary people freely express their concerns; 2) widespread education and participation in voluntary associations facilitate recruitment and mobilization; and 3) leaders challenge the prevailing regime while remaining in close communication with their "grass roots" constituents. Rachleff demonstrates that African American movement culture exercised a transformative impact not only within the city, but also throughout Virginia, on three critical occasions. The first, in 1867–9, secured a state constitution guaranteeing black male suffrage and universal public education. The second, from 1879 to

---

[22] Information for these lists was supplied by the index of Rachleff, *Black Richmond and the Knights of Labor in Richmond*, 245 (entry for Labor Organizations), 247–8 (entry for Secret Societies), together with corresponding pagination.

1883, led to legislation that eliminated poll taxes, abolished whipping posts, funded a black college, and greatly expanded public education for African Americans. The third, from 1884 through 1888, witnessed black and white workers in Richmond coalescing under the banner of the Knights of Labor in a movement that challenged labor oppression and white supremacy in a manner that was nothing short of revolutionary.[23]

INTERRACIAL POLITICS: 1865–84

Building a movement culture required reuniting hundreds of families as emancipated people flocked in from the countryside in 1865–6. Simply the logistics, let alone the legal, material, and emotional requirements of this process, would have been overwhelming, had it not been for churches and congregations. Ministers and elected deacons gave sanctification and legal standing to marriages. Lay members, women as well as men, organized new secret societies that provided services ranging from Bible studies, Sunday schools, bazaars, bake sales, and support for widows and orphans to sickness and death benefits. Their names made their purposes self-explanatory – the Good Samaritans, the Baptist Helping Society, Young Female Hope, Sisters of Emmanuel, and the Christian Union Aid Society. Next came trade-based self-help societies that also began to function as craft and labor unions with names such as the Grand Lodge of Quarrymen, the Warehouse Combined Industrial Society, the National Laboring Club, the Bakers Union, and the Railroad Helpers. There were still other organizations, which, aided by Northern missionaries, established schools for adults and children. What in 1865 had been estimated as a literate black population of two thousand jumped to seven thousand by 1870, a full third of all black Richmonders. By then the Freedman's Savings Bank had attracted more than seven thousand depositors.[24]

Five years after Emancipation, in 1870, over four hundred societies of all types were acting on the precept of being one's brother's or sister's keeper. This nutrient-rich ecology was now giving sustenance to black Richmond's movement culture, which, in turn, led the community deep into politics, attempts at interracial alliance building, and labor organizing. Frustrating and repressing them at nearly every turn were white

---

[23] Lawrence Goodwyn, *Democratic Promise: The Populist Movement in America* (Oxford and New York: Oxford University Press, 1976).
[24] Rachleff, *Black Richmond and the Knights of Labor in Richmond*, 25–33.

supremacists, politicians, and hard-fisted factory owners. Invariably, hard-headed interracial self-interest, not moral or religious idealism, explains the significant gains (however temporary) that Richmond's black community secured between 1865 and 1900.

In 1867–8, for example, Virginia's defeated Confederates boycotted voting for delegates to the Convention that met in Richmond to frame the new constitution required for the state's readmission to the Union. That decision led white Republicans bent on preserving their electoral supremacy to coalesce with black Republican delegates bent on securing racial equality. To encourage their delegation, Richmond's blacks walked out of the city's factories, filling the convention hall and issuing petitions demanding that former Confederate leaders be disenfranchised, dispossessed of their property, and required to sign loyalty oaths. Their delegates, in response, called for redistribution of leading Confederates' lands; free, integrated public schools; and desegregated streetcars, restaurants, and hotels. When white Republicans rejected these demands, Richmond's black activists occupied the white-owned toll bridges that connected their neighborhoods and attempted to integrate the city's streetcars. In the end, the black–white Republican coalition approved a constitution that extended suffrage to all adult male citizens and established the state's first (segregated) public school system, complete with mandatory funding and attendance – partial results to be sure, but crucially important to both blacks' and whites' self-interests and to the common good.[25]

The value of interracial coalition building confirmed itself again, in 1879, when Virginia's white politicians divided sharply over whether or not to write off or "readjust" their state's debts. With the white electorate split, African American voters held the balance of power, and Richmond's blacks launched a three-year political mobilization that spread all over the state. The election sent fifteen black Readjuster delegates to the state legislature, who joined with their white counterparts to create an historic record of mutual interest legislation. In exchange for black support of a drastic reduction of taxes and the election of a leading Readjuster to the United States Senate, the General Assembly funded the state's first public black college, more than doubled the funding for public schools, abolished the poll tax as a prerequisite for voting, and eliminated the brutal, humiliating whipping post, left over from slavery days, used for punishing incarcerated African Americans. Statewide, black school

[25] Ibid., 45–51.

enrollments jumped from 36,000 in 1879 to 91,000 in 1883. In that same span, the number of African American teachers tripled, while African Americans were appointed to administer Richmond's black schools and to sit on Richmond's Board of Education. To be sure, the black delegates also issued unsuccessful demands that cut decisively against whites' self-interest and prejudices, specifically, legislation to suppress lynching and to integrate public conveyances. Nevertheless, once again, politics based on interracial self-interest had proven remarkably effective.[26]

To be clear, none of this added up to irrevocable "progress." Instead, it provoked a vicious counterrevolution led by the white supremacist Democratic Party that suppressed the statewide networks Black Richmonders had created. Facing threats of violence, black voting plummeted statewide in the 1883 election. Riots exploded in nearby Danville, where black Readjusters had made significant gains, leaving one white and four African American people dead. White supremacist Democrats swept into power, cut school budgets, and unseated black office holders. At the same time, however, this desperate moment quickly evolved into a compounding crisis that upended Richmond's regime of racial segregation and white supremacist politics. In 1884, Richmond's history changed course with astounding rapidity.[27]

THE KNIGHTS OF LABOR, 1884–1900

By the early 1880s, the city's working class faced burgeoning technological unemployment. Tobacco factories were discharging laborers irrespective of race in favor of new leaf-rolling, shaping, flavoring, and cutting machines. Steam-driven barrel stave saws and planers were displacing hundreds of coopers, who also found themselves undercut by convict-leased laborers working in the state penitentiary. Whatever their complexions, unskilled widows, single mothers, and older children depended as much on factory income as did skilled male workers. The African American social "safety net," that is, the secret societies, churches,

---

[26] Jane Elizabeth Dailey, *Before Jim Crow: The Politics of Race in Post-Emancipation Virginia* (Chapel Hill, NC: University of North Carolina Press, 2000); Dailey, "The Limits of Liberalism in the New South: The Politics of Race, Sex and Patronage in Virginia, 1879–1883," in Jane Elizabeth Dailey, Glenda Elizabeth Gilmore, and Bryant Simon, *Jumpin' Jim Crow: From Civil War to Civil Rights* (Princeton, NJ: Princeton University Press, 2000), 88–104.

[27] Dailey, "Limits of Liberalism," 99–104; Rachleff, *Black Richmond and the Knights of Labor in Richmond*, 70–108.

and labor organizations, were overwhelmed. So were white churches and benevolent organizations. Never had the need for interracial labor organizing been so pressing or so obvious. How this realization evolved into direct biracial action is best explained by returning briefly to the immediate post-Emancipation years.[28]

Although black Richmonders had emerged from slavery no less conscious of being exploited as workers than they were of being oppressed by white supremacy, their initial attempts to develop their own labor unions came to naught. 1867 featured two abortive strikes, first by black stevedores and then by black coopers, both of which were easily defeated with white strike breakers. Then, in 1870, over 1,200 African American workers attempted without success to launch a Richmond branch of the short-lived National Colored Labor Union while also demanding desegregation of public facilities and the right to organize. To this the Richmond City Council responded by gerrymandering the city's black voters into a single district, drastically reducing their representation in the city's government.[29]

In 1873, after striking black railroaders had been permanently displaced by Italian immigrants, black and white laborers finally organized together. How that momentous determination was made in a city so replete with racial hostility cannot be documented. It is clear, however, that the long-standing resilience, stability, and above all spatial cohesiveness of Richmond's black community – in short, its strictly segregated movement culture – made this exceptional moment possible. It empowered black organizers, made them responsible to a well-defined constituency, convinced whites of their capacity as activists, and insulated them from white manipulation. It also assured white activists with racist proclivities that the rigid geographic boundaries defining the black community would buffer them against close-up and personal racial mixing. Neighborhood segregation actually concentrated black organizational power while reducing the threat of such power for activist whites.[30]

Ironically from our twenty-first-century perspective, biracial labor organizing went forward because it practiced "separate but equal." Yet segregation could never be completely enforced simply because

---

[28] Rachleff, *Black Richmond and the Knights of Labor in Richmond*, 109–15.

[29] Ibid., 70–85.

[30] Kim Voss, "Labor Organization and Class Alliance: Industries, Communities, and the Knights of Labor," *Theory and Society* 17 (1988), 329–64: Joseph Gerteis, *Class and the Color Line: Interracial Coalition in the Knights of Labor and the Populist Movement* (Durham, NC: Duke University Press, 2007), 76–102; Eric Arneson, "Following the Color Line and Labor: Black Workers in the Labor Movement before 1930," *Radical*

never before had contact between black and white activists been so frequent or so politicized. Partly for this reason, not surprisingly, this unstable internal color boundary would stand as an outsized target for racist attackers aiming to shatter the movement along racial lines. Though obvious to us, this problem was all but impossible to anticipate when Richmond's workers first mobilized, so unprecedented was their approach to developing a social movement. In 1877 the city witnessed two hundred black and white barrel makers closing down tobacco factories for better than two weeks in a futile effort to end competition from convict labor in Virginia's state prison. Five years later, in 1882, Tredegar ironworkers of both races, members of the internally segregated Amalgamated Association of Iron and Steel Workers, struck in an unsuccessful effort to force the reinstatement of a fired white laborer.[31]

Then, two years later, in 1884, Richmond's working class, black and white, suddenly embraced *en masse* a rising national labor organization, the Holy and Noble Order of Knights of Labor, and brought the city to the brink of revolution. With a peak national membership estimated at 800,000 and with branches in most major cities, the Knights of Labor dominated workers' movements during the 1880s by rejecting unpopular ideologies such as socialism and anarchism in favor of promoting workers' cooperatives and demanding an eight-hour day.[32]

In the view of some historically minded Richmonders, the fleeting presence of the Knights in the city (1884–8) reduces their significance to a brief reference. The importance of correcting this mis-estimate becomes obvious, however, in light of the extraordinary scope, impact, and success of the Order's organizing work. The Order's inaugural action in early 1885 bespoke a genius that only a movement culture could inspire. Instead of mounting risky strikes, the Knights launched an enormously popular boycott against every Richmond business with ties to Virginia's deeply despised convict lease system. The principal target, however, was the Haxall-Crenshaw Company, supplier of barrels to countless other city enterprises and the state's largest exploiter of incarcerated laborers. The boycott engaged entire families, not just working men, since women and children did much of the family shopping. It also developed religious

History Review 55 (1993), 53–87; Rachleff, *Black Richmond and the Knights of Labor in Richmond*, 74–82, 106–7.

[31] Rachleff, *Black Richmond and the Knights of Labor in Richmond*, 43–4, 80–1, 106–7.

[32] For the Knights of Labor generally see Melton Alonza McLaurin, *The Knights of Labor in the South* (Santa Barbara, CA: University of California Press, 1978).

and political language widely shared by black and white participants. "The divine right to boycott is accorded us by the Holy Bible ... The right to boycott is handed down to us by our [American revolutionary] forefathers ..." and so forth.[33]

As boycotting spread, the Knights' membership skyrocketed. Segregated district assemblies multiplied while coordinating their actions across racial lines. Next, the Knights established the *Labor Herald*, a boycott-driven newspaper, a "reading room," and an employment center. Black and white district assemblies had even begun sponsoring family tours to nearby Washington, D.C. that featured stops at historic sites and visits with local members of the Order. In June 1885 District Assembly 84 opened a soap manufacturing cooperative run by white women but heavily promoted in black churches. Next it established a cooperative building investment association run by whites but open to black participants to defray housing costs and stave off foreclosures.[34]

Then there appeared "the Long Strike," a highly popular romantic melodrama of working-class courage staged by the "Knights of Labor Theater Society." Blacks and whites in impressive numbers sat apart during the performance and departed together resolving to intensify their boycott of the Haxall-Crenshaw Company. Nine months into the boycott, in November 1885, Haxall-Crenshaw ceased purchasing convict-made barrels and gave published notice that it would "not discriminate against the Knights of Labor" in its personnel policies. Fear that the boycott might reach them led many wholesalers to stop dealing in other convict-produced products. Enormous by any measure, the victory erased all doubt about the Order's capacity to deliver. As membership swelled, the Knights turned to capturing the city's government and announced the creation of the Workingman's Reform Party. By now they estimated their number at over 12,000, a potential electorate that could easily outvote the Republicans and the Democrats – which, in city elections held in May 1886, they did.[35]

The Knights carried every city ward save one while promising governmental reforms that opened working-class employment opportunities.

[33] See Campbell, *Richmond's Unhealed History*, 136–7, for an abbreviated treatment. For discussions of the political culture of the Knights of Labor, see Robert E. Weir, *Beyond Labor's Veil: The Culture of the Knights of Labor* (University Park, PA: Pennsylvania State University Press, 1996).

[34] Rachleff, *Black Richmond and the Knights of Labor in Richmond*, 128–42.

[35] Leon Fink, *Workingman's Democracy: The Knights of Labor and American Politics* (Champaign-Urbana, IL: University of Illinois Press, 1988), 155–7.

Reformers comprised a majority on a city council that included five African Americans and gained half of the alderman seats, two occupied by blacks. Allied but independent from one another, black and white leaders of the Knights had secured political power by communicating constantly with the grass roots of their respective communities. Black and white workers' politics had not fused. Each race had preserved its boundaries and immunized itself from manipulation by the other. But they had also come together around a single slate of candidates and decisively defeated political white supremacy. There seemed little point in addressing their movement's racial Achilles heel as the Knights turned from one successful strike to another. Revolution in the workplace seemingly moved apace with revolution in politics.[36]

Historian Leon Fink reports that the Knights conducted no fewer than ten strike actions during 1886 and 1887 and succeeded in no fewer than seven. In 1886 alone, strikers included painters, coopers, typographers, cotton processers, hod carriers, and iron workers. By mid-year, the Order had turned several tobacco factories into closed shops, and, following a bitter struggle, granite workers secured a nine-hour day with no reduction in pay. In one instance, cotton compress workers struck, demanding wage equality as well as a raise because black laborers were earning less than whites. Meanwhile, away from the shop floors, boycotts, and electioneering, as historian Peter Rachleff details, black leaders politicked ceaselessly to mitigate tensions between middle- and working-class interests, to stifle the instinct for political compromise and to continue working across the racial divide.[37]

The skill of these custodians of African American movement culture and the energy of their constituents speaks to the strength and the potential sustainability of black democratic politics in Richmond. One can speculate that under different circumstances what had begun with such great promise and had accomplished so much in so short a time might have evolved into a permanently enriching feature of Richmond's political landscape. In the end, however, the movement's Achilles heel – its insistence upon the "separate but equal" doctrine – proved fatal. Contention first burst forth during the Knights Annual International Conference that gathered in Richmond in the fall of 1886. When a prominent black delegate from New York City objected vehemently to Richmond's segregated hotels and restaurants, the Order's national

---

[36] Rachleff, *Black Richmond and the Knights of Labor in Richmond*, 150–6.
[37] Fink, *Workingman's Democracy*, 154–5.

leader, the white Pennsylvanian Terence V. Powderly, quite publicly supported him.[38]

White racists, Republicans and Democrats alike, factory owners and the ranks of Richmond's white middle class now had ammunition aplenty for bombarding the Order with charges of miscegenation. Slowly but steadily, collaboration veered into bitter contention as white workers chose to protect their racial purity instead of their working-class interests. In the final analysis, "separate but equal" had given black and white workers too little opportunity to know, to learn from, and to trust one another, dooming them finally to compounding stereotyping and misunderstanding. "Both black and white workers," historian Rachleff concludes, "thirsted for 'independence.' Yet each pursued its quest alone. Separate camps became hostile camps."[39]

By 1889 few, if any, traces of the Knights of Labor remained in Richmond. Once (white) Virginians had adopted a new state constitution in 1902 ironclad segregation, wholesale disenfranchisement, and racial terrorism ruled the commonwealth. African American resistance continued, but retreated from public view behind an ever more substantial wall of segregation. There, black Richmonders created what anthropologist James Scott has termed a "hidden transcript" of resistance, inscribed in their music, leisure activities, spiritual expression, church-centered benevolence, fraternal organizations, and informal economic exchanges. Only with the coming of the struggle for civil rights would their hidden transcript again become visible as the foundation for building a renewed movement culture.[40]

In the face of the Knights of Labor's brief existence, painful demise, and devastating aftermath, what deeper historical truths should be derived from its history? First, the Knights incontestably demonstrated that black and white workers could act productively together. Second, they established beyond doubt that a working-class movement structured around racial coalition building could profoundly challenge the prevailing order. And third – surely the most important – the existence of the Knights themselves would have been inconceivable apart from the vital legacies passed on to them by Richmond's antebellum black community. Before the Civil War in the shadow of the slave mart and the gallows,

[38] Rachleff, *Black Richmond and the Knights of Labor in Richmond*, 171–91.
[39] Ibid., 204.
[40] James Scott, *Weapons of the Weak: Everyday Forms of Peasant Resistance* (New Haven, CT: Yale University Press, 1985).

Richmond's African Americans, enslaved and free, had come together to improvise their own underground government and their own rich networks of mutual support, rooted in their churches, secret societies, and informal economy. These supplied the raw material from which a powerful movement culture came into being that inspired a vision of economic justice and racial equality. For the Knights the promise of democratic struggle depended profoundly on the accomplishments of African Americans who preceded them, just as is the case in racially divided Richmond today.

A NEW MOVEMENT CULTURE IN RICHMOND

How could anyone believe that such a complicated and unfamiliar history could compete with, let alone displace, the deeply entrenched, pervasive myths of the "lost cause"? Activists, not historians or public policy scholars, possess the commitment, knowledge, and insight into Richmond's political culture required to supply substantive answers. More generally, however, it seems clear that complex historical narratives can be transmuted into compelling political knowledge around which a new movement culture can be organized. Might not YouTube videos, Twitter feeds, blogs, smart phone apps, poetry slams, art exhibits, and designer T-shirts prove the equivalent of the Knights of Labor's "Theatre Society" and its play, "The Long Strike"? Might not street-level voluntary organizations, churches, and community agencies network together as they did in the post-Civil War black community? What this deep plunge into history makes possible, in our opinion, is the opportunity to discover a truthful past, to learn from it, embrace it, enrich it by recasting it into accessible formats, to teach it as widely as possible, and then to act on its implications. These, it seems to us, are the surest ways to develop creative, historically informed policy recommendations that address the ills of racism and exploitation in the Capital of the Confederacy today – structural racism, systemic poverty, and enslavement in its various twenty-first-century forms. Despite the best efforts of museum directors, public historians, and activists, symbols of the "lost cause" remain the most visible signs of Richmond's political, racial, and historic identity. The vital work of transmuting truthful history, however it is accomplished, returns us to a group with whom we are now familiar, the DFJE.

Were Richmond's nineteenth-century black activists whisked into our time and introduced to the members of DFJE, we imagine that they would warmly embrace these modern activists as "family." The DFJE has led protests against the Monument Avenue statues and is working to level the city's historical landscape by creating a Memorial Park to honor the roughly 300,000 black Virginians uprooted by Richmond's participation in the interstate slave trade. In truth, the site for the park is what was quite literally home to our activist time-travelers. Its location in Shockoe Bottom (where the "Joker/Obama" wall poster recently hung) was, as mentioned earlier, the epicenter for Richmond's nineteenth-century working-class community, home to many African Americans, to poor whites, immigrant Jews, Huguenots, and Haitians. Its 9-acre setting is today replete with deeply buried African American sites and artifacts of historical significance, including the aforementioned Lumpkins' slave jail notorious for auctioning off human beings, a significant African burial ground, and a gallows site from which thousands were hanged, white as well as black, including those Africans convicted after Gabriel's 1800 slave insurrection. When working on the Memorial's design, the DFJE has also consulted widely with businesses, civic groups, museums, religious groups, institutions of higher learning, urban planners, and graphic designers. The project has been endorsed by the National Trust for Historic Preservation, Preservation Virginia, the Richmond Branch of the NAACP, the Richmond Crusade for Voters, and Historians Against Slavery, an international alliance of antislavery scholars and activists.

Since the heartbeat of Richmond's history of African American struggle animates Shockoe Bottom just as Monument Avenue pulsates with the history of slaveholding, the DFJE's demand that the city fund the Memorial Park should stand as a new movement culture's most obvious and most pressing priority, but not just because of its obvious historical logic. This demand also reprises the success of the Knights of Labor's boycott campaign against convict labor that gained it so many supporters. Back then, grass roots interest groups responded by mobilizing across racial lines and around shared interests. Today, in our judgment, the DFJE's drive to establish the park offers similar opportunities for coalition building. But with whom to collaborate and why? While this is obviously a question that can only be decided by Richmonders themselves, groups professing objectives seemingly supportive of the DFJE's are easily identified. For this reason, our initial suggestion is that DFJE engage with Initiatives of Change (IFC),[41] a respected Richmond organization noted for promoting racial healing and reconciliation. Although it has not thus far

[41] Initiatives of Change, http://us.iofc.org/HH2015.

supported the DFJE's work, its values are clearly similar, its emphasis unequivocally historical, and its programs bring together a multitude of actors, agencies, and organizations. It has sponsored two expansive city-wide Healing History Conferences, the overall objectives of which have been to convene people from many walks of life to deal openly with Richmond's excruciating racial history.

Titles of conference break-out sessions convey the potential "fit" of its priorities with those of the DFJE; for example, "Connecting Memory, Legacy and Social Change"; "Museums and Public History Sites for Education & Healing"; "Linking Racial History, Healing, and Systems Change." "Social capital," a concept developed by political scientist Robert Putnam, clarifies what IFC would contribute. His term refers to the grass roots social relations that create political coalitions around causes that reinforce mutual trust with mutual self-interest. Putnam defines the concept as "a wide variety of quite specific benefits that flow from the trust, reciprocity, information, and cooperation associated with social networks. Social capital creates value for the people who are connected and, at least sometimes, for bystanders as well."[42] What the IFC offers the DFJE is precisely what Putnam posits, a vehicle for legitimizing and amplifying public support for the Memorial Park. What the DFJE offers the IFC likewise reflects Putnam's observations. The Memorial Park, when up and running, would solidify and extend the personal relationships and projects initiated by IFC events, all critical steps for initiating an activist "ecology."

Yet campaigning for the Memorial Park in and of itself only hints at what the Knights of Labor attempted back in the late nineteenth century: the comprehensive challenging of racial and class barriers citywide. Might the new movement culture we are envisioning be able to reach for something equally ambitious and, by so doing, to develop an "ecology" comprising a truly wide spectrum of organizations? As we are about to explain, it's certainly possible. Perhaps, as of 2017, it's already starting, much as it did for Richmond's black and white workers when they adopted an emerging national movement and made it their own, the Knights of Labor.

RESTORATIVE JUSTICE IN RICHMOND

The national movement in this case involves the Kellogg Foundation. In February 2016, national leaders of activist organizations met in

---

[42] "About Social Capital," *Harvard Kennedy School: The Saguaro Seminar, Civic Engagement in America*, www.hks.harvard.edu/programs/saguaro/about-social-capital.

Richmond with representatives of that organization to consider a national response to the ongoing state-sanctioned violence leveled against African American people. Since Richmond's history is rooted in the earliest years of colonial enslavement, they reasoned, the city offers an aptly symbolic site for launching a national program to promote restorative justice. And since Richmond served as the Capital of the Confederacy, the doubled symbolic power of their choice is undeniable.[43] But in addition, as we see it, the idea of organizing a national project in Richmond adds weight to our policy recommendations that: (1) efforts to resolve racial problems in Richmond must be grounded in deep understandings of the city's history of African American struggle; that (2) to this end, establishing the Defenders of Freedom, Justice and Equality's Shockoe Bottom Memorial Park is imperative for moving Richmond closer to equality and democracy. Seconding the suggestions of the Kellogg Foundation group, here is a third recommendation: (3) that the city government should initiate a broad-based public–private partnership to plan for and help finance the Kellogg Foundation's national restorative justice initiative. To the extent that the city first faces up to its racial past, so then can the Republic.

Since the 1970s, more than two dozen truth and reconciliation commissions have convened across the world, ranging from South Africa's 1990s tribunals in the aftermath of apartheid to Canada's 2008 programs for restorative justice for brutally disrupted indigenous families. Their wide variety sets no precedents – certainly not within the United States, where only one such commission has ever addressed African Americans' claims, specifically, in that case, involving the 1979 murder of (both black and white) Communist Workers' Party demonstrators in Greensboro, North Carolina.[44] Unless such historical silence is broken, it seems to us that opportunities to heal racial trauma in Richmond or anywhere else are negligible. One can, however, imagine the convening of just such a national inquiry on the grounds of a recently opened, DFJE administered, Shockoe Bottom Memorial Park.

Specifying a national restorative justice agenda is light years beyond this essay's mandate. Two points, however, seem beyond dispute. It is not

---

[43] Yessenia Funes, "Finally, the US Steps Closer to Racial Healing with a National Truth and Reconciliation Commission," *Moyers and Company*, April 21, 2016, http://billmoyers.com/story/finally-the-us-steps-closer-to-racial-healing-with-a-national-truth-and-reconciliation-commission/.

[44] Eric A. Posner and Adrian Vermeule, "Reparations for Slavery and Other Historical Injustices," *Columbia Law Review* (2003), 689–748, http://chicagounbound.uchicago.edu/cgi/viewcontent.cgi?article=2787&context=journal_articles.

worth the effort if the expectation is simply an apology, or if the central concern comes down to nationwide financial reparations. Both outcomes let history "off the hook": the first is far too easy and the second far too contentious. Instead, let us reflect upon the number $150,735,000,000,000. That's the estimated value of the unpaid labor performed by enslaved African Americans from 1619 to 1865, compounded at 6 percent interest through 2016.[45] If nothing else, this gargantuan number removes all doubt that the nation's indebtedness to African American people is incalculable. This intimidating total also suggests that we restrict our attention to Richmond. How might one develop a restorative justice project that does justice to the city's past by extending the prospect of justice into the present? Answers involve designing a Richmond Restorative Project that begins a multiyear program of specific projects to enhance equality and democracy, not simply a one-off event.

To prepare for such an initiative, a full accounting is required from Richmond of its historical complicity with slavery and its seemingly endless consequences, a subject not fully addressed by any means by the account presented above. If the purpose is to find healing in history, that first requires standing up to and accepting all of it. To get specific:

First, consider the number 300,000. That figure, already cited, closely approximates the number of enslaved individuals who passed through the city after having been uprooted from the countryside and marched into the Deep South. Add the family members they left behind, and the total number becomes incalculably high, and that's only a fractional accounting of the costs of slavery for Virginia's African Americans. It does, however, make this larger point.

Next, grapple with some grim benchmark dates that extend far beyond our account of the Knights of Labor: 1902, the year that the Virginia legislature banned its black citizens from voting; 1919, when existing racist laws were revised by the legislature to enforce still more stringent segregation in every aspect of public life; 1924, when the legislature passed the Racial Integrity Law, banning interracial marriage and requiring a complete statistical account of "the racial composition of any individual as Caucasian, negro, Mongolian, American Indian, Asiatic Indian, Malay or any mixture thereof ...," thereby creating a database leading to the forced sterilization of thousands deemed inherently

---

[45] The aggregated worth of enslaved labor in 2016 dollars derives from Samuel H. Williamson and Louis B. Cali, "Measuring Slavery in 2016 Dollars," www.measuring worth.com/slavery.php.

criminal or "feeble minded" – whites as well as Native Americans and blacks; 1925, when the average per white pupil expenditure in Richmond was $40.27 annually as compared with $10.47 for black students, and when Richmond's new mayor was elected while promising "no Negroes on the City's payrolls – city jobs for hard working white men"; 1935, when every Richmond home in every African American neighborhood was officially certified unfit for mortgage financing, further entrenching segregated and vastly inferior housing; 1956, when Richmond followed the state's lead in responding to federally mandated desegregation by closing its entire public school system, a conflict which continued over the next two years; 1957, when the city exercised its right of eminent domain to construct the Richmond–St. Petersburg Turnpike by cutting an eighteen block swathe through Jackson Ward, demolishing close to a thousand homes and displacing 10 percent of the population in the historic center of the black community (thus making the Memorial Park Project all the more imperative.)[46]

Readers can easily extend this narrative through the civil rights movement, the resultant white backlash and the end of "welfare as we know it," the election of Barak Obama, and so forth. But in any event, we find ourselves finally in the Richmond of today, afflicted as so many cities are with disproportionately race-based poverty and achievement gaps, rancor over policing and police brutality, shockingly biased incarceration rates, and despair over the "school to prison pipeline." Given all this, one must take seriously the contention of social psychologist Joy DeGruy that many African Americans today, Richmonders included, presumably, labor under what she terms Post Traumatic Slave Syndrome (PTSS).[47] PTSS, DrGruy explains, arises from multigenerational trauma rooted in 250 years of enslavement, more than an additional century of racist repression, and the well-founded conviction that white supremacy denies black Americans benefits and privileges open to everyone else. The science of epigenetics confirms this reality. A 2015 study published in *Scientific American* found that descendants of Holocaust survivors tended to have to have stress hormone profiles differing from those of their peers, which predispose them to reflexive anxiety disorders.[48]

---

[46] This grim narrative of white racism's expression and impact is compellingly reviewed in Campbell, *Richmond's Unhealed History*, 135–74.

[47] Joy DeGruy, *Post Traumatic Slave Syndrome: America's Legacy of Enduring Injury and Healing* (Portland, OR: Uptone Press, 2005).

[48] Tori Rodriguez, "Survivors Have Altered Stress Hormones: Parents' Traumatic Experience May Hamper Their Offspring's Ability to Bounce Back from Trauma,"

Considering DeGruy's disturbing findings, never has a history that leads to restorative justice and healing seemed more urgently needed. Fortunately for Richmonders, never has potential access to a rich cache of exactly such a history been greater or closer at hand. Evidence that brings this past directly to life is packed into Shockoe Bottom. The proposed Memorial Park would offer it to the public much as we have narrated it here. It is an inspiring chronicle in which the citizens of Richmond should find not only factual substance but also hope, pride, and understanding, featuring as it does roughly two centuries of African American inventiveness, resilience, risk taking, accomplishment, and interracial coalition building.

Richmond also possesses social capital aplenty for bringing this history before the public, and in particular to scholars, students, museum curators, librarians, teachers, civil rights activists, elected officials, and business owners. Apart from governmental agencies, some of the nonprofit organizations able to contribute to a new movement culture might well include the following, to which others can doubtless be added:

Defenders of Freedom Justice and Equality, Initiatives of Change, the University of Richmond, the University of Virginia, Virginia Commonwealth University, the American Civil War Museum, The Library of Virginia, The Richmond Slave Trail Commission, The Black History Museum and Cultural Center of Virginia, Richmond NAACP, Black Action Now, Justice RVA, the Richmond Crusade for Voters, the *Richmond Free Press*, Non-Denominational Black Churches (87 listed), Black Baptist Churches (296 listed).

All told, it's an impressive listing that recalls that dense list of secret societies, church organizations, and labor groups from the immediate postbellum period. And while it is not our place to recommend a program of restorative justice, we can confidently predict that if a group such as this one did unite around a common agenda, city officials would become deeply interested. So would the Kellogg Foundation.

Anticipating what the future may well bring adds urgency to these recommendations. By 2050, white Americans will comprise only 47 percent of the population, down from 85 percent in 1960.[49] As this transformation goes forward and as deindustrialization and declining prospects

---

Scientific American, March 1, 2015. See also Jenna Wortham, "Racism's Psychological Toll," *The New York Times*, June 24, 2015, www.nytimes.com/2015/06/24/magazine/racisms-psychological-toll.html?_r=0, which details the research of University of Louisville social psychologist Monnica Williams.

[49] Paul Taylor, "The Next America," *Pew Research*, April 10, 2014, www.pewresearch.org/next-america/#Americas-Racial-Tapestry-Is-Changing.

continue demoralizing ordinary Americans, so too does a skyrocketing rise in the number of white hate groups, which has doubled, from 457 in 1999 to 892 in 2015.[50] In the decades to come, neo-Confederates such as the Virginia Flaggers, so vocal when defending white power on Monument Avenue, might well be joined by a multitude of new supporters. Office seekers who emulate the likes of Donald Trump all but guarantee a continuing white backlash, greater fear and defensiveness among people of color, and more Michael Browns, Eric Garners, and Trayvon Martins.

And as this is being written, in February 2018, racial conflict in Richmond is at best at a stalemate. According to a January 9, 2018 poll conducted by Virginia Commonwealth University, close to 50 percent of the state's residents want Confederate monuments left in place. A Mayor's Commission appointed in June 2017 to consider the "monuments question" has remained silent since. At the same time, several community groups continue to promote interracial trust-building and healing, and the University of Richmond is planning similar initiatives. As with Richmond's history, the prospect for restorative justice remains "up for grabs."[51]

Whatever the future, by far the most persuasive reasons for pursuing restorative justice come from young black Richmonders, such as the ones who participated in meetings held in 2015 to discuss the design of the proposed Memorial Park. Referring to the Shockoe Bottom project, the meeting's report concludes that "Richmonders want a place that is authentic – that tells the WHOLE story that communicates real emotions and allows people to experience that way at Lumpkin's Jail Site and be broad in scale ... a full immersive experience in which visitors can explore the historic artifacts and remains of the site in detail, shedding much more light on what the experience of enslavement was like for African

[50] "SPLC's Intelligence Report," *Southern Poverty Law Center*, February 1, 2016, www .splcenter.org/news/2016/02/17/splcs-intelligence-report-amid-year-lethal-violence-extremist-groups-expanded-ranks-2015.

[51] "Mayor Lavar Stoney Has Established a Monuments Commission" www .monumentavenuecommission.org/#home-section "VCU Poll: Nearly Half of Virginians Want Confederate Monuments Left in Place," www.richmond.com/news/virginia/vcu-poll-nearly-half-of-virginians-want-confederate-monuments-left/article_3e77c215-57c5-582c-8c00-c25bee51237e.html. "Richmond Councilman Vows to Reintroduce Failed Monument Avenue Proposal in Spring," www.richmond.com/news/local/city-of-richmond/richmond-councilman-vows-to-reintroduce-failed-monument-avenue-proposal-in/article_92e78d9f-2819-598a-8953-7739c303ec18.html. For information on community restorative justice group initiatives, see www.richmondhillva.org/learn/koinonia-school-of-race-justice/; https://richmondpledge.org; http://us.iofc.org/ctf.

Americans."[52] Moreover, they stressed, "the Park must be an active site of learning and connected to the schools of Richmond and the commonwealth: elementary, secondary, and higher education." One student succinctly captured the non-negotiable requirement for beginning a process of reparation and reconciliation. "I want to know WHY? Why did people think it was okay to do that [slavery] to another person?" So did a second student when insisting that there "Finally [be] an acknowledgment that all these lives matter. We were taught those black lives didn't matter. Now we want to find out as much as possible about those lives." A third put the same thought this way: "There is a darkness in Shockoe Bottom ... it won't be healed until the whole ugly story is told."

EMANCIPATING RICHMOND?

"The whole ugly story" raises a disturbing final question: Can Richmond truly pursue restorative justice while it is common knowledge that human beings continue being bought and sold today? Recall the racist poster of President Obama as 'The Joker" (see Figure 12) and the image of the strip club that displayed it. Sexual exploitation, particularly of underage girls, is a problem in Richmond[53] and in much of the nation. In other locales, enslaved people can be found sequestered as household workers and as laborers in restaurants, laundries, landscaping companies, hair and nail salons, and a variety of other small businesses.[54] A very great many, we know, remain undetected and are transient, shuttled as they so often are along the interstate highway system which passes through Richmond and where Interstate Highways I-64 and I-95 conjoin, making it a hub of human trafficking.

How many enslaved people reside in Richmond? No one knows. For Virginia as a whole, the National Human Trafficking Resource Center (NHTRC) reports that in 2014, 175 cases of human trafficking were documented, including 114 cases of sex trafficking and 49 cases of labor trafficking. All told, these cases involved 124 adults, 49 minors, 61

---

[52] "Richmond Speaks about Lumpkins Site: Draft Report on Community Engagement," http://rvanews.com/wp-content/uploads/2015/12/lumpkins-site_key_findings_report_online.pdf.

[53] Shelby Brown, "Henrico Prostitution Bust Leads to Underage Sex Trafficking Charges," *CBS 6 News*, March 16, 2016, http://wtvr.com/2016/03/17/henrico-prostitution-bust-leads-to-underage-sex-trafficking-charges.

[54] National Human Trafficking Resource Center, https://humantraffickinghotline.org/state/virginia.

foreign nations, and 58 US citizens. But these figures barely hint at the realities, because slavery today remains all but invisible to law enforcement officials and practically everyone else. This is not only because of its illegality, but also because it differs so profoundly from the images of slavery from the antebellum South deeply etched in the minds of so many Americans, those in the Capital of the Confederacy particularly, one suspects. The "Virginia Aristocracy" that gave us Washington, Jefferson, and Madison is all but impossible for most Richmonders to square with today's criminal networks, entrepreneurial pimps, hyper-exploitative industries, avaricious landholders, and cynically abusive state enterprises. For all these reasons and more, the extent of enslavement today remains a great unknown and that makes it natural to assume the worst, particularly when global estimates of the total number of enslaved people vary between 21 to 46 million, and when the annual total of women and children sexually enslaved in the United States is said to be in the tens of thousands.[55]

Three high-profile organizations work full time against slavery in Richmond today: the Richmond Justice Initiative,[56] founded in 2009, the Gray Haven Project,[57] founded in 2010, and Impact Virginia,[58] founded in 2014. These organizations focus on victim advocacy, community education, survivor care, crisis intervention, and recuperative services for victims. Despite the connections between forced labor and racial marginalization – past and present – these groups are not connected with the work DFJE does. How can restorative justice be undertaken in Richmond if those who detest slavery (past and present) most deeply and are most fully committed to overcoming its consequences operate in silos, missing the opportunity to leverage truths and strength from each other's expertise and networks? Can a vibrant antislavery movement united in its demand for restorative justice be brought together in the shadow of Monument Avenue? Surely those who endure slavery today are as much entitled to restorative justice as are those struggling against centuries of white racism. Surely the wisdom accrued by African American people over centuries of struggle has significant value for those opposing slavery today. Surely the case for each approach to antislavery is powerfully

---

[55] See, for example the *Global Slavery Index*, www.globalslaveryindex.org, and Kevin Bales et al., eds., *Hidden Slaves: Forced Labor in the United States* (Berkeley, CA: University of California, Berkeley, Human Rights Center: 2004).

[56] Richmond Justice Initiative, http://richmondjusticeinitiative.com.

[57] Gray Haven Project, http://thegrayhaven.org.

[58] Impact Virginia, www.impactvirginia.org.

amplified by a demand for both. Surely such antislavery unity is required in order to respond in full voice to the claims of Monument Avenue. Or is such a proposal a step too far?

While only Richmonders can determine an answer, the Frederick Douglass Family Initiatives (FDFI), located in Washington, DC, can be of assistance.[59] Founded by direct descendants of Frederick Douglass and Booker T. Washington, the FDFI combats today's human trafficking with acclaimed educational programs that are being implemented in cities across the country, which transform knowledge of the history of American slavery into the keys for acting against enslavement and racial prejudice today. Their focus is on reaching young people from all cultures and walks of life, the only group whose outlooks may not yet have been fatally tinctured with racism and resentment and who want most of all to "to know WHY? Why did people think it was okay to do that [slavery] to another person?" In this respect, the expertise of the Douglass Family Initiatives is uniquely tailored to bridging generations, skin colors, the "parallel universes" highlighted above, and, in our estimate, to doing what is required in order to initiate a comprehensive antislavery movement culture in Richmond.

RECOMMENDATION SUMMARY/RESTORATIVE JUSTICE

These recommendations are offered in all seriousness as a full measure of the history that we believe the City of Richmond would be required to overcome in order to redirect its future toward greater equity and democracy. We are well aware of the enormous expenditures of time, commitment, and resources required, which again measures well the power of history that Richmond needs to overcome and the promise of the "healing history" that can begin to replace it.

1 Establish a broad-based coalition with the immediate goal of funding construction of the Shockoe Bottom Memorial Park financed by a public–private partnership. Begin funding construction.
2 Employ this public–private partnership to leverage the Memorial Park project as the platform for building a citywide Restorative Justice Initiative. Begin defining the initiative as a multiyear program development project, not simply an event.

[59] www.fdfi.org.

3 Enlist foundation financial support, Kellogg and others, and political support for government funding for citywide initiative.

4 Initiate a citywide, historically based educational program in support of the citywide initiative involving all age groups and levels of learning.

5 Initiate the Richmond Restorative Justice Project and begin to evaluate the city's suitability to host a National Restorative Justice Initiative.

Annotated Bibliography for Future Research

James Brewer Stewart and Elizabeth Swanson

PLANTATION SLAVERY AND ABOLITION, AND THEIR LEGACIES IN THE AMERICAS

Alexander, Michelle. *The New Jim Crow: Mass Incarceration in the Age of Colorblindness*. New York: The New Press, 2010.
Chronicles the targeting of black men through the "War on Drugs" and the transformation of United States prisons into a stringent system of racial control.

Beckert, Sven, *Empire of Cotton: A Global History*. New York: Vintage, 2014.
A historical examination of the counterpoint between cotton production, enslavement, and the development of global capitalism.

Berlin, Ira, *Generations of Captivity: A History of African American Slaves*. Cambridge, MA: Belknap Press of Harvard University Press, 2003.
A comprehensive scholarly examination of the development and evolution of African American enslavement from 1700 onward.

Berlin, Ira, *The Long Emancipation: The Demise of Slavery in the United States*. Cambridge, MA: Belknap Press of Harvard University Press, 2015.
Presents the history of slave emancipation in the United States while stressing its gradual elimination in the North as well as the struggle for emancipation in the South.

Blackmon, Douglas A. *Slavery by Another Name: The Re-Enslavement of Black Americans from the Civil War to World War II*. New York: Anchor Press, 2008.
An authoritative historical account of the re-enslavement of post-Civil War African Americans through systems of convict leasing, debt peonage, and mass incarceration.

Blight, David, *Race and Reunion: The Civil War in American Memory*. Cambridge, MA: Belknap Press of Harvard University Press, 2002.
Examines how post-Civil War Americans explained that war to themselves and one another in terms of race, region, and nationality.

Child, Denis, *Slaves of the State: Black Incarceration from the Chain Gang to the Penitentiary*. Minneapolis, MN and London: University of Minnesota Press, 2015.
An in-depth, interdisciplinary investigation of the origins, evolution, and impact of the contemporary carceral state.
Daniel, Pete R. *The Shadow of Slavery: Peonage in the South, 1901–1969*. Champaign-Urbana, IL: University of Illinois Press, 1990.
Examines the history of debt peonage as a method of re-enslavement of emancipated African Americans.
Davis, David Brion. *The Problem of Slavery in the Age of Emancipation*. New York: Vintage, 2014.
  The Problem of Slavery in the Age of Revolution, 1770–1823. New York and Oxford: Oxford University Press, 1999.
  The Problem of Slavery in Western Culture. Ithaca, NY: Cornell University Press, 1966.
  Inhuman Bondage: The Rise and Fall of Slavery in the New World. Oxford and New York: Oxford University Press, 2006.
The author of these four volumes is recognized the world over for his richly informed transnational accounts of the problem of slavery in the Western world from the Middle Ages through the end of the American Civil War.
Drescher, Seymour. *Abolition: A History of Slavery and Antislavery*. Cambridge and New York: Cambridge University Press, 2009.
A detailed history of the rise and evolution of Western abolitionist movements from the late eighteenth century onward.
Eltis, David, and Richardson, David, *The Atlas of the Transatlantic Slave Trade*. New Haven, CT: Yale University Press, 2010.
The authoritative historical source of the size, scope, and dynamics of the Atlantic slave trade.
Follett, Richard, Eric Foner, and Walter Johnson. *Slavery's Ghost: The Problem of Freedom in the Age of Emancipation*. Baltimore, MD: Johns Hopkins University Press, 2013.
In three provocative essays, the authors assess the meaning of freedom for enslaved and free Americans in the decades before and after the Civil War, excavating local and national histories of reconstruction from the perspectives of the newly emancipated and of both Northern and Southern white Americans.
Foner, Eric. *"Nothing but Freedom": Emancipation and its Legacies*. Baton Rouge, LA: Louisiana State University Press, 1987.
Traces the evolution of post-Emancipation black labor in the Southern United States in local, regional, and comparative settings.
Glickstein, Jonathan. *Concepts of Free Labor in Antebellum America*. New Haven, CT: Yale University Press, 1991.
A historical analysis of American beliefs regarding free and slave labor that illuminates abolitionists' perceptions and moral judgments.
Hardesty, Jared Ross. *Unfreedom: Slavery and Dependence in Eighteen Century Boston*. New York: New York University Press, 2016.
Hardesty constructs a broad history that challenges the dichotomy slavery v. freedom by showing the many forms of dependence and servitude that

shaped the lives of eighteenth-century white and black Bostonians, and by revealing the struggles of enslaved people for autonomy and recognition even within the bonds of the slave systems.

Hartman, Saidiya. *Scenes of Subjection: Terror, Slavery, and Self-Making in Nineteenth Century America*. Oxford and New York: Oxford University Press, 1997.

A close examination of rituals of dominance practiced by antebellum slaveholders and expressions of resistance by the enslaved.

Jackson, Maurice. *Let This Voice Be Heard: Anthony Benezet, Father of Atlantic Abolitionism*. Philadelphia, PA: University of Pennsylvania Press, 2009.

Jackson offers a robust intellectual biography of eighteenth-century anti-slavery activist Anthony Benezet, chronicling his mobilization of Enlightenment and Quaker philosophies alongside narratives of enslaved persons and slave traders themselves to help found a thriving transnational abolitionist movement.

Johnson, Walter. *River of Dark Dreams: Slavery and Empire in the Cotton Kingdom*. Cambridge, MA: Belknap Press, 2013.

Walter Johnson writes a transformative history of the Cotton Kingdom of the old South, centering the damage done to Native American communities and to enslaved persons as the Mississippi Valley was made into the capital of the cotton economy that fueled the rise of transnational capitalism on the backs of those bought and sold in the transatlantic slave trade.

LeFlouria, Talitha, L. *Chained in Silence: Black Women and Convict Labor in the New South*. Chapel Hill, NC: University of North Carolina Press, 2016.

A scholarly historical examination of the re-enslavement of African American women in the Deep South and their responses to their exploitation.

Oshinsky, David M. *"Worse Than Slavery": Parchman Farm and the Ordeal of Jim Crow Justice*. New York: Free Press, 1996.

An in-depth historical portrayal of post-Emancipation Southern enslavement as practiced in one particularly notorious state prison.

Resendez, Andres. *The Other Slavery: The Uncovered History of Indian Enslavement in America*. New York: Houghton Mifflin, 2016.

A path-breaking study of the enslavement of Indian Americans throughout the Western Hemisphere from the time of the Spanish Conquest to the opening of the twentieth century.

Schermerhorn, Calvin. *The Business of Slavery and the Rise of American Capitalism 1815–1860*. New Haven, CT: Yale University Press, 2015.

This volume presents the intertwined history of capitalism and slavery in the nineteenth-century United States, demonstrating how the highly destructive institution of slavery also contributed greatly to the growing capitalist economy of the country.

Sharpe, Christina. *Monstrous Intimacies: Making Post-Slavery Subjects*. Durham, NC and London: Duke University Press, 2010.

An exploration of how sexual violence and sadism have constructed both black and white subjectivity during the era of plantation slavery and beyond.

Sinha, Mansiha. *The Slave's Cause: A History of Abolition*. New Haven, CT: Yale University Press, 2016.

The most in-depth and complete historical account currently available of the American abolitionist movement.

Stewart, James Brewer. *Holy Warriors: The Abolitionists and American Slavery.* New York: Hill and Wang, 1997.

The most accessible history of the American abolitionist movement currently available, notable for its focus on the role of women in the movement.

Walters, Ronald. *The Antislavery Appeal: Abolition after 1831.* Baltimore, MD: The Johns Hopkins University Press, 1978.

A wide-ranging analysis of American abolitionists' ideological convictions regarding religion, family economy, sexuality, and enslavement.

Warren, Wendy. *New England Bound: Slavery and Colonization in Early America.* New York: Liveright Publishing, 2016.

Shifting the typical focus of slavery studies from the Southern US, Warren chronicles the central role of enslavement to the earliest days of colonial settlement in New England.

Wheat, David. *Atlantic Africa and the Spanish Caribbean 1570–1640.* Chapel Hill, NC: University of North Carolina Press, 2016.

Wheat's important study resituates the Spanish Caribbean as an important part of the combined Portuguese and Spanish empires, studying the impact of Luso-Africans in the Spanish Caribbean at the start of the transatlantic slave trade.

HUMAN TRAFFICKING AND CONTEMPORARY GLOBAL SLAVERY

Augustin, Laura Maria. *Sex at the Margin: Migration, Labor Markets and the Rescue Industry.* London: Zed Books, 2007.

Critiques the "savior complex" that motivates some opponents of sexual enslavement and offers a careful investigation of what motivates those who become sex workers.

Bales, Kevin. *Disposable People: The New Slavery and the Global Economy.* 3rd edition. Berkeley and Los Angeles, CA: University of California Press, 2012.

Offers an accessible overall introduction to the problem of today's slavery.

Bales, Kevin. *Blood and Earth: Modern Slavery, Ecocide, and the Secret of Saving the World.* New York: Spiegel and Grau, 2016.

Explores linkages between enslavement and the destruction of natural environments, arguing that abolitionist activism is also environmental activism.

Bales, Kevin. *Ending Slavery: How We Free Today's Slaves.* Berkeley and Los Angeles, CA: University of California Press, 2008.

Develops the case for a global economic strategy for eliminating contemporary slavery.

Bales, Kevin, Zoe Trodd, and Alex Kent Williamson. *Modern Slavery: The Secret World of 27 Million People.* New York: One World Press, 2009.

An overview accompanied by statistics of the various forms of enslavement across the globe.

Bales, Kevin, and Ron Soodalter. *The Slave Next Door: Human Trafficking and Slavery in America Today.* Berkeley and Los Angeles, CA: University of California Press, 2010.

An instructive introduction to the problem of slavery in the twenty-first century within the United States.

Bales, Kevin, and Trodd, Zoe. *To Plead Our Own Cause: Personal Stories of Today's Slaves.* Ithaca, NY: Cornell University Press, 2009.
Presents a rich and varied collection of personal testimony given by survivors of contemporary slavery.

Brysk, Alison, and Austin Choi-Firzpatrick. *From Human Trafficking to Human Rights: Reframing Contemporary Slavery.* Philadelphia, PA: University of Pennsylvania Press, 2012.
Effectively critiques overly broad and/or restrictive definitions of contemporary slavery and argues for the application of human rights approaches.

Craig, Gary, ed. *Child Slavery Now: A Contemporary Reader.* Bristol, UK and Portland, OR: Policy Press, 2010.
Essays by nineteen leading authorities convey a global picture of child slavery and offer strategies for opposing it.

Davidson, Julia O'Connell. *Modern Slavery: The Margins of Freedom.* London and New York: Palgrave Macmillan, 2015.
A comprehensive critique of the "modern abolitionist" movement's ideological and programmatic inconsistencies that argues for human rights solutions to problems of labor exploitation.

Duane, Anna Mae, ed. *Child Slavery before and after Emancipation: An Argument for Child-Centered Studies of Slavery.* Cambridge and New York: Cambridge University Press, 2017.
Eleven original essays consider child slavery in historical and contemporary contexts while examining ethical and definitional problems within the field of slavery studies more generally.

Hoang, Kimberly Kay, and Rhacel Salazar Parrenas, eds. *Human Trafficking Reconsidered: Rethinking the Problem, Envisioning New Solutions.* New York: International Debate Education Association Press, 2014.
Original essays that analyze the effectiveness of current anti-trafficking regimes and the problems facing anti-trafficking advocates on the ground.

Kara, Siddharth. *Bonded Labor: Tackling the System of Slavery in South Asia.* New York: Columbia University Press, 2014.
An extended account based on personal experience and governmental reports of the many forms of labor exploitation practiced in India, Pakistan, and Nepal.

Kara, Siddharth. *Sex Trafficking: Inside the Business of Modern Slavery.* New York: Columbia University Press, 2010.
A broad survey of sexual enslavement grounded in personal observations and detailed with statistics derived from governmental and law enforcement agencies.

Linden, Marcus van Der, and Magaley Rodriguez Garcia, eds. *On Coerced Labor: Work and Compulsion after Slavery.* Boston, MA and Leiden: Brill Academic Publishers, 2016.
A collection of scholarly essays that examines coercive forms of post-Emancipation labor substitution that have persisted into our time.

Miers, Suzanne. *Slavery in the 20th Century: The Evolution of a Global Problem.* New York: Altamira Press, 2003.

Places modern slavery in comparative historical context while tracing the development of the international antislavery movement over the last hundred years.

Miller, Joseph C. *The Problem of Slavery as History: A Global Approach*. New Haven, CT: Yale University Press, 2012.

A challenging historical critique of conventional academic understandings of slavery in the past and today that proposes radically new approaches.

Murphy, Laura, ed. *Survivors of Slavery: Modern Day Slave Narratives*. New York: Columbia University Press, 2014.

An accessible collection of first-hand testimony of slavery survivors from many walks of life.

Patterson, Orlando. *Slavery and Social Death: A Comparative Study*. Cambridge, MA: Harvard University Press, 1982.

An influential historical analysis of enslavement that defines that condition as "social death."

Quirk, Joel. *The Antislavery Project: From the Slave Trade to Human Trafficking*. Philadelphia, PA: University of Pennsylvania Press, 2011.

A comprehensive, substantial historical examination of the evolution of abolitionist movements in response to evolving manifestations of slavery.

Samarasinghe, Vidyamali. *Female Sex Trafficking in Asia: The Resilience of Patriarchy in a Changing World*. New York: Routledge, 2008.

A feminist, field-research-based exploration of sex trafficking in Nepal, Cambodia, and the Philippines, focusing on strategies for combatting such exploitation.

Shelley, Louise. *Human Trafficking: A Global Perspective*. Cambridge and New York: Cambridge University Press, 2013.

Presents a global picture of contemporary slavery while employing a historical approach that explains national and regional variations.

Skinner, E. Benjamin. *A Crime So Monstrous: Face to Face with Modern Slavery*. New York: Free Press, 2008.

A compelling personal account of a journalist's encounters with contemporary slavery.

Wong, Kent, and Monroe, Julie. *Sweatshop Slaves: Asian Americans and the Garment Industry*. Los Angeles, CA: UCLA Center for Labor Research Education, 2006.

Focuses on Asian American workers in the garment industry, particularly in California, and the organizations that have worked to eradicate sweatshops.

Wright, Robert E. *The Poverty of Slavery: How Unfree Labor Pollutes the Economy*. New York: Palgrave MacMillan, 2017.

An analysis of the stultifying consequences of enslavement, past and present, for growth and diversification in national economies.

Index